This book presents a new paradigm for the interpretation of Plato's early and middle dialogues as a unified literary project, displaying an artistic plan for the expression of a unified world view. The usual assumption of a distinct "Socratic" period in Plato's work is rejected. Literary evidence is presented from other Socratic authors to demonstrate that the Socratic dialogue was a genre of literary fiction, not historical biography. Once it is recognized that the dialogue is a fictional form, there is no reason to look for the philosophy of the historical Socrates in Plato's earlier writings. We can thus read most of the so-called Socratic dialogues proleptically, interpreting them as partial expressions of the philosophical vision more fully expressed in the *Phaedo* and *Republic*. Differences between the dialogues are interpreted not as different stages in Plato's thinking but as different literary moments in the presentation of his thought. This indirect and gradual mode of exposition in the earlier dialogues is the artistic device chosen by Plato to prepare his readers for the reception of a new and radically unfamiliar view of reality: a view according to which the "real world" is an invisible realm, the source of all value and all rational structure, the natural homeland of the human soul.

PLATO AND THE SOCRATIC DIALOGUE

Portrait bust of Plato in the Fitzwilliam Museum, Cambridge.
One of the two best preserved ancient copies of a lost Greek
original, presumably the statue by Silanion mentioned in Diogenes
Laertius III.25. See G. M. A. Richter, *The Portraits of the Greeks*
(London, 1965), vol. II, p. 167, no. 16. *Photo*: Fitzwilliam Museum.

PLATO AND THE SOCRATIC DIALOGUE

The philosophical use of a literary form

CHARLES H. KAHN

Professor of Philosophy, University of Pennsylvania

CAMBRIDGE
UNIVERSITY PRESS

Published by the Press Syndicate of the University of Cambridge
The Pitt Building, Trumpington Street, Cambridge CB2 IRP
40 West 20th Street, New York, NY 10011-4211, USA
10 Stamford Road, Oakleigh, Melbourne 3166, Australia

First published 1996

Printed in Great Britain at the University Press, Cambridge

A catalogue record for this book is available from the British Library

Library of Congress cataloguing in publication data
Kahn, Charles H.
Plato and the Socratic dialogue / Charles H. Kahn.
p.   cm.
Includes bibliographical references.
ISBN 0 521 43325 8 (hardback)
1. Plato.   2. Socrates.   3. Imaginary conversations.   1. Title.
B395.K24   1996
184 – dc20   95-48307 CIP

ISBN 0 521 43325 8 hardback

AO

for Edna,
loving and joyful companion

Contents

ix

Preface

I offer here an interpretation of Plato's early and middle dialogues which aims to do justice to the genius of Plato not only as a thinker but also as a writer. For Plato is the only major philosopher who is also a supreme literary artist. There is no writer more complex, and there is no other philosopher whose work calls for so many levels of interpretation. Plato was the first author to offer a systematic definition of the goals and methods of philosophy. But he was also a social reformer and an educator, whose conception of philosophy entailed a radical transformation of the moral and intellectual culture of his own time and place. Much of his writing is designed to serve this larger cause. Hence a perceptive interpretation of Plato's dialogues calls for attention to his revolutionary cultural enterprise as well as to the literary and philosophical dimensions of his work.

My understanding of Plato reflects three quite different traditions. As a student at the University of Chicago, I learned from David Grene to read Plato as a great dramatist who belongs in the company of Shakespeare and the Attic tragedians. As a doctoral student in Classics at Columbia University, I was initiated into the mysteries of historical philology by Ernst Kapp and Kurt von Fritz. There I came to see Plato's dialogues as central texts for Greek culture of the fourth century BC, in the perspective of the great Plato commentaries of John Burnet and E. R. Dodds. Finally, for the last thirty years I have taught Plato to philosophy students, in an intellectual setting where the natural parallel is not with Shakespeare or Euripides but with Aristotle and Descartes, Kant and Wittgenstein.

Thus what I have to offer is a comprehensive interpretation, at once literary, historical, and philosophical, the fruit of a lifetime of reading and teaching Plato. My starting-point is Plato's career as a writer, one who makes use of the Socratic dialogue form that was practiced by other Socratic authors of his generation. But Plato is the only Socratic writer to turn this popular genre into a major art form, in rivalry with the great works of fifth-century Attic drama. He was also the only Socratic writer to utilize the dialogue form as the device for presenting a full-scale philosophical world view. However, as a result of Plato's choice of this form of discourse, in which he himself never appears, his thought is presented to us in a manner very different from that of a treatise. The task of the interpreter is inevitably compounded by the fact that the exposition of Plato's philosophy in the dialogues is deliberately indirect, ingressive, and incomplete.

The Plato presented here is a thinker with a unified world view, consistent throughout his life. That is to say, he belongs rather with philosophers like Descartes or Hume, whose philosophical position remains essentially unchanged once their thought attains maturity, than with philosophers like Kant and Wittgenstein, whose conception of philosophy undergoes radical change. Thus I firmly dissent from the standard view of Plato as an author who defends fundamentally different philosophies at different stages of his career.

Since the dialogues are so diverse, both in form and in content, even great scholars have been tempted to suppose that Plato changed his mind as often as he changes the literary presentation of his thought. And the traditional division of the dialogues into early, middle, and late encourages the belief that we can trace Plato's philosophical development through these successive phases. However, this developmental approach systematically underestimates Plato's cunning as an author. Not only does it assume (as Jaeger put it) that Plato must say in each dialogue everything he thought at the time. It also assumes that what Socrates says is also what Plato thinks. I shall argue that this is occasionally true, for example for many passages in the *Gorgias, Phaedo,* and *Republic,* but that in most of the early dialogues Plato's use of Socrates is more devious and artistically more complex.

The developmental view also presupposes that Plato writes dialogues like other philosophers write essays or treatises: in order to solve problems for himself, or to announce his solutions to the world. But this, I believe, is to misconstrue Plato's motive in writing. His principal aim, above all in the earlier works, is not to assert true propositions but to alter the minds and hearts of his readers. Plato's conception of philosophical education is not to replace false doctrines with true ones but to change radically the moral and intellectual orientation of the learner, who, like the prisoners in the cave, must be converted – turned around – in order to see the light. It is, I suggest, with this end in view that most of the early and middle dialogues were composed. Accordingly, the dialogues in question must be interpreted primarily from the point of view of this intended impact on the reader, an impact designed to be provocative, stimulating, and bewildering.

Since the earlier dialogues are so indirect in form and so frequently and deliberately inconclusive, it is not given to us to see Plato's thought in the making. What we can trace in these dialogues is not the development of Plato's thought, but the gradual unfolding of a literary plan for presenting his philosophical views to the general public. One function of Plato's sustained use of the aporetic dialogue form, including such literary masterpieces as the *Protagoras*, must have been to create as wide an audience as possible before presenting his own unfamiliar and very unconventional views in the *Symposium*, *Phaedo*, and *Republic*. In Plato's eyes, the traditional Greek world view, as represented by Sophocles and Thucydides as well as by Homer and Hesiod, was radically false. In developing the Socratic dialogue as a major literary form to rival his great predecessors, Plato sought to replace Achilles, Oedipus, and Pericles with his own hero, Socrates. In this Plato was at least partially successful, since Socrates did in fact become the hero figure for a new tradition, in which philosophy takes the place of religion for the educated public. At stake for Plato, then, was a different view of the meaning of human life, embedded in a radically new view of the nature of reality. When exactly this world view and this literary plan were formed, we cannot know. But they must predate many of the dialogues that are traditionally classified as Socratic. For it is only from the moral and metaphysical standpoint defined by the *Phaedo* and *Republic* that we can properly understand Plato's philosophical intention in composing such dialogues as the *Laches*, *Charmides*, *Euthyphro*, and *Protagoras*. Such is the central thesis of this book.

My interpretation is to this extent unitarian, in that I contend that behind the literary fluctuations of Plato's work stands the stable world view defined by his commitment to an otherwordly meta-

physics and to the strict Socratic moral ideal. These views were
formed relatively early and maintained consistently throughout his
life. But to claim that the general framework of Plato's philosophy
remained unchanged is not to imply that his thought was ever
stagnant or ossified.

The continuity of Plato's metaphysics is marked by the fact that
the Parmenidean dichotomy between unchanging Being and variable Becoming, first hinted at in the *Protagoras* (343D–344A) and
announced in the *Symposium*, continues to structure his thought,
not only in the *Phaedo* and *Republic* but also in the *Statesman*,
Philebus, and *Timaeus*. On the other hand, the classical doctrine of
Forms, which serves to articulate this dichotomy, is formulated
differently each time it appears. The Forms can even be ignored in
the *Theaetetus*, and subjected to criticism in the *Parmenides* and
Sophist. We can see that this doctrine, although never abandoned,
was frequently and substantially revised. Thus the notion of participation proposed in the *Phaedo*, as a relation between sensibles
and Forms, is given up in later works, and replaced in the *Sophist*
by a participation relation between Forms. Plato's substitute for
the rejected notion of participation, the sensible imaging of
Forms, is given an entirely new dimension in the *Timaeus* by his
introduction of the Receptacle as the locus within which such
imaging takes place. These innovations, together with the new direction given to dialectic in the later dialogues, demonstrate the
extent to which Plato's philosophy retains its creative vitality. But
these and all other advances are worked out within the fixed
framework of the Parmenidean dichotomy.

To defend this thesis in any detail for the later dialogues would
require another book. I am concerned here with the early and
middle dialogues, and with what I take to be a unified literary
project that comes to a conclusion in the *Republic* and *Phaedrus*. I
count all these dialogues as Socratic in a literary sense, since in all
of them Plato makes use of the popular genre of "Conversations
with Socrates" (*Sōkratikoi logoi*). These works of Plato, like those of
the other Socratic authors, are designed to be read by a broadly
educated public. After the *Phaedrus* the literary form changes.
Other speakers replace Socrates; and even in the *Theaetetus* and
the *Philebus*, where Socrates remains the chief speaker, the content
becomes much more technical and the discussion is addressed to a
narrower, more professional audience. Hence a different, less lit-

erary mode of interpretation would be called for in dealing with these later works. I limit myself here to exploring the essential unity of Plato's thought, and the literary devices by which it is articulated, in the so-called early dialogues and in the great central works.

I want to take this opportunity to reflect briefly on the background of this book, and thus to acknowledge my debt to various persons and institutions.

My general understanding of Plato's work began to take shape in my student days. But the first occasion for a public presentation of my views came in 1979–80, in a paper entitled "Did Plato Write Socratic Dialogues?" which was read in Paris and Cambridge. In the Paris audience was Pierre Aubenque, who asked me what I intended to say about Aristotle's account of Socrates, since this account seemed to support the standard view of Plato's earlier dialogues as representing the philosophy of Socrates, and since it was on this notion of an early Socratic period that the developmental conception was based. Having learned in work on the Presocratics never to take Aristotle's report on his predecessors without a large measure of salt, I did not at first see this as a serious objection to my denial of the alleged Socratic period in Plato's own work. After all, no student of the Presocratics would accept Aristotle's account as taking precedence over the original texts. And in Plato's case we do have the relevant texts, namely the dialogues, on which Aristotle's own view was based. Hence it was only later, in reflecting on Aubenque's point (as reiterated by others, including Gregory Vlastos, in his book on Socrates) that I came to understand what a long shadow the Aristotelian account of Socrates has cast over our belief in the "Socratic" element in Plato's early dialogues – a belief that goes back to Hermann's work in the early nineteenth century. And so I came to see the need for the systematic critique of Aristotle's report that is given here in Chapter 3.

Another important moment in the genesis of this book was provoked by the generosity of Gabriele Giannantoni, who donated free copies of the preliminary version of *Socratis et Socraticorum Reliquiae* to participants in a conference in Amalfi in 1985. This fundamental publication of the material on Socratic literature enabled me to see the importance of the fact that the Socratic genre was well developed, and practiced by at least half a dozen different authors, before Plato transformed it into his own philosophical instrument. This led directly to my composition of the typescript entitled *Sōkratikoi logoi*, which began to circulate in 1986, and which appears here in briefer form as Chapter 1. The comments of Klaus Döring were particularly helpful on the earlier version of this chapter. (The section on Aeschines was published separately in Vander Waerdt [1994].)

The first draft of this book was largely written on sabbatical leave in Cambridge in early 1991, where it benefited from discussion and criticism by a number of friends and colleagues, including David Sedley and Malcolm Schofield. The critical comments of Myles Burnyeat were exceptionally valuable in awakening me from my dogmatic slumber on the subject of the Socratic reading of the earlier dialogues. I had innocently supposed that the old developmental view of these dialogues had by then collapsed of its own weight, and hence that the world was ready and waiting for my alternative interpretation. (Gregory Vlastos' *Socrates* had not yet appeared ...) Myles' comments made clear to me the need for a full statement of the case against a Socratic reading of the *Protagoras* and the dialogues of definition, and in favor of a unitarian view. The result was a general presentation of my argument in Chapter 2 and a radical rewriting of Chapters 6 and 8.

A number of other friendly critics have helped to make this work less imperfect than it might otherwise be. As readers for the Cambridge University Press, Anthony Price and Christopher Rowe both contributed extremely useful comments. Diskin Clay read long stretches of the typescript and persuaded me that what I was calling the "pre-middle" dialogues would be more felicitously referred to as "threshold" works, immediate preliminaries for the middle dialogues. My colleague Susan Sauvé Meyer read several chapters and improved them with her criticism. In Athens my friend Vassilis Karasmanis did likewise. Michael Ferejohn offered penetrating comments on the *Protagoras* interpretation. Others who made helpful comments on one or more chapters include John Cooper, Daniel Devereux, George Klosko, Alexander Nehamas, and Gisela Striker. It is not possible for me to acknowledge individually all the colleagues and graduate students who responded with helpful criticism, or occasionally with encouragement, to parts of this book presented in various colloquia and seminars over the last ten years. But I must single out for special thanks my two research assistants, Mary Hannah Jones who worked with the manuscript in 1990–1, and most particularly Michael McShane, who has loyally tended it since 1993. To all of these, my thanks.

It remains only to express my gratitude to the institutions that have helped to make this work possible. First to the Guggenheim Foundation for a Research Fellowship in 1979–80, and to Balliol College, Oxford, for a Visiting Fellowship in the same year, when the initial spade work for this project was begun. Next to the American Council of Learned Societies for a research grant in 1985–6, and to Clare Hall, Cambridge, for a Visiting Fellowship in fall, 1985, when the research for *Sōkratikoi logoi* was carried out. Then to the National Endowment for the Humanities for a research fellowship in 1990–1, when the first draft of eight or nine chapters was completed. Finally to my own institution, the University of Pennsylvania and its Philosophy Department, which have loyally supported my research throughout this time, and to the University's Research Foundation which has twice provided grants towards the preparation of this manuscript for publication.

I want also to thank my faithful typist, Connie Cybulski Donnelly, who has persevered through every chapter and every revision. At Cambridge University Press I am grateful to my editor, Pauline Hire, for her patient and helpful support over the last few years, and to my copy-editor, Glennis Foote, for an outstanding job in preparing the typescript for printing.

Finally, I want to acknowledge the contribution of my wife, Edna Foa Kahn, who has not only put up with the long labors involved in completing the manuscript and supported me with her enthusiasm for the project, but who has often offered penetrating criticism. And it was she who, browsing in the Fitzwilliam Museum on a Sunday afternoon, discovered the Cambridge Plato which appears here as frontispiece. It is with love and gratitude that I dedicate this book to her.

C.H.K.
Philadelphia, November 1995

Addendum, June 1996

While correcting proof I have been able to see Andrea Nightingale's *Genres in Dialogue: Plato and the Construct of Philosophy* (Cambridge,

1995). Her discussion of the relations between Plato and Isocrates provides an important supplement to my account of the contemporary context of Plato's work in Chapter 1.

I want to add a word of gratitude and appreciation for my three students, Michael McShane, Daniel McLean, and Satoshi Ogihara, for their invaluable help in reading proof and preparing the indexes.

C.H.K

Abbreviations

DK   H. Diels and W. Kranz, *Die Fragmente der Vorsokratiker*, 5th edn., Berlin, 1951

D.L.   Diogenes Laertius, *Lives of the Philosophers*

LSJ   Liddell–Scott–Jones, *A Greek–English Lexicon*, 9th edn., Oxford, 1940

RE   *Realencyclopädie der classischen Altertumswissenschaft*, ed. Wissowa, Kroll, *et al.*

SSR   *Socratis et Socraticorum Reliquiae*, ed. G. Giannantoni, Naples, 1991

CHAPTER I

Sōkratikoi logoi: *the literary and intellectual background of Plato's work*

I. THE SOCRATIC LITERATURE

We begin this study of Plato's Socratic dialogues with a survey of what is known about other Socratic writings in the same period. That is not a familiar starting-point. In other fields, and notably in biblical scholarship, genre studies have become commonplace. Students of the New Testament, for example, have found it fruitful to compare the literary form of narrative and discourses in the different Gospels. It may come as a surprise, then, to realize that (as far as I can tell) there has never been a comparative study of the Socratic dialogue form.[1] This may be due in part to the mistaken belief that Plato was not only the perfecter but also the inventor of this form. But such was certainly not the case. Aristotle in his *Poetics* refers to the *Sōkratikoi logoi* ("Socratic discourses," or "Conversations with Socrates") as an established literary genre. And in his lost dialogue *On Poets* Aristotle is said to have named a certain Alexamenos of Teos as the originator of this genre.[2] Unfortunately, nothing more is known of Alexamenos.

What is known is that quite a number of friends and followers of Socrates celebrated his memory in literary form, after his death. Aside from Plato's work, only the writings of Xenophon have survived intact. Nevertheless, we have significant remains from at least four other Socratic authors: Antisthenes, Aeschines, Phaedo, and Eucleides. And we have at least anecdotal information concerning a fifth author, Aristippus. Until recently the fragmentary material for these other "minor Socratics" had rarely been studied with care. That situation has been altered in the last few decades by a

1. Perhaps the closest thing to a precedent is Hirzel (1895). For a modest start, see Kahn (1990).
2. Arist. *Poetics* 1447b11; *De Poetis* fr.3 Ross (= Rose² 72).

number of important publications, culminating in the monu-
mental *Socratis et Socraticorum Reliquiae* edited by G. Giannantoni.[3]
It is now possible as never before to survey the Socratic literature.
The results are of considerable interest for an understanding of
Plato's own work.

There is no evidence that any of these writings were composed
during Socrates' lifetime. There were of course caricature portraits of Socrates presented in Aristophanes' *Clouds*, and in other
fifth-century comedies now lost. Aside from this comic material,
however, the Socratic writings known to us (including the dialogues of Plato) all belong to the fourth century BC, after Socrates'
death. The importance of this will become clear in a moment.

Our aim in this first introductory chapter is, first of all, to situate Plato in his own time and place, and thus to overcome what
one might describe as the optical illusion of the dialogues. By this
I mean Plato's extraordinary success in recreating the dramatic
atmosphere of the previous age, the intellectual milieu of the late
fifth century in which Socrates confronts the sophists and their
pupils. It is difficult but necessary to bear in mind the gap between
this art world, created by Plato, and the actual world in which
Plato worked out his own philosophy. That was no longer the
world of Protagoras and Gorgias, Hippias and Thrasymachus.
With the exception of Gorgias (who was unusually long-lived),
these men were probably all dead when Plato wrote. Protagoras,
in particular, must have died when Plato was a child, and the dialogue named after him is situated before Plato's birth. The intellectual world to which Plato's own work belongs is defined not by
the characters in his dialogues but by the thought and writing of
his contemporaries and rivals, such as the rhetorician Isocrates
and the various followers of Socrates.

Our comparative survey of the Socratic literature is thus designed to correct the misleading historical perspective that is built
into Plato's work. But it can do more. At least one feature of the
genre can be of decisive importance for an interpretation of Plato's
thought. This is the imaginative and essentially fictional nature of
Socratic literature.

3. Giannantoni, *Socratis et Socraticorum Reliquiae* (hereafter *SSR*), Naples, 1990, 4
volumes. See also the works by Caizzi (1964, 1966), Döring (1972), Ehlers
(1966), Mannebach (1961), A. Patzer (1970), and Rossetti (1980). Important
earlier work was done by Dittmar (1912) and Gigon (1947).

Plato's success as a dramatist is so great that he has often been mistaken for an historian. Hence the history of philosophy reports Socrates' thought on the strength of Plato's portrayal in the dialogues. And it is not only modern scholars who fall victim to this illusion. Like Guthrie or Vlastos, Aristotle himself finds the historical Socrates in the *Protagoras* and *Laches*; and the Stoics do much the same. Now Aristotle and the Stoics are interested in philosophy, not in history as such, and for them the figure of Socrates serves to define a certain position in a theoretical debate. But the modern scholars who follow in their footsteps claim to be writing history. And since they treat Plato's literary creations as if these were historical documents, the result is a pseudo-historical account of the philosophy of Socrates.

Even more unfortunate are the consequences for an understanding of Plato's own work. In current English-language scholarship on Plato, the belief still prevails that the philosophy of Socrates is somehow faithfully represented in Plato's earlier writings. And this supposedly historical datum is then used to define a distinct Socratic period in Plato's philosophic development. It is not clear that such a belief in the historical fidelity of the dialogues can survive a critical study of the Socratic literature. Hence, one function of my introductory survey is to undermine the foundations of the traditional view, insofar as this depends upon the assumption of an early Socratic period in Plato's work. We can then proceed to develop an alternative view, resting upon entirely different assumptions.

This enterprise of deconstruction is not the only insight to be gained from such a comparative survey. There is also the striking diversity to be found in the portraits of Socrates given by Aeschines, Phaedo and Xenophon. These differ from one another as much as they differ from Plato, despite the fact that there is something like a family resemblance that unites all four portrayals. This diversity points up what is peculiar to Plato's version of Socrates and helps us bear in mind the distance between the literary and the historical reality. In addition, there is the important literary phenomenon known nowadays as intertextuality. We have at least two passages from Antisthenes and three from Aeschines that are so closely related to passages in Plato that it is natural to assume either that Plato is alluding to an earlier text or that the other Socratic author is responding to Plato. We can thus situate Plato within a literary community of Socratic authors reacting to one another's work. (For the numerous echoes of Plato in Xenophon, see the Appendix pp. 393–401.)

Finally, a catalogue of the philosophical topics discussed by other Socratics can serve to locate Plato's own discussion in its contemporary setting. I list here some of the topics common to Plato and one or more other Socratics; details will be given in the survey that follows in §§ 2–7.

1. The relative importance of knowledge or theory (*logos*) and moral toughness (*enkrateia, karteria*) in the conception of virtue. (Contrast Antisthenes.)

2. The existence of many names for one thing (Eucleides) or only one *logos* for one thing (Antisthenes).

3. The use of *epagōgē* or reasoning from parallel cases (in Aeschines), and the criticism of this argument form (by Eucleides).

4. The relation between knowledge and opinion (*doxa*). (A book title by Antisthenes.)[4]

5. The role of poets and poetry in education (Antisthenes).

6. The attitude to pleasure (Antisthenes hostile, Aristippus indulgent).

7. The roles of friendship and *erōs* in philosophy, and Socrates as a specialist in matters erotic (Antisthenes, Aeschines, Phaedo, Xenophon, with a book title for Eucleides).

8. Critical judgment on the major statesmen of fifth-century Athens (Antisthenes).

Given the paucity of our information regarding much of the Socratic literature, this list can only serve to suggest how extensive was the thematic overlap between questions discussed in Plato's dialogues and in the other Socratic writings.

Our discussion of the six other Socratic authors will focus on the theme of Socratic *erōs*, since this is the topic most fully represented in the surviving material.

2. ANTISTHENES

In the first fifteen years after Socrates' death, Antisthenes was probably regarded as the most important follower of Socrates.

---

4. Compare also the phrase from Antisthenes' *Ajax*, where *diagignōskein* is contrasted with *diadoxazein* (*SSR* v A 53, line 43).

The dominant position of Plato, both as author and as leader of a school, was only established later, probably after 385 BC.[5] Antisthenes' dates are uncertain, but the evidence suggests that he lived from about 445 to about 365 BC, which would make him some twenty years older than Plato.[6] According to an ancient tradition, Antisthenes was already a teacher (of rhetoric, perhaps) before encountering Socrates, but he then instructed his students to follow his own example and become disciples of Socrates (D.L. VI.2). The story may not be reliable in this form,[7] but it clearly presupposes that Antisthenes ranked as an older, more established figure among the followers of Socrates in his last years. And this impression is confirmed by Xenophon's portrayal. Thus Xenophon represents Socrates as consulting Antisthenes for an independent judgment on matters of worldly wisdom, in contrast to the treatment of younger interlocutors, who typically receive advice from Socrates.[8] Antisthenes was clearly one of Socrates' most devoted followers. He is present at the death scene (*Phaedo* 59B), and is described by Xenophon as one of the two disciples who were inseparable from Socrates, because they were captivated by his "love potions and spells."[9]

Antisthenes was a prodigious author. The catalogue of his works in Diogenes Laertius lists over sixty titles, some of which may represent very short pieces like the two extant display speeches *Ajax*

5. See Eucken (1983) 25ff. and *passim*.
6. For Antisthenes' dates see Caizzi (1966) 118; *SSR* vol. IV, pp. 199–201.
7. See Patzer (1970) 251.
8. See *Mem.* II.4.5. Antisthenes is one of the guests in Xenophon's *Symposium*, which has a fictive date of 422 BC. This is not exactly historical evidence, but it tends to confirm the other indications.
9. *Mem.* III.11.17. The other inseparable companion named here is Apollodorus, the first narrator of the *Symposium* and the most emotional of the group at Socrates' death (*Phaedo* 59A 9, 117D 3). It is noteworthy that Plato never mentions Antisthenes by name except to record his presence at the death scene, just as he never mentions Aeschines except as being present there and at the trial (*Ap.* 33E 2). He mentions Aristippus only to record his absence in the *Phaedo* scene. Thus Plato carefully excludes from his portrayal his three most notable rivals among the Socratics (treating them, in effect, as he treats himself), whereas nearly all other members of the inner circle appear from time to time in the dialogues: Apollodorus, Crito, Critoboulus, Hermogenes, Ctesippus, Menexenus, Simmias, Cebes, Eucleides, Terpsion, and Phaedo himself, to take the names from *Phaedo* 59B. Of those present there only Epigenes and Phaidondes (besides Antisthenes and Aeschines) fail to appear elsewhere in Plato.

and *Odysseus*. But others seem to be of considerable length, for example, three *Protreptics on Justice and Courage*, five books *On Education, or on Names*, four books *On Opinion and Knowledge*. At least nine of these works were in dialogue form. The range of subjects covered was very wide, from the discussion of Homer and poetry to topics in natural philosophy and philosophical method. Unfortunately, except for the two speeches mentioned, we have no substantial verbatim quotations.[10]

After Socrates' death Antisthenes emerged as an important moral teacher in his own right. The ancient sources represent him as maintaining something like a regular school, with lectures or discussions in the Cynosarges gymnasium, where the students were apparently supposed to take notes.[11] But it is clear that Antisthenes did not organize a school for professional training and research, like Plato and Aristotle, or for the development and teaching of a system of thought, like Zeno and Epicurus. His instruction must have been a much more informal affair, consisting partly in worldly advice and exhortations to virtue as Antisthenes conceived it, and partly in the model of his own life and moral attitudes.[12] We can perhaps best imagine the "teaching" done by Antisthenes and the other Socratics (other than Plato) along the lines of Socrates' own procedure in Xenophon's portrait, where Socrates figures as moral guru and head of a circle of like-minded, younger men.

In many respects Antisthenes differed radically from Socrates. Both in Xenophon's portrait and in the anecdotes reported by Diogenes Laertius, Antisthenes is outspoken to the point of rudeness. His social manners were unpolished, and his language could be rough. After quarreling with Plato he wrote a book against Platonic dialectic entitled *Sathōn*, which rhymes with *Platōn* but means "a large prick" (D.L. III.35: cf. VI.16).

Since our focus here is on the theme of *erōs*, we are particularly interested in Antisthenes' moral doctrine and especially in his atti-

---

10. For a survey of what is known about Antisthenes' writings see Caizzi (1966) 77ff., A. Patzer (1970) 91–101, *SSR* vol. IV, pp. 235ff. For an example of his Homeric exegesis, see below, 121–4.

11. D.L. VI.3–4 and 13; note the reference to writing materials in VI.3 and apparently to school fees in VI.4 and VI.9. Antisthenes' own *hupomnēmata* mentioned in VI.5 sound like lecture notes.

12. Cf. von Fritz (1931) 718, line 48: "eine Erziehung und Ausbildung der Schüler für das Leben," referring to the Socratic schools generally. Similarly Döring (1972) 94f.

tude to sex. He followed Socrates in regarding *aretē* or moral excellence as the most important thing in the world, so that philosophy was simply the rational pursuit of a life of *aretē*. Virtue was apparently closely associated with wisdom in the Socratic manner: thus the good man is also called "the sage" (*ho sophos*). There is a strong intellectualist streak in Antisthenes' thought. "The safest wall is wisdom (*phronēsis*) ... One should construct one's defenses in one's own impregnable calculations (*logismoi*)" (D.L. VI.13). At the same time "*aretē* is a matter of deeds; it does not require much theory (or arguments, *logoi*) or much learning (*mathēmata*)" (D.L. VI.11). In fact in his conception of excellence Antisthenes adopted the stance of a counter-culture puritan or proto-cynic: he emphasized those elements of toughness (*karteria*), self-mastery (*enkrateia*), indifference to sensual pleasure and worldly goods which he regarded as the essential traits of Socrates' own life.

Antisthenes' goal was *autarkeia* or self-sufficiency: "virtue is sufficient (*autarkēs*) for happiness; it requires nothing but the strength of Socrates" (D.L. VI.11 = *SSR* V A 134). His non-conformism (and probably his debt to Socrates as well) shows up in the claim that the *aretē* of a man and a woman is the same (D.L. VI.12). And his anti-hedonism is expressed in two famous sayings: "I would rather go mad than enjoy pleasure," and "If I could catch Aphrodite I would shoot her down with my bow, because she has corrupted so many excellent and beautiful women" (D.L. VI.3 = *SSR* V A 122–3). He is said to have regarded sexual love as a vice of nature; "its unhappy victims call their disease a god", i.e. Eros (*SSR* V A 123). It is not clear whether he disapproved of *all* pleasure or only that which leads to moral softening and distraction from the arduous pursuit of *aretē*.[13] With regard to sex his attitude seems at first sight crassly utilitarian: "one should frequent women who will be grateful" (*SSR* V A 56). For the satisfaction of a bodily need any woman will do, like simple food for a hungry man. (Cf. Xen. *Symp.* IV.38.) Hence the adulterer, who in Athens is risking his life if caught, is a great fool; he could have avoided the danger by paying an obol to a prostitute (D.L. VI.4). The wise man, however, "will marry for the sake of children, joining with women who are best endowed by nature," that is, best endowed for the production of good chil-

13. Cf. *SSR* V A 126: "One should pursue the pleasures which follow toil and effort (*ponoi*), not those which precede it." See the note in Caizzi (1966) 116.

dren. "And he will be in love; for the sage is the only one who knows whom one should love (*eran*)" (D.L. VI.11 = *SSR* V A 58).

It seems that Antisthenes' deeper concern is always with moral excellence, as he understands it. "It is the good man who is worthy of love and good men (*hoi spoudaioi*) who are friends" (D.L. VI.12). Or, in another version, "It is the sage who is worthy of love and friend to one like himself (*tōi homoiōi*)" (D.L. VI.105 = *SSR* V A 99). So in Xenophon Antisthenes claims to be in love with Socrates (*Symp.* VIII.4). The topic of friendship is certainly one that Antisthenes developed at length, in connection with his own conception of *aretē*. It is precisely on this question, on the value of friends, that Xenophon's Socrates calls upon Antisthenes for an expert opinion (*Mem.* II.5.2). In his long speech in Xenophon's *Symposium* Antisthenes emphasizes his debt to Socrates, who has taught him the freedom and happiness of being contented with what he has. What he values most is the leisure to spend all his time with Socrates (*Symp.* IV.43–4).

Antisthenes composed a dialogue entitled *Aspasia*, probably before Aeschines' dialogue of the same name. From Antisthenes' *Aspasia* we have only two or three quotations. One involves an attack on Pericles' sons for keeping unsavory company (*SSR* V A 142). This apparently formed part of a more general attack on Pericles; Antisthenes and Plato seem to have agreed for once in a negative judgment on the great leaders of the fifth-century democracy.[14] The *Aspasia* focused its attack on Pericles' private life. Pericles had previously been married to an Athenian woman of high station, mother of his two legitimate sons whom we meet in Plato's *Protagoras*. But he divorced her in order to take Aspasia as his semi-legal wife. His love for her was "rather erotic," as Plutarch says in his *Life*, probably following Antisthenes: "they say he embraced her twice a day with tender kisses (*meta tou kataphilein*), when he left for the agora and when he returned."[15] Presumably this sensual behavior on Pericles' part was supposed to be reflected in the dis-

14. See *SSR* V A 204: his dialogue *Politikos* contained an attack on "all the popular leaders of Athens." Dittmar (1912: 15, n.48, citing Dümmler) remarks that Plato (in the *Gorgias*) and Antisthenes seem to have been the only Socratics to express an unfavorable view of the leading statesmen of Athens.

15. Antisthenes fr. 1 Dittmar (p. 299) = *SSR* V A 143. (Dittmar and Giannantoni include the Plutarch passage as Antisthenean; Caizzi [1966: 98f.] is more cautious.)

solute life of his sons. Grim results followed from the fact that the great statesman chose the life of pleasure rather than that of virtue and wisdom (fr.3 Dittmar = *SSR* v a 144).

This does not give us much information about Antisthenes' treatment of Aspasia, but it fits in with his known attitude on the subject of sensual pleasure, and it is enough to serve as a more conventional foil against which to understand the strikingly different interpretation of Aspasia that we find in Aeschines, Plato, and Xenophon.

Much less is known about Phaedo, Eucleides, and Aristippus: three non-Athenians among the followers of Socrates. The remains of these more shadowy figures will serve nevertheless to illustrate the density of thought, discussion, and literary output in the early post-Socratic period.

3. PHAEDO

Phaedo from Elis in the western Peloponnese is familiar to us as narrator of the Platonic dialogue that bears his name, and best remembered for the scene in that dialogue where Socrates plays with the long hair that Phaedo will soon cut in sign of mourning (89B). The story of Phaedo's life that we read in Diogenes Laertius and other ancient sources is a fantastic melodrama whose historicity is impossible to control. He is said to have been of noble birth but enslaved after the capture of his native Elis and brought to Athens as a male prostitute. He managed to attract Socrates' attention, who thereupon persuaded one of his wealthy friends to purchase Phaedo's freedom and thus permit him to pursue the life of philosophy.[16] This story is likely to be invented, or at least distorted, to suggest the dubious background of some of Socrates' associates and to cast discreditable light on the tenderness shown by Socrates in the famous scene in the *Phaedo*.[17]

All we know is that Phaedo eventually returned to Elis, founded some sort of school there, and composed at least two Socratic dialogues, entitled *Simon* and *Zopyrus*. These both deserve to be better

16. D.L. ii.105 with parallels at *SSR* iii a 1; discussion in *SSR* vol. iv, pp. 115–19.
17. For unscrupulous invention and distortion in the anti-Platonic tradition of Hellenistic biography, see Düring (1941). The Phaedo story seems to be accepted as historical by most scholars, despite the fact that no such capture of Elis is recorded.

known. In antiquity they enjoyed an extraordinary literary fame, and at least one of them was still read by the Emperor Julian as late as the fourth century AD (*SSR* III A 2). Phaedo's wise shoemaker Simon served as the model for a whole literature of shoemaker dialogues, "the sayings of sage Simon"; while his figure of the physiognomist Zopyrus can also be traced through the Roman period down to late antiquity, with echoes in medieval treatises on physiognomy. It seems likely that these two extraordinarily successful character types were both creatures of Phaedo's imagination.[18] Nevertheless, optimistic archaeologists digging in the Athenian agora claim to have found traces of Simon's workshop.[19]

Simon is a representative of the solid artisans whom Socrates liked to frequent and whom he so often invokes to prove a point. In Phaedo's dialogue, Socrates, Alcibiades and their friends gather

18. So rightly Wilamowitz (1879) 187–9. Simon gets a chapter of his own in D.L. (II.122–3), but I can see no good reason to believe in his historical reality. This is one of the many examples where the imaginary creation produced by a Socratic author has become the source of a pseudo-historical tradition. Compare n.48 below, on the liaison between Aspasia and Lysicles. On Simon see the skeptical considerations of Zeller (1889) 243n. Zopyrus is the name of a famous Persian in Herodotus (III.153–60), whose grandson of the same name took refuge in Athens and ended badly. (See *RE*. s.v. Zopyrus 2, 2.Reihe, XA, 1972, 767f.) The name was originally used for foreigners (Zopyrus 4 is Alcibiades' Thracian *paidagōgos*), and later for Greeks. But the physiognomist seems to be Phaedo's invention, inspired perhaps by Antisthenes' work *Peri tōn sophistōn physiognōmikos*.

19. In the initial excavation report in *Hesperia* 23 (1954) 54f., Homer Thompson was quite cautious. Sufficient hobnails were found "to justify the view that the establishment had been occupied for a time by a shoemaker. It is perhaps the name of this shoemaker that occurs, in the genitive case, ΣΙΜΟΝΟΣ, incised in letter forms of the late fifth century" on the broken foot of a cup "found at an appropriate level in the area." Thompson is aware that Simon the Shoemaker "is a very shadowy figure, but," he adds, "if any reliance at all is to be put in Diogenes, one can scarcely resist the association with our establishment."

In a fuller publication entitled "The House of Simon the Shoemaker" in *Archeology* 13 (1960) 234–40, Dorothy Burr Thompson is somewhat more assertive. "Was the owner of the cup the owner of the shop? Why not? We can never be sure, but there is a good chance that the cup was broken in the house and tossed out into the street" (p. 238).

It is clear, I think, that such archaeological speculation cannot establish the historical existence of Phaedo's shoemaker, which it presupposes. The evidence proves only that Simon was a genuine name (like Zopyrus), not that it was the name of a shoemaker.

in the shoemaker's workshop for their conversation.[20] Antisthenes himself seems to have been present, and the earthy, democratic character of Simon's wisdom shows some affinity with Antisthenes' conception of philosophical training. But we can form a clearer picture of Phaedo's conception of Socratic "care of oneself" from the remains of his other dialogue.

The scene in which Zopyrus encounters Socrates must have been one of the most striking passages in all Socratic literature. An oriental magus comes to town who claims to be able to read people's character in their faces and in their bodily appearance.[21] He is confronted with Socrates, who is unknown to him. Zopyrus declares Socrates to be dull and stupid, on the strength of his bull neck, and also subject to sensuality, a womanizer in fact, probably judging from his protruding eyes.[22] At this point Alcibiades bursts out laughing. Socrates' friends are beginning to ridicule the physiognomist when the philosopher interrupts them. These are indeed his native weaknesses, he says, but they have been overcome by rational training. So from an initial interest in the contrast between external appearance and inner reality, the conversation turns to the power of nurture over nature. We have one verbatim quotation in which someone, perhaps Zopyrus himself, is telling Socrates an oriental tale about a lion cub given as a gift to the youngest son of the Persian King. "And I think the lion got so used to the boy that when he was a young man the lion followed him wherever he went. So the Persians said the lion was in love with the boy" (*SSR* III A 11 = fr. 1 Rossetti). Here we have a striking example from the animal kingdom, where one might

---

20. See Wilamowitz (1879) and von Fritz (1938), with additions from Rossetti (1973) 364–81. Rossetti (p. 373) quotes a passage from Plutarch (*Moralia* 776A, missing in Giannantoni) which describes Socrates as seated next to Simon (cf. *para se kathezesthai* in the spurious letter addressed to Simon by Aristippus, *Socrat. Ep.* 13 = *SSR* IV A 224, line 6).
21. The relevant texts are missing from *SSR*; they are printed *in extenso* in Rossetti (1980) 184ff. The fullest report is in the Syriac version (fr. 9 Rossetti, p. 186), while Cicero (frs. 6–7), the Persius scholiast (fr. 8) and Alexander (fr. 10) give only Zopyrus' diagnosis with Socrates' response. The best discussion is by von Fritz (1938) 1540.
22. *Mulierosus* in Cicero (fr. 6 Rossetti), *libidinosus* in the Persius scholia (fr. 8), "the eyes of a pederast" in Cassianus (fr. 11). A reference to Socrates' eyes is common in the later literature (frs. 12–17 Rossetti; cf. fr. 18 where Zopyrus is mentioned but not Socrates).

suppose that nature was supreme, for the victory of nurture and training: instead of being the enemy of man the lion became his friend.

It is clear that Phaedo's *Zopyrus* gave a very personal twist to the standard theme of moral self-improvement and the teachability of virtue that we know from Antisthenes, Aeschines, and presumably from Socrates himself. It may be from the same dialogue that the Emperor Julian quotes Phaedo's conviction "that nothing is incurable for philosophy; by its power everyone can be purified from all ways of life, from practices, desires and all such" (*SSR* III A 2). If we can believe the story of Phaedo's escape to philosophy from a life of vice, we may be inclined to recognize in this statement a reference to his own experience. There is one more quotation, given by Seneca from an unidentified dialogue, that expresses a similar sense of the therapeutic action of philosophy. "As Phaedo says, when some minute animals bite we do not feel it, so slight and deceptive is their power. Only a swelling marks the bite, and even in the swelling we see no wound. The same thing will happen to you in conversation with wise men: you will not notice how or when you profit, but you will notice that you *have* profited" (*SSR* III A 12).

This is all we know of the dialogues of Phaedo. But it is enough to reveal a writer of some talent, with a literary grace unknown to Antisthenes and a straightforward moral earnestness that we will not find in Aeschines. It was perhaps these qualities, together with a certain personal sensitivity and a deep commitment to the transforming power of philosophy, that led Plato to make Phaedo the narrator of the dialogue that contains both the scene of Socrates' death and the first systematic statement of Plato's own philosophy. For it is of course Plato who, by celebrating Phaedo in this way, has made his name more familiar to us than those of much more influential Socratic authors such as Antisthenes and Aeschines.

4. EUCLEIDES

Eucleides of Megara was probably not very gifted as a writer. At all events, we know nothing of his literary work except the titles. But we do have some substantial information concerning his philosophical views. In fact Eucleides may have been the only Socratic (other than Plato) to have done important technical work in philosophy.[23] That fact is probably reflected in the role Plato gives him as narrator of the *Theaetetus*, one of the more technical of Plato's own dialogues. It was to Eucleides in Megara that Plato and other Socratics went from Athens after the death of Socrates. The *Theaetetus* shows that this friendly relationship still existed thirty years later.

Eucleides is depicted in the Hellenistic histories of philosophy as founder of a Megarian school, whose doctrines are discussed and opposed by Aristotle in the next generation. Of the nature and structure of this "school" we know almost nothing, except that it seems to have focused on what was known in Hellenistic times as dialectic, that is, on questions of logic and language.[24] This logical bent is also characteristic of what little we know of Eucleides' own work.

The doctrines reported for Eucleides are the following: "the good is one, called by many names; sometimes it is called wisdom (*phronēsis*), sometimes god (*theos*), also intelligence (*nous*) and so forth" (D.L. II.106). Elsewhere "the Megarians" are said to hold that it is *aretē*, virtue rather than the good, which is one but called by many names (D.L. VII.161). This may indicate that *aretē* and "the good" (*agathon*) were treated as equivalent, as they might well be for a follower of Socrates. There is also a suggestion that the individual virtues were regarded like *phronēsis* and *nous* as so many alternative designations for the same principle.[25] This is the strongest of the three views of the unity of virtue formulated by Socrates

23. It is difficult to say whether or not Antisthenes made any significant contribution to technical philosophy. He was certainly concerned with topics in epistemology and philosophy of language.
24. For a survey of the evidence, see Döring (1989) 293–310.
25. Döring (1972: 86) suggests that the individual virtues are implied by "and so forth" (*kai ta loipa*) at D.L. II 106. The doctrine in this form is later ascribed to Menedemus (a pupil of Stilpon of Megara, and hence a "follower" of Eucleides): "He denied the multiplicity and diversity of the virtues; virtue is one and employs many names; for the same thing is called *sōphrosunē* and courage and justice, just as the same thing is called mortal (*brotos*) and human being (*anthrōpos*)" (Plut. *De virt. mor.* 2, 440E cited by Döring, *loc. cit.*) A heavily intellectualist slant is suggested by the occurrence of *phronēsis* and *nous* as names for the good in the doxography for Eucleides; and this is reinforced by the parallel view reported for Menedemus "that all good is located in the mind and in the cognitive faculty (*mentis acies*) by which truth is apprehended" (Döring [1972] fr. 26A), where *mentis acies* must be Cicero's translation for *nous*.

in Plato's *Protagoras* (329D 1, 349B). We might wonder whether
Plato is indebted to Eucleides for this formulation, or vice versa.
For all we know, they may have worked it out together in conversation. What the parallel certainly shows is that "the question of the
unity of the virtues was under discussion among the Socratics in
the form in which Eucleides answered it."[26]

Eucleides' teaching, then, is probably in the background when
Plato in the *Protagoras* discusses the unity of virtue. And again Eucleides' conception of the good in terms of wisdom (*phronēsis*) is
likely to be in Plato's mind when in *Republic* VI he canvasses various opinions on the good: "most people think pleasure is the good
but the more refined sort think it is *phronēsis*" (505B).

Diogenes Laertius reports several other views for Eucleides.[27]
Of particular importance are two comments on methods of philosophical reasoning. Eucleides objected to an argument "by attacking not the premises but the conclusion." And he rejected the argument by analogy (as used in a Socratic *epagōgē*) on the grounds
that if the cases are not similar, the comparison is irrelevant;
whereas if they *are* similar, one should deal directly with the case
in question rather than with what resembles it (II.107). The meaning of the first report is not entirely clear, but both remarks testify
to a concern with logical rigor that must have had an impact on
Plato's own work. It can hardly be a coincidence that, whereas in
the *Gorgias* reasoning by analogy seems to support conclusions of
"iron and adamantine strength" (509A), in the *Charmides* Socrates
is twice criticized for employing an argument from parallel cases,
since the interlocutor (Critias) insists that the case in dispute is not
parallel. (See below, p. 194)

Eucleides is reported to be the author of six dialogues, including a *Crito*, an *Aeschines*, an *Alcibiades*, and an *Erotikos* (D.L. II.108).
Since Alcibiades is the figure with whom the erotic streak in Socrates is most closely associated, that theme is likely to have played

---

26. Döring (1972) 86.
27. D.L. II.106: Eucleides "eliminated the things opposed to the good and said
    they were not real (or "did not exist," *mē einai*)." The precise import of this
    is not clear, but it may involve an ontology in which negative concepts are
    defined by the absence or privation of the corresponding positive principle.
    This would then be the view that Plato is denying in his claim (in *Theaetetus*
    176A) that there must be something opposed to the good. But for other inter-
    pretations see Döring (1972) 86 n.1.

a role in Eucleides' dialogue of that name; and this will certainly be true for a work called *Erotikos*. The existence of these two titles bears witness to the intensity with which this theme was treated in the Socratic literature, even though we do not know what Eucleides' treatment was like.

5. ARISTIPPUS

Aristippus of Cyrene is the mystery figure among the prominent Socratics: the only one absent from the death scene[28] and perhaps the only one who did *not* write Socratic dialogues. On the other hand the account of his life in Diogenes Laertius is the longest of any Socratic except Plato, longer even than the chapters on Antisthenes and Xenophon, but it consists almost entirely of anecdotes and witticisms. We are given a vivid portrayal of Aristippus' rapid repartee, his social pliability, and his love for gourmet dishes, wine, women, and good conversation; but we are offered precious little information about his philosophical ideas and his image of Socrates.[29] A typical *mot d'esprit* is his reply to someone who reproached him for passing so easily from Socrates to the court of the tyrant Dionysius: "But I went to Socrates for education (*paideias heneken*), to Dionysius for entertainment (*paidias*)" (D.L. II.80). Aristippus' style of life was obviously expensive, and he is said to have been the first of the Socratics to teach for pay (D.L. II.65). When reproached for taking money from his associates, he said he did it not for his own sake, but in order for them to know how to make good use of their money. A series of stories connect him with the famous courtesan Lais. To those who complained of this connection he replied: "I possess her, but am not possessed by her. The best thing is to master pleasures, not to avoid them" (D.L. II.75).

28. Except for Plato of course (if we are to believe him on this point: in the *Phaedo* Plato's absence is artistically so convenient that it seems more likely to be fictional than historical), and except for Xenophon, who was still in Asia. But we may doubt whether Xenophon was ever a member of the inner circle.

29. We also have no definite information about his birth or death. He seems to be roughly of the same age as Plato, with whom he is said to appear at the court of Dionysius. But is this the first Dionysius, whom Plato probably visited *c.* 390–387, or is it his son (whom he visited twice, in the 360s)? Presumably the latter, but then Aristippus scarcely passed "from Socrates to Dionysius"! The whole chronology is extremely vague. See *SSR* Vol. IV, pp. 137f.

It has been pointed out as a measure of the extraordinary personal magnetism of Socrates that a man like Aristippus, an unrepentant pleasure-seeker and his opposite from almost every point of view, was nevertheless wholly bound to him in friendship and admiration.[30]

Aristippus seems to have remained on friendly terms with Aeschines but not with other members of the Socratic circle. It is hard not to see anti-Platonic animus in his attack on mathematics, based as it is on the charge that, unlike practical arts such as carpentry and shoemaking, mathematics "takes no account of what is good or bad, better or worse" (*SSR* IV A 170 = Arist. *Met.* B.2, 996b1). This would most naturally be directed against Plato's proposal in *Republic* VII that mathematical studies are an indispensable preparation for knowledge of the Good.

Xenophon's portrayal of Aristippus is clearly hostile, though not very different from the image conveyed by the jokes and anecdotes.[31] In Xenophon's account Socrates cross-examines Aristippus "because he [Socrates] noticed that one of his companions was rather self-indulgent (*akolasterōs echonta*) in matters of food, drink, sex, and sleep and [reluctant to endure] cold, heat, and toil" (*Mem.* II.1.1). Aristippus agrees with Socrates that the tough life is better training for anyone who has to assume the responsibilities of governing the city; but *he* has no such ambitions. Taking care of one's own needs is hard enough, says Aristippus; he wants his life to be as easy and as pleasant as possible. He has no desire to neglect his own interests in order to look after the

---

30. *SSR* Vol. IV, p. 142, citing Ivo Bruns. Compare the story in Plutarch (*De curios.* 2, 516c = *SSR* IV A 2) of Aristippus' conversion to philosophy by hearing a few samples of Socratic conversation at second hand in Olympia: "he was so powerfully affected that his body began to deteriorate; he became very pale and thin," until he could reach Athens and make contact with the man and his philosophy "whose goal was ⟨for each⟩ to recognize his own faults (*kaka*) and be rid of them." This is probably from a dialogue of Aeschines; see Dittmar (1912) 60f.

31. The opprobrium of "those who received a few things from Socrates and sell this to others for a high price" (*Mem.* 1.2.60 = *SSR* IV A 3) must be directed against Aristippus, although it might apply to Antisthenes as well. See above, n.11.

    It has frequently been suggested that the anecdotal tradition in Diogenes draws upon material from Aristippus' lost works. This would explain the convergence between this tradition and Xenophon, who must also have consulted Aristippus' writings.

needs of the city (*Mem.* ii.1.8–9). "Precisely for this reason I do not shut myself up in the confines of a political community (*politeia*), but I am a stranger (*xenos*) everywhere" (ii.1.13). A foreigner in Athens as in Syracuse, Aristippus revels in this role and so prefigures the cosmopolitan philosopher of Hellenistic times.

Our sources thus provide us with a clear and vivid picture of Aristippus' lifestyle. What is much less clear is how far he was interested in giving any theoretical formulation to the principles underlying such a life of agreeable dissipation.[32] His writings seem to have perished relatively soon and, unless their contents are reflected in the anecdotes and witticisms preserved in the Hellenistic tradition, we know almost nothing of them. Our picture is again distorted for Aristippus by the Hellenistic tendency to construe the history of philosophy in terms of "successions," and thus to represent Aristippus as the founder of a later school. Aristippus seems to have returned to his native Cyrene towards the end of his life, where the philosophical tradition was subsequently carried on by his daughter Arete and her son Aristippus the younger, known as *mētrodidaktos* "taught by his mother." It was probably only in these later generations that the so-called Cyrenaic school began to develop the hedonistic doctrines for which it was famous, defining pleasure as "smooth motion," welcome to all animals, pain as "rough motion," repellent to all (D.L. ii.86–7). The Cyrenaics held that the *telos*, or what is choiceworthy for its own sake, is particular pleasure; happiness as the overall system or balance of pleasures is chosen not for its own sake but for particular pleasures (ii.87–8). It seems unlikely that any of these Cyrenaic doctrines was propounded by Aristippus himself.[33]

It is also difficult to establish any connection between Aristippus and the two versions of hedonism presented in Plato's *Gorgias* and *Protagoras*. But it is probably important to bear in mind that Plato's treatment of pleasure is conditioned by the fact that Aristippus,

32. See in this connection W. Mann, "The Life of Aristippus," in *Archiv für Geschichte der Philosophie* (forthcoming, 1996), who suggests that for Aristippus philosophy was essentially a style of living. Similarly *SSR*, Vol. iv, p. 181.

33. The crucial text is fr. 155 Mannebach = *SSR* iv a 173: "He said nothing clear concerning the *telos*, but in effect he placed the reality (*hupostasis*) of happiness in pleasures. For since he was always talking about pleasure he led his followers to suspect that he meant the *telos* was to live pleasantly." As Mannebach (1961: 110) recognizes, all doxographical reports concerning a *telos* are formulated in the technical terminology of a later period.

one of the supposed "followers" of Socrates, had become notorious for his pursuit of pleasures of the most unabashedly sensual
type, in a lifestyle that turned its back on all traditional notions of
virtue and self-respect. (We may recall the anecdote in which Aristippus endures being spat upon by Dionysius and answers with a
bon mot, suggesting that this is a small price to pay for a good dinner, D.L. II.67.) There may be a passing allusion to Aristippean
sensualism here and there in the dialogues, but Plato probably regarded his stance as too disreputable, too lacking in moral fibre to
be taken seriously as a philosophical position.[34] Aristotle might
well have chosen Aristippus as a model for what he calls the *apo-
laustikos bios*, the life of enjoyment (*NE* 1.5, 1095b17). But he too
seems to think that such a view stands in no need of refutation; it
is enough to call it "the life of cattle" (1095b20).

6. AESCHINES[35]

With Aeschines (from the Athenian deme of Sphettos) we come to
the only Socratic, other than Plato and Xenophon, for whom we
have substantial literary remains. Aeschines' dialogues were widely
read down to the time of Plutarch, Lucian and beyond; and the
quotations from his *Alcibiades* and *Aspasia* are extensive enough for
us to form a relatively full picture of these two dialogues. From
the literary point of view, Aeschines can be regarded as the originator of the notion of Socratic *erōs*. Of course there must have
been some historical basis for this notion in the personality of
Socrates himself. But the literary presentation of this theme in the
dialogues of Aeschines and Plato refers in every case to a period in
Socrates' life of which neither Aeschines nor Plato can have had
any personal knowledge. What we have, then, is not historical
documentation but the literary development of a Socratic theme.
As far as we can tell, this development began with the two dialogues of Aeschines to be discussed here.

Important as an author, as a personality Aeschines is a kind of
poor relation among the Socratics. His place as a member of the
inner circle is guaranteed by Plato's references to him in the

---

34. Compare the inarticulate role assigned to Philebus as advocate of unqualified
hedonism in Plato's dialogue of that name. We might think of "Philebus" as
a pseudonym for Aristippus.

35. For a fuller version of this section on Aeschines, see Kahn (1994).

Apology (33E) and *Phaedo*, but his life in Diogenes Laertius is extremely meager (D.L. II.60–4: among the Socratics, the only shorter life is that of Phaedo). We know nothing of when he was born or when he died. The reference in the *Apology* to his father as present in court suggests that he may have been younger than the others, and one anecdote definitely represents him as junior to Aristippus (D.L. II.83). According to one tradition it was Aeschines who urged Socrates to escape from prison; Plato transferred this role to Crito "because Aeschines was too friendly with Aristippus" (II.60). Aeschines was a poor man, and his poverty drove him to write speeches for the lawcourt and perhaps to give lectures for pay (II.62–3).

It is above all for his dialogues that Aeschines was remembered; they were admired for their lifelike portrayal of Socrates. Ancient critics praise these works for their natural style and purity of diction, and some authors prefer them to Plato's.[36] We know the names of seven dialogues, and there may have been more. We can detect a strong literary interaction between the two pest-known works of Aeschines and several of Plato's earlier dialogues.

6.1 The Alcibiades of Aeschines

The *Alcibiades* was a narrated dialogue, in which Socrates reports to an unidentified audience a conversation he has had with Alcibiades. The external form is thus the same as that which Plato adopted in his *Charmides* and *Lysis*, apparently following Aeschines' example. Plato has made the internal structure of the dialogue more elaborate, since in the reported conversation of Aeschines' dialogue Socrates has only one interlocutor, whereas in Plato's *Charmides* he has two (and one more in the prologue) and in the *Lysis* he has four. On the other hand the form of Aeschines' dialogue is more complex than the (presumably earlier) *Alcibiades* of Antisthenes, which seems to have had the simple mime structure of a direct conversation, without any narrative frame.[37] We probably

---

36. "There are seven dialogues of Aeschines which have captured the *ēthos* of Socrates" (D.L. II.61). For other literary judgments see Dittmar (1912) 260–5.

37. Antisthenes *Alcibiades* fr. 3 (Dittmar p. 309) = *SSR* V A 200. The mime form is attested only to the extent that this brief dialogue quotation is typical of the whole work. That would not prove that Antisthenes' dialogue was earlier (though it probably was), only that it was artistically less complex, as we

have the opening words of Aeschines' dialogue in the sentence: "We were seated on the benches in the Lyceum, where the judges organize the games" (*SSR* VI A 43). The gymnasium setting reminds us of the *Lysis*, where Socrates is initially heading for the Lyceum until he is stopped by Hippothales (*Lysis* 203A–B).

Aeschines' readers may have been familiar with the dialogue in which Antisthenes described (from personal experience, *autoptēs gegonōs*) the extraordinary physical strength, courage, and beauty of Alcibiades, which was such that "if Achilles did not look like this, he was not really handsome" (*SSR* V A 198–9). Some such picture was either presented or presupposed by Aeschines. Alcibiades appears here as so proud of his talents, his wealth, and his family connections that "he might easily have found fault with the twelve Olympian gods" (fr. 5 Dittmar = *SSR* VI A 46), and he regards his Athenian competitors as beneath contempt. Socrates undertakes to expose to him the folly of his self-conceit and the need for some serious moral and political training for a political career. Thus the situation is structurally the same as in the pseudo-Platonic *Alcibiades* I, where Socrates says to him: "You are in the depths of ignorance (*amathia*), and so you rush into politics before being trained" (118B). In both dialogues the task of Socrates is to bring Alcibiades to a more realistic view of himself and hence to a desire for improvement.

"I noticed that he was jealous of Themistocles," says Socrates (fr. 7 Dittmar = *SSR* VI A 49). So Socrates develops, in a long and eloquent speech that is largely preserved, the intellectual achievements of Themistocles in organizing the Greek victory over Xerxes while at the same time securing Xerxes' favor, so that when he was later exiled from Athens he was able to enjoy great esteem and power among the Persians (fr. 8 Dittmar = *SSR* VI A 50). The missing sections must have referred to the effort of self-improvement or "care for himself" (*epimeleia heautou*) which led to this success, since the preserved text emphasizes that his achievements were due to his superiority in *aretē*, his skill in deliberation (*bouleuesthai*), his intelligent planning (*phronein*), in short to his knowledge (*epistēmē*). But even such intellectual mastery was not

might expect. Notice that the two pseudo-Platonic dialogues entitled *Alcibiades* also have the simple mime form. This is presumably the "primitive" form of the Socratic dialogue, which we have in Plato's *Crito*, *Ion*, and *Hippias Minor*, and again in the *Meno* and many later dialogues.

sufficient to prevent Themistocles' failure in Athens and his exile in disgrace (VI A 50, lines 34–41).

The effect of this speech upon Alcibiades is overwhelming. He burst into tears and "weeping, laid his head upon my knees in despair" (VI A 51) as a sign of supplication, begging Socrates to rid him of his depraved condition and help him to gain *aretē* (VI A 52). (We may find an echo of this passage in Plato's *Symposium* 215E, where Alcibiades reports being moved to tears by Socrates' words.) Alcibiades had come to see that so far from being Themistocles' equal, he was, in his ignorance and lack of education, no better than the meanest laborer in the city (VI A 47, with Dittmar, pp. 99f.). The dialogue closes with a return to the narrative frame, where Socrates reflects upon the reasons for his success with Alcibiades and upon the limits of his powers. This final section is important enough to quote in full:

If I thought that it was by some art (*technē*) that I was able to benefit him, I would find myself guilty of great folly. But in fact I thought that it was by divine dispensation (*theia moira*) that this was given to me in the case of Alcibiades, and that it was nothing to be wondered at.

For many sick people are made well by human art, but some by divine dispensation. The former are cured by doctors; for the latter it is their own desire (*epithumia*) which leads them to recover. They have an urge to vomit when it is in their interest to do so, and they desire to go hunting when it is good for them to have exercise.

Because of the love (*erōs*) which I have for Alcibiades I have the same experience as the bacchantes. For when the bacchantes are possessed (*entheoi*), they draw milk and honey from wells where others cannot even draw water. And so although I know no science or skill (*mathēma*) which I could teach to anyone to benefit him, nevertheless I thought that in keeping company with Alcibiades I could by the power of love (*dia to eran*) make him better. (fr. 11 Dittmar = *SSR* VI A 53)

In the Socrates of this text, who denies that he has any *technē* to make men better by teaching them something, we immediately recognize the Socrates of Plato's *Apology*, who speaks with ambiguous admiration of the art of educating people in the virtue of man and citizen but who also firmly denies that he possesses any such art (19E–20C). We may plausibly count this as a well-documented attitude on the part of the historical Socrates, deliberately distancing himself from the sophists as professional teachers.[38]

38. So rightly Döring (1984).

Now the *aretē* in which Themistocles excelled is precisely what young men of Alcibiades' generation flocked to the sophists to learn. Instead, we find Alcibiades in the company of Socrates. Will Socrates teach him political *aretē* in Themistocles' sense? Certainly not. Will he teach him, or rather will he help him to release within himself the desire to acquire the kind of knowledge and excellence in which Themistocles was *deficient?* Perhaps so. At least the first step has been taken. Alcibiades has come to recognize his own ignorance, his nullity as far as the excellence of man and citizen is concerned. To that extent he has already been made "better." But what is the *next* step? How are *erōs* and knowledge related to one another? And how is *erōs* related to the kind of wisdom that Themistocles lacked?

The answer to these tantalizing questions is not clear from the preserved sections of the *Alcibiades*. And it seems to be an essential part of Aeschines' art to leave the reader in doubt, to stimulate us to think further about the issues raised,[39] in particular about the pursuit of excellence and wisdom and about the impact of Socrates upon his associates. The one thing that is unmistakable is the important role assigned to *erōs* in this connection. In the concluding passage of the *Alcibiades erōs* is presented as a kind of divine gift, like Philoctetes' bow, an almost irrational power, in contrast both with the worldly wisdom of Themistocles and with the technical training or *mathēmata* of the arts and crafts.

We must assume that there were historical grounds, in fact or at least in gossip, for Aeschines and Plato both to represent Socrates as the lover (*erastēs*) of Alcibiades. Of course Alcibiades' speech in the *Symposium* has the ring of truth about it, but that is simply the extraordinarily deceptive power of Plato's art. The events in question, when Alcibiades was in his "bloom," belong before the time of Plato's birth; and Aeschines was probably even younger. Plato was in no position to know the truth about this relationship, and in the convoluted narrative structure of the *Symposium* he has taken pains to disclaim any direct knowledge of the facts. We may accept Plato's account as the most likely story available to us; but it is probably correct to regard Aeschines as his predecessor. Aeschines does not tell us how he understood the relationship. But perhaps he is saying in his simpler way, through the ambiguous

39. See the perceptive comments of Gaiser (1969) 200–9.

syntax of *dia to eran* in the last words of the dialogue (which seem to mean "because of my love for Alcibiades" but might also mean the converse), what Plato indicates more explicitly in the Alcibiades speech: that what looked to the world like Socrates' flirtatious interest in handsome young men was in fact his way of focusing upon them the magnetic power of his own personality and thus drawing them to him "through the power of love," instilling in them a desire to imitate in their own lives the philosophical pursuit of *aretē* which they saw embodied in his. If this was not what Aeschines intended to say in comparing Alcibiades' impulse to the *epithumia* that leads a sick man to spontaneous recovery, that is at any rate what Plato understood when, following Aeschines' lead, he came to give his own literary portrayal of Socratic *erōs* in the *Charmides*, *Lysis*, and *Symposium*.

6.2 The Aspasia of Aeschines[40]

Since there are fewer verbatim quotations here than from the *Alcibiades*, the external form of the dialogue is not so definitely known. There is no clear evidence of a narrative frame; we seem rather to have a direct dialogue between Socrates and Callias. The internal structure is more complex. Socrates makes several long speeches, including the full report of a conversation in which Aspasia, playing the part of Socrates, cross-examines Xenophon and his wife. Thus the literary form is like Plato's *Menexenus* but even more variegated, since the dialogue contains at least one play-within-the-play, namely the Aspasia–Xenophon conversation enclosed within the Socrates–Callias dialogue.

Callias begins by asking Socrates to recommend a teacher for his son. In the *Apology* Callias is the father cited by Socrates as the one to whom this very question might be addressed: "whom would you select to train your sons in *aretē*?" (*Ap.* 20B). If, as seems likely, the *Apology* came first, this may have suggested to Aeschines the starting-point for his own dialogue, but with the ironical twist that this time it is Socrates who must answer questions.[41] In any case

40. Except where noted otherwise, my reconstruction of the *Aspasia* follows Ehlers (1966).
41. On this reversal of the usual situation see Ehlers (1966) 43. Note that in the *Apology* passage Callias actually recommends a teacher, namely Euenos of Paros.

we may be surprised to find that a man like Callias, who has spent a fortune on the sophists (*Ap.* 20A 5), should be turning to Socrates for advice on educating his son. Even more surprising, however, is Socrates' answer: send your son to Aspasia (fr. 17 Dittmar = *SSR* VI A 62).

As Pericles' semi-legal wife Aspasia was the most famous woman in Athens and the butt of a thousand jokes, above all in comedy. Her image is, on the one hand, that of the hetaira or courtesan and, on the other hand, that of the dominating female who has Pericles under her thumb. Aristophanes has her getting Pericles to start the Peloponnesian war in order to take revenge on the Megarians for kidnapping two of her prostitutes (*Acharnians* 526–39). It was apparently this somewhat disreputable character that Antisthenes represented in his own dialogue *Aspasia*. (See above, pp. 8f.)

Given her public image, the provocative nature of Socrates' recommendation of Aspasia will be unmistakable. Callias must have reacted with shock and disbelief. What? send a man to study with a woman? and with *such* a woman!

Socrates stands his ground. He himself regards Aspasia as his teacher; he goes to her for instruction on matters on which she is expert, presumably matters of love.[42] The rest of the dialogue consists of three different kinds of examples introduced by Socrates in defense and explanation of his claim that Aspasia is the best teacher of *aretē*; and all three sets involve the power of love. The examples are as follows:

1. Two other outstanding women: Rhodogyne and Thargelia.
2. Aspasia as a teacher of political excellence: Pericles and Lysicles.
3. Aspasia as a teacher of moral excellence: Xenophon and his wife.

1. The fictitious Persian queen Rhodogyne is presented as a woman whose military success and devotion to duty displayed all the qualities of an exceptional man. Thargelia was a (legendary?) Milesian hetaira who married a Thessalian prince and ruled over the Thessalians for thirty years.

---

42. Fr.19 Dittmar = *SSR* VI A 62. Since we do not have the literal text, we do not know whether or not Aeschines said explicitly that Socrates went to Aspasia for lessons in love (*ta erōtica*), as later sources report. Given Aspasia's reputation, that was certainly implied.

2. The example of Thargelia prepares us for the transition to Aspasia, another Milesian concubine turned queen: she rules Pericles and Pericles rules Athens. It has been plausibly conjectured by several scholars that the story of Thargelia was told in a speech *composed by Aspasia* that Socrates recites from memory, as he recites Aspasia's funeral oration in the *Menexenus*. That could explain why the one literal quotation that we have from the Thargelia episode is in extreme Gorgianic style (fr. 22 Dittmar = *SSR* VI A 65). For, as we shall see, Aspasia is presented by Aeschines as a teacher of rhetoric in the manner of Gorgias. In any case, the Thargelia speech anticipates another Platonic piece of virtuoso writing, namely the speech of Agathon in the *Symposium*. For Aeschines here (in fr. 22), as Plato there, has produced an imitation of Gorgias' diction exaggerated to the point of caricature.

Aspasia is praised for her role in Pericles' political career. She was not only the source of wise political advice; she also taught him rhetoric. She made Pericles into a powerful political orator by "sharpening his tongue on Gorgias" (fr.24 = *SSR* VI A 65). Thus Aeschines presented Aspasia as Pericles' teacher in public speaking, just as Plato was to do in the *Menexenus*. And Aeschines' Aspasia not only made Pericles into an effective speaker; she repeated the performance with Lysicles the sheep-merchant (fr.26 = *SSR* VI A 66).

Lysicles must be the Athenian general who died in Caria in 428, scarcely a year after Pericles' death (Thucydides III.19.1). His fame lived longer, above all in comedy, where he serves as a model for jokes about vulgar tradesmen with successful political careers.[43] To demonstrate that Aspasia's achievement with Pericles was due to her talent and not simply to his own gifts, Aeschines has her perform the same feat with Lysicles, where her decisive influence would be undeniable: she raised Lysicles from humble origins to the height of power and made a man of no talent and training into "a skillful orator and an admired general,"[44] just like Pericles.

---

43. So in Aristophanes' *Knights*, produced in 424 BC, the oracle which announces Cleon's imminent overthrow by the sausage-seller mentions as precedents a rope-seller overthrown by a sheep-seller (Lysicles) who is in turn overthrown by a leather-seller (Cleon). See verse 132 with scholia; Lysicles is mentioned by name at verse 765.

44. This is from the Syriac version cited by Ehlers (1966) 75–7. Compare frs.26–7 Dittmar = *SSR* VI A 66 and 68.

This comparison must have sounded strange to anyone who remembered Lysicles' image in Aristophanes, or the disastrous campaign recorded by Thucydides, which ended in Lysicles' death.

3. By contrast with the stories of Aspasia's liaisons with Pericles and Lysicles, Socrates' last example presents Aspasia in the respectable role of advisor to a young married couple: no other than Xenophon and his wife!

The Xenophon episode is preserved in Cicero's Latin translation.[45] We have first a conversation between Aspasia and Xenophon's wife, then one between Aspasia and Xenophon himself, the whole of which is *narrated by Socrates.* This literary experiment with a genuine (reported) dialogue-within-a-dialogue seems to have no exact parallel in Plato. The closest thing is the reported conversation with Diotima in *Symposium* 201Dff. And Diotima is in many ways Plato's response to Aeschines' Aspasia. But there is a significant formal difference, since in the *Symposium* Socrates is represented as narrating a conversation in which he himself was a participant, which makes the report more natural. In this respect, as in the overall form of the reported dialogue as we found it in the *Alcibiades*, and also in the parody of the Gorgianic style, Aeschines seems to be the inventor but Plato the perfecter of each technical innovation.

The passage has the form of a Socratic *epagōgē* or, as Cicero calls it, an *inductio.* So Aspasia figures here as "a female Socrates."[46] She asks Xenophon's wife, first, whether if her neighbor possessed finer gold jewelry she would prefer her neighbor's gold to her own, and next whether, if her neighbor had more precious clothes and ornaments, she would prefer her neighbor's clothes or her own. In both cases the wife answers that she would prefer her neighbor's portion. The third question is: "If she had a better man as husband than you have, would you prefer hers or yours?" At this point the wife blushes, and Aspasia begins to question Xenophon. When asked concerning a better horse and a better estate, Xenophon answers as expected, like his wife, that he would prefer the better share. And then comes the third question: "What if the neighbor had a better wife than you, would you prefer yours or his?" And here Xenophon too falls silent. Then Aspasia speaks.

45. *De Inventione* 1.31.52F. See fr.31 Dittmar = SSR VI A 70.
46. Hirzel's apt phrase, quoted by Dittmar (1912) 51.

"Since neither of you answered the question I wanted most to hear answered, I will say what each of you was thinking. You, the wife, want to have the best husband, and you, Xenophon, want to have the most excellent wife. Hence unless you bring it about that there is no better man and no more excellent woman on earth, you will both be lacking in what you regard as most desirable (*optimum*), namely, that you have married the best possible wife and she the best possible husband."

Here end the quotations from Aeschines' *Aspasia*. We do not know how far Socrates' final remarks will have elaborated the point of this little conversation and of the whole dialogue. But it would seem that Aspasia is appealing to the love which Xenophon and his wife have for one another in order to urge them on to a mutual effort of self-improvement.[47] Hence Aspasia in her "Socratic" role serves to generalize the principle that Socrates embodies at the end of the *Alcibiades*: to make someone better *dia to eran*, through the power of love.

We thus have several different versions of that deep, somewhat mysterious link between *erōs* and the urge to *aretē* that was brought out in the conclusion to the *Alcibiades*. In the absence of a complete text for either dialogue, it is impossible to see precisely how Aeschines meant this link to be understood. The three long quotations from the *Alcibiades* and *Aspasia* suggest that the dialogues of Aeschines were composed like an artful short story, a strange mixture of truth and fantasy where we as readers are left free to work out our own interpretation.

What should be clear, on any interpretation, is just how fantastic and implausible are the components of this extraordinary dialogue. The figures of Aspasia and Lysicles are taken from comedy, and transformed.[48] Aeschines has borrowed the story of Thargelia from Hippias the sophist, who apparently reported that she was

---

47. So Ehlers. The passage is open to other interpretations.
48. Aspasia and Lysicles are both historical, of course, but only Aeschines brought them together. Plutarch reports as follows: "Aeschines says that Lysicles the sheep-merchant, of humble birth and undistinguished talent, became first among the Athenians by living with Aspasia after Pericles' death" (*Life of Pericles* 24 = SSR vi A 64). Since Lysicles died within a year of Pericles' death, this story should never have been taken seriously by modern historians. Yet Kahrstedt has Lysicles married to Aspasia (*RE* 13 [1927] 2550–1); Gomme (1956: 279) is more cautious.

so beautiful and wise that she was married to fourteen men.[49] In Aeschines her story begins with Antiochus and ends with Xerxes, which appears to be chronologically impossible.[50] Pericles learning Gorgianic rhetoric from Aspasia is certainly chronological non-sense: Gorgias' only recorded visit to Athens was in 427, two years after Pericles' death. Writing a generation later, Aeschines is as indifferent to the historicity of his Aspasia stories as he is when describing the exploits of his imaginary Persian queen. And Aspasia was surely dead before Xenophon was old enough to have a wife. Thus *not one* of the five episodes (Rhodogyne, Thargelia, Pericles, Lysicles, Xenophon and wife) cited by Socrates in the *Aspasia* is historically accurate, or even historically plausible.

Before leaving Aeschines we may take note of some points of literary contact between these two dialogues and several of Plato's earlier writings. These connections not only suggest a good deal of mutual influence but also permit us to reconstruct some of the chronology of composition. There is an obvious link between Aeschines' *Aspasia* and Plato's use of Aspasia in the *Menexenus*, where she is said to be the author of the funeral oration that Socrates recites, and which he claims she composed with the leftovers from the speech she wrote for Pericles. It seems clear that Plato is the debtor here, and that it is from Aeschines that he has taken the motif of Aspasia as teacher of rhetoric for Pericles and Socrates.

Now in the case of the *Menexenus* we have that very rare thing, an absolute date. Because of the nature of its reference (at 245B–E) to the King's Peace of 386 BC, the *Menexenus* must have been written in the same year or immediately thereafter.[51] So Aeschines' *Aspasia* will have been composed before 386, but perhaps not by much. We can provisionally situate it in the early 380s. And if we follow Ehlers in interpreting the *Aspasia* as a kind of sequel to the *Alcibiades*, then the latter must also fall before 386.

On the other hand, in Plato's *Ion* we find a verbal reminiscence

---

49. DK 86B.4; cf. Dittmar (1912) 30. Aeschines seems to have married her only to Antiochus, the "ruler" of Thessaly (frs.21–2; *SSR* VI A 64–5). Ehlers' attempt (1966: 52ff.) to reconstruct the historical facts behind this fantastic tale seems unconvincing and unnecessary.
50. See Ehlers (1966) 53, n.66 for the problem of dating Antiochus.
51. The King's Peace is much more than a *terminus post quem*, if I am right in seeing the *Menexenus* as a kind of moral protest against the terms of that peace. See Kahn (1963) 220–34.

that seems to point in the opposite direction: here Aeschines must be the borrower. In Aeschines' *Alcibiades* (fr.11c Dittmar, cited above on p. 21), Socrates compares himself to the bacchantes who draw milk and honey when possessed, just as they do in *Ion* 534A. Since the imagery of possession is deeply embedded in the *Ion* context but somewhat surprising in Aeschines (where Socrates does not *seem* to be possessed), it is natural to suppose that in this case Aeschines is echoing Plato.[52] Now the *Ion* is plausibly dated in or shortly after 394 BC.[53] So we have the following coherent picture.

Plato's *Ion*, *c.* 394–392
Aeschines' *Alcibiades*
Aeschines' *Aspasia*
Plato's *Menexenus* 386–385

I do not attempt to locate Antisthenes' *Alcibiades* and *Aspasia* here, although I imagine that both of them belong before the corresponding dialogues of Aeschines.

It would be unreasonable to insist on this chronology as historically established.[54] But it is internally consistent and intrinsically plausible. And it fits with the evidence from another early Platonic dialogue, the *Hippias Minor*, which (as we shall see in Chapter 4 §7) implies a polemical relation to a work by Antisthenes. At this early stage of his own literary career, Plato seems to have engaged in frequent exchanges with his fellow Socratic authors.

7. XENOPHON AND THE FICTIONAL CHARACTER OF SOCRATIC LITERATURE

The Socratic writings of Xenophon (*Memorabilia, Apology, Symposium, Oeconomicus*) are too extensive to be surveyed here. And there is no reason to believe that these writings made any impact whatsoever on Plato.[55] To the contrary, on the subject of Socrates

52. So Ehlers (1966) 22, following Flashar (1958) 61.
53. Flashar (1958) 101f.
54. For a fuller defence of my proposed chronology, see Kahn (1994) 103–5.
55. The only case known to me where Plato takes account of a text in Xenophon is not in reference to anything Socratic but in his polemical allusion to the *Cyropaedia* at *Laws* III.694cff., where the education of Cyrus is criticized. See the discussion in Tatum (1989) 216ff. and 226ff.

Xenophon seems rather like a sponge, soaking up ideas, themes, and even phrases from Antisthenes, Aeschines, and Plato. This is to be explained by the fact that, whereas the other Socratics were writing in the 390s and 380s, within ten or fifteen years after Socrates' death, Xenophon's Socratic works were apparently composed much later, perhaps in the 360s, after the first generation of Socratic literature had made its appearance.

Xenophon left Athens as a young man in 401 BC, two years before Socrates' death, to pursue a career of military adventure in Asia. When he returned to Greece in 394, he was exiled from Athens and lived in a remote village in the western Peloponnese until at least 370 BC. The *Memorabilia* may have been begun during Xenophon's long exile, but the work seems to have been completed only after his return to Athens in the 360s.[56]

Since Xenophon is the only Socratic author other than Plato whose works have been preserved, he is a key witness for the extent to which such writings mix fact and fantasy in ways to which we are unaccustomed. From one point of view, as works of imaginary biography, Xenophon's Socratic writings can be compared to his *Education of Cyrus*, which a recent commentator has rightly described as an "imperial fiction."[57] In the *Memorabilia*, of course, Xenophon's imagination was nourished by his youthful memories of Socrates. But these memories were in turn filtered through the Socratic literature that had been published in the meantime. We may first consider some marks of this earlier literature in Xenophon, before documenting the fictional element in his work.

It is particularly easy to trace the influence of Antisthenes, since he appears in person in both the *Memorabilia* and the *Symposium*. Gigon has shown how Xenophon begins his depiction of Socrates' character (in the second chapter of the *Memorabilia*, 1.2.1) with three virtues that correspond closely to the moral ideal of Antisthenes: self-mastery (*enkrateia*), endurance (*karteria*), and self-sufficiency (*autarkeia*).[58] Xenophon, despite his somewhat unfavorable presen-

---

56. This is the judgment of Lesky (1957/58: 468): the Socratic writings were "hardly composed before the 360s." Lesky's judgment is obviously correct for Book III of the *Memorabilia*, which presupposes the situation after the battle of Leuctra in 371 (III.5). See Delatte (1933) 73, 172; and Breitenbach (1967) 1811.

57. Tatum (1989).

58. Gigon (1953) 27.

tation of Antisthenes' personality, clearly finds Antisthenes' conception of manly virtue largely in harmony with his own view.[59] So perhaps we should speak of affinity rather than influence when we find Xenophon's Socrates warning against the enslavement of passionate sexual attachments – above all from kissing beautiful boys – and preaching the need for training in self-restraint and for indulgence only in pleasures that are not overwhelming. The true *erōs* is the love of one wise man for another (*Symp.* VIII.3–4). But sexual urges should be satisfied with unattractive women, as hunger with simple foods (*Mem.* 1.3.14-15; cf. *Symp.* IV.38). Wives should be chosen for their qualities in producing good children (II.2.4). The adulterer is the human equivalent of sensual birds like quails and partridges, who are caught in traps because they cannot resist the allurements of the female (II.1.4–5). This attitude towards sexual indulgence which we find developed in the first two books of Xenophon's *Memorabilia* coincides to a very large extent with doctrines that are attested for Antisthenes.

Since Aeschines introduced Xenophon into his *Aspasia*, we naturally look for some response on Xenophon's part. Aeschines' name is never mentioned by Xenophon, but we do find several echoes of this literary scene. At *Memorabilia* II.6.36 Xenophon's Socrates quotes Aspasia as his authority for the view that good matchmakers are successful in arranging good marriages only by telling the truth about the candidates for marriage. And at *Oeconomicus* III.14, when Socrates is asked whether men with good wives have trained them themselves, he responds: "I will introduce you to Aspasia, who is more knowledgeable than I and will explain the whole matter to you." We recall that it was precisely as the teacher of husband and wife that Aspasia appeared in the Xenophon episode of Aeschines' dialogue.

These examples may serve as a specimen of Xenophon's use of material from his Socratic predecessors. His indebtedness to Plato can be so abundantly documented that I treat this topic in an Appendix (pp. 393–401). Several passages of particular importance for the interpretation of Socrates will be analyzed in Chapter 3 §3.

59. Compare Caizzi (1964) 96: in Xenophon's eyes "Antisthenes was the closest to Socrates, the one who was most worthy of his legacy, despite the divergences of temperament that he himself [sc. Xenophon] rather humorously points out."

We turn now to the dimension of fiction in Xenophon's Socratic writings. It is at first sight quite astounding but in the end perfectly obvious that when Xenophon says, "I remember" or "I was there," there is no reason at all to take him at his word. We have simply to get used to a quite different, essentially fictitious use of the first-person narrative, without any attempt even at what we might expect as fictional plausibility. For example, Xenophon begins his *Symposium* with the statement that he was present, but no mention is made of him in the rest of the work, and we know that at the fictive date of Callias' party in 422 BC Xenophon must have been less than ten years old. He does not expect us to believe, or even to imagine, that he was present at this imaginary party. Similarly, the *Oeconomicus* opens with the remark: "I once heard him discussing as follows the subject of household management." But it is clear in the sequel that what we have is Xenophon speaking, not Socrates.

The *Oeconomicus* is an extreme case of fictive implausibility, since Xenophon makes Socrates refer explicitly to the death of Cyrus and the events of 400 BC (at IV.16–19), although Xenophon never saw Socrates after 401 BC.[60] To speak of anachronism here would be misleading; there is simply no attempt made to keep up the pretense that it is Socrates speaking, much less that Xenophon is present. In the *Symposium*, on the other hand, a good deal of care is given to fictional verisimilitude, that is, to creating the artistic illusion of a scene in the 420s. (Here Xenophon is surely following the precedent set by Plato in his construction of dialogues with well-defined fictive dates, such as the *Charmides* and *Symposium*.) But chronological consistency is not to be pressed too far even here. When Socrates in his long speech on love refers to the views of "Pausanias the lover of Agathon," he is clearly referring to the speaker in Plato's *Symposium*. (It does not matter that he has partially mixed up Pausanias' speech with that of Phaedrus.) Even in the imaginary world of Socratic literature this is impossible, of course, since the fictive date of Plato's *Symposium* is six years later than that of Xenophon's. But that is really irrelevant. There is simply no consistent interest on Xenophon's part in fictive dates. So Charmides in a party dated in 422 BC can refer to his loss of property after 404 (*Symp.* IV.32).

In the *Memorabilia* anachronisms are inevitable, given the ram-

60. This was noticed by Maier (1913) 19f.

bling structure of that work. But more striking than anachronisms are the first-person formulae already mentioned, such as "I will write everything I remember" (1.3.1) and "I will state what I once heard him say" (1.4.2). Such statements must be understood as literary fictions designed to introduce a new section of the work or to call attention to an episode that Xenophon regards as particularly important.[61] Since these are presented as recollections, the larger fiction is that Xenophon was present at *all* the speeches: how else could he know what is said? But as Momigliano has pointed out, we are scarcely expected to believe "that Socrates was waiting for the arrival of Xenophon to lecture his own son Lamprocles on his duties towards his mother" (*Mem.* II.2).[62] The format of reminiscences is as much a literary fiction as the particular statements of "I heard him say." It is no accident that Xenophon's only unmistakably genuine recollection of Socrates occurs in an historical work, the *Anabasis*, where he reports how he evaded the advice that Socrates gave him to consult the Delphic oracle on whether to join the expedition of Cyrus (*Anabasis* III.1.5–7). In an historical work such reports are intended to be believed. But entirely different conventions prevail in the *Sōkratikoi logoi*.

We know very little about the format of Antisthenes' Socratic dialogues, but I suspect that he provided the model for Xenophon's introduction of himself in the first person, a device that we do not find in Aeschines or Plato. For we do know that Antisthenes gave a description of Alcibiades from his own experience;[63] and this would be most naturally done in a dialogue introduced or narrated in the first person. We can say for the *Memorabilia* and *Symposium* what Momigliano has said for the *Cyropaedia* (where again Antisthenes is the precedent, with two dialogues entitled *Cyrus*): "The existence of previous Socratic writings of the same type may explain why Xenophon felt no need to warn his readers about the fictitious character of his biography: this was understood."[64]

---

61. Caizzi (1964) 90 has pointed out that two important theological discussions in the first and last books of the *Memorabilia*, which have many points in common, are formally linked by the fact that in both cases Xenophon introduces the conversation as one at which he was personally present (1.4.2 and IV.3.2), "perhaps to give greater prominence to what he says."
62. Momigliano (1971) 54.
63. *autoptēs* in *SSR* V A 198. See above, p. 20.
64. Momigliano (1971) 55. Momigliano notes the role of Antisthenes in this connection (*ibid.* p. 47).

Xenophon was clearly no innovator in the use of fictional narratives. If we look back at Aeschines' *Aspasia*, we recall that the element of fantasy is predominant there. (Are we expected to believe that Socrates actually recommended Pericles' mistress as the moral tutor for Callias' son?) Since Xenophon can scarcely have been married during Socrates' lifetime, much less during Aspasia's, the Xenophon episode in this dialogue has always been recognized as unhistorical. What has not been sufficiently noticed is that every single episode in the *Aspasia* is not only fictitious but incredible.

Thus it was the Socratics as a group, and the literature they produced, that "moved to that zone between truth and fiction which is so bewildering to the professional historian."[65] Plato seems to be an exception only if we forget the *Menexenus*, where Aspasia produces the funeral oration for 386 BC, if we ignore the anachronisms of the *Ion*, which led one scholar to give it a "fictive date" of 394 BC[66] (five years after Socrates' death ...), and if we are so willing to twist or disregard chronology as to suppose that Parmenides and Zeno actually visited Athens around 450 BC (to give Socrates the opportunity of explaining to them Plato's doctrine of Forms ...).

We shall not understand what biography was in the fourth century if we do not recognize that it came to occupy an ambiguous position between fact and imagination ... The Socratics experimented in biography, and the experiments were directed towards capturing the potentialities rather than the realities of individual lives. Socrates, the main subject of their considerations ... was not so much the real Socrates as the potential Socrates. He was the guide to territories as yet unexplored.[67]

This fact is to a large extent obscured for us by the extraordinary realism or verisimilitude of Plato's dialogues. Plato's portrayal of Socrates is just as free, just as much his own, as that of Aeschines and Xenophon, Antisthenes and Phaedo. But he is unique in his ability to produce a work of art in which the characterization of

---

65. Momigliano (1971) 46. Cf. the remarks of Wilamowitz (1879: 192): Xenophon uses free inventions, "like all the Socratics (for to believe in the historical reality of his Socratic conversations is a hopeless naiveté, and just as good as to treat them as inauthentic)."
66. So Méridier (1931: 24): "la date *supposée* de l'entretien se place entre 394 et 391."
67. Momigliano (1971) 46.

the speakers and their way of expressing themselves are so convincing that the reader feels as if he or she had been present at an actual conversation. T. S. Eliot once said of Shakespeare that in his tragedies he treated the death of the hero much like other Elizabethan dramatists "except only that Shakespeare does it both more poetically and more lifelike."[68] Analogously we may say of Plato that he invents the conversations of Socrates with the same freedom as other Socratic authors, but that Plato does it both more philosophically and more lifelike. A lifelike picture of the past is one in which time and place, character and action are not only internally consistent but do not conflict conspicuously with well-known facts. Hence Plato's dialogues are relatively free of anachronism; that is simply a consequence of their dramatic realism. But if, by way of contrast, we do not take full account of the fantastic disregard for historical plausibility in Aeschines and Xenophon, we will fail to recognize one of Plato's greatest literary achievements: the creation of the "realistic" historical dialogue, a work of imagination designed to give the impression of a record of actual events, like a good historical novel.

68. T. S. Eliot (1932) 111.

CHAPTER 2

The interpretation of Plato

I. THE PROBLEM OF INTERPRETING THE DIALOGUES

An anecdote reports that, when Plato was about to submit a set of
tragedies for competition at the Dionysian festival, he encountered
Socrates on his way to the theater. After this conversation with
Socrates, so the story goes, Plato returned home and burnt all
his poetic compositions.[1] If this story is not true, it is certainly *ben
trovato*. Plato had the dramatic gifts of a Sophocles or Euripides,
but he decided to exploit them in a different literary form. In the
preceding chapter we surveyed the new genre that the development of Greek letters had provided for his use: the *logos Sōkratikos*, or
"conversation with Socrates." Since it was Socrates who had made
Plato a philosopher, it was by writing about Socrates – more exactly, by representing Socrates in his writing – that Plato could le-
gitimately deploy his dramatic powers in the service of philosophy.

Plato's compositions in the dramatic dialogue form achieved an
immense literary success. But Plato's use of this form, in which
he himself never appears, creates formidable difficulties for the
interpretation of his thought. The anonymity of the dialogue form
presents the interpreter with a problem that is unparalleled for
any other philosopher. According to a Platonic doctrine suggested
in many places and crystallized in the *Republic*, the philosophical
vision tends to see things together, to seek for unity in the midst
of diversity and plurality.[2] But where is the unity to be found in
Plato's own vision? Since we never hear Plato's own voice, how can
we know where, and to what extent, what Socrates says represents
what Plato thinks? The problem is made more acute both by the

1. D.L. III.5.
2. "One who sees things together (*ho sunoptikos*) is a dialectician, one who does
   not is none" (*Rep.* VII, 537C 7).

36

formal independence of the dialogues from one another, and by the discrepancy between the positions attributed to Socrates in different contexts.

We deal in this study with some eighteen dialogues,[3] from the *Apology* to the *Phaedrus*, covering almost two-thirds of Plato's entire corpus. Now it is a formal feature of these works that they make no explicit reference to one another: each dialogue presents itself as an autonomous unit, existing in its own literary space.[4] This situation changes with later dialogues. The *Sophist* and *Statesman* claim to continue a conversation begun in the *Theaetetus*; the *Critias* is a continuation of the *Timaeus*, and the *Timaeus* itself contains what appears to be an ambiguous reference back to the *Republic*. But the dialogues that we will discuss contain no such instance of overt cross-reference. In each case Socrates begins an entirely new conversation with new interlocutors. Although Socrates and his interlocutors will often refer to previous conversations, these conversations are not recorded in any of Plato's dialogues.

This formal autonomy makes it tempting, even desirable, to read each dialogue as if it were a complete literary unit and a thought-world of its own, like the individual plays of Shakespeare or Molière. At the same time, anyone who is interested in Plato's philosophy must find a way to relate the intellectual contents of these works to one another. We cannot ascribe to Plato eighteen different philosophies. In part, then, the problem of interpreting Plato's work can be seen as the problem of how the philosophical contents of the different dialogues are to be connected with one another.

At first sight the positions presented in separate works seem not only distinct but in some respects incompatible. To take an extreme example: Socrates in the *Gorgias* consistently denies an identity between pleasure and the good that Socrates in the *Protagoras* seems to affirm. Has Plato changed his mind? If not, how are we to explain the fact that in at least one of these two cases he makes Socrates expound a view that he, Plato, believes to be false? Is

3. The *Apology*, of course, is not a dialogue but a set of courtroom speeches. In the next chapter we take account of this difference. To avoid pedantry, in most contexts I simply count the *Apology* among the dialogues.

   Among the dialogues proper I ignore the *Hippias Major*, which many scholars regard as Socratic or "transitional." I have given elsewhere my reasons for believing that this dialogue was not written by Plato. See Kahn (1985).
4. See Clay (1988). Clay is developing an observation of Tigerstedt (1977) 99.

Plato then not committed to Socrates' position in *either* work? And why do so many of the dialogues end in an *aporia* where no satisfying conclusion seems to be reached?

I maintain that the unifying links between dialogues, and the hints of conclusions not explicitly stated, are more deliberate, more subtle, and more ubiquitous than is generally recognized. Now the existence of thematic connections between dialogues is not itself a matter of dispute. Where interpreters differ is in the philosophical intention they attribute to these connections. Do different treatments of the same topic, such as the unity of virtue or the method of hypothesis, represent a change of views on Plato's part? Alternatively, is Plato simply exploring different possible positions, without a definite commitment to any one?[5] Or can these separate discussions ultimately be seen as different aspects of a single philosophical view? These are the central questions that any interpreter of the dialogues must confront.

2. TWO ALTERNATIVE READINGS OF THE DIALOGUES

Since the early nineteenth century the interpretation of Plato has been divided between two major tendencies: a unitarian view going back to Schleiermacher, and a developmental view introduced by Karl Friedrich Hermann. The unitarian tradition tends to assume that the various dialogues are composed from a single point of view, and that their diversity is to be explained on literary and pedagogical grounds, rather than as a change in the author's philosophy. Different dialogues are seen as exploring the same problem from different directions, or as leading the reader to deeper levels of reflection. According to Schleiermacher, the order of the dialogues is the order of a philosophical education. The unitarian tradition has been represented in this century (in different ways) by von Arnim, Shorey, Jaeger, Friedländer, and the Tübingen school.

The developmental tendency, on the other hand, assumes that Plato has changed his mind, and that the diversity of the dialogues reflects different stages in the evolution of Plato's thought. K. F.

---

5. The classical statement of this view is that of Grote (1875): "Plato is a searcher, and has not yet made up his mind" (I, 246). "Each of his dialogues has its own point of view, worked out on that particular occasion" (II, 278).

Hermann is credited with being the first to recognize a "Socratic" period in Plato's earlier work and to interpret the sequence of dialogues by reference to Plato's intellectual biography.[6] The developmental approach was reinforced at the end of the last century by the chronological study of Plato's style that began with Lewis Campbell's work in 1867 and which, by the end of the century, had successfully divided Plato's dialogues into three consecutive groups. Since all of the dialogues traditionally regarded as Socratic belong in the earliest of these groups, such stylistic studies seemed to confirm the developmental approach. After all, Plato began as a disciple of Socrates. Why should he not have established his own point of view by moving gradually away from, or beyond, the position of his master?

This approach presupposes that we can locate with some accuracy the philosophical position of Socrates within the dialogues, in order to trace Plato's movement from that point. Thus Guthrie recognized a group of dialogues in which Plato "is imaginatively recalling, in form and substance, the conversations of his master without as yet adding to them any distinctive doctrines of his own."[7] A more subtle and extreme formulation of this developmental view has been given by Gregory Vlastos, who finds an essentially Socratic philosophy in some ten or twelve Platonic dialogues. According to Vlastos, in these dialogues Plato is still under the spell of his master, whose philosophy is not only distinct from but antithetical to Plato's own mature thought. When Plato becomes an original philosopher, he departs from, and reacts against, his original Socratic position.[8]

By contrast, my interpretation will stress the elements of continuity in Plato's thought, and reject the notion of any sharp break between the earlier dialogues and the metaphysical doctrine of the *Phaedo* and *Republic*. But I should make clear that in denying the existence of a distinct Socratic period I do not mean to deny either the historical reality of Socrates or the importance of his influence on Plato. It is probably fair to say that no philosopher ever had a greater impact on his pupil or successor than Socrates had on Plato. It is the Socratic moral ideal, the total commitment to

6. Hermann (1839).
7. Guthrie (1975) 67.
8. Vlastos (1991). See ch. 2, "Socrates *contra* Socrates in Plato."

justice or righteousness (*dikaiosunē*) consecrated by Socrates' own martyrdom, that guides Plato throughout his life. The relationship between the two men will be more fully explored in the next chapter. What I deny is not the influence of Socrates but the usual biographical assumption that localizes this influence in Plato's earlier period.

It is also no part of my thesis to deny that we can plausibly recognize different stages in the formulation of Plato's thought. On the contrary, I will suggest that the traditional conception of a Socratic period confounds several distinct moments in Plato's development as a writer. But this traditional view also tends to conceal the fundamental continuity of thought between stages, and in particular between what I call the threshold dialogues and the next, more explicit statement of Plato's position in the great middle works: *Symposium, Phaedo,* and *Republic.*

It is on this point that my view is most resolutely unitarian. I want to deny any fundamental shift in philosophical position between such so-called Socratic dialogues as the *Laches, Charmides,* and *Protagoras,* on the one hand, and the *Phaedo* and *Republic* on the other hand. There is obviously a great deal of doctrine in the latter works that is absent from the former. But the argument from silence has no grip on an author as cunning as Plato. As Jaeger pointed out, the developmental interpretation often seems to assume that Plato must put into every dialogue everything that he knows or thinks at the time of writing.

Of course there are also better arguments for the developmental view, arguments that rely not upon silence but upon the appearance of doctrinal incompatibility, for example between the immanent essences of the *Euthyphro* and *Meno* and the metaphysical Forms of the *Phaedo,* or between the treatment of *akrasia* in the *Protagoras* and the moral psychology of the *Republic.* These arguments will be considered at length in Chapters 6 and 8, respectively.

Before proceeding with the interpretation, let me make the main outlines of my position clear. Concerning the *Gorgias* and the three very short dialogues, *Crito, Ion,* and *Hippias Minor,* my interpretation does not deviate very far from the traditional view. However, I do argue for more doctrinal continuity between these four works, and more distance from Socrates' own position, than is generally recognized – specifically with regard to Plato's unSocratic conception of a moral *technē.* And I emphasize that, formally speaking, the three shorter dialogues belong to the genre of "Socratic discourses" studied in Chapter 1. It is with the *Gorgias*, I suggest, that Plato first established himself as a major writer and transformed the *logos Sōkratikos* into an appropriate vehicle for constructive philosophy. But in its dogmatic tone the *Gorgias* is not typical. At the same time or, as I suppose, shortly thereafter, Plato created an essentially new form, the aporetic dialogue with a pseudo-historical setting. This form is exemplified in the seven works I call "pre-middle" or threshold dialogues to emphasize their proleptic relationship to the later group: *Laches, Charmides, Euthyphro, Protagoras, Meno, Lysis*, and *Euthydemus*. Plato here embarks upon a sustained project of philosophic authorship that reaches its climax in the three great middle works: *Symposium, Phaedo, Republic*. My view is that this group as a whole and each of its members are best understood from the perspective of the *Republic*. It is precisely for this threshold group that I would endorse Jaeger's somewhat extravagant claim:

For Plato the goal was fixed and the outlines of the whole scheme were already visible to him, when he took up pen to write the first of his "Socratic" dialogues. The entelechy of the *Republic* can be traced with full clarity in the early dialogues.[9]

I regard this, however, not as a strictly historical claim but as a hermeneutical hypothesis, a proposal for the most insightful reading of the dialogues. Except for what he tells us in the *Seventh Epistle*, we know nothing about Plato's intellectual biography.[10] And it is a mistake to think that we can make straightforward inferences from the dialogues concerning Plato's philosophical development. That would be impractical even if we knew the chronological sequence of the dialogues, which we do not. (The limits of our knowledge on this point will be traced in the next section.) The anonymity of the dialogue form, together with Plato's problematic irony in the presentation of Socrates, makes it impossible for us to see through these dramatic works in such a way as to read the mind of their author. To suppose that one can treat these dialogues as a direct statement of the author's opinion is what I call

9. Jaeger (1944) 152 = English tr. 96. I have modified the translation where necessary.
10. As I shall argue in Chapter 3, Aristotle's account of the origins of Plato's philosophy is not historically reliable.

the fallacy of transparency, the failure to take account of the doctrinal opacity of these literary texts. What we can and must attempt to discern, however, is the artistic intention with which they were composed. For in this sense the intention of the author is inscribed in the text. It is precisely this intention that my exegesis is designed to capture, by construing the seven threshold dialogues together with the *Symposium* and *Phaedo* as a single complex literary enterprise culminating in the *Republic*. And that means to see this whole group of dialogues as the multi-faceted expression of a single philosophical view.

Such, in outline, is the interpretation to be presented here. Since it involves a chronological component, I begin in the next section with a survey of our knowledge and ignorance concerning the chronology of the dialogues down to the time of the *Republic*. And since the prevailing view has a plausible biographical story to tell about Plato's philosophical development, tracing his progress from Socratic apprenticeship to mature Platonism by way of contact with mathematics and Pythagorean philosophy, to replace that story I shall sketch an alternative, equally speculative account of Plato's intellectual biography for the period of the early and threshold dialogues. In §5 I give a preliminary review of the evidence in support of my central thesis, the reading of these seven dialogues as deliberate philosophical preparation for the views to be presented in the *Symposium, Phaedo,* and *Republic*. This thesis implies that Plato had reached these views long before he expounds them in the middle dialogues. Why then should he withhold such information from readers of the earlier works? That is the question I attempt to answer in §6.

3. QUESTIONS OF CHRONOLOGY

The early nineteenth century had no reliable clues as to the order of the dialogues. The only fixed point was Aristotle's report in *Politics* II.6 that the *Laws* was written later than the *Republic*. F. A. Wolf had pointed out (in his edition of 1782) that the *Symposium* seemed to refer to events of 385 BC; and of course the *Apology* and other works referring to Socrates' trial and death had to be later than 399. But the rest was speculation. Schleiermacher put the *Phaedrus* first, because of its youthful spirit. Many dialogues were dated before the death of Socrates. The *Theaetetus, Sophist,* and *States-*

man were thought to be relatively early, the *Republic* very late, along with the *Timaeus* and the *Laws*.

All this was changed in the last quarter of the century by the insights of two scholars of genius, Lewis Campbell and Friedrich Blass, and by the careful work of a succession of diligent word- and phrase-counters, of whom the most distinguished was Constantin Ritter. The story is a fascinating one, and it is told most dramatically by Lutoslawski for whom it was still fresh.[11]

In 1867 Campbell published an edition of the *Sophist* and *Statesman* in which he argued for the late date of these dialogues on the basis of an amazing number of observations, both literary and stylistic, of features common to them and to the *Philebus, Timaeus, Critias,* and *Laws.* He thus identified what has come to be known as the late group or Group III. Campbell also noticed that the *Theaetetus, Phaedrus,* and *Republic* have more traits of diction and sentence structure in common with this group than do the other dialogues. He thus implicitly recognized the existence of what has since been identified as the middle group or Group II.

Campbell's work was revolutionary, but it remained unnoticed for nearly thirty years, until Lutoslawski brought it to the attention of the German scholars who, beginning with Dittenberger in 1881, had independently undertaken to establish the chronology of the dialogues on linguistic grounds. In the meantime an epoch-making discovery was contributed by Blass in his history of Attic rhetoric.[12] Blass observed that the avoidance of hiatus, systematically practiced by Isocrates, is adopted by Plato in only a few of his works, including the *Phaedrus,* but above all in the six dialogues independently identified by Campbell as the late group. Thus the identity of this group was clearly established by two independent investigators, using quite different observations, before the stylometricians began their work.

What Dittenberger (in 1881), Ritter (in 1888) and the others have done is above all to confirm the division of the dialogues into three groups. It was Campbell again in 1896 who definitively assigned the *Parmenides* to the middle group, together with the *Repub-*

---

11. Lutoslawski (1897). I am largely reporting information provided by Lutoslawski and Brandwood (1990). Brandwood gives a more reliable and up-to-date critical survey of work in the field, but Lutoslawski gives a fuller report of the early studies.

12. Blass (1874).

lic, *Theaetetus*, and *Phaedrus*[13]. (Ritter had found the style of the *Parmenides* so anomalous that he doubted its authenticity.) The same result concerning the three groups was reached independently by von Arnim, in a publication in the same year.[14]

In my opinion, this division of Plato's dialogues into three separate groups – early, middle, and late – can be regarded as a fixed point of departure in any speculation about the chronology of the dialogues. These groups were identified a century ago by three scholars working independently of one another, and their results in regard to the late group were confirmed by the hiatus observations of Blass and Janell.[15] The careful statistical studies begun by Dittenberger in 1881 and summarized by Brandwood more than a century later, have done nothing whatsoever to undermine this division into three groups.[16] This is the one solid achievement of stylistic studies.

Can stylometry do more? One may reasonably doubt it. What has occurred in the study of Platonic chronology since 1896 is (I am afraid) mostly confusion, not progress. There is first of all confusion about the term "middle dialogues," which was originally a name for the stylistically intermediate group, but is now applied to the dialogues of Plato's so-called "middle period" defined in terms of content, with reference to the doctrine of transcendental Forms. The "middle" period so defined includes two or three stylistically early dialogues (*Symposium*, *Phaedo*, *Cratylus*); whereas the

13. Campbell (1896) 129–36.
14. See the account of von Arnim's 1896 publication in Brandwood (1990) 96–109; more briefly in Lutoslawski (1897) 136–8.
15. Lutoslawski emphasizes the extent to which the early investigators worked in ignorance of one another's results. The three pioneers – Campbell, Blass, and Dittenberger – were completely independent of one another, but all three identified the same group of six dialogues as late. Ritter (1888) knew Blass and Dittenberger but not Campbell. Von Arnim (1896) knew Dittenberger but apparently neither Campbell, Blass, nor Ritter. See Lutoslawski (1897) 101, 103, 121, and 136. It was Lutoslawski who first brought all of these studies together.
16. Brandwood (1990: 108), commenting on the work of Ritter and von Arnim, notes "their complete agreement on the division into three chronological groups, and at exactly the same points." Elsewhere (p. 8) he recognizes that Campbell had already identified the same three groups. In another recent study, G. R. Ledger recognizes "the sharp difference between early and late works," and implicitly confirms the division between Groups II and III. See Ledger (1989) 224f. But these fundamental results are obscured by Ledger's attempt to establish a sequence for all of the dialogues.

intermediate chronological group, defined stylistically, excludes these but includes *Parmenides* and *Theaetetus* which are often thought of as "late" dialogues. To avoid this confusion it would be better to speak simply of stylistic groups I, II, and III, recognizing that today the terms "middle dialogue" and "middle period" are regularly used with reference to content rather than style. I submit, however, that it is only the stylistic division into three groups that offers any basis for an intersubjective agreement on chronological order.

A second source of confusion is even more radical. This is the attempt to employ stylometry to establish a chronological order for dialogues *within* the three groups. In effect, what Campbell, Ritter and others discovered was that, in the course of his long career, Plato's style changed basically *twice*: once when he undertook to write the *Republic*, a composition on an entirely new scale; and once again when he began systematically to avoid hiatus and hence adopt more unnatural word order and sentence structure. (This change occurred between the *Theaetetus* and the *Sophist*, marking the break between Groups II and III.) But there is really no reason to suppose that Plato's style changed significantly every time he wrote a new dialogue, and no reason to exclude the possibility that he was working on several dialogues at the same time.

The attempt to establish a complete linear ordering for the dialogues on stylometric grounds has produced no reliable results, no agreement after a century of work.[17] And this is what we might expect, since the attempt is based upon the fallacious assumption that chronological order will in every case be reflected in stylistic change. Although many if not all studies confirm the division into three groups, two different studies – even two studies by the same scholar[18] – rarely if ever produce the same ordering for dialogues *within* each group. In seeking to establish a linear ordering, stylometry in the last hundred years has attempted to do the undoable.

17. This lack of agreement is documented in the reviews of Brandwood's and Ledger's books. See, e.g. Schofield (1991) 108f.; Keyser (1991) and (1992); Young (1994).
18. The most striking case of this is von Arnim, who in his first (1896) study put the *Lysis* and the *Laches* at the very end of Group I, with the *Phaedo* and *Symposium*; but in his second (1912) study he placed both these dialogues near the beginning of this group, after the *Ion* and *Protagoras*. See the report in Brandwood (1990) 107 and 215.

This prolonged and continuing endeavor has served only to obscure, and hence undermine confidence in, the one solid, objective (or at least, reliably intersubjective) result of the chronological studies that began with Campbell. This is the modest but decisive achievement of dividing the dialogues into three groups.[19]

As far as stylistic evidence goes, then, the *Apology* and the *Crito* might have been written at the same time as the *Symposium* and the *Phaedo*. All we really know is that these works are, as a group, earlier than the *Republic*. I think it is reasonable to believe that the *Apology* and *Crito* were written early, soon after Socrates' death, and that the three dialogues presenting the metaphysical conception of Forms (*Symposium, Phaedo*, and *Cratylus*) were written much later, shortly before the *Republic*. But there seems to be no sound philological basis for arguing this point against a doubter. There is no significant stylistic change. Thus, if we rely on Ritter's figures as reported by Brandwood, the *Symposium* has only three features of Plato's late style, the same number as the *Ion* and *Charmides*, and only one more than *Apology* and *Crito*.[20]

I have presented elsewhere the case for dating the *Gorgias* before the *Protagoras*, against the prevailing view.[21] Although I believe that the *Gorgias* was written first, I do not suppose that I have proved this. Conceivably, these dialogues were written at the same time. We really do not *know* the order of dialogues within Group I. Hence a responsible scholar has the right to arrange them in any

---

19. The only systematic study known to me that does not fully confirm the division into three groups is that of Thesleff (1982). Thesleff (p. 70) does recognize the identity of Group III as "valid beyond any reasonable doubt," but he does not accept the standard view of Group II as a chronological unit. Thesleff's method of dating combines stylistic criteria with considerations of philosophical content and he introduces hypothetical revisions by Plato and rewriting by a secretary. In my view, this means giving up any basis for intersubjective agreement.

20. Brandwood (1990) 66. Compare the situation for the *Euthydemus*, which some scholars have wanted to date after *Republic* VII, because the *Euthydemus* ranks dialectic above mathematics in a way that recalls the *Republic* text (*Euthyd.* 290c). The burden of proof is on a supporter of this view to explain why the *Euthydemus* has only four late features, the same number as the *Protagoras*, whereas *Republic* VII has sixteen – roughly the same number as the *Parmenides*, which has seventeen – despite the fact that the *Euthydemus* is one-third longer than *Republic* VII. (For these figures see Brandwood (1990) 66 and 72.)

21. Kahn (1988a).

sequence that he or she finds persuasive. There are very few exceptions, one of which I will mention in a moment. But in general the ordering must be decided by literary tact, historical imagination, or personal hunch. This hermeneutical choice is not to be confused with the kind of solid philological result, intersubjectively confirmable, that is represented by the division into three groups.

Perhaps the one clear exception in Group I is the chronological priority of the *Meno* to the *Phaedo*. This is guaranteed, not by the absence of the Forms from the former and their presence in the latter (for nothing justifies us in supposing that Plato must assert every one of his doctrines in every dialogue), but by definite textual indications that the author of the *Phaedo* intends the reader to recognize that the *Meno* is presupposed. Whereas the doctrine of recollection is introduced as a surprising novelty in the *Meno* (81A–E), in the *Phaedo* it is presented as a familiar view that Socrates "often used to assert" (72E). The whole context in the *Phaedo* (with the mention of leading questions and geometrical diagrams) comes close to being a direct reference to the *Meno*.

This is, I think, almost the only case in Group I where Plato himself has marked a sequence for the dialogues. (The closest parallel is provided by those passages in the *Crito* that refer to what Socrates said in court, and that in fact correspond to passages in the *Apology*.) Otherwise, the dialogues prior to the *Republic* are composed in such literary independence of one another that any sequential ordering is left up to us.

My own preference, then, is to arrange the dialogues of Group I in six successive stages, moving towards the position of the *Republic*. This is illustrated in the following list. The division into three groups represents a well-established consensus; the order of dialogues within each group is a matter of personal conjecture.

The ordering of Plato's dialogues

Group I
1. Apology, Crito
2. Ion, Hippias Minor
3. Gorgias, Menexenus
4. Laches, Charmides, Euthyphro, Protagoras
5. Meno, Lysis, Euthydemus
6. Symposium, Phaedo, Cratylus

Group II
  Republic, Phaedrus, Parmenides, Theaetetus
Group III
  Sophist–Statesman, Philebus, Timaeus–Critias, Laws

I once believed that my arrangement of the dialogues in Group I was a chronological sequence, but I now think it is a mistake to make any claims about a matter on which we have so little evidence. Even if they are taken as chronological, however, my six stages do not pretend to represent the development of Plato's thought. They represent different moments in his literary presentation of Socrates and different approaches to the philosophical position of the *Republic*. In the last analysis, it is this systematic orientation towards the *Republic* that ties all or most of these dialogues together and offers the most enlightening perspective on their interrelationship. Such is my basic claim.

Since the dialogues of Group I are earlier, I have described their relation to the *Republic* as proleptic. But this term "proleptic" may seem too chronological. It does not greatly matter in what order these dialogues were actually composed or in what sequence they are in fact read. My six stages may be thought of as the proposal for an ideal reading order. Perhaps the better metaphor will be spatial rather than temporal: instead of before and after we can speak of exoteric and esoteric, of relative distance from the center as defined by the *Republic*. As a variant on the notion of prolepsis, this mode of interpretation might equally well be called *ingressive*. The different stages of Group I provide us with various points of entry, various degrees of ingress, into the Platonic thought-world that finds its fullest expression in the *Republic*.

4. A SPECULATIVE BIOGRAPHY

In the case of ancient authors we are generally without any serious documentation concerning the personal context of their literary work. For Plato, however, there is one exception. His *Seventh Epistle* offers a brief sketch of his early life, as seen from the vantage point of his old age.[22] As Dodds and others have recognized, this

22. Plato would have been about seventy-four at the time the letter was written. I have no doubt that the letter was written by Plato. Most twentieth-century Plato scholars have recognized the letter as authentic, but in the last gen-

account is most plausibly read as Plato's own self-portrayal of the events that led to the composition of the *Gorgias*. The letter gives us a picture of Plato's concerns in the 390s that seem quite different from the preoccupation with the theory and teaching of virtue that we find in the *Protagoras* and the dialogues of definition.

The narrative begins with the statement that "when I was young I had the same attitude as many others: I thought I would enter public life as soon as I came of age" (*Ep.* VII, 324B 8). Plato descended, in fact, from a great public family. He often mentions with pride his family connections with Solon; and his stepfather and great-uncle, Pyrilampes, was a close associate of Pericles.[23] It would have been natural for him to aspire to an eminent public role, like the ambitious young men he depicts in the dialogues, such as Hippocrates in the *Protagoras* (316B 8). But the letter recounts a series of events that prevented Plato from pursuing a normal political career. First there was the collapse of the extreme democracy after the defeat of Athens in 404 BC. In place of this constitution "which was reviled by many" came the oligarchic regime of the Thirty.

> Some of these leaders were relatives and acquaintances of mine,[24] and they invited me to join them as a natural associate. And my attitude was not surprising, in view of my youth. [Plato was twenty-three at the time.] I thought that they would lead the city from an unjust way of life to a just form of government. So I paid close attention to what they would do. And I saw that these men in a short time made the previous regime look like a golden age. (*Ep.* VII, 324D)

Plato particularly mentions their treatment of "my older friend Socrates, whom I would not hesitate to call the justest man of his time" (324E). The Thirty attempted to involve Socrates in their own crimes by ordering him to carry out a death-squad arrest of Leon of Salamis, which Socrates refused to do at the peril of his life.

> When I observed these events and many others of the same kind, I was disgusted and I withdrew from the evils of that time. But shortly after-

eration the doubters were more conspicuous. The *communis opinio* seems now to be swinging back in favor of authenticity.

23. *Charmides* 154E–155A, 157E–158A; *Timaeus* 20E–21D. For Pyrilampes see Dodds (1959) 261. On Plato's family see also below, pp. 186f.
24. Critias, ringleader of the Thirty, was Plato's first cousin; Charmides, one of the Thirty, was his uncle.

wards the Thirty fell and their whole constitution collapsed. Once more I was drawn, more slowly this time but nevertheless, by the desire for a public role in politics.

On the whole the restored democracy was quite moderate and resisted the temptation to take revenge on their political opponents. But by some chance they accused and put to death "our same companion, Socrates."

As I considered these matters and the men engaged in politics, and our laws and customs, the more I observed and the more I advanced in years, the harder it seemed to me to direct political affairs in the right manner. (325B)

It was difficult to find trustworthy allies, while both the political mores and the letter of the law seemed progressively more corrupt.

So despite my initial enthusiasm for a public career, seeing this general disorder I ended by becoming dizzy. And I did not give up watching for things to improve ... and waiting for an opportunity for action, but I finally understood that all the cities of today are badly governed. For the situation of their laws is practically incurable without an extraordinary stroke of good luck. And I was obliged to say, in praise of true philosophy, that it gives insight into what is just both for the city and for private individuals. So the races of mankind will not be released from evils until the class of true and genuine philosophers gain political power or until the rulers of the cities come by divine dispensation to practice true philosophy. It was in this frame of mind that I set out for my first trip to South Italy and Sicily. (*Ep.* VII, 325E–326B)

This is a document of extraordinary importance for anyone who assumes, as I do, that the letter was written by Plato. We could not have known of his youthful and persistent ambition for a political career, lasting until he was almost forty, if he had not told us himself. We might rather have imagined his early years preoccupied with philosophical inquiries, as in Socrates' description of his own youth in the *Phaedo*. But once we comprehend Plato's passionate concern for political action, many things fall into place. The deep yearning for political reconstruction explains why his three longest works, spanning his whole career, are devoted to the question of how to impose a moral order on the life of the city: *Gorgias*, *Republic*, and *Laws*. The same preoccupation helps us to understand his two fruitless voyages to the court of Dionysius II in Syracuse, when he thought he had some chance to influence the course of events in the most powerful city in the Greek world. From the repeated reference in this letter to the treatment of Socrates as a kind of measure of the health of a political regime, we can see the unique importance of Socrates in Plato's own life as a model for his moral and political thinking. And it is a model to which he still remains loyal in this letter, written almost half a century after Socrates' death. (The letter dates itself in 353 BC, just six years before Plato's own death.) By showing us how difficult it was for Plato to give up his political ambitions, the letter explains how important it was for him to conceive the life in philosophy as the continuation of politics by other means, so that his Socrates, at the end of the *Gorgias*, can paradoxically claim to be the only true politician in Athens (521D).

The letter tells us that Plato was about forty when he left Athens for Sicily and Magna Graecia. Looking back on this moment thirty-five years later, Plato reports that he had already reached the radical conclusion expressed in a famous passage of the *Republic*, that until political power and philosophic wisdom could be joined in the same hands, "there will be no cessation of evils for the cities, or even for the human race" (*Rep.* V, 473D). It seems entirely natural that in the letter Plato should quote this formula as the mature expression of his radically new view of politics. But this does not mean that the *Republic* was written when Plato was forty years old. Many scholars have recognized that the choice in the *Gorgias* between the Two Lives, the life in philosophy and the life in politics as usual, directly reflects Plato's own life decision as reported in the *Seventh Epistle*. A classic statement of the connection between the two documents is that of Dodds.

The secret of the peculiar emotional power of the *Gorgias* is, I think, that its author felt the issue as a deeply personal one, and has communicated the resulting tension to his readers ... Here behind the figures of Socrates and Callicles, we can for once catch sight of Plato himself. For in the light of the *Seventh Letter* it is fairly clear that the *Gorgias* is more than an *apologia* for Socrates; it is at the same time Plato's *apologia pro vita sua*.[25] Behind it stands Plato's decision to forgo the political career towards which both family tradition and his own inclinations (*Ep.* VII, 325E 1) had urged him, and instead to open a school of philosophy. The decision was, as he tells us, the outcome of a long internal struggle, and that

25. "That the *Gorgias* is 'Plato's Apology' was first said by Schleiermacher in the introduction to his translation of the dialogue (pp. 15f. of the 3rd edition)." (Dodds' note in Dodds [1959].)

struggle seems to have left its mark on certain pages of the *Gorgias*: we shall hardly be wrong in hearing an echo of it in Socrates' bitter words about the cloud of false witnesses from the best Athenian families whom Polus can call to prove him mistaken (472A–C); or in the sneer of Callicles at people who turn their backs on public life "to spend the rest of their days whispering in a corner with three or four young lads" (485D); or in Socrates' final call to a new way of living, without which there can be no true statesmanship (527D–E). These personal tones give the *Gorgias* a unique place among the dialogues.[26]

In the *Gorgias* the figure of Socrates has become the emblem for Plato's own choice of the life in philosophy. The *Seventh Letter* tells us that this choice became definitive before Plato left for Italy around 388 BC. It is because we seem to find the direct reflection of this decision in the *Gorgias* that we can plausibly date the dialogue either just before or just after the voyage to the West.[27] In my judgment, the tone of bitterness and the relentless condemnation of Athenian politics and culture are more likely to mark the *Gorgias* as a farewell to Athens composed by the disappointed politician-philosopher leaving the city in disgust, rather than as a homecoming gift after his sojourn in other cities whose moral life he found even more depraved (*Ep.* VII, 326B–D). So I conjecture that the *Gorgias* was composed in 390–388 BC, before the trip to the West and only a few years after the *Ion* and the *Hippias Minor*.

The *Gorgias* says explicitly what the *Seventh Epistle* implies: that Socratic soul-tendence is both the prerequisite and the goal for political activity, so that philosophy pursued in the Socratic spirit is the only realistic way of working for political improvement. I suggest that with this new conception of politics came a new conception on Plato's part of his own role as writer and teacher. The project of teaching will be pursued in his activities in the Academy, following his return to Athens. The project of writing will take shape in a new series of dialogues that begins with the dialogues of definition and culminates in the *Republic*. The novelty of this project will appear more clearly if we situate it against the background of what I assume to be Plato's earlier work.

The *Apology* and the *Crito* are Socratic in an historical sense, in that they attempt to explain and justify Socrates' actions in court

26. Dodds (1959) 31. Dodds is here following the insight of Wilamowitz (1920) I, 232–8.
27. So Dodds (1959) 26f.; Guthrie (1975) 284f.

and in prison, and thus to interpret the meaning of his life and death. The *Ion* and the *Hippias Minor* (which I take to be the only other dialogues composed in the 390s before the *Gorgias*) are Socratic in the literary sense: they represent imaginary conversations in which Socrates develops ideas (about poetry and about morality) that are somehow connected with the historical Socrates but freely developed in Plato's own way. Here Plato is amusing himself in the new literary genre of "conversations with Socrates," while at the same time developing certain themes and modes of argument that betray his involvement with philosophy in a more technical sense (as we shall see in Chapter 4). As I have suggested, it is in the *Gorgias* that Plato first sets out to formulate his own philosophical position and to compose a major literary work. Of course the *Apology* and *Crito* are small-scale masterpieces, revealing an exceptional literary talent; but the *Ion* and the *Hippias Minor* suggest that Plato was not ready to exploit that talent fully. It is, I assume, in the *Gorgias* that he does so for the first time. And the *Gorgias* will be followed or accompanied, after Plato's return to Athens, by an unceasing stream of dialogues, beginning perhaps with the *Laches*, and constituting the most extraordinary body of philosophical literature ever composed. Thus the man who, on my view, was only an occasional author before the composition of the *Gorgias* in his late thirties, became from then on something like a full-time writer, despite the fact that, as he tells us both in the *Seventh Letter* and in the *Phaedrus*, he never considered writing to be the most important part of his philosophical activity.

In the *Gorgias* we have, as Dodds recognized, "the first statement of Plato's personal views on ethics and politics, later to be developed in the *Republic*."[28] But the defense of Socratic ethics in the *Gorgias* is above all a negative achievement, in the brilliant refutation of Polus and Callicles. The positive argument for the life of Socratic virtue is much less satisfactory, as we shall see. And so Plato will be obliged to undertake once more the defense of justice and the moral life, as he will do in the *Republic*. But to do so with greater success he must first accomplish a major constructive work of philosophic thought and writing.

28. Dodds (1959) 16, n.1. For the central importance of political reconstruction in all of Plato's thought, see the remarks of Jaeger *à propos* of the *Seventh Letter*, (1944) 137 = English tr. 83f.

We can only guess how much philosophy Plato was discussing with his friends in those first ten years after Socrates' death, when his chief concern seems to have been the search for political allies and for an opportunity of political action. What we learn from the *Gorgias* about his early philosophical preoccupations, in addition to his moral-political program and his extraordinary skill in deploying arguments, is above all a keen interest in the mystical view of the soul that is usually described as Orphic or Pythagorean, and which in the dialogue is attributed to "someone from Sicily or South Italy" (493A 6). It was of course not necessary to travel to the West to encounter such ideas; they are introduced in the *Gorgias* by a quotation from Euripides (492E). But it may well be this interest in a view of the afterlife much cultivated in the West, as much as curiosity about Pythagorean science and mathematics, that decided Plato to undertake his voyage to the New World.[29] It may also be that he simply felt the need for a radical change of scene, for the opportunity to reflect upon life in Athens from a perspective both culturally and geographically remote.

Plato seems to have returned to Athens within a year or two, probably in 387 BC.[30] We have another very unusual document that reflects his passionate concern with Athenian politics shortly after his return. This is the funeral oration contained in the dialogue *Menexenus*. This is the only time we know of that Plato spoke out publicly on a matter of Athenian policy. And as usual he chose to speak anonymously and indirectly, in the guise of a dialogue where Socrates pretends to deliver a funeral oration composed by Aspasia "from the scraps left over from the funeral oration she composed for Pericles" (236B). The criticism of Athenian policy is itself indirect, conveyed by ironical praise of the Athenians for the courage and loyalty they no longer displayed in 386 BC. But the message must have been unmistakable for Plato's contemporaries. It constitutes an immediate application to the current political

29. The ancient tradition has it that Plato traveled to Italy to meet Archytas and the Pythagoreans. See the references to Cicero in Guthrie (1975) 17, n.3; cf. D.L. III.6.

I see no reason to believe in Plato's travels to Egypt and other lands, although the unreliability of the ancient sources who report such trips is not in itself proof that they did not take place.

30. So Guthrie (1975) 19, on slim evidence. But the *Menexenus* strongly suggests that he was back in Athens by 386.

crisis of the general critique of Athenian policy that Plato had formulated in the *Gorgias*.[31]

After this moment in 386 Plato's attitude towards Athenian politics seems to be summed up in his statement many years later in the *Seventh Epistle*:

[It is impious to use violence against one's parents.] If they are fixed in a way of life that pleases them, though it may not please me, I shall not antagonize them by useless scolding nor yet flatter them by contributing to the satisfaction of desires that I would myself rather die than approve. A reasonable man would live with the same attitude in regard to his city. He will speak out, if he thinks her politics are bad, and there is a prospect that he will be listened to and not put his life in danger by his speech . . . [But if his goals cannot be achieved without violence] he will keep his peace and pray for what is good both for himself and for his city. (331C–D)

Plato's conditions for speaking out in Athens were apparently satisfied at the time of the *Menexenus*, but never again. In the *Republic*, Plato compares the philosopher in an unjust city to the man caught in a dust-storm who takes refuge behind a wall and "who, when he sees the others filled with lawlessness, takes comfort if he is himself able to live his life here free from injustice and crime, and will cheerfully take his departure from this life with good hope for the future." This would be no small achievement, answers Adeimantus. "Nor the greatest either," says Socrates, "unless he meets with an appropriate commonwealth (*politeia*). For in a fitting constitution he will himself grow greater and together with his own welfare he will be a savior of the common good" (VI, 496D–497A). In this sense Plato never abandoned his political aspirations. Not only did he succumb twice to the temptation to try his hand in Sicilian politics. At the end of his life he was still preparing his last and longest work, the *Laws*, as his philosophical legacy to Athens and to the future of political thought.

In the years after 387 or 386, however, Plato was busy with other concerns. There was above all the organization of teaching and research that we have come to know as the foundation of the Acad-

---

31. For connections between the *Gorgias* and the *Menexenus* see Dodds (1959) 23f. followed by Guthrie (1975) 317. Dodds correctly saw that *Gorgias* and *Menexenus* "convey the same criticisms of Athenian democracy and Athenian foreign policy," but he underestimated the seriousness of Plato's protest against the humiliating terms of the King's Peace. See Kahn (1963) 220–34.

emy. Concerning the details of Plato's teaching activity and the conditions of study in the Academy we are not very well informed. What we do know is that he established the first permanent institution of higher education and scientific research, the paradigm for all academies, universities, and research centers down to our own time. Thus Plato's school not only served to train Aristotle and a host of other important thinkers and scientists; it also provided the model for Aristotle and later philosophers to form their own schools. And it seems that Plato's Academy never lost sight of its political mission, to serve as a "nursery of statesmen" by training men who would play an important role as political leaders or royal advisors.[32]

I suggest that at the same time when he was organizing this educational enterprise in the Academy, in the middle and late 380s, Plato began to write a new series of dialogues concerned with the theory of education and the unity and definition of virtue, and that these dialogues were planned as a natural complement to his activity as an educator. It is important to bear in mind that the publication of the *Gorgias* must have catapulted Plato from the ranks of the minor Socratics to his permanent position among the supreme masters of Greek letters. On the traditional assumption that Plato composed the *Protagoras* and several other dialogues before the *Gorgias*, his ascent will have been more gradual but still dramatic enough. Both the *Gorgias* and the *Protagoras* must have been recognized as literary masterpieces as soon as they appeared.[33] Even their titles, referring to the major intellectual figures of the previous age, would have attracted considerable attention. The *Gorgias* alone will have established its author as the out-

32. The quotation is from Marrou (1950) 104. Marrou lists more than a dozen names of members of the Academy who played an important part in politics. (Most of the names are given by Plutarch *Adversus Colotem* 1126c–d.) For recent, more critical studies of the political mission of the Academy see Saunders (1986) 200–10, and a skeptical view argued at length in Brunt (1993) 282–342.

33. Athenaeus (*Deipnosophistae* XI, 505D) tells of Gorgias himself reading Plato's dialogue named after him and remarking to his friends, "How well Plato knows how to make fun of people (*iambizein*)!" (DK 82A.15a). Aristotle reports the story of a Corinthian farmer who, after encountering the *Gorgias*, abandoned his fields in order to study with Plato. (See below, Chapter 5, p. 141 with n.17.) Whether true or not, such stories reflect the reputation which the dialogue soon acquired.

standing Greek thinker and writer of his generation: not only the principal heir to Socrates as a philosopher but the successor to Euripides as an intellectual dramatist and the rival of Thucydides as a political thinker.

It was (I imagine) from this position of eminence that Plato embarked upon the creation of a new kind of Socratic dialogue, a set of rigorous discussions on virtue and education without any definite conclusions, designed to perplex and provoke his readers and thus to produce in them the kind of intellectual stimulation he had himself received from Socrates. We will discuss later Plato's interpretation of *aporia* as the first stage in philosophical enlightenment.[34] Here we are concerned with the literary innovations of this threshold group.

The aporetic dialogue makes its appearance in a new literary form, the "historical dialogue," anticipated only in the *Crito*. A careful proem sets the scene of the dialogue in a definite location with a fictive date.[35] In several cases a vivid description of the setting and the interlocutors is provided by a frame narrative, in which Socrates reports the conversation to a friend (*Charmides*, *Protagoras*, *Lysis*, *Euthydemus*, as later in the *Republic*). The extraordinarily lifelike characterization of the participants gives the reader the illusion of overhearing an actual conversation. It is the same art that reaches its highest achievement in the *Symposium* and *Phaedo*, where, for a fuller representation of Socrates as the central figure, the role of narrator is assigned to someone else.

As an extension of Plato's own educational activities, this great series of dialogues must have been designed to serve many different functions. But one thing these dialogues do not attempt to do is to represent Plato's own train of thought. His own position at any moment tends to be hidden from view by the artfulness of the dialogue form. Thus the doctrine of recollection is presented in the *Meno* as the teaching of wise priests and priestesses, just as the transcendent Form of Beauty itself is revealed in the *Symposium* as the mystic teaching of Diotima. When these two doctrines come together in the systematic arguments of the *Phaedo*, it is reasonable to see Socrates as speaking finally for Plato himself. And in the

---

34. See below, Chapter 3 § 6 and Chapter 6 § 7.
35. Note the absence of any specific location and any definite fictive date in the *Ion*, *Hippias Minor*, and *Gorgias*.

Republic Plato's personal signature is indirectly but unmistakably conveyed by the choice of Socrates' interlocutors, Plato's own brothers, the two "sons of Ariston": Glaucon and Adeimantus.[36]

In dialogues before the *Phaedo* and *Republic*, however, the rhetorical focus is on the reader, or rather on the various overlapping sets of readers. There is the loving portrait of Socrates for the general public, to honor his memory and propagate his moral ideal; there is the protreptic to philosophy for gifted young men (and perhaps a few women) who can be drawn into the educational enterprise; and there are the technical subtleties to be studied by those who are already ripe for training in philosophy. It is for all these audiences that the series of "popular" dialogues from the *Laches* to the *Symposium* is composed, in order to create the new audience that will be capable of entering the more unfamiliar philosophical world of the *Phaedo* and *Republic*.

We do not know when this large literary project took shape, just as we do not know when Plato first formulated the doctrine of Forms for himself and for his friends. What we may reasonably believe is that when Plato begins to write the *Laches*, for example, he does so in the perspective of a much larger undertaking, one whose outlines may be dim but whose goal is clear: to lay the philosophical basis for a systematic defense of Socratic ethics and their application to the political domain. Thus to write the *Laches* is to prepare to write the *Euthyphro*, the *Charmides*, the *Protagoras*, the *Meno* . . . and ultimately the *Republic*.[37]

How old was Plato when this plan was formed, and when it was carried out? We cannot know, but we can at least make some plausible conjectures. The *Gorgias* is reasonably taken to mark the moment of Plato's commitment to the philosophic life, in his late thirties or early forties – the moment dated *c.* 388 BC by his own statement in the *Seventh Epistle*. The *Symposium*, on the other hand, provides the first explicit reference to his transcendental metaphysics, in the years after 385. (The dialogue is postdated by the anachronism at *Symposium* 193A.) Hence on my hypothesis the seven threshold dialogues, from the *Laches* to the *Meno* and *Euthy-*

---

36. See Sedley (1995: 4f.) for two strategic uses of the phrase "son of Ariston" as a subtle device by which Plato manages "to project his own authorial voice."
37. For my suggestion that the *Laches* was composed as the introduction to this new literary project, see Chapter 6 § 2.

demus, will fall in between, in the middle and late 380s. The *Republic* was composed after the *Symposium*, in the decade 380–370, when Plato was in his fifties. If these calculations are sound, the plan itself, and the composition of seven so-called early dialogues, will belong in the middle or late 380s, when Plato was about forty-five years old.

5. A SKETCH OF THE INGRESSIVE INTERPRETATION

If by the meaning of a text we understand the message that the author intends to transmit to the reader, then the meaning of a Platonic text is accessible only at the cost of a considerable effort of interpretation. The reader must be as cunning in interpreting a dialogue as the author has been artful in composing it.[38]

This distance between text and message, or between what Plato writes and what he means to convey, is the first problem that any interpretation must confront. Behind it looms a larger problem: the distance between what Plato means to say in a specific passage and what he thinks in general, or, to put it differently, the place of a particular text within the larger world of Plato's philosophy. My notion of ingressive exposition is a proposal to deal with the first problem in the light of the second: to identify the meaning of a particular argument or an entire work by locating it within the larger thought-world articulated in the middle dialogues.

This proposal may be regarded as begging the question against the developmental reading: I assume that Plato did not change his mind in any fundamental way between the *Laches* and *Protagoras*, on the one hand, and the *Phaedo* and *Republic* on the other. But since in any case we do not have access to Plato's mind, the issue is: which assumptions provide us with the best interpretation of the texts? In this sense, the whole of Chapters 6 to 11 will constitute my argument against the developmental view and in favor of the hypothesis of ingressive exposition. By this hypothesis I mean the claim that the seven threshold dialogues are designed to prepare the reader for the views expounded in the *Symposium*,

38. Compare Tigerstedt's remarks (1977: 99) on "the reader's responsibility": "Nothing is a matter of course; everything can be called into question. To read Plato demands a far higher degree of vigilance and activity than any other philosopher asks for. Time after time, we are forced to make our choice, to decide how we should interpret what we are reading."

Phaedo, and *Republic,* and that they can be adequately understood only from the perspective of these middle works.[39]

Evidence in support of this claim will be of two kinds. On the one hand we find passages in the threshold dialogues that are enigmatic, puzzling, or somehow problematic, for which the solution or clarification will be provided by a text or a doctrine in the middle dialogues. And on the other hand, we find texts in the middle dialogues that deliberately emphasize their continuity with ideas and formulations familiar from the earlier works. An example of the first sort is the gradual emergence of the terminology for dialectic. An example of the second sort will be the formula for the Forms, presented in the *Phaedo* and repeated in the *Republic,* which unmistakably echoes the *what-is-X?* question of the dialogues of definition. I begin with the first example.

The terminology for dialectic provides what is perhaps the clearest case of progressive disclosure. In Plato as elsewhere in Greek, the verb *dialegesthai* means "carry on a conversation." In three dialogues of Group I – the *Hippias Minor, Gorgias,* and *Protagoras* – this verb serves to describe the Socratic technique of discussing a topic by question and answer, in contrast to the rhetorical practice of making long speeches. (These three dialogues belong to what I count as stages 2–4 in Group I: see above, p. 47.) In three other dialogues of Group I we find forms derived from the corresponding nominal stem *dialekt-.* (These three dialogues belong to my stages 5–6.) Thus we have in the *Meno* 75c–d the adverbial form *dialektikōteron,* which characterizes a friendly method of inquiry as "answering questions more gently and *more conversationally,*" in contrast to the hostile, competitive techniques of eristic disputation. If the distinction between dialectic and rhetoric is in some sense pre-Platonic, this contrast between dialectic and eristic, as drawn in the *Meno,* is presumably Plato's own. And the term *dialektikōteron* seems in fact to be his invention.

The next step in terminological elaboration is marked by the expression *dialektikos* for the dialectician, literally someone who is "skilled in the art of conversation." (This term also seems to be a Platonic creation. The feminine form for the art itself, *dialektikē,*

---

39. I am here assuming (what we cannot prove) that the *Symposium* and *Phaedo* are later than the other dialogues of Group I, with the exception of the *Cratylus,* which is also presumably one of the latest members of this group.

does not appear until *Republic* VII.) This word for dialectician turns up in only two passages in Group I: in the *Euthydemus* and in the *Cratylus*. In both contexts the *dialektikos* is unexpectedly introduced as someone in possession of a superior art, which enables him either to make use of the truths discovered by mathematicians (*Euthyd.* 290C), or to judge the correctness of the words which the namegiver has assigned to things (*Cratylus* 390C). These two passages are truly proleptic, in that they must strike the reader as enigmatic in their context.[40] They require an explanation that will be provided only in a later text. The *Euthydemus* passage is explicitly marked as mysterious, the utterance perhaps of some higher power (290E–291A). Neither the term *dialektikos* nor the corresponding conception of dialectic as the highest form of knowledge can really be understood without reference to the central books of the *Republic*. Only in the discussion of the Divided Line at the end of Book VI, and in the following references to dialectic as the sequel to mathematical studies in Book VII, does Plato explain why the *dialektikos* is in a position to judge the results of mathematical work and the correctness of names. (These passages are discussed in Chapter 10 §5.)

We can follow a similar pattern of progressive disclosure for the knowledge of good and bad. Introduced in the *Laches* as a covert answer to the question: "What is virtue?" (199E), the knowledge of good and bad reappears in the *Charmides* as the implied definition of *sōphrosunē* (174B–D). What is striking here is that in neither dialogue does either Socrates or his interlocutor recognize the implicit solution. Both *Laches* and *Charmides* end in overt *aporia*, and we the readers are left to puzzle out the answer on our own.

The *Euthydemus* treats a related theme as the topic for an infinite regress: Knowledge is the only good, but good for what? If it is beneficial, it must produce more knowledge. What will *this* knowledge make us good for? For making others good? But good for what? (*Euthyd.* 292E–293A). The regress is broken only in *Republic* VI, where the Form of the Good is introduced as the *megiston mathēma*, the highest object of knowledge.

Now when Socrates introduces the Form of the Good as ultimate object for knowledge, he repeatedly asserts that "you have

40. Compare the role of enigmatic utterance in the technical sense of prolepsis developed by Lebeck (1971) 1–2.

often heard this before" (VI, 504E 8, 505A 3); which is perhaps as close as Plato ever comes to commenting on his own use of proleptic composition. The whole context resonates with echoes of earlier dialogues.[41]

> Furthermore, you know this too, that most people think the good is pleasure [as in the *Protagoras*], whereas the more refined sort think it is wisdom (*phronēsis*) [as in the *Euthydemus* and the *Meno*] ... And those who hold the latter view are not able to indicate *what kind of wisdom*, but they end up being forced to say: knowledge of the good ... [This is ridiculous] if those who complain that we do not know the good go on to speak to us as if we know it. For they say it is knowledge (*phronēsis*) of good, as if we understood what they say when they pronounce the word "good." [Compare the regress of *Euthydemus* 292B–E.] But what about those who define pleasure as good? ... Are not they too forced to agree that some pleasures are bad? [So Callicles in the *Gorgias*, 499 Bff.] (*Rep.* VI, 505A–C)

Having reached the climatic moment of his exposition, Plato here looks back over the whole range of anticipatory discussions in earlier works. He thus makes clear that they are all to be understood in the light of this ultimate conception of the Good. (For more on the topic of knowledge as beneficial or good-directed, see Chapter 7 §8.)

Chapters 6–11 will deal with other themes for which an expository progression can be traced from threshold to middle dialogues. I conclude this preliminary sketch with the theme of the Forms themselves. It is well known that the *what-is-X?* question of the dialogues of definition serves as a direct antecedent for the theory of Forms. The most striking evidence of this is the fact already mentioned that, in the *Phaedo* and later dialogues, the technical designation for the Forms is the inverted form of the *what-is-X?* question, "the very what-X-is", *auto to ho esti* (*Phaedo* 75B 1, D 2, 78D 4, 92A 9; *Rep.* VI, 507B 7, and often). The essences of the *Euthyphro* and the *Meno* become the Forms of the middle dialogues. The continuity is explicitly marked by the fact that the three Forms

---

41. In this connection Adam (1902: II, 51) comments that the claim that, without knowledge of the good, nothing else is of any use, is "one of Plato's commonplaces," and he cites as parallels *Charmides* 173Aff., *Laches* 199C, *Euthyd.* 280Eff., 289Aff., 291, *Lysis* 219Bff. Adam adds: "The *Euthydemus* and *Charmides* already forecast the city of the Philosopher-king, in which Knowledge of Good shall 'sit alone in the helm of the state' (*Euthyd.* 291D)."

mentioned when the metaphysical doctrine is generalized at *Phaedo* 65D 12 (namely, Magnitude, Health, and Strength) are exactly the same as the three examples cited in the *Meno* for a uniform *eidos* applying to different cases. (For more indications of continuity on this point see below, Chapter 11 §3.)

Such unmistakable signs of continuity are often interpreted as so many marks of development. The *what-is-X?* question of the *Laches* and *Euthyphro* is seen as the original, Socratic form of the search for definitions. It is only later, in mature Platonism, that this search is reinterpreted as the pursuit of metaphysical definienda, construed as items of eternal, intelligible Being. For this developmental view, the turning-point comes in the *Meno*, with the doctrine of recollection and the new importance of mathematics. But it is only in the *Symposium* and *Phaedo* that the new epistemology of the *Meno* is completed by the corresponding ontology, in the classic theory of unchanging Forms.

There is no disagreement, then, on the literary fact of continuity of content and gradual disclosure leading from the *Laches* and *Euthyphro* to the *Phaedo* and *Republic*. But are these lines of continuity to be read as stages in the development of Plato's thought? Or are they rather, as I am proposing, stages in the aporetic introduction and progressive exposition of elements in a unified view? I have shown elsewhere how the thematic structure of the *Republic* is characterized by techniques of proleptic composition that rise to a crescendo in Books VI–VII.[42] I suggest that an analogous plan of ingressive exposition, using similar techniques, leads from dialogue to dialogue to the very same climax in the central books of the *Republic*. At this point the developmental and the ingressive interpretations are strictly incompatible, since on my view there is no more reason to speak of Plato's intellectual development between the *Laches* and the *Republic* than there is to speak of his development between Book I and Book X of the *Republic*. Plato's thought processes in the course of composition are inaccessible to us. What we have is his authorial design, inscribed in the text of the dialogues. I suggest that the evidence for a comprehensive artistic plan should be seen as a reflection of the underlying unity of Plato's philosophical position. To put my view in its most drastic form: we may read some ten dialogues of Group I (from the *Laches* to the

42. See Kahn (1993a) 131–42.

Phaedo and the *Cratylus*) as if Plato had written them all at the same time, but offered them to the world in successive stages.

Some readers may balk at my suggestion that we can attribute to Plato an authorial design that is only conveyed indirectly. Appealing to rigorous principles of philogical method, they may well ask: what right do we have to ascribe to Plato an intended meaning that is not explicitly spelled out in the text? For example, I shall argue in Chapter 6 that the conception of metaphysical Forms, though never mentioned in the *Meno*, is in fact entailed by the use made there of the doctrine of recollection as a response to Meno's paradox. For unless the prenatal cognitive experience of the disembodied psyche was radically different from learning in this life, the hypothesis of learning in a previous existence would simply produce a regress, in which the paradox would immediately recur. But what right do we have to assume that the author of the *Meno* was aware of this problem and left the solution for an insightful reader to discover?

Now it is easy to show that such indirect writing is a characteristic of Plato's art, and to show this from a closely related example in the *Meno* itself. The doctrine of recollection is illustrated there by a geometry lesson, in which an untutored slave learns (or "recollects") how to double the area of a given square. Socrates shows him that you can double the square by constructing a new square on the diagonal through the given square. Now this construction also illustrates two important mathematical results. First, the construction is an instance of the Pythagorean theorem, since the new square takes as its side the hypotenuse of the triangle formed in the original square by drawing the diagonal. And in the second place, this construction also illustrates the existence of incommensurable magnitudes or, as we say, irrational numbers, since the side of the new square stands to the side of the original square as $\sqrt{2}$, the most elementary case of an irrational number.

Why does the *Meno* make no mention of these important mathematical truths? Plato is clearly writing for a double audience. He expects his more intelligent and better informed readers to do some thinking on their own. The case is similar for the link between recollection and the Forms. Just as anyone trained in geometry will see what is involved in doubling the square, so anyone familiar with Plato's metaphysical thought will see what the objects of recollection must be.

In conclusion, I must admit that we cannot refute the developmental hypothesis, since we do not know Plato's intellectual biography. We can only challenge such a reading by pointing out how many unsupported assumptions it must make, and how many problems it leaves unsolved, by asking (for example) why the early dialogues contain so many puzzles – not only aporetic conclusions but so many deliberately undeveloped hints (like the knowledge of good and bad in *Laches* and *Charmides*) and so many enigmatic challenges, such as the references to dialectic and knowledge of the good in the *Euthydemus*, and the mysterious allusions to a virtue based on knowledge in the arguments of the *Protagoras* and the conclusion to the *Meno*. What kind of knowledge are we to suppose Plato has in mind in these cryptic references in *Protagoras* and *Meno*? If he is not leading us here in the direction of *Republic* v–vii, why are there so many questions that must remain unanswered for the reader who has not reached these central books? Why are there so many different lines of thematic development converging on the same point?

The most plausible explanation for the abundant and diverse evidence of meaningful design leading from the earlier dialogues to the *Republic* is the hypothesis of authorial intent. It is, I suggest, because we all implicitly recognize such a design and such an intent that we know that it is Plato speaking, and not merely the dialogue *persona* of Socrates, in the central books of the *Republic*. Plato for us is the author of the dialogues. And it is the pattern of unity created by the network of thematic lines connecting the dialogues and meeting one another in the *Republic* that permits us to say: this is the author's intention. He has designed these dialogues in such a way that, despite the anonymity of the dialogue form, we can securely recognize here the point of what he has written, the philosophic message he means to convey.

6. PLATO'S MOTIVE FOR HOLDING BACK

Why so much deviousness on Plato's part? Why do dialogues like the *Charmides*, *Meno*, and *Euthydemus* obscurely hint at doctrines or conceptions we cannot fully understand unless we have read the *Phaedo* and the *Republic*?

The motivation guiding the work of a great writer will be complex, and presumably not always transparent even to himself. In the case of Plato his lifetime loyalty to the dialogue form suggests a temperamental aversion to direct statement, reinforced by much reflection on the obstacles to successful communication for philosophical insight. But there are two more specific considerations that can help explain his choice of the technique of gradual disclosure in the threshold dialogues.

The first consideration is the pedagogical advantages of *aporia*. As Aristotle put it, a problem must be well knotted before it can be resolved. As pupil of Socrates and author of Socratic conversations, Plato would be peculiarly attentive to the salutary shock of perplexity and the effectiveness of this as a stimulus on inquiring minds.

The second consideration that lies behind Plato's reluctance to disclose his philosophical position goes deeper and is more difficult to formulate. The ingressive mode of exposition has, I suggest, been chosen by Plato because of his acute sense of the psychological distance that separates his world view from that of his audience. The frame of mind implied by Diotima's final revelation in the *Symposium*, more fully expressed in the extra-celestial vision of the *Phaedrus*, taken for granted in the allegory of the Cave and the otherworldly longings of the *Phaedo*, is essentially the frame of mind of a metaphysical visionary. Such a person is convinced that the unseen, intangible world, accessible only to rational thought and intellectual understanding, is vastly more meaningful, more precious, and more real than anything we can encounter in the realm of ordinary experience.[43] For such a visionary, the domain of unseen reality is the place of origin from which the human spirit or the rational psyche has come, and to which it may under favorable circumstances return. Philosophy is essentially the practice of spiritual liberation by which the rational psyche prepares itself for a successful voyage back to its transcendental homeland.

The metaphysical vision just described is recognizably that of Plotinus and the Neoplatonists, as it is also that of rational mystics in the philosophical tradition of India. This is the vision articulated by Plato in the pre-natal myth of the *Phaedrus* and in the opening apologia of the *Phaedo*, when Socrates explains why a philosopher should be ready to die, since only the disembodied soul

43. For the fundamental importance of this aspect of Plato's thought, see Vlastos' sensitive discussion in "A Metaphysical Paradox (1973: 50–6)."

can hope to achieve fully the knowledge that it seeks. This vision continues to dominate Plato's later work, as when the *Theaetetus* speaks of escaping from the evils of this world by assimilation to the divine (ὁμοίωσις θεῷ), or when the Athenian Stranger in the *Laws* remarks that human life is of little account, a mere plaything of the gods (VII, 803C, 804B).

This otherworldly vision is entirely at home in the spiritual atmosphere of late antiquity, in the age of gnosticism and theurgy. But it would be difficult to overstate the discrepancy between this view of human destiny and the typical attitudes and values of Greek society in the fifth and fourth centuries BC. The world we know from Attic tragedy and comedy, from the history of Thucydides and the pleading of the orators, is a world of petty pride, heroic passion, ordinary lust and greed, unlimited ambition and utter ruthlessness. In such a world the metaphysical vision just described seems almost grotesquely out of place.

This radical discrepancy is, I suggest, a fundamental factor in the shaping of the Platonic dialogue. On the one hand Plato's dialogues are firmly planted in Athenian soil, in the social and political reality of the Socratic age. Thus we have Nicias and Laches, Critias, Charmides, and Alcibiades, the sons of Pericles, and the grandsons of Aristides and Thucydides as the typical actors and audience for these dramas. On the other hand, the dialogues are also destined to reflect the celestial, otherworldly vision. That is as true for certain passages in the *Gorgias* and *Meno* as it is for the *Phaedo* as a whole and the climax of Diotima's speech. This discrepancy is of course one explanation for Plato's use of myth: myth provides the necessary literary distancing that permits Plato to articulate his out-of-place vision of meaning and truth.

For Plato's new world view, his only ally would be the Orphic-Pythagorean doctrine of reincarnation, with its associated teaching that we are dead in this life, buried or imprisoned in the body, but destined for a more divine existence. Hence it is precisely the Orphic-Pythagorean conception of the soul that is invoked in the *Meno* as background for Plato's doctrine of recollection. This new notion of recollection, understood not as a Pythagorean recall of previous incarnations but as a mode of a priori knowledge, is the brilliant link by which Plato connects his own metaphysical vision – whose rationality is guaranteed by its grounding in mathematics – with the old, weird teaching about a transmigrating soul. It is above all Plato's allegorical reinterpretation of Orphic-Pythagorean doctrine that made such views respectable in the West.[44]

In the *Gorgias* Plato hints at the otherworldly vision, when he quotes Euripides: "who knows if life be death, but death be really life?" (492E). But the judgment myth of the *Gorgias* is relatively conventional. Plato is here not ready openly to commit himself (or Socrates) to the Orphic-Pythagorean conception of rebirth, as he will do in the myths of the *Phaedo, Republic,* and *Phaedrus.* The *Meno* contains the first unmistakable disclosure of this transcendental conception of the soul; but essential features of the larger view remain unstated. Before that, Plato has been deliberately holding back, as a strategy for dealing with an exoteric audience. The ordinary Greek reader or auditor, whom we may conjure up from the world of comedy and oratory, from the lectures of the sophists and the writings of Xenophon, is wholly unprepared to take seriously Plato's metaphysical vision. Plato must first write in such a way as to engage the attention of readers who can identify with a blunt soldier like Laches or an amateur intellectual like Nicias or Meno. His Socrates will stimulate and puzzle such readers with topics that concern them directly, like the nature of courage and piety or the teachability of virtue.

In discussing these topics of interest to every thinking Athenian, the Platonic Socrates is no doubt following in the footsteps of his historical namesake, who called upon his interlocutors to examine their lives and reflect upon their aspiration to *aretē*. But in turning the discussion of courage, piety and virtue into an unsuccessful search for essences that explain why things are as they are, the Platonic Socrates is dispensing a new kind of *aporia*, in order to prepare his audience for a new kind of knowledge and a new view of reality.

It is in the *Symposium* that the delicate literary junction between Plato's vision and his contemporary audience is effected, by the cunning artifice of Diotima. The figure of Diotima is clearly designed to remind us of those wise priests and priestesses who teach reincarnation in the *Meno.* But Diotima is careful never to mention

44. Plato was preceded in this by Pindar, whom he loves to quote in this connection (*Meno* 81B–C, *Rep.* I, 331A). Empedocles' claim to divinity, by contrast, would have seemed wildly eccentric. Note the satirical tone of Xenophanes' reference to reincarnation (DK 21B.7) and the guarded way in which Herodotus mentions these doctrines (II.123).

either reincarnation or any conception of immortality that might be laughed to scorn by the urbane company at Agathon's dinner party.[45] She (or rather Plato's Socrates, by the use of her voice) inserts the otherworldly vision into a philosophical account of erotic passion, the conventional topic for the evening's entertainment. Instead of appealing to outlandish conceptions of the psyche, Diotima founds her vision on the strictly rational ground of Eleatic ontology. The doctrine of eternal, unchanging Being, originally formulated by Parmenides, appears here in Diotima's account of the one and (as far as the *Symposium* goes) only representative of the Forms, the Beautiful itself, the object of metaphysical *erōs*.[46]

The otherworldly atmosphere that thus intrudes into Agathon's victory celebration is subtly reinforced by the repeated description of Socrates' fits of abstraction. But the seismic gap between world views is most vividly dramatized in the frustrated passion of Alcibiades, who is unable to establish emotional contact with Socrates even in bed, because they inhabit different worlds. The ironical contrast between two kinds of beauty that Alcibiades would propose to exchange with Socrates, "like gold for brass" (219A 1), echoing the contrast between the two wisdoms that Agathon and Socrates might transfer to one another by sharing the same couch (175C–E), confirms the sense of two radically opposed conceptions of what is true and significant.

The *Symposium* thus provides a decisive but still only partial disclosure of the otherworldly view. In the *Symposium* as in the *Meno*, Plato as consummate artist is careful not to lose touch with his audience by levitating too long or too far from the Athenian earth. Just as in the *Meno*, where the doctrine of rebirth was presented as background for recollection, the discussion quickly turns aside to a more pedestrian exercise in the method of hypothesis, so in the *Symposium* we are acquainted with the doctrine of Forms only in a momentary glimpse of the one transcendent object of desire. The dialogue ends in riotous drinking, with Socrates' interlocutors falling asleep. It is only in the *Phaedo* that we get a full disclosure of the transcendental world view, systematically anchored in the

---

45. The Orphic-Pythagorean verses of Euripides, cited with respect by Socrates in the *Gorgias* (429E 10 = fr. 638 Nauck²), are repeatedly mocked by Aristophanes in the *Frogs* (1082, 1477f.)

46. See the passage from *Symposium* 210Eff. cited and discussed below, pp. 342ff.

doctrine of Forms, with Socrates sanctified by his approaching death. Here the strong doctrine of immortality (from the *Meno*) can finally be joined with the Parmenidean metaphysics (from the *Symposium*) to construct the distinctly Platonic atmosphere of rational spirituality that pervades the entire dialogue, and that takes poetic shape in the first overtly Pythagorean myth of judgment.

In later chapters we return to a discussion of the literary tact with which Plato gradually familiarizes his reading audience with the new world view. But first we must begin where Plato himself began, with Socrates.

CHAPTER 3

Socrates

Socrates is ... not so much the mask behind which Plato is hiding as rather the enigmatic paradigm figure whose secret drives Plato on to ever new doctrinal and literary interpretations and who motivates his philosophical advances; his philosophizing is embedded in ever new attempts at a poetical modeling of his master. The obligatory participation of Socrates in all Platonic dialogues (except for the *Laws*) is, then, the visible testimony that Plato throughout his life remained a Socratic, who strove to fulfill the unfinished work of his master.

Harald Patzer[1]

I. THE IMPORTANCE OF SOCRATES

In Plato's work the presence of Socrates is overwhelming. Out of twenty-five or more dialogues, Socrates is absent from only one: the *Laws*. (And this is so exceptional that Aristotle, in a slip, can refer to the *Laws* as one of the "discourses of Socrates," *Politics* II.6, 1265a11.) Even in Plato's latest period, where Socrates, though present, is normally replaced as chief speaker by a visitor from Elea or Locri, he can still surprise us. In the *Philebus* he resumes once more the role of protagonist when the topic under discussion returns to familiar Socratic territory, the relation between pleasure and the good.

1. "Sokrates ist also ... nicht so sehr die Maske hinter der sich Plato verbirgt, als vielmehr die ratselhafte Vorbildgestalt, deren Geheimnis Plato zu immer neuen sachlichen und dichterischen Deutungen antreibt und die sein Philosophieren eingebettet in immer neue Versuche einer dichterischen Gestaltung des Meisters vorwartsbringt. Das obligate Mitwirken des Sokrates in allen platonischen Dialogen (ausser den Nomoi) soll also sichtbar bekunden, dass Platon zeit seines Lebens Sokratiker blieb, der das unvollendete Werk des Meisters zu erfüllen bestrebt war." (Harald Patzer [1965] 43)

It is not simply Socrates as *dramatis persona* who persists throughout Plato's work. It is Socrates as the martyred embodiment of a
moral ideal and also Socrates as the paradigm philosopher, tire-
lessly pursuing intellectual inquiry by the method of question and
answer. If for Plato the highest form of philosophical activity is
named "dialectic," the art of conversational discussion, that is an
obvious reminder that the method of Socratic conversation remains Plato's model for philosophic teaching and research. And
the twin paradoxes of the Socratic moral position – that vice is a
sort of ignorance and that no one does wrong voluntarily – are
firmly embedded in Plato's latest work.[2] Finally, in the *Seventh
Epistle*, written when he was in his seventies, Plato (as we have
seen) refers to Socrates as "my older friend, whom I would not
hesitate to call the justest man of his time." And he implies that
the fate of Socrates had served him as a touchstone by which the
moral health of a political regime could be evaluated.[3]

The central importance of Socrates is not a matter for dispute.
What is in question is how much philosophy Plato learned from
him. In this regard the problem of the historical Socrates is not
only vexed but perhaps insoluble. Our only contemporary reports
are from Aristophanes and other comic poets, who love to make
fun of his bulging eyes, his bare feet and unkempt appearance,
and his ardent pursuit of idle conversation.[4] But except for locating him in the intellectual circles represented by Euripides and the
sophists, these comic caricatures tell us nothing of the content of
Socrates' thinking.[5] For information on Socrates' philosophy we
are entirely dependent upon the later writings of his followers,
above all Plato and Xenophon, and the second-hand report of
Aristotle (who arrived in Athens in 367, more than thirty years
after Socrates' death). How far can we trust one or more of these
three authors for a faithful representation of Socrates' own thought?
The question has been debated for more than two centuries, with

2. See *Timaeus* 86D–E, *Laws* V, 731C, IX, 860D.
3. *Ep.* VII, 324E, 325B; cf. *Phaedo* 118A: "of all the men we have encountered of his
   time, the best and also the wisest and most just."
4. See e.g., *Clouds* 359–63 and the passages in *SSR* Vol. I, pp. 3–6.
5. Bruno Snell suggested that the connections between Plato's *Protagoras* and two
   passages in Euripides reflected a debate about *akrasia* between Euripides and
   Socrates in 431–428 BC. (See below, Chapter 8 §3 with n.5.) The suggestion is
   attractive; but the passages in Euripides can be perfectly understood without
   reference to Socrates.

no signs of any consensus emerging from such prolonged controversy.[6] On the contrary, the most recent scholarly treatments of the subject go in diametrically opposed directions. I will briefly summarize the traditional reconstruction of Socrates' philosophy and then give my reasons for preferring a more agnostic position.

2. THE HISTORICAL SOCRATES: A MAXIMAL VIEW

Since Plato's portrayal of Socrates is by far the richest in intellectual content, many scholars have relied on the earlier dialogues, and in particular on the *Protagoras* and the dialogues of definition (*Laches, Charmides, Euthyphro,* and *Meno*) for a reconstruction of Socrates' own philosophical position. By thus limiting themselves to dialogues in which the theory of Forms does not appear, scholars such as Zeller and Guthrie have been able to recognize a set of doctrines that can apparently be confirmed as historically Socratic by parallel evidence from Xenophon and Aristotle.

This traditional conception of Socratic philosophy includes the following views: (1) that virtue (*aretē*) is some kind of knowledge or wisdom, so that moral understanding is not only necessary but sufficient for virtuous action; (2) that in this sense all the virtues are one, namely, something like knowledge of what is good and bad; (3) hence, no one acts badly (pursues what is bad) voluntarily, but only out of ignorance, and (4) *akrasia,* or acting against one's better judgment, is impossible: what looks like being overcome by pleasure or passion is in fact an intellectual mistake. It is these views which have come to be known as Socratic "intellectualism," a purely cognitive moral psychology that ignores or denies the role of emotion as an explanatory cause of human action.

The supreme importance assigned to moral knowledge accounts for the urgency of Socrates' elenctic mission, examining interlocutors who pass for wise, and exposing false claims to knowledge on the part of those who lack it. His own modest claim is simply the recognition of his own ignorance; and his endeavor in discussion with others is to help them achieve this same recognition. That is an essential part of what Socrates means by "caring for one's soul": to come to self-knowledge by acknowledging one's lack of

6. For a survey of the controversy, beginning with Brucker in the eighteenth century, see A. Patzer (1987) 6–40.

wisdom. But Socratic self-care also involves a more positive moral dimension: to make one's soul as good as possible (*Apology* 30B). It seems to be this conception of *aretē* as psychic goodness that lies behind Socrates' insistence that one must under no circumstances act unjustly. Socrates' personal commitment to this principle of avoiding all unjust action is manifested by his action at the trial of the generals of Arginousae, his refusal to arrest Leon of Salamis under the Thirty Tyrants, and his refusal to escape from prison when condemned to death.

The traditional view also accepts Aristotle's account of Socrates' philosophic method as including both *epagōgē*, or inductive inference by analogy from similar cases, and universal definition as the search for essences. Now the argument from analogy is in fact found everywhere in the Socratic literature, and there seems no reason to doubt its authenticity as a practice of the historical Socrates. The question of definition is more complicated, as we shall see.

So much is common ground for many accounts of Socrates. An important recent study by Gregory Vlastos goes further, and claims as historically Socratic the whole range of philosophic ideas, theses, and methods of argument illustrated in the earliest eight or ten Platonic writings, down to and including the first section of the *Meno*, before the doctrine of recollection is introduced.[7] On this view, the early dialogues depend not only on Plato's memory of Socrates' words but also on his imaginative continuation of Socratic lines of thought. But this continuation is so faithful to the thought of the master that we can safely treat Plato's early dialogues as reliable documents for the philosophy of Socrates.

I have elsewhere argued the case against this historical reading of the dialogues.[8] Here I simply recall three principal objections. In the first place, it is highly implausible to assume that a philosopher as creative as Plato should remain fixed in the position of his master for a dozen years or more after Socrates' death. Secondly, it is a fundamental misunderstanding of the nature of Socratic writings to see them as aiming at a faithful portrayal of the historical Socrates. As we have seen in Chapter 1, the Socratic literature, including the dialogues of Plato, represents a genre of

7. Vlastos (1991).
8. See my review of Vlastos' *Socrates* in Kahn (1992), especially pp. 235–40.

imaginative fiction, so that (with the possible exception of Plato's *Apology*) these writings cannot be safely used as historical documents. Finally, there is good reason to doubt that the testimony of Aristotle can serve as a reliable guide to the views of the historical Socrates.

These last two considerations – the unsuitability of the fourth-century Socratic writings as an historical source for the fifth-century philosopher, and the problematic nature of Aristotle's testimony – will tell not only against a maximal interpretation like that of Vlastos but also against more traditional attempts to reconstruct the philosophy of Socrates, as in the histories of Zeller and Guthrie. So we are led to review this evidence more critically.

3. A SKEPTICAL CRITIQUE: XENOPHON

Socrates is not a character of fiction. The contemporary caricatures by Aristophanes and other comic authors, together with two explicit references in Xenophon's historical works,[9] are enough to guarantee the reality of the man portrayed at such length in the writings of Plato and other Socratics. His physical appearance, his conversational talent, and several of his public actions are well attested. Furthermore, the character portrayal of Socrates in Plato's *Apology*, *Crito*, *Symposium*, and *Phaedo* is sufficiently striking, internally consistent, and compatible with what we hear from Xenophon and others, to make it reasonable to believe that Plato has given us a lifelike portrait of the man he so loved and admired.[10] We know, or may reasonably believe, a great deal about Socrates as a human being. What can we know about Socrates as a philosopher?

Here the question of evidence is more delicate. The traditional view tends to rely upon the principle that philosophical information from Plato's dialogues can be accepted as historically Socratic when it is confirmed by parallel information from Xenophon or Aristotle. But of course the testimony of Xenophon and Aristotle can count as confirmation only to the extent that it is independent of the Platonic texts in question. If it is not independent, such

9. Xenophon, *Hellenica* 1.7.15; *Anabasis* III.1.5–7.
10. See de Strycker (1950) 199–230; German translation in A. Patzer (1987) 323–54. For the physical description of Socrates, see Guthrie (1969) 386–90.

parallels show only that Xenophon or Aristotle found the Platonic picture useful for their purposes, which were not necessarily historical. A critical review of the evidence for Socrates' philosophy must begin by examining the claims of Xenophon and Aristotle to provide information that is independent of their reading of Plato's dialogues.

As far as Xenophon is concerned, I list in the Appendix (pp. 393–401) a dozen passages from the *Memorabilia* and *Symposium* where he apparently makes use of material from Plato in order to add philosophic spice to his otherwise bland account of Socrates' moral teaching. Now if one accepts the *general* fact of Xenophon's dependence upon Plato, in no particular instance can we have much confidence that his testimony is independent of Plato. We must remember that Xenophon left Athens two years before Socrates' death to engage in a series of adventures in Asia, that he was then banished and not able to return to Athens for at least thirty years. Xenophon's Socratic writings were thus begun, and perhaps largely completed, in exile. His memories of Socrates, and above all his acquaintance with Socrates' philosophical practice, are in constant need of enrichment from the writings of those (like Antisthenes, Aeschines, and Plato) who had known Socrates better, had stayed with him till the end, and had remained in personal contact with the Socratic community after his death. Where a previous generation of scholars looked to Xenophon for a more reliable historical report of Socrates' philosophy, a critical reader today will see him as largely reflecting (and refracting through his own personal lens) what he has read in the works of Socratics better informed than himself.

For our purposes, the key passage is a section from *Memorabilia* Book IV that is particularly rich in borrowings from Plato. In IV.2–4 we can recognize no fewer than six echoes of Platonic texts.[11] At the end of the following chapter, IV.5, Xenophon introduces the notion of dialectic (*dialegesthai*) in a way that reveals both his familiarity with Platonic material and his inability to master Plato's conception. Xenophon's Socrates has been praising the virtue of self-control (*enkrateia*). Only those with self-control, he says, "are able to consider matters of the greatest importance and, by distinguishing them according to kinds (*dialegontas kata genē*) in word

---

11. See Appendix below, pp. 396f.

and in deed, are able to choose what is good and abstain from what is bad" (*Mem.* iv.5.11).

And in this way, he said, men become most excellent, most happy, and most capable of discussion (*dialegesthai*). He said that discussion (*dialegesthai*) took its name from coming together to deliberate in common by distinguishing things according to kind (*dialegontas kata genē*). Therefore one should make every effort to prepare oneself for this and to have a care for this. For from this source men become most excellent, the best leaders, and most skilled in discussion (*dialektikōtatoi*). (iv.5.12)

Coming as it does at the end of a long account of the advantages of *sōphrosunē* and self-control (*enkrateia*), and the disadvantages of *akrasia* or lack of self-control, this passage clearly understands skill in *dialegesthai* to consist in prudent deliberation concerning what is good and what is bad, so that the person who is *dialektikōtatos* is the one who is most skillful in choosing what is good, avoiding what is bad. That is how Xenophon understands the notion of "sorting things according to kind" in iv.5.11. Thus Xenophon has managed to convert a technical notion from Platonic philosophy (dialectic as the capacity to distinguish things according to their natural kinds[12]) into a mundane conception of practical wisdom, by means of an un-Platonic etymology, taking *dialegein* to mean "sorting things out."

In the next chapter of the *Memorabilia* (iv.6) Xenophon expands on the notion of Socratic *dialegesthai* by applying it to the pursuit of definitions. He begins as follows: "I will try also to say how he made his associates more skilled in discussion (*dialektikōteroi*)." This terminology is unprecedented in Xenophon or in other Greek authors, but it is of course familiar from Plato. As was noted in Chapter 2, in the *Meno* Plato introduces the comparative form *dialektikōteron*, which is probably his invention. (The comparative is used again at *Statesman* 285D 6 and 287A 3.) The notion of a *dialektikos*, a dialectician or someone skilled in conversation, is mentioned in the *Euthydemus* and the *Cratylus*. (See below pp. 306–9.) But it is only in the *Republic* that the concept of dialectic is explained, as the highest form of training for philosopher-kings.

Xenophon was apparently struck by this conception of dialectic as the training for a political elite. It is something of this Platonic notion (together with the new terminology of *dialektikos* in comparative and superlative forms) that he has absorbed. Furthermore,

12. See below, pp. 298f.

Xenophon has understood from Plato that only the dialectician is able to give an account of essences or *what a thing is* (*Rep.* VII, 531E 4, 532A 6, 534B 3). Hence he proceeds to illustrate Socratic training in "dialectic" by the pursuit of definitions, although Xenophon understands this training in purely practical terms.

Socrates believed that those who know what each thing is (*ti hekaston eiē tōn ontōn*) are also able to explain it to others,[13] whereas it is not surprising that those who do not have this knowledge go wrong themselves and make others go wrong (*sphallein*). For this reason in his inquiries with his associates he never ceased to ask what each thing is (*ti hekaston eiē tōn ontōn*).

Now it would be a great task to describe how he defined all things (*panta hēi diōrizeto*). I will say enough to make clear his mode of inquiry.

First, he investigated piety in this way.

Tell me, he said, Euthydemus, what sort of thing (*poion ti*) you believe piety to be.

By Zeus, he answered, most excellent (*kalliston*).

Can you say what sort of person the pious man is?

I think, he said, he is someone who honors the gods.

Is it permissible to honor the gods in any way one wishes?

No, there are laws and customs (*nomoi*).

So the person who knows these laws will know how one ought to honor the gods?

I think so, he said.

Then will the one who knows how one ought to honor the gods think that he ought to do this otherwise than as he knows?

Certainly not.

Does someone honor the gods otherwise than as he thinks he ought?

I think not.

So the person who knows what is lawful concerning the gods will honor the gods lawfully?

Certainly.

Therefore anyone who honors them lawfully honors them as he ought?

Of course.

But the person honoring them as one ought is pious?

Certainly.

So the pious person is rightly defined by us as the one who knows what is lawful concerning the gods?

I think so. (IV.6.1–4)

As an account of Socratic religion, this is banal and conventional. If Xenophon read the *Euthyphro*, he has learned nothing from its

---

13. For the notion that "knowing what a thing is" permits you to explain it to others (*Mem.* IV.6.1), compare *Laches* 190B–C and *Charmides* 159A.

contents. The reasoning here is best understood as an awkward imitation of Socratic arguments in, for example, the *Protagoras*; and the implicit conclusion (that piety is a form of knowledge) is what a reader of the *Protagoras* will expect Socrates to say. From other texts we know that Xenophon is familiar with the *Protagoras*.[14] So in the following passage he will offer definitions of justice and courage in terms of knowledge (*epistēmē*, *Mem.* IV.6.6 and 6.11). Xenophon's zeal and lack of insight even lead him to define wisdom (*sophia*) in terms of knowledge (*epistēmē*), whereas for Plato the two terms are interchangeable (*Mem.* IV.6.7).

This passage (IV.6.1–11) is the only text in all of Xenophon's writings that depicts Socrates in the pursuit of definitions.[15] Now this is just the sort of case where the agreement between Xenophon and Plato has been taken as a warrant of historical reliability. But once we recognize the probability, or near certainty, that Xenophon has borrowed his notion of Socratic dialectic from Plato, he can no longer serve as independent evidence for the practice of the historical Socrates.[16]

4. A SKEPTICAL CRITIQUE: ARISTOTLE

The evidence from Aristotle is of greater interest for the history of philosophy, since Aristotle draws a clear distinction between the philosophical positions of Socrates and Plato. For example, according to Aristotle Socrates pursued essential definitions, but he did not "separate" the Forms as Plato did.

Before we look at the evidence for Socrates, it will be well to review Aristotle's general performance as an historian of philosophy.

In the most important text, chapters 3–6 of the first book of the *Metaphysics*, Aristotle gives a highly schematic account of his predecessors. His survey of previous philosophers (beginning with Thales and ending with Plato) is explicitly motivated by the desire to see how far they have anticipated his own explanatory system of four causes or principles. Thus he deliberately interprets the thought of his predecessors in terms of his own conceptual scheme for the analysis of nature. To begin with, all the Ionian philosophers

14. See below, pp. 394f.
15. There is a vague parallel at *Mem.* 1.1.16. See below, p. 95 with n.45.
16. For similar considerations leading to the same conclusion, see A. Patzer (1987) 438–42.

before Anaxagoras are characterized as material monists, who explain the world of nature by reference to a single elementary principle that Aristotle identifies with his own material cause or substrate (*hupokeimenon*). Hence for these thinkers, according to Aristotle, "the substance (*ousia*) [of things] remains [the same] but changes in its properties" (*Met. A.3, 983b10*).

Now it is questionable whether this interpretation is accurate even for the Milesians; it is certainly misleading for Heraclitus, whom Aristotle includes in this account. Furthermore, both here and elsewhere he reports that these early philosophers did not believe in radical or unqualified coming-to-be and perishing, since the elementary substrate remains the same (983b12). But this is quite anachronistic. The arguments of Parmenides are directed precisely against the view that, according to Aristotle, no one maintained. And the polemical rejection of coming-to-be and perishing by both Anaxagoras and Empedocles would be unintelligible if Aristotle were correct in attributing this Parmenidean denial of Becoming to the earliest philosophers.[17] But Aristotle is not really interested in reconstructing the historical dialectic of fifth-century cosmology, in which the Eleatic critique of Ionian natural philosophy gave rise to these new conceptions. Instead he construes his predecessors as interlocutors in a timeless discussion that leads to the formulation of his own system.[18]

Historians of Presocratic philosophy have learned to make use of Aristotle's account with all due caution, and to correct it wherever possible by close attention to the original texts. His report on Socrates has not been subjected to similar scrutiny. Let us look at the context in which it appears, just three chapters later in this same historical survey.

Aristotle has been explaining how the Pythagoreans were the first to show interest in the essence or formal cause (*to ti esti*), but they identified this with numbers in a rather superficial way (A.5,

17. Aristotle may have been encouraged to do so by the fact that Diogenes of Apollonia, a post-Parmenidean representative of the Ionian tradition, had proposed a revision of Milesian monism that prefigures Aristotle's conception of the material substratum (DK 64B.2 and 5).
18. On this see the classic study by Cherniss (1935). For typical judgments see Vlastos (1995) 1,326 who recognizes Aristotle's "constitutional incapacity to respect a set of categories that cut across his own"; similarly Inwood (1992) 70f.: "Aristotle tends to assume that Empedocles was grappling with the same issues as he himself faced."

987a20ff.). Next came Plato, who followed the Pythagoreans in many respects, but made some innovations.

For in his youth Plato had become acquainted with Cratylus and the Heraclitean doctrines that all sensible things are always in flux and there is no knowledge of them; and this is what he later believed. Plato afterwards took Socrates as his teacher, who was concerned with moral philosophy and not with the study of nature; but in these matters Socrates sought for the universal (*to katholou*) and was the first to focus attention on definitions. Plato therefore came to the conclusion that this [concern with universal definitions] referred to something else and not to sensible things. For it was impossible that the general definition should be of the sensible things, since these were always changing.

Plato, accordingly, called such entities Forms (*ideai*), and held that sensible things were distinct from these and named by reference to them. For things are named after Forms (*eidē*) on the basis of participation [in the corresponding Forms]. But he only changed the name "participation" (*methexis*). The Pythagoreans say that things exist by imitation (*mimēsis*) of numbers; Plato changed the name to participation. (A.6, 987a32–b12)

Many historians of philosophy have followed this account of the origin of Plato's theory of Forms. I submit, however, that it is just as arbitrary and schematic as Aristotle's account of Plato's predecessors. There is no reason to suppose that Aristotle had any good evidence for the early development of Plato's thought. When he arrived in Athens as a youth of seventeen, Plato was sixty years old and had probably recently completed the *Phaedrus, Parmenides*, and *Theaetetus*.[19] So Aristotle had in front of him, as given, all the early and middle dialogues, all the writings in Groups I and II. (Of the dialogues in which Socrates is the chief speaker, only the *Philebus* was composed after Aristotle's arrival in Athens.) The importance attributed by Aristotle to the theory of flux probably reflects the fresh impact of the *Theaetetus*. ("This is what he later believed.")[20] And the exaggerated estimate of Pythagorean influence certainly corresponds to the intellectual atmosphere of the Academy in Plato's later years.

It is sometimes supposed that Aristotle is relying here on an oral

19. The memorial dedication to Theaetetus dates this dialogue in or shortly after 369 BC. Aristotle arrived in Athens in 367.
20. There is no reference to the flux of sensible things in any Platonic dialogue before the *Cratylus*, and no characterization of the sensibles as such before the *Symposium* and *Phaedo*. Aristotle's retrojection of all this back into Plato's youth seems devoid of any historical basis.

tradition in the Academy, or even that he had discussed these matters with Plato himself.[21] Such an assumption seems entirely gratuitous. We know nothing of the personal relations between Plato and Aristotle (who was his junior by nearly forty-five years). And what we do know of Plato as a writer does not suggest any readiness to speak openly about his intellectual development. The only solid piece of historical information here is that the theory of Forms belongs to Plato, not to Socrates. But that would presumably be a fact well known to everyone in the Academy. (No one in antiquity took as historical the proem to the *Parmenides*, where the theory of Forms is ascribed to the young Socrates.) The rest of Aristotle's report is more likely to represent his own speculation, based upon his reading of the dialogues and supplemented in some cases by information from Xenophon.[22]

The essentially non-historical character of Aristotle's account is demonstrated both by what it omits and by what it includes. We are struck above all by the absence of any reference to what an historian examining the texts would recognize as the most important single influence on Plato's theory of Forms: the Parmenidean conception of eternal, changeless Being. On the other hand, it is difficult to believe that Plato had learned from Cratylus the neo-Heraclitean doctrine he develops in the *Theaetetus*. This attribution to Cratylus looks like an Aristotelian inference from an over-hasty reading of the dialogue that bears that name.[23] A more perceptive reading of this same dialogue indicates that Cratylus was not someone from whom Plato thought he had anything to learn. Both

21. Ross (1924: I, xxxvii) speaks of "the supposition that all he [Aristotle] knew of Socrates he learnt from the Academy, and perhaps even from Plato himself."

22. Although Aristotle's account of Socrates is largely drawn from Plato, there are one or two unmistakable examples of his dependence on Xenophon's *Memorabilia*. See Deman (1942) 57–60, texts XVI and XVII (*Rhet.* 1393b3–8 and *EE* 1235a35–b2, reflecting *Mem.*I.2.9. and 1.2.54). The dependence of Aristotle on Xenophon was recognized (and perhaps over-emphasized) by Maier (1913) 92–102.

23. Aristotle seems to know more about Cratylus than he can have learned from Plato's dialogue: for example, that he ended by only moving his finger, and that he criticized Heraclitus on the grounds that you could not step into the same river even once (*Met.* Γ5, 1010a12–15). This may come from the un-identified dialogue of Aeschines in which Cratylus was described as "hissing and waving his hands" (Arist. *Rhet.* III.16, 1417b1 = *SSR* VI A 92). In the latter context Aristotle implies that Cratylus was notorious for such behavior.

in the *Cratylus* and *Theaetetus* Plato makes clear that the contemporary Heracliteans were not willing or able to give a coherent account of their doctrine. The flux theory of the *Theaetetus* must be Plato's own, not something he learned from Cratylus.[24] (Philosophically speaking, however, Aristotle's pseudo-historical remark about Cratylus represents a correct intuition on his part, that the flux theory is an indirect argument for positing Forms, corresponding to the statement at *Parmenides* 135B–C that Forms are required as the stable object of thought and the basis for rational discourse. There is a parallel claim at *Sophist* 249C.)

Aristotle's account of Pythagorean influence is also incredible as an historical report. It is only intelligible in its context, as a survey of antecedents for Aristotle's notion of formal cause. That Plato's doctrine of participation was borrowed from a Pythagorean theory of imitation is not only implausible on its face; it is contradicted by Aristotle's own statement that the Pythagoreans before Plato made no distinction between sensible things and numbers. They said (according to Aristotle) that things *are* numbers, or that the Limit and Unlimited are the principles of things (A.5, 986a3, a15–21; cf. Philolaus frs. 1–2, 6). It is Aristotle who attributes to them a doctrine of resemblance (985b27, 33, 986a4), for which there is no independent evidence. And there is nothing in the fragments of Philolaus that could be correctly construed as an anticipation of the theory of Forms. On the other hand, except in the *Phaedo* and *Parmenides*, the notion of imitation or resemblance plays a more important role than participation does in Plato's own formulation of the theory of Forms. (See below, Chapter 11 §5.5.) So this statement of Aristotle is doubly misleading, both in regard to Plato and in regard to the Pythagoreans.

Is Aristotle a more reliable historian concerning Socrates than he is concerning Plato and the Presocratics? Aside from the use of

24. The picture of Plato as a student of Cratylus seems to be one of the earliest examples of the Peripatetic tendency (continued by Theophrastus) to construct lines of philosophical succession, corresponding to what historians today would call influence. For doubts as to the historicity of Aristotle's claim here, see Kahn (1985) 241–58. Compare Woodbury's comment on a parallel case: "the teacher–pupil relationship between Archelaus and Socrates ... is a doxographic construction of the school of Aristotle in the fourth century and is without corroboration in fifth-century sources or in any good historical evidence" (Woodbury, 1971: 309).

inductive or analogical arguments (*epagōgē*), which is well documented in the Socratic literature, there are three main points in
Aristotle's account of Socrates:

1. The pursuit of universal definitions
2. The identification of virtue with knowledge
3. The denial of *akrasia*.

It is these three Aristotelian claims, together with some parallels in
Xenophon, that form the textual basis for our traditional view of
the historical Socrates. For it is precisely these claims that have
authorized modern scholars to find a faithful reflection of Socratic
practice in the *Protagoras* and the dialogues of definition.

   1. Aristotle's report about Socrates' search for universal definitions, cited above from A.6 (987b1–4) is paralleled by a fuller text
in *Metaphysics* M.4. Here again Aristotle is describing the origin of
the theory of Forms. He begins once more by referring to Heraclitean flux, and he now makes explicit the argument that is adumbrated in the *Cratylus* and implied in the *Theaetetus*: "if there is
going to be knowledge and wisdom (*phronēsis*), there must be other,
unchanging natures besides the sensibles" (1178b15).[25] He then proceeds to Socrates.

Socrates concerned himself with the moral virtues, and in reference to
these he was the first to seek universal definitions ... It was reasonable
for him to seek the essence (*to ti esti*), because he was looking for deductive inference (*sullogizesthai*); and the starting-point for deductions is
the essence. For dialectic was not yet strong enough to be able to examine contrary theses without an essential definition. [I.e., the method of
hypothesis did not yet exist.] For there are two things that one can
rightly assign to Socrates: inductive arguments (*epaktikoi logoi*) and universal definition (*to horizesthai katholou*). And both of these are concerned
with the starting-point (*archē*) of science.
   Socrates, however, did not make the universals (*ta katholou*) separate,
nor did he separate the definition. But they [the Platonists] separated
them, and they called such entities Forms (*ideai*). (M.4, 1078b17–32)

Despite Aristotle's evident care here to assign to Socrates a distinct and limited contribution, there is no reason to accept this account as historically more reliable than the earlier report of what
Cratylus and the Pythagoreans had to contribute to the doctrine
of Forms.

   25. See my reconstruction of this argument in Kahn (1973) 169–71.

We can see here that the motive ascribed to Socrates for his interest in definitions presupposes Aristotle's own theory of science
and dialectic, according to which scientific first principles are provided by definitions, whereas (Aristotelian) dialectic can function
hypothetically on the basis of alternative opinions. On the other
hand, Aristotle's reference to the pursuit of definitions for "the
moral virtues" shows that he (like Xenophon) has Plato's dialogues
of definition in view, and is prepared to treat them as evidence for
the historical Socrates. Aristotle also insists upon the point that,
unlike Plato, Socrates did not separate the object of universal definition from sensible particulars. Furthermore, adds Aristotle, Socrates was right *not* to separate them (*Met.* M.9, 1086b3–5). Thus it
turns out that Aristotle's acceptance of the dialogues of definition
as historical evidence for Socrates is essential not only for his account of the origins of the theory of Forms but also for his criticism of that theory. He lays the basis for this criticism by, in effect,
attributing his own notion of universals to Socrates.

We recognize, then, that Aristotle had good doctrinal reasons
for taking Plato's portrayal as evidence for Socrates' pursuit of
definitions, evidence reinforced perhaps by Aristotle's acquaintance with the passages we have examined from *Memorabilia* IV.6.
But if Aristotle's information is, like Xenophon's, derived from his
familiarity with Plato's dialogues, there is a serious question
whether either report can be regarded as having any independent
value.[26] The same question arises in respect to the other two controversial items in Aristotle's account.

2. The thesis that virtue in general, and courage in particular, is a form of knowledge, is repeatedly ascribed to Socrates
by Aristotle.[27] The same thesis can be found scattered through
Xenophon's *Memorabilia*, above all in Books III and IV. (See the passages cited above from IV.6 and the explicit statement in III.9.5:
"justice and all the rest of virtue is *sophia*.") Both authors are

---

26. For other scholarly doubts on Aristotle as an independent source, see Maier
(1913); Taylor (1911) 41, 46; and more recently H. Patzer (1965) 28f.; A. Patzer
(1987) 435f.; similarly Döring, in his contribution on Socrates to a forthcoming volume of Ueberweg-Flashar, *Die Philosophie der Antike*. For the dependence of Xenophon on Plato, see Robin (1910), 1–47; A. Patzer (1987)
438–40.

27. *NE* VI.13, 1144b14–21; III.11, 1116b3–4, etc. Texts in Deman (1942) 82–5,
98f.

clearly familiar with the *Protagoras*, where this thesis is argued for at length; and the doctrine can be confirmed by some passages in the *Laches* and *Meno*. However, in the *Laches*, where the definition of courage as knowledge is proposed by Nicias (and apparently refuted by Socrates), what Nicias ascribes to Socrates is something much less categorical: "I have often heard you say that each of us is good in those matters where he is wise (*sophos*), bad in those where he is ignorant" (*Laches* 194D). Now this regular connection between wisdom and goodness falls considerably short of a definitional identity between the two. It is compatible with the claim that moral knowledge *causes* one to be virtuous, as moral ignorance is the cause of vice. And this is a view that we will find represented in the *Apology*, where there is no question of definition. The convergence between the *Apology* and the *Laches* on this point may well be historical, and hence the notion of a fundamental connection between knowledge and virtue will be genuinely Socratic. Nevertheless, its presentation as a *definition* of virtue is probably a Platonic innovation – an innovation that is subsequently reflected in the pages of Xenophon and Aristotle.

3. Aristotle's direct dependence upon Plato is most obvious for the denial of *akrasia*. Aristotle is literally quoting the text of the *Protagoras* when he reports that Socrates found it strange that "if knowledge is present in a person, something else should dominate and drag it around like a slave."[28] Now Xenophon also makes a confused attempt to render the motivational theory expressed in the same section of the *Protagoras*.[29] Here again, Aristotle may have been encouraged by the parallels in Xenophon to rely on the *Protagoras* as a source for the philosophy of Socrates. But modern scholars are surely ill advised to follow suit. It is reasoning in a circle to cite Xenophon's and Aristotle's borrowings from Plato as evidence for the historicity of Plato's portrayal in the *Protagoras*.

It has long been recognized that nearly everything that Aristotle

---

28. *NE* VII.2, 1145b23, from *Protagoras* 352B 5–C 2. Like a good historian, Grote draws the right conclusion: "We see from hence that when Aristotle comments upon *the doctrine of Sokrates*, what he here means is, the doctrine of the Platonic Sokrates in the *Protagoras*" (1875) II, 62n. And Grote observes that at *NE* IX.1, 1164a25 Aristotle is again drawing on the *Protagoras* for the way the sophist allowed his students to assess their own fee.

29. *Mem.* III.9.5. See the Appendix, pp. 394f.

tells us about Socrates can be derived from the dialogues of Plato.[30] Of course Aristotle does not simply identify the literary *persona* with the historical figure. He seems to make a systematic stylistic distinction between the two, and he does not attribute the doctrine of the *Phaedo* and *Republic* to Socrates.[31] But did he have a reliable oral account to support his conception of Socrates? If there was any oral tradition in the Academy, we may well doubt that it could contain accurate information on the unrecorded teachings of the master, some thirty or forty years after his death. In Aristotle's day, it must have been extremely difficult for anyone in Athens to distinguish between what they remembered of Socrates' words and teaching and what they had read – or written – during an entire generation of Socratic literature.

I conclude that neither Aristotle nor Xenophon is in a position to tell us anything about the philosophy of Socrates that he has not learned from Plato's dialogues. Aristotle is unable to do so because he arrived on the scene too late; he was separated from Socrates by the dazzling screen of Plato's portrayal. Xenophon is unable because he has no personal understanding of philosophy at all. (Xenophon did of course have other sources, notably Antisthenes, for Socrates as a model of moral toughness, that is, of *karteria* and *enkrateia*; but, as far as we can tell, this information had no direct bearing on the doctrinal issues discussed here.) We ourselves have direct access to the primary source for both writers' accounts of Socrates' philosophy: namely, the works of Plato. That means that we have both the freedom and the responsibility to evaluate these texts from the critical standpoint of modern historical philology, without bowing to the authority of Xenophon or Aristotle.

30. See e.g., Zeller (1889) 95n. The exception, of course, is that Socrates did not "separate" the Forms, i.e., that the Socrates of the *Phaedo* and *Republic* is not historical.
31. See the discussion of "Fitzgerald's Canon" in Ross (1924) I, xxxix–xli: When Aristotle refers to the historical Socrates, he omits the article before the proper name; but ὁ Σωκράτης means a figure in the dialogues. So, for example, in *Politics* II.1–6 in the criticism of Plato's *Republic* Aristotle's regular formula is ὁ Σωκράτης φησί. The rule is, however, not inflexible. The *Rhetoric* twice cites a line from the *Menexenus*, attributing it once to Socrates with the article (I.9, 1367b8), once without (III.14, 1415b31). See the texts in Deman (1942) 61.

5. THE HISTORICAL SOCRATES: A MINIMAL VIEW

If the argument of the previous section is correct, any historical account of Socrates' philosophy (as distinct from his personal actions, appearance, and character) must be drawn from the writings of Plato alone. But Plato is one of the most original thinkers of all time, as well as a great creative artist. How can we distinguish the history from the art? How can we tell where Plato's memory of his master's teaching ends, and his own development and transformation of this teaching begins?

If we survey the Platonic writings with this question in mind, we are struck by the fundamental contrast between the *Apology* and the rest of Plato's work. There is first of all a sharp difference of literary form. The *Apology* belongs to a traditional genre, the courtroom speech revised for publication; the dialogues all belong to the new genre of "Conversations with Socrates." But underlying this literary contrast there is a more fundamental difference. The *Apology* reflects a public event, the trial of Socrates, which actually took place, and at which Plato and hundreds of other Athenians were present. The dialogues represent private conversations, nearly all of them fictitious. In the one case where the setting of a dialogue is unquestionably historical, namely in the death scene in the *Phaedo*, we are explicitly told that Plato was not present.[32] So none of Plato's dialogues purports to be an actual event witnessed by the author. Plato has deliberately given himself almost total freedom to imagine both the form and the content of his Socratic conversations.

The situation is quite different for the *Apology*. As the literary version of a public speech, composed not by the speaker but by a member of the audience, the *Apology* can properly be regarded as a quasi-historical document, like Thucydides' version of Pericles' Funeral Oration.[33] We cannot be sure how much of the speech as we have it reflects what Socrates actually said, how much has been added or altered by Plato. But if, as we imagine, Plato composed the speech to defend Socrates' memory and to show to the world

---

32. As indicated above (p. 15, n.28), I assume that Plato's absence is artistic, not historical, but that makes the point even clearer.

33. The comparison is drawn by Vlastos (1991) 49, n.15. Compare H. Patzer (1965) 27: "Although the *Apology* is obviously literature (*Dichtung*), it intends to be a document for Socrates (*Sokratesdokument*)."

that he was unjustly condemned, it was essential to present a picture of Socrates in court that could be recognized as authentic.
Even admitting the large part played here by Plato's literary elaboration, there are external constraints that make his *Apology* the
most reliable of all our testimonies concerning Socrates.[34]

Insofar, then, as we can know anything with reasonable probability concerning Socrates' own conception of philosophy, we
must find this in the *Apology*. What we find there is often quite different from what we learn from the dialogues. It is nevertheless
confirmed at several crucial points by evidence from Aeschines. It
is tempting, and perhaps legitimate, to supplement this information by relying also on the *Crito*. For the *Crito* presents itself as a
kind of sequel to the *Apology*, designed to explain and justify to the
world Socrates' decision not to escape from prison. But here we
must proceed with more caution. The *Crito* is an imaginary conversation, and the external constraints are not so strong. The minimal view should limit itself to the *Apology* as far as possible.

1. Philosophy is the search for wisdom (*sophia*). Socrates is devoted to the search, but he can find none. Or rather, he concludes
that wisdom concerning "the greatest things" (how to make men
better, what constitutes a good life, what awaits us after death,
and the like) is not available to human beings at all, but is a possession of the gods alone (23A–B). He does not rule out the possibility of genuine knowledge concerning the world of nature. But
he personally has none of this, and he implies that what generally
passes for knowledge in this domain is probably not knowledge at
all (19C). Above all, Socrates himself has no *technē* (20C 1), no *mathēma* (33B 5), no kind of knowledge that would permit him to teach
others.[35] His wisdom is at best the "human wisdom" of recognizing his own ignorance, of realizing that he "is truly deficient in
regard to wisdom" (23B 3).

2. Socrates represents himself not as a teacher but as a seeker,
and his search consists in examining himself and others in respect

---

34. This has now been recognized by a number of German scholars, beginning
(as far as I know) with Harald Patzer. See also A. Patzer (1987) 442ff.; Döring
(1992) 1–16, with reference to his earlier publications, nn.3 and 4.
  For a plausible attempt by a great scholar to distinguish the historical
from the literary elements in Plato's *Apology*, see Wilamowitz (1920), II, 50–5.
35. *Apology* 33A–B; cf. 19B 8ff. This point is explicitly confirmed in the conclusion
to Aeschines' *Alcibiades* (fr. 11 Dittmar = *SSR* VI A 53, 61). See above, p. 21.

to wisdom and excellence. The examination (*exetasis*) and testing (*elenchos*) is largely negative in its immediate outcome. Socrates seeks to bring the interlocutor to a proper sense of his own inadequacy, and hence of his need "to care for himself" (*epimeleisthai heautou*) or "to care for his soul (*psuchē*)," that it should be as good as possible (29E–30B).[36] The positive moment is thus the call to self-examination and self-improvement, with the concept of excellence (*aretē*) internalized as the intrinsic character of the person himself or, equivalently, of his soul. This represents a radical (if not entirely unprecedented) break with traditional views, which regard *aretē* as dependent upon birth, fortune, or external success.

3. Care for the excellence of the soul includes the pursuit of practical intelligence or understanding (*phronēsis* 29E 1, *phronimōtatos* 36C 7). So in Aeschines' *Alcibiades* we find Socrates attempting to make the young aristocrat aware of his own need for knowledge and training.[37] Thus the Socratic conception of *aretē* certainly includes a cognitive or intellectual element. But nothing in the *Apology* suggests that virtue is simply a kind of knowledge, or identical with wisdom.[38] On the contrary, Socrates denies possession of genuine wisdom or knowledge of what is most important, but he never denies that he has practical good sense (*phronēsis*) and moral excellence (*aretē*). In fact he makes it quite clear that he regards himself as morally superior to Meletus and Anytus (30D 1), and that, as a good man, he is protected by the gods from evil (41D 1).

4. Care for the soul also entails a refusal to do anything unjust or shameful. The conception of justice as the healthy condition of the soul, injustice as its disease or corruption, is expressed in the *Crito* (47D–E), not in the *Apology*. But the *Apology* makes clear that, for Socrates, a person who is worth anything will not calculate the risks of danger or death, but "when he acts, he will consider only

36. The phrase *epimeleisthai heautou* occurs in *Apology* 36C and in Aeschines fr. 8 (Dittmar = *SSR* VI A 50, line 42); Plato prefers the expression *epimeleisthai tēs psuchēs* (*Ap.* 29E 2, 30B 2).

37. See the references to *phronein* and *epistēmē* in the Aeschines fragment *SSR* VI A 50, lines 31, 30, 45. It is possible that Socrates regarded competence in governing the city as a *technē*, by analogy with the arts and crafts. But there is nothing in the *Apology* to indicate that he thought of himself as possessing the *politikē technē*, as conceived by Plato in the *Gorgias*, *Euthydemus*, and elsewhere. See below, pp. 129–31, 208 and 214.

38. Contrast Antisthenes' view of *aretē* as requiring deeds rather than much doctrine (*logoi*) or learning (*mathēmata*): D.L. VI.11.

whether the action is just or unjust, the deed of a good man or a bad" (28B 6–9). His recital of his own behavior under the extreme democracy and under the oligarchy of the Thirty is designed to show that his primary concern was "to do nothing unjust or impious" (32D): as in the case of the illegal trials and arrests that he refused to condone or perform, so later in his refusal to escape from prison before his execution.

5. In the *Crito* the refusal to act unjustly under any circumstances includes a refusal to do deliberate harm or injury to anyone, even to someone who has previously wronged you. This is said to follow from the principle, which Socrates has often agreed to in the past, that one should never act unjustly, since "acting unjustly is in every way both bad and shameful for the doer" (49A–B 6). This dramatic break with the traditional principle of retaliation, of returning wrong with wrong or harm with harm, is fully attested only in the *Crito* (and then echoed in *Republic* I, 335B–E). However, its authentic Socratic origin is strongly suggested by its introduction in the *Crito* as part of what "we have often agreed to on previous occasions" (49B 6). And this seems to be confirmed by the argument, against Meletus, that it is unreasonable to want to harm one's neighbors (*Ap.* 25D–E).

6. The testing of oneself and others in the light of these normative principles is described as "the greatest good for a human being," since the unexamined life is not worth living (38A). In the pursuit of this negative testing and positive exhortation to self-improvement, Socrates sees himself as a benefactor of his fellow Athenians, since his goal is to make them better men and better citizens (despite the fact that he has no *technē* for this: *Ap.* 20B 4–C 3).

7. Socrates' practice of this elenchus is conceived by him as a task assigned by the gods, the exercise of a capacity which is his "divine allotment" (*theia moira*)[39]. Socrates' personal assignment, which consists in "living the life of philosophy, pursuing the search for wisdom, examining myself and others" (28E 5), has been confirmed by the Delphic oracle, by dreams, by Socrates' own *daimonion* or personal divine sign, "and in every way by which any

---

39. For Socrates' use of the expression *theia moira* in reference to his capacity to help Alcibiades, see Aeschines fr.11A Dittmar = *SSR* VI A 53, line 6 (cited above, p. 21).

other divine dispensation (*theia moira*) has commanded a human being to perform any action" (33C).

8. What about the most famous of all Socratic paradoxes, that no one does wrong willingly or that no one is voluntarily bad? We find no explicit statement of this paradox either in the *Apology* or the *Crito*. But several passages in the *Apology* seem to allude to such a thesis. Socrates' statement in the second speech, "I am convinced that I have not voluntarily (*hekōn*) done wrong to anyone" (37A 5), may but need not imply the paradox. More telling is Socrates' argument against Meletus that, since "no one wants to be harmed," it would be the height of folly voluntarily (*hekōn*) to corrupt one's fellow citizens. For corrupting them is making them bad, and "bad people will do bad things to those around them" (25D–E). Now if I corrupt them involuntarily, says Socrates, what I need is not punishment but instruction. "Clearly, if I learn better, I will stop doing what I do unintentionally (*akōn*)" (26A). This falls short of a general claim that no one does bad actions voluntarily. But it does suggest that ignorance is the cause of vicious action, moral knowledge the cause of virtue. More specifically, Socrates' argument here may be seen as an instance of the moral paradox (no one does evil voluntarily) defended by an appeal to the prudential paradox (no one voluntarily does something *bad for himself*, i.e. something disadvantageous).[40]

This survey of Socratic philosophy as represented in the *Apology* (with a few points from the *Crito*) leaves unaccounted for the three principles ascribed to Socrates by Aristotle:

(i) the definition of virtue as knowledge or wisdom
(ii) the denial of *akrasia*

and (iii) the pursuit of universal definitions or essences.

Now (i) and (ii) can naturally be seen as part of a theoretical working-out of the paradox that no one does evil intentionally. If a person performs wrong acts involuntarily, out of ignorance, then knowledge of what is good should guarantee that he will act

---

40. For the distinction between prudential and moral versions of the paradox, see below, Chapter 8 §5. The prudential paradox is pretty clearly implied at *Ap.* 25C 5–D 3; the moral version is suggested at 25E 2 (*mochthēron*).

That the paradox is genuinely Socratic is confirmed by the claim in Antisthenes' *Odysseus* that ignorance (*amathia*) is involuntary, since it is the greatest of evils (*SSR* V A 54, lines 22 and 78).

rightly. ("Clearly, if I learn better, I will stop doing what I do un-intentionally," *Ap.* 26A 4.) Knowing what is good would thus seem both necessary and sufficient for virtue. What is called *akrasia* must then actually be a result of ignorance. A theoretical development along these lines is precisely what we find in Plato's *Protagoras*. The maximal view will assign this doctrine to Socrates. On the more cautious reading proposed here, this is Plato's own elaboration of one possible response to the Socratic paradox.

That leaves us with the question of definition, of which there is no trace in either the *Apology* or the *Crito*, nor in the other two short dialogues that may reasonably be regarded as among Plato's earliest writings: the *Ion* and the *Hippias Minor*. In the absence of appropriate documentation, do we have any reason to follow Ar-istotle in ascribing this practice to Socrates? Or should we regard the *what-is-X?* question of the *Laches*, *Euthyphro*, and *Meno* as a Pla-tonic innovation?

I believe that the answer to this second question must be "Yes." At the same time I recognize that the argument from silence is not decisive. Just as the fact that Aristotle anachronistically assigns his own conception of universals to Socrates does not prove that Soc-rates had no interest in definitions, so Plato's failure to mention definitions in the *Apology* and three early dialogues is not enough to show that Socrates never asked "what is courage?" or "what is piety?" At the very least, however, there is a striking difference between Aristotle's report (together with the parallel passage in Xenophon, *Mem.* IV.6) on the one hand, and the dialectical prac-tice of Socrates in the *Apology* and three of the earliest dialogues, on the other hand.

This discrepancy can be alleviated if we distinguish two kinds of requests for definition. (1) I may ask "What do you mean by X?" in order to be sure that I and my interlocutor are both talking about the same thing. In this case, agreement on a definition of terms is a useful preliminary to discussing a controversial topic. This corresponds to a requirement of clarity, or a rule of good method. It is this sense that, in the *Gorgias*, Socrates extracts from Gorgias a definition of rhetoric. The result is by no means philo-sophically innocent, but it does not claim any kind of epistemic priority or metaphysical depth. (2) On the other hand, when the *ti esti?* question is introduced in the *Laches* and *Meno*, there is much more at stake. There is, first of all, the principle known in recent scholarship as the Priority of Definition. This is the epistemic claim that you cannot *know* (in some strong sense of "know") that X is Y unless you know *what X is*.[41] Furthermore, the definitions sought in the *Euthyphro* and the *Meno* aim at more than semantic clarity. In those contexts, knowledge of *what X is* involves knowing a nature or essence (*eidos, idea, ousia*) which explains *why* things are X or what makes them X. It is this stronger notion that Aristotle has in mind when he compares Socratic definition to the search for what he calls the *ti esti* or the *ti ēn einai* and *ousia*, the essences of things.[42]

The distinction between these two kinds of definitional projects will be discussed further in Chapter 6 §3. Here I want only to point out that whereas the request for a definition in the first sense, as an agreement for the sake of methodical clarity, is entirely compatible with the Socratic conception of philosophy represented in the *Apology*, the pursuit of definitions in the second sense is not. Definitions can claim epistemic priority only if they aim to reveal the explanatory essences or natures of things. But to achieve such definitions would be to attain the kind of knowledge that Socrates in the *Apology* ascribes to the gods alone, or the kind of teachable *technē* that he explicitly disavows.[43]

In the dialogues of definition Plato has skillfully disguised this disparity by focusing on moral concepts above all,[44] and seeing to it that the central quest for definition in these dialogues never succeeds, so that the conversation ends in *aporia* and Socrates can maintain his claim to ignorance. The fact remains that, if pursued

41. See Chapter 6 §4 for discussion of this principle.
42. For Socrates and *to ti esti* see *Met.* M.4, 1078b23; for *ti ēn einai* and *ousia* see *Part. An.* 1.1, 642a26.
43. Paul Woodruff (1982: 141) rightly recognizes that, in terms of the *Apology*, the search for essential definitions sets "superhuman standards of justification, but we should not be surprised that Socrates does so. For Socrates does not count on finding the knowledge he seeks among human beings, not after his many failures." This is an ingenious suggestion for reconciling the search for essential definitions with the avowal of ignorance, but it takes for granted the point at issue here, namely, whether the search for such definitions forms part of the Socratic practice as described in the *Apology*. I maintain, on the contrary, that the notion of epistemic priority for essential definitions represents a radically new and specifically Platonic departure. See the discussion in Chapter 6.
44. The *Laches*, however, offers a definition of speed (192B), and the *Meno* indicates that the search is quite general (72D–E, 74B–77A).

with any chance of success, the search for essential definitions (as represented in the *Laches*, *Euthyphro*, and *Meno*) is formally incompatible with the epistemic stance of Socrates in the *Apology*. This search for an explanatory account of things would be a search for knowledge that qualifies as *technē*. Thus the request for a definition of virtue or courage in the *Laches* serves as a test of technical competence in the corresponding subject matter. The Socrates who systematically pursues such definitions does not fit the picture of the questioner who knows only his own ignorance, and who is not in search of an explanatory science of nature. I suggest that Socrates' pursuit in the dialogues of definition prefigures what the *Phaedo* describes as a *deuteros plous*, the quest for an explanation in terms of *logoi* as an alternative to Anaxagorean physics. But the Socrates of the *Phaedo* has come a long way from the Socrates of the *Apology*. If the *Apology* is our measure for the historical Socrates, then the Aristotelian ascription to him of the search for essential definitions cannot be historically correct.

It is quite possible, on the other hand, that the pursuit of a clarifying definition like that of rhetoric in the *Gorgias* could find a place in the historical practice of Socrates.[45] Socrates may well have asked "what is piety?" or "what is virtue?" in order to provoke his interlocutors into giving more careful thought to conceptions they take for granted. But the search that Plato initiates in *Laches*, *Euthyphro*, and *Meno* is something new and more ambitious, linked from the start to epistemic and metaphysical aspirations that are distinctly un-Socratic.

6. THE FUNCTION OF *APORIA*: PLATO'S REINTERPRETATION OF SOCRATES

As presented in the *Apology*, there is something profoundly puzzling about Socrates' philosophical position. How is his total disclaimer of knowledge concerning the most important human concerns compatible with the absolute certainty that Socrates displays in moral matters, not only in the judgments that particular acts

---

45. That might be what Xenophon has in mind in the list of definitional questions in *Mem.* 1.1.16 ("What is pious? what impious? ... what is just? what unjust?", etc.). By contrast, however, both the context and content of the definitions at *Mem.* iv.6 bear the mark of Platonic influence, as was pointed out above.

are unjust but in the readiness, on principle, to accept death rather than perform an unjust action? How can his theoretical agnosticism be so strong without leaving any trace of moral doubt in regard to practical decisions? Whence came this absolute serenity with which he faced his judges, and with which he later faced his death? A similar puzzle is posed by the contrast between the negative and the positive moments of the Socratic elenchus. How does the drive to refute others and deny wisdom to oneself co-exist with the positive exhortation to moral improvement and making one's soul as good as possible? How, without wisdom, can Socrates know what makes a soul good?

This contrast between the negativity of the elenchus and the positive stance of Socrates as a man and citizen has been described by one scholar as the riddle of the *Apology*, which serves only to magnify its hero, by "representing this conceptual contradiction in the unity of a great human personality."[46] Other readers may be tempted to suspect that the irony of ignorance was after all insincere: Socrates must really have known very well what justice meant, and why it was never in anyone's interest to be unjust. Plato, at any rate, certainly felt that this was his task as Socrates' successor. It was up to him to defend the Socratic conception of virtue in fully rational terms, as he undertakes to do in the *Gorgias* and again, on a grander scale, in the *Republic*. And to do so will require him precisely to give positive content to the notion of wisdom, so that philosophy can be reconstrued as a form of knowledge, a teachable *technē*, and not only as a search.

In the *Apology*, however, Socrates betrays no need for the wisdom he does not possess. He is calmly confident that his actions have been just and that he has nothing to fear in death. Whence comes this confidence? At the level of the text, there is really no riddle. The *Apology* itself gives a perfectly clear answer. Socrates is convinced that he has been guided by a divine command, that the oracle from Delphi together with the voice from within and the dreams to which he refers, all combine to reassure him that he is acting correctly and that his destiny is in good hands. From the first mention of the oracle (at 20E) to the last word of the third speech, Socrates repeatedly justifies his life and his conduct by reference to the divine mission that he is carrying out.

46. H. Patzer (1965) 37.

It may be that, in the context of a trial for impiety, either Socrates himself or Plato writing in his name has exaggerated this religious aspect of Socrates' moral commitment. But the *Apology* is
our best source, and we have no basis for correcting its emphasis.
And the fact is that the *Apology* represents Socrates not as a rationalist in the usual sense but as a deeply religious man, one who
believes in the gods "more than any of my accusers do" (35D 6). To
speak of religious faith here can be misleading, since that term
suggests a dogmatic *credo* based upon divine revelation, and hence
a potential conflict between faith and reason that is quite alien to
pagan thought. But we may speak instead of Socrates' religious
confidence, his intellectual poise that rests upon supernatural reassurance. The *Apology* is not alone in this; Socrates' trust in dreams
as divine messages is reaffirmed in the *Crito* (44A–B) and again in
the *Phaedo* (60E–61B). And in one of the two historical reports in
Xenophon, Socrates sends Xenophon to consult the oracle at
Delphi.[47]

It is likely, then, that in the *Apology* Plato has given us a true
picture of the man as he saw him. But for Plato Socrates is much
more than the dear friend who died in 399 BC. He is also the
paradigm philosopher. And philosophy as such cannot rely on religious reassurance. Plato will have to construct a rational basis for
his own Socratic commitment to the moral life. We can perhaps
see this process beginning in the *Crito*, where Socrates makes no
reference to his divine sign but insists instead that he has always
been "such as to obey nothing other than the *logos* which seems to
me best upon reflection (*logizomenos*)" (*Crito* 46B). But to construct a
positive philosophical position, Plato will be obliged to transform
the Socratic elenchus into something quite different, namely into
the method of hypothesis that he introduces in the *Meno*. And between the *Apology* and the *Meno*, the Platonic Socrates will have the
occasion to play several different roles.

The elenchus described in the *Apology* is a testing of persons, not
of propositions. (This conception of the elenchus is occasionally
expressed in the dialogues, for instance at *Laches* 187E–188B and
Protagoras 333C. See below, pp. 170 and 302.) This is also true for

47. *Anabasis* III.1.5. As Grote recognized, "Sokrates was a very religious man,
    much influenced by prophecies, oracles, dreams, and special revelations"
    (1875) II, 195n.

the *Ion*. The rhapsode defends no thesis; like the poets in the
Apology, his lack of *technē* is demonstrated by his inability to give a
coherent account of what he knows and what he does. Much the
same can be said for the refutation of Gorgias in the dialogue
named after him. But with the elenchus of Polus and Callicles the
burden shifts from the man himself to the thesis that he defends.
The arguments are still *ad hominem*, and in this sense it is not only
the thesis but the man as well who is tested and refuted. The negative case against these defenders of immorality is successfully argued, but the positive justification of the Socratic moral ideal is
less effective, as we shall see in Chapter 5. Beside the negative
elenchus leading to contradiction (as in the cross-examination of
Meletus), the old Socratic tool-box seems to have contained only
one form of positive argument, the *epagōgē* or inference by analogy
from parallel cases. It is just such reasoning from analogy that is
used in the final, constructive section of the *Gorgias*; but this
method lacks the rigor that is needed for compelling philosophical
argument. So after the *Gorgias*, I suggest, Plato has reason to begin
with something new: the aporetic dialogue.

Formally aporetic are the three dialogues of definition (*Laches*,
Charmides, *Euthyphro*) as well as the *Protagoras*, *Meno*, and *Lysis*.[48]
These dialogues will be discussed in later chapters. Here I am concerned only with their place in the transformation of the negative
elenchus of the *Apology* into the positive method by which Socrates
will develop systematic theories in the middle dialogues.

The three dialogues of definition are all characterized by a tension between the overtly negative conclusion and some implicit
positive thesis about the virtue in question. (In the case of the
Laches and *Charmides* the implicit thesis has to do with the knowledge of good ∟nd bad; in the *Euthyphro* it concerns the potential
definition of piety as the part of justice concerned with the gods.)
The same holds for the *Protagoras*, except that in this case the argument for the positive thesis (the unity of the virtues in the knowledge of good and bad) is more fully worked out. We shall see (in

---

48. Among later dialogues the *Theaetetus* returns to the aporetic form. In this
case the philosophical motivation for *aporia* will be significantly different:
coming (in all probability) after the critique of the *Parmenides*, the *Theaetetus*
begins a new phase of Platonic writing and thinking. The aporetic form is
designed here to give the reader the impression that we must start all over
again, investigating knowledge as it were from the beginning.

Chapter 9 §3) that the *Lysis* also develops a positive thesis about friendship (*philia*) that is ignored at the conclusion of the dialogue. And the *Meno* introduces a number of constructive ideas: learning as recollection, the method of hypothesis, the distinction between knowledge and true belief. I shall argue that these positive initiatives of the *Meno* and *Lysis* are designed to prepare the way for the central doctrines of the middle dialogues. But here I want to consider the negative function of these works, which all conclude with what amounts to a Socratic avowal of ignorance, in their failure to succeed in the inquiry that was proposed.

The moment of transition from the negative to the positive mode is clearly signaled in the *Meno*, in the geometry lesson with the slave boy. Here the new Socrates, who has learned about transmigration and recollection from wise priests and priestesses, makes use of the example of the slave boy to explain to Meno the epistemic advantage of being at a loss (*aporein* 84B 6). Meno had complained that Socrates had bewitched him by infecting him with *aporia* and numbness on the subject of virtue, on which he had previously been quite eloquent (80A–B). But the slave boy, who previously thought that the task of doubling the square was an easy one, has now learned (after two failures) to recognize his ignorance, and he is now willing to search for a solution. So he has after all been benefited by being numbed (84C 8).

These remarks may be read as Plato's comment on the aporetic dialogues generally,[49] at the moment of transition to new methods and new forms of dialogue. The aporetic technique can bring the student to the first stage of philosophical enlightenment: the recognition of a problem whose importance and difficulty he had not understood. (In the Cave allegory, the corresponding moment is the prisoner's recognition that the shadows on the wall are not real things.) So in the *Sophist* the Socratic elenchus is described as a noble cathartic art, the first stage of education, which must purify the mind of opinions that prevent learning, and in particular the opinion that one knows what one does not know (*Sophist* 230A– 231B). In both dialogues Plato recognizes the negative elenchus as a necessary preliminary, preparing but not constituting the constructive search for knowledge.

These meta-dialogical reflections on the function of *aporia* may

---

49. I owe this observation to a remark by David Sedley.

serve us as a guide for divining Plato's motive in creating the aporetic dialogue. This is his literary device for reinterpreting the
Socratic elenchus as the preparation for constructive philosophy.
The reader is to accompany the interlocutor in the recognition of
a problem. But the more astute reader will also recognize some
hints of a solution. Hence the tension between the surface conclusion in *aporia* and the implicit hints of positive doctrine. These
dialogues embody in their literary form the notion of creative perplexity that is Plato's reinterpretation of the Socratic elenchus.

Unlike Moses, however, Socrates is allowed to enter the promised land. Since Plato conceives his own philosophy as the continuation of Socrates' initiative, his Socrates is not confined to the
stage of elenchus and *aporia*. After learning about the deathless
soul and its powers of recollection from certain priests and priestesses, Socrates will be initiated into the mysteries of metaphysical
love, culminating in the vision of transcendent Form, by that wise
woman Diotima. He will consequently be enabled, in the *Phaedo*
and *Republic*, to speak in his own name about the true objects of
knowledge, and about the philosophic life and the just city that are
grounded in such knowledge. In these great didactic dialogues, the
ignorant inquirer of the *Apology* has almost disappeared.

Thus Plato is perfectly aware of the difference in principle between the stage of creative *aporia* and elenctic argument, on the
one hand, and that of constructive theory-building on the other
hand. He has in a sense formally reproduced this distinction in
the contrast between Book 1 of the *Republic* and the following
nine books.[50] But the goal of wisdom is one, and philosophy as the
pursuit of wisdom is also ultimately one. So, from Plato's point of
view, there is no fundamental discrepancy between the philosophy
of Socrates and that of Plato himself.

50. See Kahn (1993a).

CHAPTER 4

Plato as a minor Socratic: Ion *and* Hippias Minor

I. INTRODUCTION: TWO EARLY DIALOGUES

We do not know how Plato's career as a writer began. But it is reasonable to suppose that the *Apology* came first, not long after the event of the trial, and perhaps before the new genre of "Socratic discourses" had taken on definite shape. Plato's first venture in this new form would probably then be the *Crito*, since this is a sort of sequel to the *Apology*. Like the *Apology*, the *Crito* is still closely connected to the final events in Socrates' life, and concerned to explain the meaning of his life and death to a larger reading public. With the *Ion* and *Hippias Minor* we encounter something new.

These two dialogues are, with the *Crito*, the shortest of all Plato's works, and they are likely also to be the earliest. For the *Ion* we have some evidence pointing to a date in the late 390s, before Plato had decided to abandon hopes of a political career and become a full-time philosopher and writer.[1] It seems natural to think of these brief pieces as the apprentice exercises of a master craftsman, practising his art on the small jar.

Formally speaking, the *Ion* and the *Hippias Minor* are quite similar to one another. Like the *Crito*, both are in simple mime form, without a prologue or narrative frame. In the *Ion* Socrates has a single interlocutor (as in the *Crito*); in the *Hippias Minor* he has two interlocutors, although one of them, Eudikos, speaks only very briefly. Both dialogues consist of two symmetrical sections in which Socrates questions his interlocutors, separated by an intermediate

---

1. The *Crito* covers 12 Stephanus pages, the *Ion* 12 1/2, the *Hippias Minor* 13 1/2. For dating the *Ion* between 394 and 391 BC see Méridier (1931) 23f., 28. So Flashar (1958: 100f.) dates it in 394 or shortly thereafter.

passage in which he develops positive views of his own. The two dialogues are further linked to one another by the abundance in both of quotations from Homer. Read retrospectively, from the point of view of what comes later, both dialogues point to important continuities in Plato's life work. The _Ion_ is designed to undermine the intellectual prestige of poetry, represented here by the rhapsode. And the _Hippias Minor_ explores a pair of perverse moral paradoxes, leading indirectly to the central Socratic paradox that no one does wrong voluntarily. The _Hippias_ thus engages central problems in what is called Socratic intellectualism, problems to be discussed here in Chapter 8. Both dialogues have been relatively neglected in recent scholarship on Plato. I propose to examine them in detail, as a window into Plato's philosophical topics and techniques at what I take to be the very beginning of his career as an author.

The common philosophical thread running through these two works is a concern with the notion of _technē_ or craft knowledge. In the _Ion_ Socrates denies that the rhapsode (and, by implication, the poet as well) possesses a _technē_. In the _Hippias Minor_ it is by a specious parallelism between virtue and the arts that Socrates is able to establish his extravagent thesis that the person who does wrong on purpose is better than the one who does wrong involuntarily. Thus both dialogues lead us to reflect upon the concept of _technē_ and its application to the domain of moral action and character.

2. THE SOCRATIC BACKGROUND OF THE PROBLEM OF _TECHNĒ_

In the _Apology_ Socrates insists upon his lack of knowledge or wisdom (_sophia_). He does not of course claim to be ignorant in every respect. He claims to know that it is bad and shameful to do wrong or to do an unjust act under any circumstances (_Apology_ 29B 6; cf. 28B 8, 32B–C, 33A). He firmly maintains that the most important thing in life is self-examination in the concern for _aretē_, moral excellence (38A; cf. 31B 5, 41E), the concern for "intelligence (_phronēsis_) and truth and making one's soul as good as possible" (29E, 30B 2). This is what it means to spend one's life "in the practice of philosophy (_philosophein_) and in testing myself and others" (28E 5). If this practice involves, as the name _philosophia_ suggests, the search for wisdom "concerning the greatest things" (22D 7), it certainly does not imply the *possession* of such wisdom. As we have seen, Socrates denies that he has anything of this sort. Specifically he denies any share in the kind of scientific knowledge pursued by the natural philosophers (19C) and in the skill or art (*technē*) by which the sophists claim to educate people (*paideuein anthrōpous* 19D–20C), the art which he describes as that of an "expert (*epistēmōn*) in human and civic excellence" (20B 4).

The wisdom that Socrates lacks but seeks is indiscriminately referred to as *sophia*, *epistēmē*, and *technē*; but the latter term more particularly implies an ability to teach others.[2] Since there is independent evidence (from Aeschines) that Socrates denied possession of any such expert knowledge or *technē*, we may reasonably infer that this was a characteristic attitude of the historical Socrates.[3] But when we turn to the *Crito* the situation is not exactly the same. In responding to the popular view, urged by Crito, that it would be cowardly to let the city put him to death when he might escape, Socrates appeals to other opinions, opinions held by men who judge wisely in moral matters just as the doctor or trainer judges well in matters of bodily health. This analogy between physical welfare and moral excellence serves to introduce the notion of an expert in moral matters, corresponding to the position of the doctor in matters of health. So in questions of what is good or bad, right or wrong, it is not the opinion of the many which counts, since they have no special knowledge. In such matters too "we should follow the opinion of the one person, if there is someone who has knowledge" (*Crito* 47D 1), "the one who knows (*ho epaiōn*) about what is just and unjust, that one person and the truth itself" (48A 6).

Nowhere in the *Crito* does Socrates claim to possess such expertise. He claims only to follow "the reasoning (*logos*) which upon reflection seems to me the best" (46B). But his whole life has been spent in such reflection, in the concern for *aretē*; and he remains loyal to certain moral principles (*logoi*) that have been agreed upon often before (45D 8, 46B–C, 49A–B). If the *Crito* does not represent Socrates as an expert (*epistēmon*) in matters of right and wrong, it certainly presents him as referring in positive terms to the possibility of such knowledge. This does seem to constitute a significant

2. See Kube (1969) 4 and *passim*.
3. For the Aeschines passage see above, p. 21.

shift from the skepticism of the *Apology*, where Socrates' fruitless search for wisdom led him to the conclusion that only a god can be wise "but human wisdom is worth little or nothing" (23A). The ideal of "the one who knows about matters of right and wrong" is formulated in the *Crito* without the irony that Socrates generally applies to human pretensions to wisdom in the *Apology* and elsewhere.[4]

This notion of a moral *technē*, which puts in an ambiguous appearance in the *Crito*, will play an increasingly important role in other dialogues such as the *Gorgias* and *Protagoras*. Its most famous exemplar will be the philosopher-kings of the *Republic*, but we find it still later in the royal or political art of the *Statesman*. It is not surprising, however, that what is likely to be the first positive reference to the possibility of such an art should be introduced in cautious conditional form: "if there is someone who has such knowledge" (*Crito* 47D 1). Given Socrates' emphatic disclaimer in the *Apology*, the possibility of genuine knowledge concerning what is good and bad must inevitably be regarded as problematic. Later on, however, Plato's own position will be equally clear: virtue in the individual and justice in the city must depend ultimately upon moral cognition, upon knowledge in the strongest sense. The two short dialogues now under discussion are best read in the light of these concerns. In order to establish the existence of a moral *technē*, Plato must first clarify the notion of *technē*, as he begins to do here.

In discussing the *Ion* and the *Hippias Minor*, I treat first the substantive content of each dialogue and then the form of argumentation by which the conclusions are reached. This material is of particular interest if I am right to suppose that these two dialogues (together with the *Crito*) represent the earliest stage in Plato's work as a philosophic author.

3. THE *ION*: WHY POETRY IS NOT A *TECHNĒ*

Although Ion is proud of his recent victory at the poetic competitions in Epidaurus, it is Socrates who pointedly calls attention to

---

4. The contrast between the *Crito* and the *Apology* in this respect was clearly discerned by Grote (1875: 1,308f.), who sees Socrates as assuming here the role of expert in moral matters.

the pretensions of his craft. "Ion, I have often admired you rhapsodes for your art (*technē*). First of all, your body is adorned in a way fitting to your art (*technē*), to make you appear as fine as possible; and secondly, you must spend your time with many excellent poets and above all with Homer, the best and most divine of poets" (530B). (We cannot miss the irony implied in taking the rhapsode's costume as a mark of his *technē*.) Socrates emphasizes, and Ion agrees, that the chief distinction of the rhapsode is to understand the poet's thought and to interpret that thought for the audience (530C). By thus focusing attention on the exegesis of poetry and not simply on its performance, Plato points to the fundamental role in Greek education played by poetry in general and Homer in particular. It is as a moral and intellectual influence rather than as an art form that poetry becomes an object for Plato's criticism, both here and elsewhere.

The discussion that follows falls into three parts. In section I, Socrates argues *ad hominem* against Ion that his success as a rhapsode cannot be due to *technē*, since he is competent only on Homer. If he possessed the relevant art or science (*technē, epistēmē*), he would be able to speak on poetry as a whole. The second section is more positive: here Socrates gives his alternative explanation of Ion's success in terms of divine possession or inspiration, making use of the famous image of the magnet. The Muse is the magnet who transmits her power to the poet, who passes it on to the rhapsode or actor, who in turn exercises the power of possession over the audience, just as the magnetic stone attracts iron rings that in turn attract other rings and pieces of iron. Poet and rhapsode are conceived as the passive instrument by which the Muse herself exerts her power on the auditors. We notice that this conception gives a non-cognitive explanation for the achievement of the poet as well as for that of the rhapsode, and thus undermines any claim for the poet's thought (*dianoia*) to make an intellectual contribution to education.

Ion is unconvinced by this explanation of his success as the result of possession or being "out of his mind" (536D 5; cf. 534B 5–6). He would like to think that he knows what he is doing. Hence in the third section of the dialogue Socrates provides a more general argument to show that the rhapsode has no *technē*. The basic premiss is a version of what will appear in the *Republic* as the principle of specialization, the principle on which the division of labor is founded: "Has not some specific task (*ergon*) been assigned by the god to each of the *technai*, for it to have knowledge of?" (537c 5). This is then reformulated as a principle of individuation for the arts:

I call two arts distinct when each one is knowledge of a different subject matter (*pragmata*). (537D 5)

From this it follows that if the subjects known are distinct, the *technai* are distinct, and conversely. So "what we know by one art, we will not know by a different art" (537D 2). Socrates then applies this principle to a variety of passages in Homer and proceeds to show that, for any topic mentioned in the poems, there seems always to be an expert more competent than the rhapsode to judge this particular subject matter. The rhapsode has no subject that is specifically his own.

Ion grants the case for the charioteer, the doctor, the fisherman, and a host of other professions, but he insists that the rhapsode knows best "what is appropriate for a man to say, and what for a woman, what is appropriate for a slave and a freeman, and for a ruler and a subject" (540B). Socrates can show that this breaks down for specific cases (the rhapsode does not know what is appropriate for a ship captain to say if his ship is caught in a storm). But Ion firmly resists in the case of a general knowing what to say in order to encourage his troops. He insists that he is not only an excellent rhapsode but also an excellent general, "having learned this from the works of Homer" (541B 5).[5] He even maintains that the two arts are one and the same.

Against this extraordinary claim Socrates tries several logical moves, none of which succeeds in getting Ion to admit defeat. Socrates nevertheless concludes that Ion is deceiving him and that he refuses to reveal "how clever you are in the wisdom concerning Homer" (542A 1). He then confronts Ion with a final dilemma: "If you really have a *technē* ... it is unjust of you to deceive me; if however you are possessed by divine dispensation ... you do no wrong. Choose which you prefer: to be regarded by us as unjust or as divine." Faced with such a choice, Ion naturally opts for the more attractive alternative.

---

5. In Aristophanes' *Frogs* (verse 1036) Homer is praised for teaching men "battle formations, prowess, and putting on armor."

What do we find in this brief conversation by way of substantive philosophical content? We have (1) a positive theory of poetry, (2) an incipient theory of *technē*, and (3) the negative application of the *technē* theory to poetry via the rhapsode.

(1) The theory of poetry which reinterprets the traditional notion of poetic inspiration as divine madness or possession was perhaps anticipated by Democritus, who is quoted by Clement of Alexandria as saying "whatever a poet writes with divine frenzy (*enthousiasmos*) and holy inspiration (*pneuma*) is exceedingly beautiful."[6] But if the notion of poetic possession may have been borrowed, Plato has here developed it systematically by the parallel to Corybantic ecstasy, prophetic frenzy, and the supernatural powers of the Bacchae when possessed. The magnificent simile of the magnet with its chain of iron rings is certainly Plato's own, and it has the deliberate effect of giving the same explanation for poetic creation as for rhapsodic performance. The attack on Ion thus becomes an attack on Homer and the poets.[7] It was of course the poets who claimed to be divinely inspired; and it was their "wisdom" and their "thought" which played such an important role in Greek education. By eliminating the intellectual component from their achievement, Plato, like Heraclitus before him,[8] challenges their claim to be counted as *sophoi*. He thus pursues the line indicated by Socrates in the *Apology*, whose examination of the poets led him to conclude that "it was not by wisdom or skill (*sophia*) that they compose their poems, but by some natural gift (*physei tini*) and frenzy, like the prophets and oracular seers. For the latter also say many fine things, but they don't know what they are talking about."[9] The theory of the *Ion* is a systematic working out of this hint from the *Apology*. The ultimate target is not only the

---

6. DK 68B.18. The quotation does not seem to be verbatim, and Clement's language may be influenced by our passage in the *Ion*, which he has just referred to. Linguistically more convincing is Democritus B 21: "Since Homer was allotted a godlike nature, he constructed a glorious ordering of manifold verse." But this text does not imply possession. For critical discussion see Tigerstedt (1970) 163–78.

7. This was correctly seen by Méridier (1931) 13, following Schleiermacher and others.

8. Heraclitus B 42, 56, 57 (DK).

9. *Apology* 22B 9, on which Burnet comments: "It is well to remember here that *sophia* was the regular word for artistic skill, especially in music and poetry."

poets of contemporary Athens but their great predecessor, Homer himself.[10]

There can be no doubt of the enormous influence exerted by the Homeric poems on the intellectual development of the Greeks from childhood on. Many commentators assume, however, that Plato's attack is directed not only against this general influence of poetry but specifically against the use of the poets by professional sophists as part of their training program.[11] We find such a practice illustrated in the *Protagoras*, where the famous sophist is made to remark, apropos of the interpretation of Simonides' poem, that "it is a very important part of a man's education (*paideia*) to be competent on the subject of poetry, that is, to be able to understand what is well said by the poet and what is not well said, to know how to judge with discernment and to give an explanation when questioned" (*Prot.* 338Ef.). This is essentially what Ion promises to do for Homer. Plato's contempt for this notion of education is reflected in Socrates' comment that to converse about poetry is to act like banqueters who require a floor show because they are unable to enjoy their own conversation; furthermore, the poets are not there to answer our questions, and hence the conversation is futile (*Prot.* 347C–348A). Is Plato attacking the teaching of such long-dead figures as Protagoras and Hippias? Or does he have some more contemporary educational practice in view? We return to this question in discussing the *Hippias Minor*, where the interpretation of Homer is again an issue. (See §7 below.)

(2) Plato's theory of *technē* gets its start in the *Ion* with the fundamental principle of a one-to-one mapping between a science and its subject matter. This principle is so carefully articulated in our dialogue (537C–538A) that it can be taken for granted in other discussions of *technē* (e.g., *Gorgias* 462B–465A, *Charmides* 171A). A variant of this principle, extended to cover capacities (*dunameis*), will be used to distinguish the object of Knowledge from the object of Opinion in *Republic* v, 447D. The original principle is clearly defensible if the notion of subject matter is taken intensionally, that is, as *defined* by the approach of the science. In that case, the prin-

10. Compare Woodruff (1983: 6) "To attack Homer he [i.e. Socrates, but I would rather say Plato] would have to attack his representatives, the rhapsodes."

11. E.g. Flashar (1958) 32; Friedländer (1964) 129.

ciple *one science if and only if one subject matter* becomes something like
a conceptual truth. The *Ion* can be seen as formulating the insight
that to have a definite subject matter is part of the notion of what
it is to be a science. On the other hand, the principle is more
problematic if "subject matter" is taken extensionally to refer to
different slices of the world, different sets of objects or individual
entities. In this sense, it would seem that different sciences can after all study the same objects. The set of human beings, for example, might constitute the object for anthropology and psychology,
linguistics and human genetics. A critic of Plato could claim that
the *Republic* argument for two kinds of objects corresponding to
Knowledge and Opinion trades on just this ambiguity between the
intensional and the extensional reading of "object." A fuller discussion might defend Plato against this charge by a more profound analysis of the notion of intensional object. But that is not
our topic here.

(3) The principle of a one-to-one mapping between *technē* and
subject matter is already implicit in the first, *ad hominem* argument
that relies on Ion's admission that his talent is limited to Homer.
Since poetry is a single subject, the corresponding art of exegesis
would have to be similarly general. If it were by *technē* that Ion
could explain Homer, he would be equally capable of speaking
about the other poets, "for I suppose that the whole thing is poetry" (532c 8). By a slight readjustment, the same principle will
apply to the work of the poet as well as to that of the exegete.
This allows us to reconstruct the argument that Aristodemus could
not remember, how at the end of the *Symposium* Socrates was obliging a sleepy Agathon and a tipsy Aristophanes "to agree that it
belongs to the same man to master the art of composing comedy
and tragedy, and that he who was a tragic poet by art (*technēi*)
would be a comic poet as well" (*Symp.* 223D). If there was a *technē*
of composing tragedy or comedy, it would have to be the same for
both, since "the whole thing is poetry." It is simply because they
are inspired by different Muses that one poet composes tragedy,
another composes comedy, one composes epic, another composes
invectives, "and each of them is no good at the other kinds of
poetry" (*Ion* 534c).

The one-to-one mapping principle, implicit in this first argument against Ion, is formally stated in the more rigorous argument

of the third section (537C–538A). If the rhapsode had a *technē*, there would have to be a corresponding subject matter that it was uniquely qualified to know. As we have seen, however, for any particular passage of Homer there seems to be a different art that is better qualified to judge the action described. (If the action is a chariot race, the charioteer is a better judge than the rhapsode, and so forth.) But at this point we must observe that, even for cases where the mapping principle is assumed to be valid, there is something tricky or perverse in Socrates' use of it. For its application in this argument has the effect of making the work of art disappear: one looks *through* the poem to focus only on the various human actions described. The description itself, the poetry as such, never comes into view. Ion makes a desperate effort to direct attention to the poet's art of character portrayal when he specifies, as the rhapsode's proper subject matter, "what is appropriate for a man to say, and what is appropriate for a woman, and for a slave … and for a ruler" (540B). But Socrates forces him back onto the extra-poetic terrain of the first-order arts. ("Does the rhapsode know better than the pilot what the ruler of a ship should say in a storm at sea?") The poem as an art work has no independent status. This must be a quite deliberate move on Plato's part, as it directly serves his purpose of undermining the claims of poetry to be counted as *sophia*. A similarly depreciative conception of art is developed in Book x of the *Republic*, when the poet and the painter are represented as imitating reality at third hand. The theory of art sketched in the *Ion* is less merely hostile, since it also takes account of the positive, "divine" impact of poetry on the audience. But that impact is seen as entirely devoid of intellectual understanding.

4. ARGUMENTATION IN THE *ION*

It is often assumed that the standard form of argumentation in Plato's early dialogues is the Socratic elenchus. Now if by elenchus we mean any rigorous examination or refutation, any testing of the interlocutor's beliefs in which these beliefs are shown to be false or incoherent, then this is indeed typical of Socrates' procedure in the *Ion* as in other early dialogues. But since Richard Robinson's classic study, the term "elenchus" has been used to designate something more precise: an argument in which the interlocutor states a thesis which Socrates then refutes by deriving its denial from premises that the interlocutor accepts.[12] Now the elenchus in this sense may well be historically Socratic, since it is exemplified in the cross-examination of Meletus in the *Apology*. Furthermore, it is abundantly displayed in the *Gorgias*, the *Protagoras*, and the dialogues of definition, as well as in the first book of the *Republic*. Interestingly enough, however, there is no formal elenchus of this kind in the *Ion*. Socrates does not begin by extracting from the interlocutor a proposition that he then proceeds to refute.

In this dialogue we have what is presumably the original Socratic elenchus: a testing of persons, not of propositions. The thesis to be refuted (namely, that the rhapsode as such possesses a *technē*) is never asserted by Ion. (It is of course taken for granted by him, e.g., at 530c 8. But to be formally refuted it would have to be formally affirmed.) On the other hand, the contradictory thesis, that the rhapsode operates not by *technē* but by divine gift or possession, is asserted by Socrates but never accepted by Ion as the consequence of an argument. He does accept it verbally at the end, but only to avoid the charge of being unjust. This is Plato's elegant way of showing that Socrates has won the argument, even though Ion will not grant his point.

The central portion of the dialogue is not an elenchus at all but the exposition by Socrates of a positive explanation of the power of poetry. In the first and third sections we do find systematic arguments in the form of a classic Socratic *epagōgē*, an inductive generalization from the arts and crafts. In section I, Socrates cites arithmetic, medicine, painting, sculpture, and various forms of music to show that a good judge of one specimen of any given art should be a good judge of other practitioners of the same art. In section III, he cites the charioteer, the doctor, the fisherman, the prophet, the cowherd, the woolworker, and the general to show that for every action described in Homer, there is a specialist who can judge this action better than the rhapsode can. If the method is historically Socratic, Plato's use of it here is certainly highly stylized.

How good are these arguments? The *epagōgē* in section I is not

---

12. See Richard Robinson (1953) 6. Gregory Vlastos' conception of the elenchus is more demanding: (Vlastos 1994: 4). For my critique of Vlastos on the elenchus see Kahn (1992) 248–56.

formally impeccable,[13] but it makes a sound point: there is really something odd about competence in a well-defined area that extends only to the leading representative of the field and to none of his peers. The argument of section III is more ambitious. The mapping principle introduced here is important historically, for its utilization in Plato's later work, and also philosophically, as defining the proper subject matter for a given science. Socrates' application of this principle to the rhapsode and (by implication) to the poet is more dubious, as we have noted. If Ion had been more quick-witted, he might have blocked the second *epagōgē* by citing those passages in the *Odyssey* where a minstrel performs, as one case where the rhapsode is the privileged judge of the action described. Plato is aware of this possibility, and he has cunningly arranged for Socrates to mention the judging of rhapsodes as an example in the earlier *epagōgē*, at 533B–C. But the position of the minstrel is too marginal in Homeric society for Ion to take much satisfaction in a *technē* that would make him an expert in this function only. He opts for a more noble if less plausible role, that of the general encouraging his troops (540Dff.): his chosen models are Hector and Agamemnon, not the blind singer Demodocus.

From the logical point of view, the most interesting passages in section III are Socrates' final efforts to counter this rather silly move on Ion's part. Socrates does not succeed in refuting Ion, for the rhapsode is insensitive to logical defeat; but he displays some sophisticated techniques that go well beyond the familiar argument from analogy. When Ion insists that he knows how a general should encourage his men, Socrates suggests that Ion may possess two quite distinct arts: the art of the rhapsode and the art of the general. In developing this distinction he introduces, probably for the first time in philosophical history, the terminology *qua X* or *under the description Y*: "Suppose you were both a horseman and a

13. There is a slippery slide from (1) if one can recognize the superiority of good poets, one can also recognize that the others are inferior (531D 12–532B 2), which is trivially true, to (2) if one can understand and explain good artists, one can also explain inferior ones (532E 7–533C 3), which is a substantive claim, apparently falsified in Ion's case. (The slide is effected at 532A 3ff.: "the same person is competent about both," which is ambiguous between the two claims.) However, proposition 2 is supported by its own *epagōgē*. Proposition 1 is thus not logically needed; it is part of Socrates' rhetorical "softening-up" of his opponent before the logical kill.

lyre-player ... if I asked you, by what art, Ion, do you know when horses are well trained? Is it *qua* horseman or *qua* lyre-player?" (540D–E).[14] Ion recognizes the distinction in this case, but refuses to recognize it in the parallel case of general and rhapsode. So Socrates proceeds to a second tactic. "You say that the rhapsode and the general have a single art?" "Yes, I do." "Then whoever is a good rhapsode is a good general?" To this implication Ion willingly consents, for this is precisely his claim. But he balks at the converse, which is equally entailed by his identifying the two arts: "Whoever then is a good general is also a good rhapsode?" "No, I don't think so" (541A).

What is Socrates to do with such an interlocutor? His final ploy is to return to the implication that is acceptable to Ion, that a good rhapsode will also be a good general. He argues then from the positive to the superlative: "But if you are the best rhapsode in Greece, you are also the best general?" Ion cheerfully accepts the compliment (541B). Socrates asks him why in that case he performs only as a rhapsode and does not pursue an even more honorable career as general. The dialogue ends with an irrelevant dispute about whether someone from Ephesus, like Ion, could actually serve as general in the city of Athens. Socrates has clearly won the argument, but his victory cannot be logically consummated because of the stubborn obtuseness of Ion. He prevails only by the rhetorical maneuver of obliging Ion to choose between being thought either dishonest or inspired.

5. *HIPPIAS MINOR*: *TECHNĒ* AND MORAL KNOWLEDGE

Philosophically speaking, the *Hippias Minor* is one of the most puzzling of all Platonic dialogues, since it concludes not simply with a paradox but with a moral falsehood: that the one who does wrong voluntarily is a better person than the one who does wrong unintentionally.[15] From the literary point of view, on the other hand, the *Hippias Minor* is strikingly similar in form to the more straightforward *Ion* (as we have noted in § 1).

Hippias is a professional educator, a sophist in the strict sense of

14. Ποτέρᾳ τέχνῃ ... γιγνώσκεις ...; ᾗ ἱππεὺς εἶ ἢ ᾗ κιθαριστής;
15. Here and throughout I use "voluntary" and "intentional" interchangeably for *hekōn*, "involuntary" and "unintentional" for *akōn*.

one who offers training for a fee (364D). But he is also a mathematician, an astronomer, and a specialist in almost every conceivable art (368B–E; cf. *Protagoras* 315C). As a consequence, the twin questions of *technē* and education are raised here in a much sharper form than in the *Ion*. At the same time, the continuity with that dialogue is sustained not only by the formal parallels noted in §1 but more directly by the fact that, when the dialogue begins, Hippias has just finished an oratorical display "on Homer and other poets" (363C 2). The reader who comes to the *Hippias Minor* from the *Ion* is allowed to imagine that Hippias has as it were delivered the epideictic speech on Homer that Ion promised to give and Socrates asked him to postpone.[16] It is from Homeric material that the conversation begins, by a comparison between Achilles and Odysseus, and it is this Homeric comparison that introduces the shocking paradox with which the dialogue concludes. So a strong background theme for the *Hippias Minor*, as for the *Ion*, is the role of poetry in education.

Socrates opens the discussion by asking whether Hippias agrees with the familiar view that Achilles is a better man than Odysseus. Hippias agrees, but his interpretation of Odysseus' epithet *polutropos* as "false, deceitful" (*pseudēs*) is challenged by Socrates: "you mean that a truthful man and a false man are different from one another?" (365C). Socrates then proceeds to refute this reasonable claim by a devious argument. He first establishes that intelligent deception requires knowledge of the subject matter (365Eff.), and then shows that the *capacity* to lie effectively is always found together with the capacity to tell the truth. For example in arithmetic, which is one of Hippias' specialties: "The ignorant man who wants to lie will often tell the truth unintentionally (*akōn*) by chance, because he does not know, whereas you who are skilled (*sophos*) in this, if you should want to lie, you would always do so consistently" (367A). The coincidence of these two capacities is then illustrated by an elaborate series of examples from the arts, all of them designed to show that "the truthful person is no better

16. Hippias seems to have published works on such subjects, of which one began as follows: "Some of these things were perhaps said by Orpheus, some by Musaeus briefly here and there, some by Hesiod, some by Homer, some by other poets, also in prose works (*suggraphai*) both Greek and barbarian. But I have put together the most important of all these and arranged them according to kind, to create this new and diversified discourse" (DK 86B 6).

than the false one, since they are the same" (367c 8). Hence, this
cannot be the distinction between Achilles and Odysseus (369B).

So ends the first section of the dialogue. Hippias is unconvinced,
and offers to make a speech proving the superiority of Achilles
and the deceptiveness of Odysseus. Instead Socrates makes his
own speech, with three quotations from the *Iliad* to show that it is
Achilles, not Odysseus, who says what is false. Hippias responds
by claiming that Achilles speaks falsely "not from premeditation
but unintentionally (*akōn*)," whereas Odysseus does so "voluntarily
and deliberately" (370E). Hippias' view faithfully represents the
impression most of us have from reading Homer. But Socrates
now argues, with brilliant perversity, that Achilles deliberately de-
ceives Odysseus in the embassy scene of *Iliad* Book ix. More generally, he claims, those who lie voluntarily are better than those
who lie unintentionally.[17] More generally still, those who do wrong
voluntarily are better than those who do so unintentionally (372D–
E). At first Socrates confesses some misgivings about this thesis.
But he proceeds to support it in the third section of the dialogue
(373cff.) by a systematic *epagōgē*, with examples from a wide variety
of human arts and practices and from some animal examples as
well, culminating in the claim that "it is the mark of a good man
to do injustice voluntarily, but of a bad man to do it unintentionally" (376B 2). So the dialogue ends in confusion. Hippias is unable
to fault the reasoning, but he remains unconvinced by Socrates'
fantastic conclusion. "I cannot agree with you," he says. And Socrates replies: "Nor can I agree with myself. But from the argument
it necessarily seems this way to us now."

What has gone wrong? The fallacy of section I is easy to locate,
in the move from *is able to lie* to *is a liar*. The examples cited show
that anyone who can lie well about any matter will also be able to
tell the truth on the same subject. But to conclude therefore that
the same person lies and tells the truth is not only fallacious but
obviously false. Hippias recognizes the falsity but cannot spot the
fallacy. He has been deceived by Socrates' repeated claim that
the capacity to lie is a necessary condition for being a liar (366B,

17. At 371E 7 where this paradox is introduced, Socrates claims that it was estab-
    lished in their earlier discussion. But this claim involves a distortion of what
    was actually argued for at 366D 4 and 367A 3, namely, that the person who is
    best at a given subject matter will err more successfully and consistently,
    since he will do so voluntarily and not by accident.

367B 2–5); he is thus led to suppose that it must be a sufficient condition as well. Hence when Socrates concludes "To sum up, the liars are those who are clever and able to lie," Hippias assents (366B 5).

Now there is no reason to doubt that Plato is aware of the fallacy here. The text is peppered with hints that to be a liar requires not only the capacity to lie but also the will, desire, or intention to do so. The verb *boulesthai* "to want" appears nine times in this context (366B–367A), beginning with the definition of capacity: "a person is capable who does what he wants when he wants" (366B 6; so already at 366B 2). In Aristotelian terms the fallacy lies in collapsing the distinction between an open capacity like art or science (a *dunamis, technē,* or *epistēmē*) and a fixed disposition or character trait (*hexis*).[18] An intellectual capacity is a capacity for opposites: the doctor knows how to poison as well as to cure. A *hexis* like moral virtue, on the other hand, is a capacity turned in a fixed direction, trained to aim at a certain goal, reliably guided by what Aristotle calls "choice" (*prohairesis*). Plato speaks not of choice but of *boulesthai*, wanting or rational desire. It would seem that the main point of the first fallacy is to call attention to the importance of this factor.

More perplexing is Socrates' defense of the second paradox: that to do wrong voluntarily is better than to do so unintentionally. Now for a wide variety of physical activities and technical capacities, this proposition has a plausible application. For example, if running fast is good running and running slow is bad, then the good runner will run slowly (badly) only intentionally, whereas the bad runner will run slowly (badly) whether he likes it or not. And so also for wrestling badly, singing out of tune, missing the target in archery, playing the lyre badly, and so on. The fallacy arises with the application to justice (*dikaiosunē*): it is not the case that one who kills or steals deliberately is better than one who does so

---

18. Compare Arist. *NE* v.1, 1129a 7ff.: justice is a *hexis* which produces just action and desire (*boulesthai*) for just outcomes. "But the case is not the same for sciences (*epistēmai*) and capacities (*dunameis*) as for character traits (*hexeis*). For the capacity and knowledge of opposites is thought to be the same, but a *hexis* does not produce its opposite, as health does not produce unhealthy actions but only healthy ones." Aristotle is fascinated by the puzzles of the *Hippias Minor*, which he refers to by name in *Met.* Δ 29, 1025aff. See also *NE* vi.5, 1140b21–4.

unintentionally. Socrates is able to defend this strange conclusion only by counting justice as "a capacity or a form of knowledge or both" (375D 8). He thus assimilates justice to the arts of section I, to arithmetic and geometry, for example, where to make a mistake on purpose is the prerogative of one who has knowledge, whereas the ignorant person makes a mistake involuntarily. But this assimilation is deliberately misleading. Justice, and moral virtue generally, is not a bipolar capacity for opposites.[19]

But why not? Whether or not the historical Socrates identified virtue as a form of knowledge, that is certainly a thesis the Platonic Socrates will endorse in the *Meno*, the *Protagoras*, and elsewhere. What is the relevant difference that Socrates must ignore in order to defend his shocking paradox? How is the knowledge or *technē* of virtue unlike knowing arithmetic? Our only hint in section III of the *Hippias Minor* is Socrates' penultimate remark: "So the man who voluntarily errs and does unjust and shameful things, *if there is anyone of this sort*, will only be the good man." The conditional clause has been generally recognized as a cryptic reminder of the Socratic paradox: no one does wrong voluntarily.[20] But why not? The dialogue scarcely considers this question. Part I does offer a hint in the emphasis on *boulesthai*: *what is it that people really want?* If we knew this, we might understand why no one does wrong voluntarily, and why a moral character trait is not a capacity for opposites. Plato will pursue this line of thought in the *Gorgias*.

Even if such hints do give us some idea how the two central fallacies of the *Hippias Minor* are to be resolved, we are left with many questions. Why does Plato make Socrates argue here for propositions that both Plato and his readers must recognize as false? (Socrates himself repeatedly expresses doubts; he describes the second paradox as a fit that has taken hold of him, and he appeals to Hippias "to cure his soul" by ridding him of his error, at 372E.)

19. Alternatively (but equivalently) the fallacy can be diagnosed as the move from *good* in a relative or functional sense (*good at X*: good at running, good at arithmetic) to *good* in an absolute or moral sense: a good person, a good man. For an analysis along these lines see Sprague (1962) 74–7.
20. E.g. Sprague (1962) 76, who refers to Taylor and Shorey for the same view. She also quotes from Shorey (1933: 471) similar tip-off conditionals at *Gorgias* 480E ("If one ought to harm anyone") and *Euthyphro* 7D ("If the gods quarrel").

The rule "say what you really think," which is sometimes said to be a fundamental principle for Socratic dialectic, is certainly violated here by Socrates himself. Hippias, on the other hand, bravely but ineffectively defends the position of sound common sense (unlike the stupid character of the same name in the pseudo-Platonic *Hippias Major*). Why should Plato represent Socrates here as the unscrupulous sophist, defending false theses with fallacious arguments? We can well imagine that, if this dialogue were not expressly cited by Aristotle, many scholars would have judged it unworthy of Plato and hence unauthentic. Should we believe that Socrates was really like this, and that Plato has given us a faithful portrait?[21]

We cannot rule out this possibility. But it is more plausible to assume that Plato is operating with a large measure of artistic freedom, and that he is presenting us with these fallacies in order to make some philosophical point. The one thing that is unmistakably clear, since both the fallacies turn on it, is that moral virtue and vice are *not* to be understood simply as a trained capacity or skill. Being good as a human being is not like being good at running or good at arithmetic. If virtue is a *technē*, it must be an art and science of a quite unusual sort, involving the rational will or desire (*boulesthai*) in a quite specific way. It is true that Plato will always want to emphasize the decisive importance of the cognitive component in moral excellence: virtue at the highest level will always be represented as a *technē*, a form of knowledge. But by rubbing our noses here in the unpleasant consequences of equating justice with an ordinary skill or capacity, Plato must be alerting us to the difficulty of seeing just what *kind* of knowledge could possibly guarantee virtue for its possessor. Our only clue is the hint provided by the paradox, that the corresponding form of ignorance must make wrongdoing involuntary.

The *Hippias Minor* is not formally aporetic, but it does leave us with a problem for other dialogues to resolve. Of course, seen in a broader perspective the *Ion* and the *Hippias* are both big with the future: looking back from Plato's later work we can see that Socrates' conversation with the rhapsode portends his meeting with

---

21. This seems to have been the view of Hermann (1839: 432 with n.251), who cites Xenophon, *Mem.* IV.2.20 to show that the content is "nicht unsokratisch." So also Guthrie (1965) 197, citing Stallbaum and Grote.

the poets in the *Symposium*, just as his encounter with Hippias fore-
shadows his confrontation with more imposing sophists in the *Gorgias* and *Protagoras*. But there is an important difference between
these two works. Taken alone the *Ion* is self-contained, whereas the
Hippias Minor is open-ended. The problem raised here will be carried farther in the *Gorgias*, where justice is unambiguously construed as a *technē*, as part of the political art (464B–C), but where
the conception of *technē* is enriched by the notion of a built-in tel-
eology, *aiming at the good* in one form or another, as medicine aims
at health (464C–465A). Other dialogues speak of virtue as knowledge of good and bad (*Laches, Charmides*), or invoke a kind of wisdom and intelligence that will make the arts beneficial by guaran-
teeing their correct use (*Meno* 88E, *Euthydemus* 280Eff., 288Eff.). The
Republic will insist that such knowledge must have as its object the
Form of the Good. None of this is implicit in the *Hippias Minor*.[22]
But all of it is part of Plato's answer to one of the most profound
questions in moral theory, the question raised for the first time in
our dialogue: how are we to understand the connection between
moral knowledge and moral character, between reason and virtue?

6. ARGUMENTATION IN THE *HIPPIAS MINOR*

Part I of the *Hippias Minor* does contain a brief elenchus in standard form: Hippias assents to the obviously true proposition that
the truthful man is distinct from the liar (365C 5), which Socrates
proceeds to refute (369B). Similarly in section III, Hippias gives
implicit assent to the truism that those who do wrong intentionally
are worse than those who do so unintentionally (372A). But in each
case the logical and dramatic emphasis is not on the refutation of
a thesis asserted by Hippias (since he simply speaks with the voice
of common sense) but on the outrageous paradox defended by
Socrates. So the argumentation here, as in the *Ion*, is not a typical
example of the formal elenchus.

The paradoxes of sections I and III are each established by a
long *epagōgē* from the arts and crafts, as in the corresponding sections of the *Ion*. Unlike their parallels in the *Ion*, however, both of

22. Contrast Friedländer (1964) 140, citing the *Meno* and the *Gorgias* for the doctrine that a true act of will always aims at the good: "All this is implicit here
in the *Hippias*, as in a puzzle." Szlezák (1985: 89) rightly points out that no
one could infer such doctrine from the *Hippias* alone.

the *Hippias* arguments involve a fallacious move from a plausibly established generalization to a blatantly false conclusion. In the preceding section we have analyzed the two false moves: from an identity between the capacity to lie and the capacity to tell the truth to an identity between the liar and the truthful person; and from recognizing voluntary error as a mark of technical competence to claiming that voluntary wrongdoing is a mark of moral excellence. These fallacies are obviously designed as a challenge to the readers. We are meant to ask ourselves: what has gone wrong, and why? An analytically inclined professor of philosophy might require his students to analyze these texts in order to diagnose the logical errors. But Plato is presumably more interested in matters of substance, in this case matters of moral psychology: what is it that makes the slide from intellectual capacity to moral character both so attractive and so treacherous? This is how Aristotle understood the challenge, and here he seems to have been a perceptive reader of his master's work.[23]

Fallacies aside, the analogical arguments of the *Hippias* are not more complex than those of the *Ion*. Where this dialogue does show signs of more logical sophistication is in Plato's reflection on the process of philosophical argumentation. Arguing with a professional intellectual like Hippias is after all a more serious business than arguing with a rhapsode. As the third speaker Eudikos points out, here the interlocutors "may make a special claim to share in the practice of philosophy" (363A). So it is quite appropriate that we find here more traces of an incipient logical terminology: (1) "what has been agreed upon" (*ta hōmologēmena*) at 368E 3 for what we call the premises; (2) "what follows from the *logos*" at 369A 5 for what we call the conclusion; (3) the claim that the enumeration of parallel cases in an *epagōgē* is complete, or could easily be made so, at 368E–69A 1; (4) the practice of comparing statements to see if they are consistent (*sumbibazein ta legomena*) at 369D 5; and the standard phrase for contradicting oneself (*heautōi enantia legein*) at 371A 6. Most significant of all, perhaps, is that we find here the first deliberate contrast between the Socratic technique of short questions and answers and the sophistic prefer-

---

23. See the passages cited above in n.18. As Sprague (1962: 79, n.37) points out, Aristotle treats the dialogue as consisting of a single argument combining parts I and III.

ence for long speeches (373A). As we shall see in Chapter 10, the systematic development of this contrast in the *Gorgias* and *Protagoras* will form the basis for Plato's own articulation of the concept of dialectic.

7. ANTISTHENES AND THE *HIPPIAS MINOR*

Why did Plato write this strange little dialogue? That is not a question to which there could be a single answer. We have already outlined two answers, from the perspective of Plato's work as a whole. In the first place the confrontation between Socrates and a sophist shows how the Socratic testing of claims to wisdom, reported in the *Apology*, can be developed by Plato in dialogues such as the *Protagoras* in order to define and defend philosophy in the Socratic-Platonic sense against claims made by poets and sophists, who might describe their own activity by this very term of *philosophia*. The two little dialogues considered here represent a modest beginning for Plato's grand project, the definition of philosophy as we understand the term. And in the second place the paradoxes and fallacies propounded in the *Hippias* do point the way to deeper discussions of the nature of virtue and its relationship to knowledge. But neither of these answers accounts satisfactorily for the important place that the discussion of Homer occupies in both dialogues. A striking point of contact with a contemporary quotation from Antisthenes will provide a third perspective within which the significance of the *Hippias* can be appreciated.

The discussion began with Socrates' attempt to find out what Hippias means by calling Odysseus *polutropōtatos*, "most wily" or "turned in many ways." In response, Hippias introduced a contrast with the frank character of Achilles, which he illustrated by a quotation from *Iliad* IX, where Achilles says to Odysseus that "hateful to me as the gates of Hades is he who hides one thing in his breast and speaks a different thing" (365A = *Iliad* IX.312f.). Now precisely the same verse is cited to illustrate the same contrast in character between the two heroes in a lost work of Antisthenes, substantial excerpts from which are preserved in Porphyry's commentary on the *Odyssey*.[24] The convergence is too precise to be accidental, and it is only a question of who used the

24. *SSR* V A 187.

quotation first in such a context. Scholars have argued for both possibilities, but it seems to me most probable that Plato is here responding to Antisthenes.[25]

As we have noted (above, p. 5), Antisthenes was a voluminous author, apparently as prolific as Plato. About one-fifth of his total output seems to have been devoted to Homeric themes.[26] In most cases we have only the titles ("On Homer," "On Calchas," "On the *Odyssey*," "On Helen and Penelope," "On Proteus," etc.), but in two cases we have speeches supposedly delivered by Ajax and Odysseus in the competition over Achilles' armor. The genre of these two speeches is the display piece with a fictitious epic setting, the genre defined by the *Helen* and *Palamedes* of Gorgias. The style shows the influence of Gorgias, but the content of these speeches reflects a number of distinctively Socratic ideas: the notion that ignorance is involuntary, because it is the greatest of evils;[27] and the comparison between an expert judge of virtue and a doctor diagnosing illnesses.[28]

These two extant speeches show how Antisthenes could use a rhetorical literary device with a pseudo-Homeric setting to articulate his own ideas. (Precisely the same seems to have been true of the sophist Hippias.)[29] Furthermore, Antisthenes apparently conceived Odysseus as a kind of Socratic sage. This is even more conspicuous in the specimen of Homeric exegesis preserved by Porphyry. The passage is worth quoting in full.

First speaker (*aporia* or statement of the problem): Homer is not so much praising Odysseus as blaming him when he calls him *polutropos*. He does

25. So A. Patzer (1970) 176. Antisthenes is much the older man and the more established writer in the 390s. If we assume that Antisthenes is one of Plato's targets here, we can make much better sense both of Socrates' hermeneutical mischief in the *Hippias* and the attack on Homeric exegesis in the *Ion*. In either case we have here, as Patzer says, the earliest known example of a literary exchange (*Auseinandersetzung*) between two Socratics.

26. Approximately two tomes out of ten in the catalogue preserved in D.L. VI.15–18 (*SSR* V A 41). Note also the title "On Theognis" in Tome II, περὶ ἐξηγητῶν in Tome VIII.

27. *SSR* V A 54, lines 22f. and 78.

28. *SSR* V A 53, line 20.

29. In the *Hippias Major* he claims to have composed a speech in which Nestor, after the sack of Troy, gives advice to Neoptolemos about how a young man should prepare himself in order to achieve fame (286A–B). Compare *Protagoras* 347A 7, where Hippias offers to deliver a speech he has prepared on Simonides' poem.

not describe Achilles and Ajax this way but as simple and generous. Nor does he present the wise Nestor as shifty and cunning in character but as speaking openly to Agamemnon and the others and to the army; if he has good advice to give, he does not hold it back. Achilles is so far from approving this character (*tropos*) that he says as hateful to him as death is one "who hides one thing in his breast and speaks a different thing" (*Iliad* ix.313).

Second speaker (solution): In answer to this problem Antisthenes says: Was Odysseus called *polutropos* because he was a villain (*ponēros*) and not because he was wise (*sophos*)? After all *tropos* signifies not only character but also the use of discourse (*logos*). So we call a man *eutropos* if his character has a good turn, but we call "turns of discourse" (*tropoi logōn*) figures of different sorts ...

Now if the wise are clever in conversation (*dialegesthai*) they know how to express the same thought in many ways (*tropoi*). But since they know many tropes of discourse concerning the same thing, they will be many-troped (*polutropoi*). It is because the wise are good at dealing with men that Homer calls Odysseus *polutropos*: being wise, he knows how to associate with men in many ways.[30]

The first speaker takes *polutropos* to mean deceptive and cites *Iliad* ix.313 to that effect; his position is essentially the same as that of Hippias in our dialogue. The second speaker (perhaps Socrates, perhaps Antisthenes himself)[31] denies that Homer presents an unfavorable view of Odysseus. His interpretation takes *polutropos* to mean (a) flexible in discourse (*logoi*), skillful in conversation (*dialegesthai*), and hence (b) wise in dealing with different men in different ways, fitting one's discourse to the character of one's interlocutor. In interpreting Homer, Antisthenes seems to be giving his own version of Socrates' dialectical abilities.

We can see now how *one* motive for the Homeric material in *Ion* and *Hippias Minor* may well be a polemical response to Antisthenes, Plato's most prominent and ultimately most hostile competitor as heir to the Socratic tradition. Plato's response will have been particularly apt if, as seems quite possible, Antisthenes represented Socrates himself as engaging in this quasi-philosophical form of Homeric exegesis. Whatever Socrates' own practice may have

30. *SSR* v A 187. In dividing the text between two speakers I follow the suggestion of A. Patzer (1970) 168–90.
31. Patzer suggests Socrates as second speaker. As indicated above (p. 33), there is some evidence that Antisthenes (like Xenophon, but unlike Aeschines and Plato) may have been a speaker in his own dialogues.

been – and that we do not know[32] – Plato is adamantly opposed to
the use of poetic interpretation as a mode of doing philosophy.
That opposition is most fully expressed in the *Protagoras* passage
quoted above (347B–348A), but it is clearly implied not only in the
Ion but also in the *Hippias Minor* by (a) giving a deliberately misleading account of Achilles' character, supported by a deep knowledge of the Homeric text, and (b) using this distorted picture of
Achilles as a model for the outrageous paradox that the best man
is the one who does wrong on purpose. This might well be regarded as a kind of *reductio* of the moralizing or "allegorical" interpretation of Homer. If this is possible in Homeric exegesis, anything is possible. Philosophers concerned with moral truth should
busy themselves with something else.

32. Xenophon reports that Socrates studied texts together with his friends: "I
    peruse with my friends the treasures of wise men of old which they have
    written and left behind in books" (*Mem.* 1.6.14).

CHAPTER 5

Gorgias: *Plato's manifesto for philosophy*

I. THE PLACE OF THE *GORGIAS*

With the *Gorgias* we encounter one of Plato's greatest works, as it is also one of his longest. (Of all the dialogues, only the *Republic* and the *Laws* are longer.) Nowhere are the philosophic and dramatic components in Plato's art more powerfully blended than in the confrontation here between Socrates and his three successive interlocutors. Plato has taken up the old Greek moral theme of the choice between two lives and transformed it into a philosophical debate on the principles of morality and the nature of the good life. And by bringing both Socrates and his adversaries so vividly to life, Plato has represented these issues with unforgettable intensity.

The *Gorgias* is also a foundational text for two areas of philosophy; it is the first major work both in ethics and in political theory. Some of the same issues are discussed in the *Crito*, where Socrates gives his reasons for not escaping from prison. So Plato may be said to have founded moral philosophy twice: once in the *Crito* and a second time in the *Gorgias*. Plato was of course anticipated here by Socrates, to an extent that we cannot determine. And the power of the *Gorgias* largely derives from the fact that Socrates in this dialogue represents both the historical individual and also Plato's philosophical reflection upon the meaning of Socrates' life and death.

The *Crito* exemplifies moral philosophy by demonstrating how one can bring reason to bear on an important practical decision. Socrates is depicted as someone who is always ready "to obey the argument (*logos*) which, upon reflection, seems to me the best" (46B). The Socrates of the *Crito* is quite clear about the fact that such moral reasoning must start from somewhere, from some basic principle or *archē*. He also knows that his own principle – namely, never act unjustly, never do wrong to others, not even in return for wrong done to you – is not a principle that most people will accept. In applying this principle he formulates a systematic argument to show that to escape from prison, as Crito urges him to do, would be an act of injustice. So Socrates prefers to accept his death. "It is not living that is most important but living well, and that is living nobly and justly" (48B). Injustice is a disease of the soul, and life with a sick and corrupted soul is not a life worth living (47D–E). If Socrates is rightly regarded as the patron saint of moral philosophy,[1] this is not only because he insists upon the need for critical reflection concerning the right thing to do and develops such reflection in careful argument. In the *Crito* he also demonstrates an unconditional commitment to the guidance of reason by calmly facing a death that is in harmony with the principles by which he has lived.

In the conversation with Crito these principles can be taken for granted, since they are agreed upon by both parties. Their plausibility for the reader is reinforced by the dramatic portrayal of Socrates, by the way in which he seems to draw his extraordinary strength of character from the rational acceptance of these principles. Thus in the *Crito* we see Plato's literary talent employed in the service of one of his central philosophical projects: to justify the Socratic commitment to a life of moral integrity. In the *Gorgias* Plato pursues the same project on a larger scale and at a deeper philosophical level. For here Socrates is confronted with interlocutors who are ready to challenge his most basic convictions.

The first interlocutor, Gorgias, is the famous writer, orator, and teacher, who boasts of the power that oratory can achieve but would prefer to decline moral responsibility for any use that is made of it. His pupil, Polus, is an outspoken admirer of those who gain political power by immoral or even by criminal means. Callicles, finally, is a product of the new Enlightenment, an ambitious young politician willing to attack the very notion of justice and morality as Socrates understands it. In Callicles' mouth Plato has put "the most eloquent statement of the immoralist's case in European literature."[2] Faced with such opponents, Socrates must defend not only his moral principles but his whole way of life.

1. The phrase is William Frankena's. See Frankena (1973) 2.
2. Shorey (1933) 154. Compare Williams (1985) 22: "Once at least in the history of philosophy the amoralist has been concretely represented as an alarming figure, in the character of Callicles."

Now in the *Crito* Socrates expresses serious doubts about the possibility of rational debate with interlocutors who do not share his conviction that one should never act unjustly. "For I know that this is not and will not be the view of most people. And between those who think this way and those who do not there is no *koinē boulē*, no common basis for discussion, but each side will necessarily despise the others when they see their plans and decisions (*bouleumata*)" (49D). In the *Gorgias*, on the other hand, Plato has accepted the challenge of defending the basic principles of Socratic morality against attack from spokesmen for its most drastic alternative, the uninhibited pursuit of power and success. The mutual contempt which the *Crito* predicts is abundantly confirmed in the uncharacteristic rudeness with which Socrates responds to Polus' boorishness (461E, 463E, 466A, B 1, C 3–5), and the open hostility that occasionally peeps through the veil of benevolence covering the exchanges between Socrates and Callicles. If the passions are so intense it is because the stakes are so high. It is a question here not of who wins the argument, but how one must live one's life and, if necessary, die.

The *Gorgias* thus lies on a direct line of moral concern that leads from the *Apology* and *Crito* to the *Republic*, a concern with the defense of Socratic morality in the face of a radical challenge from the spokesmen for moral cynicism and *Realpolitik*. The explosive issues confronted in these works are largely avoided in what I am calling the threshold dialogues. These latter are concerned instead with more theoretical questions concerning the nature and teachability of virtue, the unity of virtue, and the nature of friendship. As we shall see (in Chapter 8 §8), the *Protagoras* and the *Meno* defend the Socratic paradox in its morally neutral or prudential form. Only the *Gorgias* and the *Republic* expound the paradox in its explicitly moral version: that one never voluntarily acts unjustly.

This division of labor between the *Gorgias* and the threshold dialogues must be deliberate on Plato's part. It is my conjecture that the threshold dialogues (from the *Laches* and *Charmides* to the *Meno* and *Euthydemus*) were composed later, after Plato's return from Sicily when he was busy with the new project of teaching and research in the Academy. The *Gorgias*, on the other hand, seems to reflect the earlier period of Plato's dramatic break with Athenian politics marked by his departure for Sicily at "about the age of forty" (*Ep.* VII, 324A).

Such biographical speculation is not essential to the interpretation, and readers may prefer to think of all these dialogues as composed concurrently. Nevertheless, there are a number of discrepancies that are easier to explain if one assumes that the *Gorgias* was written first. For example, the *Meno* is much more categorical in asserting the transcendental destiny of the soul (81A–E) than the rather guarded allusions to the same doctrine in the *Gorgias* (492E–493D), where the judgment myth contains no explicit reference to transmigration. The aporetic form is, I suggest, an innovation in the *Laches* and *Charmides*. Neither the *Gorgias* nor any of the very short and presumably early dialogues (*Crito, Ion, Hippias Minor*) is aporetic in form. In Chapter 6 I shall argue that the dialogues of definition in general and the *Meno* in particular are designed to prepare the way for the doctrine of Forms, of which there is no trace in the *Gorgias*. And in Chapter 7 we shall see that there are methodological innovations in the *Charmides* that seem to place it later than the *Gorgias*. So the order of exposition chosen here reflects my belief that the *Gorgias* was composed before the seven threshold dialogues.

The essential point, however, is not chronological but thematic. In contrast to the threshold dialogues, the *Symposium*, and the *Phaedo*, the philosophical motivation of the *Gorgias* is fundamentally the same as that of the *Republic*: to respond to the immoralist challenge formulated here by Callicles and Polus, and there by Thrasymachus. For all its brilliance, the defense of morality in the *Gorgias* is not philosophically adequate, as Plato himself must have felt. That is why he had later to pursue the same project again, in the *Republic*.

The argument of the *Gorgias* is too lengthy for a full analysis here. My discussion will focus on themes that bear essentially on the relation between the *Gorgias* and the rest of Plato's work.

2. TECHNĒ IN THE GORGIAS

The *Hippias Minor* leaves us with an unresolved dilemma. Either no one does wrong voluntarily, or if anyone does so, that person is better than someone who does wrong involuntarily. Since the second alternative is morally false, the first alternative should be true. But how can it be true that, despite appearances to the contrary, no one does wrong voluntarily (*hekōn*)? I assume that Socrates left

Plato with this paradox, and that the dialogues represent Plato's response to it.

One line of reflection provoked by the Socratic paradox is Plato's development of the notion of a distinctively moral *technē*, an art or science that knows what is good and bad, right and wrong. What the *Hippias Minor* shows is that such a conception of moral excellence, by analogy with the arts and sciences, can lead to falsehood as well as to truth. If there is anything that deserves to be called expert knowledge or *technē* in the domain of justice and morality, it must be fundamentally different from the other arts. This is a problem that Plato will pursue elsewhere, and notably in the *Protagoras*, where he emphasizes the contrast between moral wisdom and technical expertise. (See Chapter 8 §2.) In the *Gorgias*, on the other hand, Plato is concerned to distinguish Socratic philosophy from Gorgianic rhetoric by the systematic elaboration of the concept of a moral *technē*, on the basis of an analogy with the arts and crafts.

Plato everywhere assumes a principle that we have met in the *Ion*: that an art or science must be defined by reference to its subject matter. For any given subject matter there is one and only one *technē* (*Ion* 537D 5). In the first section of our dialogue, Socrates gets Gorgias to specify the subject of rhetoric as "what is just and unjust" (454B 7); this is later extended to "what is just and unjust, shameful and admirable, good and bad,"[3] in short to the whole moral domain. Furthermore, Gorgias agrees that the orator does not convey *knowledge* of this subject matter, but only persuasion (455A 2). He later hesitates on the question whether or not the orator must possess that knowledge himself. It is Gorgias' willingness to claim such knowledge for the orator that finally gets him into trouble (460Aff.). And when Polus enters the conversation in defense of Gorgias, he begins by renouncing this claim (461B–C). So Socrates can base his own account of rhetoric on the assumption that rhetoric is not really a *technē* at all, since it neither possesses nor conveys knowledge of the relevant subject matter.

Corresponding, however, to the subject matter in question,

3. 459D 1. So Aristotle in the *Rhetoric* will distinguish three kinds of rhetoric, each of which has its own *telos*: the deliberative considers whether something is good (advantageous) or bad (harmful); the forensic whether it is just or unjust; the epideictic, concerned with praise and blame, considers whether it is noble (*kalon*) or shameful (*aischron*) (1.3, 1058b 20ff.).

namely, to the domain of morality, there should be a genuine
technē with precisely this competence. (The possibility of such a
technē follows directly from the one-to-one mapping principle.)
This is what Socrates calls *politikē*, the true art of politics, of which
justice (*dikaiosunē*) will constitute a principal part. According to
Socrates, the ordinary rhetoric of Gorgias is simply the image
(*eidōlon*) and imitation of this sub-art of justice (463D–E).

This new notion of politics as a moral *technē* continues the suggestion in the *Crito* of an ideal moral judge, "the one who knows
about right and wrong" (as we saw in Chapter 4 §2). But whereas
in the *Crito* the existence of such knowledge is problematic, given
Socrates' own avowal of ignorance, here the concept is firmly articulated as a moral ideal, the philosophical alternative to politics
as ordinarily understood. Hence it is that Socrates, at the end of
the dialogue, can claim that "I am one of the few Athenians, not
to say the only one, to undertake the true political art" (521D).
Needless to say, the Socrates who aspires to such a *technē* is no
longer the ignorant Socrates of the *Apology*.

What is involved in such a conception is more fully spelled out
in the preceding discussion. The projected art will do for the soul
what gymnastics and medicine do for the body. Such an art will
have investigated the nature (*phusis*) that it cares for and the
causal explanation (*aitia*) of its procedures, so as to be able to give
a rational account (*logos*) of both, just like the doctor who has
studied the nature of the body and the causes of disease, and so
can give an explanation of his treatment.[4] And just as the doctor's
procedures are teleologically subordinated to the goal of bodily
health, so the theory and practice of the political art are rationally
structured by their relation to the *telos*, the moral welfare of the
citizens, "putting justice and temperance in their souls," making
their mind (*dianoia*) as noble as it can be.[5] In thus aiming at what is
good for the psyche, or for the person as a whole, the moral art
must choose what pleasures are good and beneficial and avoid

4. 465A and 501A. The textual ambiguities of the first passage are eliminated by
   the comparison with the second. See Dodds (1959) 229f.
5. 504E 1–2; 514A 1. As Dodds (1959) observes on 499E 8, this context probably
   represents "the earliest clear instance of *telos* in the sense 'purpose,' 'end of
   action,' so common in later Greek from Aristotle onwards." For a development of the same notion without the noun, but with the verb *teleutan*, see
   Lysis 219Dff., 220B 3, D 8.

those that are bad and harmful (500A). This means that it must satisfy the desires that make a person better, but not those that make one worse (503C 7, 505B 3). It must accordingly change people's desires, not yield to them, using persuasion and even force where necessary in order to improve the citizens (517B 5; cf. 521A 3), that is, to put justice and temperance in their souls and to remove injustice and debauchery (504E 1). Such is the art of the true statesman or, as Plato will sometimes say, the good and scientific orator (*ho rhētōr ekeinos, ho technikos te kai agathos,* 504D 5; cf. 503B 1). But in order to make the selection between good and bad pleasures, the expert in question must of course know *what is good and what is bad* (500B 3).

This conception of the political art in the *Gorgias* presents many of the features that characterize Plato's moral and political thought throughout his work.

1. The parallel between the statesman and the doctor.

2. The conception of moral virtue as a healthy condition of the soul.

3. The notion that a *techné* aims at the good of the subject and recipient, not at the advantage of those who exercise the art.

4. That the goal of government is the virtue of the governed: to make the citizens as good as possible.

5. This means controlling the desires of the subject, satisfying some and restraining others, making the soul temperate.

6. The political artist is able to pursue this goal because of his knowledge of what is good and what is bad.

In all these respects the political artist of the *Gorgias* prefigures the philosopher-king of the *Republic*. The *technikos* of the *Gorgias* is of course also a philosopher, since Socrates is the only one to practice this art.[6]

We can now return to the paradox of the *Hippias Minor*. If justice is an art, why will its possessor never abuse it, never voluntarily do wrong? The *Gorgias* contains a double answer. In the first place, a genuine *techné* is defined not only by its subject matter but also by its goal: whatever it does, it does for the sake of something

---

6. Because of this continuity between the *Gorgias* and the *Republic*, Plato some thirty-five years later can cite the doctrines of the *Republic* as if he had formulated them at the time of the *Gorgias*: "I was obliged to say ... that the races of mankind would not cease from evils until the class of true philosophers comes to political power" (*Ep.* VII, 326A–B).

good, in this case the moral welfare of its recipients. In the second place, since the artist in question possesses (by definition) the relevant knowledge, he or she cannot make a mistake. As Thrasymachus puts it in Book I of the *Republic*, the artist *qua* artist is infallible (*Rep.* I, 340D–E). Now in order to avoid doing wrong, two things are needed: first the desire, and second the skill or ability, not to do wrong. By hypothesis, anyone who possesses the art in question will have the necessary skill. The desire, on the other hand, can be taken for granted: "no one wants to do wrong (*mēdena boulomenon adikein*), but everyone who does wrong does so involuntarily" (509E 6). No one lacks the relevant desire.[7] Hence every act of wrongdoing must reflect a failure of knowledge, a lack of the relevant art.

The Socratic paradox is thus derived from two theses argued here against Polus: all actions are done for the sake of the good, which is what we really want (467C–468B); and since doing wrong (*adikein*, acting unjustly) is the greatest of evils (469B), it is not something we really want. Therefore all wrongs must be involuntary, done only out of ignorance. No one who has the art of justice, and consequently knows what is just, will ever act unjustly: no one knowingly and willingly (*hekōn*) does wrong. In the conditional "If anyone does wrong voluntarily, then . . . ", the antecedent is never fulfilled. Thus we successfully avoid the unacceptable conclusion of the *Hippias Minor*.

We can also see how, from the paradox as formulated here, the identification of virtue with knowledge is an easy further step. What is the state of mind or character that distinguishes a virtuous person from a vicious one? It cannot lie in the nature of their deepest desire, if it is true that everyone desires the same thing, namely, what is good. People desire to perform neutral or instrumental actions *only* to the extent that these actions contribute (or are believed to contribute) to the achievement of good ends (468A–C). Hence those who commit vicious or criminal acts do so only in the mistaken belief that these acts are, or will lead to, something good. If they had the requisite knowledge of what is good and what is bad, they would avoid such actions and act virtuously instead. Hence the possession of such knowledge is a sufficient condition for being virtuous and acting virtuously.

The identification of virtue as a form of knowledge is not an

7. Compare *Meno* 77B–78A and the discussion below, Chapter 8 §7.

explicit thesis of the *Gorgias*, as it is of the *Meno* and the *Protagoras*. Something very close to it is implied in the inference from knowing justice to being just that goes unchallenged at *Gorgias* 460A–B; but in the *Gorgias* Plato stops short of asserting either an identity or a definition of virtue in terms of knowledge. When the unity of the virtues is derived from temperance (*sōphrosunē*) at 507A–C, wisdom is conspicuously absent from the list of virtues. The characterization of *aretē* in terms of knowledge, which we know from the *Protagoras*, the *Meno*, and other threshold dialogues, appears perhaps for the first time in the *Laches*, in the "Socratic" definition of courage proposed by Nicias and rejected by Socrates – rejected precisely because, by being too general, it applies not to courage as such but to virtue as a whole! (See Chapter 6 §5.)

Why does the *Gorgias* not characterize virtue as knowledge? It may be that, if the *Gorgias* is earlier, Plato had not yet decided to develop the Socratic link between virtue and wisdom (*phronēsis*) into an explicit definition or identity. But there is also an explanation internal to the argument of the *Gorgias*. In the conception of the moral-political *technē* that is articulated here, virtue figures as the *telos*, the good condition of the souls of those on whom the art is practiced. Moral knowledge or *technē* is defined in part by reference to its product, the psychic excellence of those who are governed and/or educated. It would obscure the teleological structure of this art if virtue, its product, was identified with knowledge or *technē*, the art itself. For of course in Plato's vocabulary the words for art, knowledge, and wisdom (*technē, epistēmē, sophia*) are used interchangeably. These terms are applied here to the skill of the political artist, not to the virtue that he must generate in the souls of his subjects. Hence virtue is not identified with knowledge in the *Gorgias*, although all or most of the assumptions required for this identification are present here.

3. ELENCHUS IN THE *GORGIAS*

As we have seen, the Socratic elenchus was originally more a testing of persons than of propositions: Socrates examines his interlocutors to see whether their life is in agreement with their avowed principles.[8] The three successive refutations of Gorgias, Polus, and Callicles represent Plato's most brilliant literary portrayal of the

8. See *Apology* 29E and above, p. 97.

elenchus in action, where the character of the interlocutor plays an essential part in his dialectical defeat.[9]

All three elenchi are primarily concerned with issues of normative ethics: what constitutes a good life, and whether it is ever in our interest to act unjustly. The first exchange with Gorgias attacks these themes obliquely, by considering whether the pursuit of political power by the techniques of mass persuasion can be divorced from questions of justice and moral responsibility. With Polus the issue is squarely faced: is it better to do or to suffer injustice? Can the successful criminal lead a good life? But it is with Callicles that the challenge to morality finds its most radical expression. For Callicles, moral restraints on the pursuit of power and pleasure are mere conventions that the weak impose upon those who are their natural superiors. Callicles and Socrates thus present two diametrically opposed views of what constitutes a good life.

Against Gorgias Socrates shows that someone who is training young men for leadership and political power cannot publicly disclaim moral responsibility for the use that is made of his training. By cunningly tempting Gorgias to proclaim the omnipotence of his skill in persuasion, after he has admitted that rhetoric can produce only conviction without knowledge, Socrates makes it impossible for Gorgias to deny moral responsibility. "Is the orator himself in a state of ignorance concerning what is good and bad, right and wrong, but equipped with persuasion on these matters, so as to seem to an ignorant audience to have knowledge [concerning right and wrong] when he does not ... and to be a good man when he is not?" (*Gorgias* 459D 2–E 6). To which Gorgias is obliged to reply: "But I think, Socrates, that if the student does not know these things, he will learn them from me."

Gorgias' reply is apparently insincere. Meno tells us that Gorgias never claimed to teach virtue, and laughed at those who made such a claim (*Meno* 95C). He is forced to make this reply, however, because (as Polus points out) Gorgias is ashamed to admit that a rhetorician need not know "what is just and noble and good" and would not teach these things to a student who is ignorant in these matters (461B). His shame in this regard reflects his concern for public opinion and his exposed position as a foreigner who is edu-

---

9. For a fuller discussion of the three refutations, see Kahn (1983) 75–121.

cating the future leaders of Athens.[10] There is no conceptual contradiction in Gorgias' view of rhetoric as a value-free instrument
of political power. But there is a personal and social incompatibility between the public expression of this view and Gorgias'
position as an elite educator.

Socrates' refutation of Polus is more complex. Polus claims that
doing injustice is better than suffering injustice, although doing
injustice is more shameful. Socrates defends the opposite thesis in
deliberately paradoxical form: "I think that you and I and other
people believe doing injustice is worse than suffering injustice, and
not being punished [for injustice] is worse than being punished"
(474B). Socrates' argument depends upon showing that if doing
injustice is more shameful, it must also be worse. The validity of
Socrates' argument has been much debated.[11] What concerns us
here is not the validity of the argument but the emphasis placed
on the role of shame. Just as Polus told us that Gorgias' mistake
was due to shame on his part, so Plato makes use of the same device again when he has Callicles comment on Polus' defeat. Polus'
mistake, according to Callicles, was his admission that doing injustice was more shameful (*aischion*); he was refuted because "he
was ashamed (*aischuntheis*) to say what he thinks," namely that injustice is really admirable (482E 2).

Polus is refuted because he cannot reconcile his admiration for
power and wealth, no matter how obtained, with his recognition
that unjust or criminal acts are generally regarded as dishonorable
and "shameful." He can give no account of this moral blame in
terms of pleasure and utility, because he has no notion of the social function of morality. Callicles, on the other hand, will employ
the theoretical resources of the familiar contrast between nature
(*phusis*) and convention (*nomos*) to show that the dishonor attached
to unjust acts is based only on *nomos*, the moral conventions established by the weak in their own interest. For the strong, on the
other hand, the standard of honor and dishonor is set not by con-

---

10. See Kahn (1983) 79–84 for the pressure on Gorgias to answer as he does; I
    argue that the distinction between *knowing justice* and *being just*, important in
    other contexts, is irrelevant here.
11. See the discussion in Vlastos (1967) 454–60, and again in Vlastos (1991) 140–
    8. In Kahn (1983) 90–2, I maintain that the argument is strong enough to
    defeat Polus but not strong enough to establish Socrates' positive thesis that
    doing injustice is worse for the doer.

vention but by nature, which justifies the domination of the weak by the strong.

Socrates agrees that his two first interlocutors have come to grief because of their excess of shame: it is shame (*aischunesthai*) that has caused Gorgias and Polus "to contradict themselves before many people, on matters of the greatest import" (487B). Callicles counts as the ideal interlocutor, in part because he is not ashamed to speak his mind (487D 5): he will say openly "what others think, but are not willing to say" (492D 2).

Callicles' defeat will nevertheless also be precipitated by his sense of shame. The refutation turns on Callicles' claim that a happy life, the life of those who are strong and free from conventional inhibitions, will consist in maximizing pleasure and in gratifying any and all desires. Socrates begins by asking him whether scratching when you itch is a satisfaction of desire, like drinking when you are thirsty; and whether a life spent scratching is a happy life (494C). When Callicles protests the vulgarity of the question, Socrates warns him to be on his guard against shame, which was the undoing of Polus and Gorgias. So Callicles answers shamelessly that a life spent scratching oneself is pleasant and happy – regardless of the part of the body one chooses to scratch (494D–E). Socrates' next move is more decisive: he asks Callicles what he thinks of the pleasures of the *kinaidos*: roughly speaking, one who enjoys being the passive partner in anal intercourse. Attic law apparently treats this as equivalent to male prostitution, and sufficient to deprive the guilty party of his citizenship rights. The politically ambitious Callicles, who admires the manly virtues, cannot seriously describe the life of the *kinaidos* as fortunate or happy (*eudaimōn*), as Socrates challenges him to do; he can only call shame on Socrates (*ouk aischunēi?*) for bringing the argument to this point!

In the face of this challenge, Callicles for the sake of consistency maintains the identity of pleasure and the good (495A 5). He is in fact defeated by this first argument against hedonism, and defeated because of the shameful consequences of his thesis (*polla kai aischra sumbainonta*, 495B 5).[12] However, since Callicles will not admit defeat, Socrates provides two formal arguments against the

12. For the decisive character of the *kinaidos* objection, see Kahn (1983) 105–7. For the status of *kinaidoi* see Dover (1978) 19ff. and *passim*; Winkler (1990) 176–97. If we substitute "male prostitute" for "coward" in the third argument (498A–499A), we see that it is a more fully stated version of this first objection.

equivalence of the good and the pleasant. The second of these arguments, the one which finally leads Callicles to abandon his thesis, shows that, if pleasure and the good are not distinct, there will be no basis for the moral superiority of brave men over cowards to which Callicles is committed. Here, as in the first argument from shameful pleasures, it is certainly not hedonism as an abstract thesis that is refuted, but hedonism as a thesis defended by Callicles. It is because Callicles is a proud aristocrat and an ambitious politician that he cannot be a consistent hedonist. The thesis as such is not necessarily inconsistent. It is the link between the man and his thesis that is shown to be incoherent. That is why Socrates can claim that Callicles will reject his own thesis "when he has regarded himself correctly" (495E 1). From the beginning Socrates had warned him that his position would lead to disharmony: "Callicles will not agree with you, Callicles, but you will be out of unison in all your life. Yet I think it is better for my lyre to be out of tune ... and for most men to disagree and contradict me rather than for me alone to be out of tune and in contradiction with myself" (482B 5–C 3).

4. THE POSITIVE FUNCTION OF THE ELENCHUS

The results of all three refutations are essentially negative: to reveal the incoherence between the life and the doctrine of the interlocutor, an incoherence reflected in the inconsistency between different views held by the same man. But how can we relate these negative results to the positive moral doctrine propounded in the paradoxes against Polus and developed in the final section of the dialogue after Callicles' defeat? There is no doubt that Socrates presents his moral thesis (that to do injustice and escape punishment is the worst of evils) as established by elenctic arguments of the sort used to refute Polus and Callicles.

These conclusions in our previous discussions were bound and fastened with iron and adamantine arguments, or so it seems; and unless you or someone yet more vigorous unties these bonds, there will be no way to speak otherwise and still speak well ... Of all those I have encountered so far, no one has been able to deny these claims without making himself ridiculous, as in the present case. (508E–509A)

The conclusions established against Polus are presented as likewise binding against Callicles, and indeed against everyone else, so that no one can deny them without falling into contradiction. But how can such highly personalized refutations and, in the central case against Polus, such a complex and dubious argument, justify such strong and universal claims?

I want to suggest that the important role attributed to shame in the three refutations is a clue to their wider validity. Shame reflects a Platonic conception corresponding to our own notion of an innate moral sense, but which Plato describes as a universal desire for what is good. This is the thesis presented in the first paradox argued against Polus: that all human beings desire the good and pursue it in all of their actions (*Gorgias* 468B–C, 499E: cf. *Meno* 77C–78B, *Rep.* VI, 505D 11). Shame operates in this dialogue as an obscure intuition of the good on the part of Socrates' interlocutors. It must be on an intuition of this sort that Socrates is relying in his claim that Polus or Callicles will inevitably agree with him or be in disagreement with themselves. For (as Socrates says) everyone desires the good. And the good is in fact Socratic *aretē*, the moral and intellectual excellence of the soul. That is why no one wants to be unjust or act unjustly.

Now the invulnerability to contradiction that Socrates implies for his basic thesis – that *aretē* is what we really want, our true good and happiness – is reinforced by the dramatic appeal of the portrait of Socrates as the embodiment of this very thesis. The portrayal of Socrates tends to provide a positive complement to the negative results of the elenchus. And here too Plato's artistry lies in combining the personal and doctrinal elements, which fit together perfectly in Socrates' case, as they are hopelessly inconsistent in the case of those who disagree with him. In order to understand the *philosophical* significance, from Plato's point of view, of the enormous power exerted by his literary portrait of Socrates, we must consider some of the implications of his claim that we are all motivated by a rational desire (*boulesthai*) for the good.[13]

The first paradox against Polus (orators and politicians have no real power, because they do not do what they want, but only what they think best) rests upon the claim that *we want only good things* or only *the good*, and hence that whatever we do, we do for the sake of something good (or simply for the good, *heneka tou agathou* at 468B 1,

13. From here to the end of Chapter 5 I am borrowing freely from Kahn (1983) 113–21.

B 7). Now for Socrates what is good is primarily what is good for the psyche: an action is good for me only if it improves my soul, as acting justly does. But this is not a private truth: what is good for me is also good for everyone else. And everyone wants what is good for them. Now in fact, acting justly is good for them. Therefore *everyone wants to act justly*, whether they know it or not. *No one wants to act unjustly*, because (whether they know it or not) that will harm them; and no one wants to be harmed. Anyone who acts unjustly does so *akōn*: unwillingly (because he does not want to be harmed) and unknowingly (because he does not realize that his action is harmful).

Such a reading of the argument seems to be required by Socrates' own résumé of it at 509E: "Polus and I agree that no one wants to do wrong (*boulomenos adikein*), but all those who act unjustly do so involuntarily (*akōn*)." This implies that we all have a deep and fully rational if unconscious desire, a kind of true will, for justice and virtue, since what is good for us (our welfare or happiness) consists in the just and virtuous condition of the soul. But if we lack the knowledge or *technē* of justice and virtue, we do not know our own good: we are unable to identify the object of our own rational desire (*boulesthai*).[14] Such a *technē* is required both to recognize the true object of desire (the intrinsic good) and also to secure the means for achieving it (the instrumental good).

14. In order to avoid the concept of unconscious desire here, some scholars have analyzed Socrates' argument in terms of a distinction between the intended (or *de dictu*) object of desire and the actual (or *de re*) object desired. Thus everyone will want the good *de dictu*, that is, they will want whatever they take to be good. But they will differ in what they actually desire (*de re*, or concretely) because of differences in what they regard as good: power, wealth, or whatever. If the good is virtue, but Polus mistakenly believes it to be power, then he does not actually desire virtue. For an analysis along these lines, see Santas (1979) 186ff., followed by Vlastos (1991) 150–4.

This analysis may show why the argument is formally invalid. But it renders the paradox tame and sterile. The logical distinction between two conceptions of the object of desire cannot account for Socrates' statement that Polus and everyone else believes that doing injustice is worse than suffering injustice (474B), nor for the claim that, if he does not admit this, Callicles will be out of tune with himself for all his life (482B). These paradoxes are most naturally to be understood as implying that, whether they know it or not, what everyone really wants is the good of their soul, which is incompatible with committing injustice. That is the point of the final myth of the *Gorgias*, which attempts to show in narrative terms why happiness (what everyone desires) is, or inevitably follows from, psychic excellence.

This notion of an unconscious, or only partially conscious, rational desire for the good helps us to see how Plato can rely, both here and elsewhere, upon what we may call in technical jargon the "transparent" reading of desire, which would normally be considered a logical blunder. Contexts governed by verbs like "want" or "desire" are generally regarded as intensional (non-extensional) and hence as not admitting the substitution of different phrases referring to the same object. Although Oedipus wants to punish the murderer of Laius, and the murderer of Laius is himself, it does not follow logically that Oedipus wants to punish himself. Or if Rigoletto wants the person in the sack to be dead, but the person in the sack is his daughter, it does not follow that Rigoletto wants his daughter to be dead. Similarly, one would not normally count as valid an argument of the form: Callicles wants the good; the good is in fact virtue; therefore Callicles wants virtue. Perhaps we should construe Plato's use of such an argument as protreptic rather than deductive. If you come to see that virtue is good (and hence good for you), you *will* desire it. The function of the elenchus, reinforced by the presentation of Socrates as the exemplar of virtue, is to bring the interlocutor and the reader to the point where they can see this. And the motive force is not provided by Socrates' dialectical skill alone but by his ability to draw upon that deep desire for the good that motivates every rational agent, even when the agent himself is ignorant of the nature and object of this desire.

If this is Plato's view, we can better understand the role played by shame in the three refutations. In each case the feeling of shame marks the fact that Socrates brings into play moral concerns which the interlocutor must recognize and which, if properly understood, would lead to a correct perception of *aretē* as the good that he truly desires.[15] Such perception does not actually occur on the part of the interlocutor: the dialogue does not depict episodes of conversion to the philosophic life.[16] But it may help – and histor-

---

15. This is, I take it, what underlies Socrates' claims (at 474B and 475A) that everyone believes doing injustice is worse and that no one would prefer to do rather than to suffer it. It is not that these claims follow from premises that are actually believed by his interlocutors (as Vlastos once suggested). It is rather that these claims are protreptic: this is what everyone will believe and prefer *if they understand what is at stake*. So at 495E 1 Callicles will change his mind "when he has come to see himself correctly."

16. For allusions to such a conversion, see Apollodorus' remarks in *Symposium* 173C–E. For a full description of the personal power that makes such a conversion possible, see Alcibiades' speech there, 215B–216C.

ically speaking certainly did help – to trigger such conversions on the part of some readers. A lost dialogue of Aristotle reported the case of a Corinthian farmer who, after encountering the *Gorgias*, "immediately left his farmland and his vineyard to pledge his soul to Plato and to plant and cultivate Platonic fields."[17] This tale may serve as an emblem for one of Plato's principal aims in writing such a dialogue. Plato might say, or we may say for him, that the impact on the reader can rely upon the sense of moral truth in all of us that consists in our love for the good and our capacity to recognize the good in Socrates' life and practice of *aretē*. The fact that this impact is so widely felt by readers of the *Gorgias*, *Apology*, and *Crito*, if not as a conversion to philosophy at least as a sense of awe before Socrates' personality and a deep sympathy with his position against Callicles – this enormous impact of Plato's literary portrait of Socrates down through the centuries might be thought of as a kind of confirmation of Plato's position on the "transparency" of our desire for the good.

The effect on the reader lies outside the dialogue. What we have in the text is the impact on the interlocutors: Socrates' manipulation of their sense of shame to force them to confront the incoherence of their own position, and thus to make a first step toward that recognition of their ignorance which is the beginning of wisdom.

When shame at admitting base, unmanly, or politically disastrous pleasures into his moral scheme leads Callicles to recognize the incoherence of a life devoted both to political power and to indiscriminate gratification, he is obliged, in effect, to abandon the pursuit of *epithumia*, "appetite" or pleasure at any price, for the Socratic principle of *boulesthai*: the evaluation of impulse and gratification according to some standard of what is good. So behind the refutation of Callicles we catch sight of a fundamental distinction between two conceptions of desire, and the inadequacy of one of these conceptions as the basis for a coherent theory of the good life. Once Callicles admits that some pleasures are better, some worse (at 499B), he has in effect accepted *boulesthai* or rational choice as the decisive criterion of virtue and happiness, in place of *epithumia* or sheer desire. We thus return immediately to the notion of the good as the end and goal of action (499E–500A), and eventually to the rational desire (*boulesthai*) for happiness, which

17. Aristotle, *Nerinthos* fr. 1 (Ross [1955: 24] = Rose³ fr. 64).

can be realized only in the practice of the virtues (509C 9ff.). Hence "no one truly wants (*boulomenos*) to do injustice, but all who act unjustly do so involuntarily (*akōn*)" (509E 5–7). As we have seen, this rational desire for the good may be partially unconscious, as it clearly was in Callicles' case. But it is the function of the elenchus to bring this desire to consciousness, as Callicles is reluctantly obliged to do, at least in part. As the dialogue represents him, it is Socrates' confidence in such a desire that underlies his avowed faith in the elenchus, his conviction that, unless the ethical doctrine can be refuted, "Callicles himself will disagree with you, Callicles" (482B–C). The contradictor must end by contradicting himself, and be "out of tune in his whole life," because his conscious pursuits will never be in harmony with his deepest desire.

5. THE LIMITS OF THE *GORGIAS*

The refutation of Callicles extends beyond his admission that some pleasures are better than others at 499E to the conclusion at 505B, which affirms the direct denial of Callicles' moral thesis: that discipline and control of the appetites is better for the soul than unrestrained gratification. This conclusion is reached by an argument that relies essentially on the notion of the virtues as the order and harmony of the soul (*taxis, kosmos*). This conception is introduced here by a systematic induction or *epagōgē* from the arts. As in painting, architecture or shipbuilding, a moral-political artist will "look to his product (*ergon*)," in order to give it a form (*eidos*) and an ordered arrangement (*taxis*). Just as a house and a ship are good when characterized by order (*taxis*) and harmonious structure (*kosmos*), and similarly for our own bodies, so also for the soul: "will not the soul be good when it is characterized by order and structure rather than by disorder?" Callicles gives his assent: "From the previous cases it is necessary (*anankē*) to agree to this also" (504B 6).

The necessity that binds Callicles here is strictly one of analogy. And the same is true for the next step, which identifies psychic order with the quiet virtues, justice and temperance, by analogy with health conceived as the product of harmonious order in the body (504C–D). Thus it is entirely on the basis of this analogy from the arts that Socrates establishes the superiority of moral discipline over unrestrained gratification in the final refutation of Callicles at 505B.

An even wider analogy is introduced at 508A in support of the claim that the good man is happy, the bad man miserable (507C 3–5). The man who wants to be happy will not do as Callicles claims, letting his desires go unrestrained and trying to satisfy them all, "a limitless evil, living the life of a pirate," a friend neither to man nor to god.

For he is unable to share in any community, and where there is no sharing there is no friendship. Callicles, wise men say that heaven and earth and men and gods are bound together by community and friendship, by orderliness and temperance and justice, and for this reason they call the universe *kosmos*, world-order, not disorder nor dissoluteness. (507E–508A)

Callicles has missed this insight, because he has not seen how great is the power of geometric proportion (*isotēs geometrikē*) among gods and among human beings.

This vision of the harmonious, well-ordered soul, as akin on the one hand to the natural order of the cosmos and on the other to the successful products of the arts, is Plato's final attempt, within the limits of the *Gorgias*, to provide a theoretical backing for his conviction that the Socratic life is not only the best but the happiest life for a human being to live. From this conclusion, that it is "by the possession of justice and temperance that happy people are happy, and by wickedness the others are miserable," Socrates can now derive the paradoxes previously argued against Polus and Gorgias: that to do injustice is worse than to suffer it, and that the true orator must be a just person and must know what is just (508B–C 3). These conclusions are then reaffirmed in the strongest terms, as established by "iron and adamantine arguments" in the passage previously quoted from 508E–509B.

What are we to make of the arguments so confidently asserted here? We know that the argument against Polus is not strong enough to establish Socrates' conclusion;[18] and it is hard to believe that Plato was entirely unaware of this fact. The positive arguments against Callicles are all based upon the assumption that what makes something good is its proper *kosmos*; and that the proper order of the soul is temperance and justice. As we have seen, this view is supported by an analogy to the products of

18. See above, n.11.

human art. The further inference from goodness to happiness relies on a meaningful wordplay on "doing well" (*eu prattein*);[19] and
this conclusion is reinforced by another analogy, with the good
ordering of the cosmos. Aside from the wordplay, which expresses
a conviction rather than an argument, all the reasoning in this
section[20] takes the form of analogy or comparison: between virtue
and the products of art on the one hand, between virtue and the
products of nature and the whole order of nature on the other
hand; between politics and the building trade (514Aff.), between
politics and medicine and athletic training (514D, 517Eff., etc.), between the politician and the keeper of animals (516A), between the
politician and the charioteer (516E). When he composed the *Gorgias*, Plato may have believed that these arguments were stronger
than we would be inclined to suppose.[21] But we know that Plato's
friend Eucleides criticized the argument from analogy. And in the
Charmides Plato makes Critias express a similar criticism.[22] Sooner
or later Plato must have realized that the positive arguments of
the *Gorgias* were unsatisfactory. It was in order to do the job better
that he had later to write the *Republic*.[23]

What is lacking here is, first of all, a moral psychology of the
kind to be developed in Books IV and VIII–IX of the *Republic*, a
psychological theory that can give rational support to the intuitive
conviction that justice is the health of the soul, so that someone
with a character like Socrates must be not only virtuous but
happy. What is lacking also is a theory of knowledge that can pro-

19. "The good man will do well and nobly (*eu te kai kalōs*) whatever he does, and
    one who does well (*eu prattonta*) will be blessed and happy" (507C 3–5). The
    first occurrence of *eu prattein* is unequivocally moral; the second occurrence
    plays on the sense of good fortune and success.
20. With one exception: the deductive argument for the unity of the virtues at
    507A–C.
21. Richard Robinson (1953: 209) quotes *Gorgias* 508A on the power of geo-
    metrical equality "among gods and among men" in support of his view that
    "Plato believes that 'analogies' or 'geometrical equalities' are frequent in re-
    ality and basic to its structure." Regardless of the nature of reality, however,
    Plato is more willing to rely on the argument from analogy in the *Gorgias*
    than in the *Charmides*, as we shall see.
22. *Charmides* 165E, 166B 7–C 3. See the discussion below, Chapter 7 §4. For Eu-
    cleides' objection to reasoning by *epagōgē*, see above, p. 14.
23. So also Williams (1985: 22): Socrates' argument against Callicles is "so un-
    convincing, in fact, that Plato later had to write the *Republic* to improve on
    it."

vide more content for the notion of *technē*, more substance to the notion of moral knowledge as a decisive component of the life in philosophy. And for Plato, a theory of knowledge will also require a theory of the *object* of knowledge, in other words a metaphysics. To get from the *technikos* of the *Gorgias* to the philosopher-king we will need the doctrine of Forms. And to explain how the Forms can guide and motivate a life of virtue, we will need the theory of philosophical *erōs*.[24] Finally, in order to expound and defend such theories Plato will need a mode of argument that goes beyond the techniques of elenchus and *epagōgē* employed in the *Gorgias*. More specifically, he will need the more powerful notion of dialectic introduced in the *Meno* with the method of hypothesis.

Still, what the *Gorgias* has to offer is not negligible. Here the most cogent argument for the Socratic moral position is the total collapse of the Calliclean alternative, with a positive counterpart in the portrayal of Socrates himself. The elenchus shows that Socrates' opponents cannot give an account of good and bad, right and wrong, that is consistent with their own life and their own convictions. Socrates' ideal of psychic excellence is established by the only support that elenctic testing can give: in his case alone does his life and his death turn out to be in harmony with his doctrines. Hence the trial and death of Socrates, so often alluded to here, are part of the argument of the *Gorgias* in much the same way as the fall of Troy is part of the plot of the *Iliad*.

The *Gorgias* implies that this harmony between life and belief holds because Socrates' doctrines are, and his adversaries' claims are not, in agreement with their own *boulesthai*, their rational desire for the good. This connection between the personal dimension of the elenchus and Plato's theory of desire is perhaps the most fundamental insight of the dialogue. It explains the philosophical importance of the personal figure of Socrates, the fortunate soul whose inner strength and serene self-assurance rest upon a harmony of desire that both illustrates and confirms the psychological theory that Plato will develop in the *Republic*. It is the extraordinarily seductive power of this portrait of Socrates that helps

---

24. See below, Chapter 9. For the seeds of such a theory in the *Gorgias*, note the contrast between the *erōs* for philosophy and the *erōs* for the Athenian demos at 481Dff. It is the presence of the latter in Callicles' soul that prevents him from being persuaded by Socrates' arguments (513C7).

to make so many of us sympathetic, at least at the instinctive level, to Plato's philosophical claims.

An unfriendly critic might complain that Plato has thrown literary dust in our eyes, dazzling us by his brilliant portrayal so that we are blinded to the gaping holes in his arguments. Taking a more favorable view of the relation between literature and philosophy, I suggest that we see Plato as exploiting his artistic powers to produce in us the readers a simulacrum of the personal impact of Socrates upon the life of his original auditors, and first and foremost upon Plato himself. If I may borrow from the *Ion* the comparison to a magnetic chain, Plato as author is like the rhapsode who transmits to the readers of the dialogue that philosophical *erōs* which he himself received from Socrates, the prior magnet and analogue to the poet in the *Ion*. But as the poet draws his power from the Muses as the original magnet, so Socrates draws the enormous force of his doctrine and his personality from their archetypal source and goal, in the love and pursuit of what is truly *kalon* and good. I think Plato might say that his (and at a great remove, our own) love for Socrates is the love for a soul whose life is made beautiful by its total commitment to certain principles, a love whose power is to be explained (according to the theory of the middle dialogues) by the erotic appeal – for Socrates first of all, then for Plato, and finally for us – of what is fully real and unqualifiedly good.

In the *Gorgias* things are simpler, since our rational desire for the good is directed not towards some transcendent Form but towards the very adornment of the soul by virtue that makes a life admirable and beloved. Here, as in the *Apology* and *Crito*, the life and death of Socrates is presented as a principal support for his moral teaching, just as the personal elenchus of his adversaries undermines whatever claims their own doctrines, abstractly considered, might seem to have. Plato's philosophic justification for this dependence of the argument upon the life and character of the speaker, and also (we may add, from Plato's point of view) the psychological explanation of why this linkage between argument and character achieves such conspicuous success in the dramatic impact of the dialogues – both explanation and justification are to be found in the deep, partially unconscious desire for the good on the part of interlocutor and reader alike. We can say that for Plato the desire for the good plays the role that sympathy or the moral sense plays for a philosopher like Hume. No theory of philosophical argument and proof that ignores the role of this fundamental desire in shaping patterns of agreement and assent can give an adequate account of the practice of philosophy as it is portrayed in the Platonic dialogues.

CHAPTER 6

The priority of definition: from Laches *to* Meno

I. THE THRESHOLD DIALOGUES

On basic issues of moral philosophy Plato remains faithful to the position presented in the *Gorgias*. In particular, it remains his view that the goal of rational politics is the same as the goal of moral education: to produce virtue in human souls. That will require a *technikos*, an expert on *aretē*. But the *technikos* of the *Gorgias* is not yet the philosopher-king. For that we will need the psychology, epistemology, and metaphysics of the *Republic*. So there is room for a large development of Plato's thought between the *Gorgias* and the middle dialogues: *Symposium, Phaedo*, and *Republic*.

It is in this intervening space that I would locate the seven threshold dialogues: *Laches, Charmides, Euthyphro, Protagoras, Meno, Lysis*, and *Euthydemus*. These dialogues present and elaborate themes that come together in the central books of the *Republic*, where *technē* becomes *dialektikē*, the master art of the philosopher-king. Now for Plato a *technē* is defined by reference to its object or subject matter. The object of *dialektikē* will be the forms or essences of things. So the most decisive step in Plato's gradual articulation of the *technē* of the philosopher-king will be his introduction of the notion of essence in the dialogues of definition. I suggest that the search for essence in the *Laches, Euthyphro*, and *Meno* is from the start future-oriented, that is to say, designed to prepare the way for the doctrine of Forms. But Plato's mode of exposition is so subtly ingressive that this design can only be perceived retrospectively, from the vantage point of the middle dialogues.

The seven threshold dialogues form a diverse group. Perhaps the only feature they have in common is their aporetic structure: all of them end with questions rather than with answers. (The *Euthydemus*, which is the maverick of the group, is not directly aporetic; but it too ends without any straightforward conclusion.) The *Laches*, *Charmides*, and *Euthyphro* are all dialogues of definition: they seek to specify what courage is, what temperance (*sōphrosunē*) is, and what piety is – and they all fail. Having pursued in these dialogues the separate parts of virtue, in the *Meno* we seek to determine the unity of virtue as a whole. The question "What is virtue?" is raised here as a prerequisite for answering Meno's question: "Is virtue teachable?" The *Meno* oscillates between these two concerns, the nature and teachability of virtue, without any firm conclusion on either one. The question of teachability and the relation between virtue and its parts are also the two central topics in the *Protagoras*, a dialogue that ends precisely at the point where the *Meno* begins. In thematic content, then, these five works are tightly linked to one another: *Laches*, *Charmides*, *Euthyphro*, *Protagoras*, and *Meno*.

The other two threshold dialogues, the *Lysis* and *Euthydemus*, are more loosely tied to the group. But the *Lysis* and *Euthydemus* share with the *Laches* and *Charmides* the school atmosphere of their opening scene and a common concern with the education of the young. The narrative charm of the *Lysis* and *Charmides* is so similar that the two have been described as twin dialogues.[1] And there are many common points of topic and argument between the *Euthydemus* and *Meno*.[2] So even though there is no single theme or format characterizing every member of the set, by virtue of a series of overlapping family resemblances these seven dialogues may plausibly be seen together as forming a coherent group, the aporetic-proleptic introduction to the middle dialogues.

We begin our discussion of the group with the *Laches*. In this chapter I will present, and as far as possible defend, the following controversial claims:

1. That the three dialogues, *Laches–Euthyphro–Meno* form a unified, continuous exposition on the logic of definition.

2. That the *Laches* is the natural introduction to this series, and to the larger group of threshold dialogues.

3. That the epistemic principle of priority of definition announced in the *Laches*, and developed more fully in the *Meno*,

---

1. So Wilamowitz (1920) I, 187–9.
2. For parallels between *Meno* and *Euthydemus*, see below pp. 207, 225f.

entails Meno's paradox, and thus prepares for the doctrine of recollection.

4. That the doctrine of recollection as introduced in the *Meno* cannot resolve Meno's paradox unless the objects of recollection are radically different from the objects of ordinary experience, and hence that the recollection of transcendent Forms, as expounded in the *Phaedo*, is already implied by the use made of recollection in the *Meno*.

5. Accordingly, that the exposition of the doctrine of essences as definienda, from the *Laches* to the *Phaedo*, is the gradual disclosure of a single philosophical position, and not a movement from "early Plato" (or Socrates) to "middle Plato." The most important movement in these dialogues is from a concept of philosophical *technē* whose content is vaguely specified as the knowledge of good and bad, towards a concept of *technē* as *dialektikē*, whose content will be spelled out by the doctrine of Forms. This movement begins with the search for explanatory essences in the *Laches* and *Euthyphro*.

6. That this continuity between the essences of the *Laches–Euthyphro* and the Forms of the *Phaedo–Republic* is explicitly marked by Plato in his choice of the technical expression for the Forms: *to ho esti (ison)*, "the what-Equal-is."

7. Finally, that we can best understand the aporetic and propaedeutic function of the threshold group in terms of Plato's own reflections in the *Meno* on the function of *aporia* as a prerequisite for knowledge.

We begin, then, with the three dialogues most directly concerned with questions of definition: *Laches, Euthyphro*, and *Meno*. In the next chapter we turn to the *Charmides*, which has the external form of a dialogue of definition but is in reality focused on other issues. In Chapter 8 we deal with the *Protagoras*, and in Chapter 9 with the *Lysis*. My discussion of the *Euthydemus* is postponed to Chapter 10, in the treatment of dialectic. I thus present a partial interpretation of all seven threshold dialogues before taking up, in Chapter 11, the doctrine of Forms as presented in the middle works.

2. THE *LACHES* AS AN INTRODUCTORY DIALOGUE

There are several striking features of the *Laches* that are best explained on the assumption that Plato designed it as an introduction to a new series of dialogues, precisely those dialogues that have been regarded as typically "Socratic" because they end in *aporia*. One indication of the introductory function of the *Laches* is the unparalleled length of the dramatic prologue, which occupies the first half of this short work.[3] This prologue is remarkable both for the exceptional prestige of the interlocutors and for the unusual way in which Socrates is introduced. The *Laches* is unique among Socratic dialogues in that Socrates is not a participant in the opening conversation, and several pages of text must be perused before he intervenes. By selecting an initial speaker, Lysimachus, to whom Socrates needs to be introduced, Plato has created an occasion for the two generals, Laches and Nicias, to sing his praises as an outstanding citizen-soldier with a special interest in the education of the young. The prologue thus carefully prepares both the privileged position of Socrates and the central topic of the threshold dialogues: the training of the young in *aretē*. The discussion of this topic in the *Laches* will lead directly to the problem of defining the virtues, and hence to the principle of the priority of definition.

First the cast of interlocutors. The fathers whose sons are to be educated, Lysimachus and Melesias, are themselves sons of two of the most famous statesmen of fifth-century Athens: Aristides the just and Thucydides son of Melesias, the rival of Pericles. And the two generals whose advice is solicited, Laches and Nicias, are leading figures in Athenian political life in the years following Pericles' death. The high personal status of Laches and Nicias, and the even more distinguished family connections of the two fathers whose concern for their sons' education motivates the dialogue – all this serves to focus dramatic interest on the debate concerning the best way to train the young in excellence. Socrates ends predictably by showing these renowned soldiers that they do not know what they are talking about when they try to define courage. But in the prologue something else is going on. Socrates is presented as an eminently respectable citizen who is highly regarded by two of the most important men in the city. Furthermore,

3. The proem to the *Laches*, the longest in any dialogue, covers eleven out of twenty-three Stephanus pages, before the search for definition begins at 189E–190D. Its closest rival is the triple prologue to the *Protagoras*, which occupies ten pages in a dialogue more than twice the length of the *Laches*. Typically, a dramatic prologue is four to six pages long; the preamble to *Republic* I is less than five pages.

the conversation with Lysimachus son of Aristides shows that he has family connections with the best Athenian society. The impression made on the reader is thus very different from the *Hippias Minor*, where Socrates defends outrageous moral views, or from the *Gorgias*, where he attacks the reputation of Pericles and other great names in Athenian history. By introducing Socrates as an appropriate tutor for the young, the prologue to the *Laches* sets the stage for a series of dialogues on the nature and teaching of virtue, where Socrates will play the role of moral guide. And by presenting Socrates as an acknowledged example of courage, the virtue to be defined, the *Laches* also embeds the theoretical search for a definition within a broader practical concern for moral and political education: how should young men be trained in order to acquire *aretē*, "excellence"? At the beginning of the prologue, excellence is understood in terms of political success and public fame; by the end, Socrates has carefully reformulated the goal as making "their souls as good as possible" (186A). The tension between these two quite different conceptions of *aretē*, which dominates the passionate confrontation of the *Gorgias*, remains latent here, since the topic of courage allows for at least superficial convergence between the two views.

The direct result of the prologue is to motivate the search for a definition as the basis for a decision on educational policy. The twin issues of teachability and practical utility are raised from the beginning, in the dispute between Laches and Nicias on whether the boys should be trained in fighting in armor: is it or is it not a *mathēma*, a subject worth learning (182E)? But this question is generalized and transformed by Socrates into an attempt to specify the goal, the *hou heneka*, of moral education (185D): how can *aretē* enter the boys' souls and make them better men (190B)? This is, of course, precisely the goal of the political art as defined in the *Gorgias*, and here too we are looking for an expert, a *technikos* (185A 1, B 11, D 9, E 4, etc.). Even the credentials required of an expert are the same as in the *Gorgias*: who were his teachers? and what works has he produced?[4] Only in this case Socrates decides to take a different tack.

Another inquiry that leads to the same result, and that would be

---

4. Compare *Laches* 186E–187C, 189D 5–7 with *Gorgias* 514B–C, 515Aff.

a more fundamental starting-point, he suggests, would be to define the subject matter for which we need an expert and the goal to be pursued.[5] In order to establish such a starting-point, says Socrates, we must know what virtue is (190B). But since virtue as a whole is too large a topic, let us take the part of virtue that seems most relevant to the question first posed: should the boys be trained to fight in armor? "So let us try to say first what courage is (*andreia ti pot' estin*); and afterwards we will inquire in what manner it can be acquired by the lads, insofar as it can be obtained through practices and teaching (*mathēmata*)" (190D 7).

We return in the next section to this posing of the *what-is-X?* question. The question is introduced here as theoretical preliminary to the practical enterprise of moral training. Precisely the same connection is preserved in the fuller discussion of definition in the *Meno*, where the question "What is virtue?" is posed as a prerequisite to answering Meno's question: is virtue teachable? The priority of definition, insisted on in both dialogues, is first of all the methodical priority of theory to practice. In the other two dialogues of definition, the *Charmides* and the *Euthyphro*, the inquiry is at least superficially motivated by an equally practical concern. Socrates asks Charmides to define temperance in order to discover whether he already possesses the virtue or whether he needs the charm that will help to cure his headache; and Socrates asks Euthyphro to define piety so that he can use this knowledge to defend himself in court against the charge of impiety. In the *Laches* and the *Meno*, however, where the priority principle is explicitly formulated, the practical motivation reflects a central concern of the Socratic-Platonic enterprise: the need to define virtue as the goal of moral education.

This practical embedding of the *what-is-X?* question has often been overlooked. Aristotle complains that Socrates thought the goal (*telos*) was to know virtue, and that he asked "what is justice?" and "what is courage?" because he thought knowing justice was equivalent to being just. "So he inquired what virtue is, but not how it is acquired and from what sources" (*Eudemian Ethics* 1.5,

5. The sense of *mallon ex archēs* at 189E 2–3 is explained by the earlier reference at 185B to the need "to agree from the beginning (*ex archēs*) what it is that we are deliberating about, which of us is an expert and has acquired teachers for this purpose (*toutou heneka*), and which has not."

1216b3–10). Here Aristotle ignores the point that is so emphatically made in the *Laches*: defining the virtues is the starting-point, not the goal, for a program of moral education. This practical concern that begins with the dialogues of definition will culminate in the theory of education for the guardians in the *Republic*. But the process is in a way circular: one must first know what virtue or excellence is in order to design a program for training in it; but the highest level of training is precisely a deeper understanding of excellence and the Good.

The literary form of the *Laches* is worth noting. This is the first dialogue we have encountered with a dramatic prologue, and the first to situate the conversation at a definite fictive date (except, of course, for the *Apology* and *Crito*, which are unavoidably dated by their relation to Socrates' trial and death). Since Laches died in 418 BC and the dialogue refers to the battle of Delium (424 BC) as if it were a recent event, the fictive date must be in the late 420s, about the time that Nicias was negotiating the peace that bears his name. A dramatic prologue of this kind is typical of every threshold dialogue except the *Meno*, and of the *Symposium* and *Phaedo* as well. In several cases the prologue also begins by referring to an event that serves to fix a definite dramatic date. (The *Charmides* is dated by an opening reference to the battle of Potidaea in 432 BC, *Euthyphro* by Socrates' trial, *Protagoras* by the sprouting beard of Alcibiades, the *Symposium* by Agathon's first victory.) In this respect the *Laches* presents what looks like an innovation in Plato's literary technique. But the *Laches* is lacking in one device that is typical of the *Charmides, Lysis, Protagoras, Euthydemus* and other works, including the prologue to the *Republic*: the use of a narrative frame. The *Laches* is the only example of a dialogue with an extended dramatic introduction that is *not* reported by a narrator. From the formal point of view, then, the *Laches* still exhibits the straight dramatic ("mime") structure used by Plato in the *Gorgias* and in the three very short dialogues (*Crito, Ion, Hippias Minor*); whereas the dramatic prologue points ahead to the new form that is typical of Plato's writing from the *Charmides* to the *Republic*.[6]

---

6. Since in the aporetic dialogues (as in Aeschines) the narrator is Socrates himself, Plato had a good artistic motive for this unique instance of a long dramatic prologue *without* a narrative frame, namely, the delayed entrance of Socrates into the conversation.

3. TWO KINDS OF DEFINITION

In Chapter 3 §4 I distinguished two kinds of requests for definition, one that does and one that does not claim *epistemic* priority
over other questions. The less demanding request is illustrated in
the *Gorgias*, where Socrates presses Gorgias to specify the character of his profession (namely, rhetoric), so that they can evaluate
it. Socrates insists that the question "What is rhetoric?" must be
answered before deciding whether or not rhetoric is an admirable
thing (448E, 462C 10, 463C). Socrates will not answer the second
question until he has answered the first, because that would not be
right (*ou dikaion*, 463C 6). This is what I have called a rule of good
method: to begin by making clear what you are talking about before debating its controversial features. Once Socrates and his interlocutors have agreed on the description of rhetoric, he can go
on to show why it is not a *technē* and hence not admirable. And this
rule of priority applies equally well to speechmaking. In *Symposium*
195A and *Phaedrus* 237B–D a similar requirement is invoked: to
make clear by agreement what *erōs* is, before praising it.

In the *Laches*, on the other hand, it is a question not merely of
agreement but of knowledge. "Isn't this required of us, to know
what virtue is? For if we don't know at all what virtue really is,
how can we be advisers to anyone on how it is best acquired?"
(190B 7). This is not simply a rule of clarity but a principle of epistemic priority, the principle that real competence on any subject
requires one to know of that subject *what-it-is*. The question at issue is educating the young, and Socrates has entered the discussion by insisting that the decision should be made on the basis of
knowledge (*epistēmē*), not by counting votes: "is there among us an
expert (*technikos*) on this subject?" If not, we should look for one
(185A). (The terms *technē* and *technikos* occur seven times in the immediate sequel, 185A 1–E 11.)

However, the precise subject on which we need an expert remains to be specified. It is this specification that is called for by the
ti estin ("what is it?") question, first obscurely at 185B 6, more directly at 185B 10. And the practical orientation of the question is
clarified by the explanatory phrase *hou heneka*, specifying that "for
the sake of which" the expert is needed. An initial answer suggested by Socrates is: making the souls of the young men as good
as possible (186A 5). But the canonical form of the question, and

the insistence on its priority, comes in a later context, when Socrates begins the examination of the two generals. He has interpreted their readiness to offer advice as a claim of educational expertise: they would not have declared themselves so confidently on the subject of training the boys if they did not believe they had adequate knowledge (*hikanōs eidenai*, 186D 3). In his search for expert knowledge Socrates was about to examine their credentials: who were their teachers? whom have they improved? But instead he substitutes the search for a definition as "another inquiry leading to the same result, that would be more appropriate as a beginning (*mallon ex archēs*)" in testing their competence (189E). So the question, "What is *aretē*?" is posed at 190B. And Laches accepts the question as a test of expertise (190C).

The principle stated here is something new, although it seems familiar. It represents a convergence between two things that are in fact familiar: (a) the rule of good method, which may be historically Socratic, and which is stated here when the priority principle is first introduced at 185B 9: "I don't think we agreed from the beginning what it is we are deliberating about"; and (b) the Socratic scrutiny of claims to knowledge or wisdom, as described in the *Apology*. It is precisely in the context of the Socratic search for wisdom that the rule of good method can be reconstrued as a principle of epistemic priority. But the principle itself is purely Platonic, since it rests on the fundamental explanatory role of essences in Plato's scheme. On that subject there is more to be said in the next section, and still more in Chapter 11.

These two kinds of *what-is-it?* questions receive very different treatment. In the *Gorgias* the method of counterexamples is used to trim an over-generous definiens until it precisely matches the definiendum (at 454E). In the *Laches*, however, as in the other dialogues of definition, the very same method is employed not to improve but to eliminate proposed definitions one after another, so that a satisfactory result is never achieved. This lack of success is a direct function of the aporetic structure of these dialogues. When Plato wishes to provide workable (if not fully adequate) definitions of the virtues for constructive purposes in *Republic* IV, he has no difficulty in doing so. In fact plausible definitions of both courage and virtue are implicitly provided in the *Laches* itself. (See below, §5.) Plato's systematic failure to define the virtues in the threshold dialogues is of course deliberate.[7] It serves not only to preserve the Socratic avowal of ignorance, while at the same time illustrating the epistemic benefits of *aporia*. It manages also to suggest that the knowledge of essences, while fundamental, is very difficult to obtain.

4. THE PRIORITY OF DEFINITION

The principle of epistemic priority for definitions was identified by Richard Robinson in his classic study, *Plato's Earlier Dialectic*; but more recent discussion has been provoked by Peter Geach's attack on what he calls the Socratic fallacy. The fallacy according to Geach is to assume "that if you know you are correctly predicating a given term 'T' you must 'know what it is to be T,' in the sense of being able to give a general criterion for a thing's being T."[8] This makes it impossible to arrive at a definition of T by means of examples, since unless you already possess the definition you cannot know whether the examples are genuine cases of T, for you do not know whether you are predicating "T" correctly. As stated, the principle seems doubly fallacious, since (1) to use a predicate correctly does not normally require knowing a general definition, and (2) unless we can rely on some examples (and counterexamples), it is hard to see how we could ever get agreement on definitions.

A voluminous literature has been produced to show that Geach's case against Socrates is textually unsound.[9] The passage in the *Euthyphro* on which he seems to be relying says only that knowing the form or essence of piety would enable one to decide controversial cases (6E) – that such knowledge might be a sufficient, but not a necessary condition for applying the term correctly. This is a plau-

---

7. The definition of courage covertly implied in the *Laches* might well satisfy extensional criteria (see §5 and §6.1); to be explanatory the definition would need to invoke some psychological theory, as in *Republic* IV. Of course the definitions of *Republic* IV still fall short of an adequate account of essences, as Plato clearly indicates at 435D and 504B–D. For the limits on any literary account of the Forms see below, Chapter 12.
8. Geach (1966) 371.
9. See most recently Vlastos (1994) 67–86, with fuller bibliography in Vlastos (1990) 15.

sible claim. There is no hint of fallacy here, but also no hint of epistemic *priority*. And the reference to judging controversial cases is a special feature of this dialogue, in which Euthyphro is prosecuting his father for murder. (Euthyphro's action seems outrageous to Socrates, but Euthyphro claims that it is required on religious grounds. The judgment on this case clearly depends upon one's general conception of piety.) In other dialogues of definition there is no disagreement on examples. When the principle of epistemic priority is invoked – in the *Laches*, the *Meno*, and later in *Republic* i – the issue is quite different.

In the *Laches* the request for a definition is proposed as a test for competence on the subject of moral education, and (as we have seen) it is accepted as such by Laches: "we claim to know what virtue is . . . and if we know, we can also say what it is" (190C). So the request for a definition of virtue, or of its relevant part courage, is not presented as a criterion for the correct use of a word or for the correct recognition of examples. It is a test of the appropriate expertise, the possession of a *technē* in Plato's sense, the mastery of a given subject matter. In this case it is a test for such expertise in virtue as would qualify one to be a teacher or to give authoritative advice on moral education. Laches' failure to define courage does not call into question his recognition of Socrates' brave conduct at the battle of Delium.[10] It leads instead to a sense of frustration and the beginning of a recognition of his own ignorance: "I seem to understand what courage is, but it somehow got away from me, so that I am not able to grasp it in words (*logos*) and say what it is" (194B).

In the *Laches*, then, the failure to define courage does not show that the generals are not brave or that they cannot recognize examples of bravery. What it shows is that they lack knowledge in the strong sense, of being able to teach or give expert advice on training in virtue.[11]

In the *Meno* Socrates administers a similar lesson in epistemic modesty to his interlocutor, but instead of acknowledging his ignorance Meno responds with his famous paradox. Again the prior

10. At *Laches* 193E Socrates remarks: "Someone who overheard our conversation might say that we share in courage in deed (*ergon*) but not in word (*logos*)."
11. For this connection between definitions, expert knowledge, and teaching, compare the remarks of Woodruff (1982) 139–41 and (1990) 65–75.

question is "What is virtue?" and the subordinate question is how it is to be acquired. The difference is that here (i) knowledge is emphasized for both questions, and (ii) the principle is generalized, and illustrated by the example of knowing who Meno is:

If I do not know what a thing is, how can I know what kind of thing (*hopoion ti*) it is? Or do you think it is possible for someone who does not know at all (*to parapan*) who Meno is to know whether he is handsome or rich or of noble birth, or the opposite of these? Do you think this is possible? (71B)

Here both the generalization and the illustration introduce complications that will be exploited in the formulation of Meno's paradox.

For the sake of clarity we must begin by distinguishing between a common-sense and a paradoxical claim of epistemic priority, corresponding to the distinction between a weak and a strong sense of "to know" for the knowledge in question. The common-sense principle claims only that one must have some minimal kind of cognitive contact or familiarity[12] with the subject under discussion in order to know anything further about it. In the case of an individual like Meno one must be able to identify him as a subject for discussion; in the case of a notion like courage or virtue one must be able to recognize examples. If one is utterly ignorant of the subject – if one does not know at all (*to parapan*) what it is we are talking about – then one can scarcely know whether or not it has any given attribute. We might call this the priority of reference over description. And in this very weak sense of epistemic priority there is no question of essences or definitions, as we can see from the example of knowing who Meno is. The kind of knowing required is really no stronger than the notion of true belief. As readers of the dialogue, we all know well enough who Meno is to know that he is in fact handsome, rich, and well born. (This example clearly shows that the knowledge in question is not what philosophers have called knowledge by acquaintance: we know a great deal about Meno without being personally ac-

---

12. Of course "knowing who he is" (*gignōskei hostis estin*) includes but does not require direct acquaintance. For a nice example of this weak epistemic reading see *Meno* 92C: How can Anytus know whether the practice of the sophists is a good thing or a bad, if he has had no personal contact with them? Easily, he claims, for "I know who they are."

quainted with him.) So construed, the priority principle is a mildly epistemic version of the rule of good method illustrated in the *Gorgias*. It represents the sound principle of common sense that we should know what we are talking about.

So much for the modest notion of priority and the weak sense of "to know." But the dialogue also plays with another kind of priority and a much stronger sense of knowledge, corresponding to the requirement of expert competence in the *Laches*. This is the kind of knowledge that involves an explanatory essence, a single form (*eidos*) of virtue, which all the virtues have, "because of which they are virtues" (72C 8), and which is "what virtue actually is" (*ho tunchanei ousa aretē*) (72D 1). It is knowledge of "what virtue is" in this sense that Socrates requires, before he is willing to say whether or not virtue is teachable. So understood, the generalized principle of priority claims that without knowledge of the essence of X, for any subject X, one cannot know anything about X.[13] No knowledge is possible without knowledge of essences. But in that case, how is the knowledge of essences to be acquired in the first place?

We should recognize that, at the dramatic level, Socrates' initial request for a definition is fully intelligible. Socrates and Meno have radically different conceptions of excellence or *aretē*.[14] And the answer to the question of teachability will obviously depend upon what it is one is trying to teach. It is part of Plato's art to make use of this reasonable need for a clarifying definition, together with the ordinary notion of familiarity with the subject under discussion, in order to motivate the quite different and extraordinary request for prior knowledge of explanatory essences. For it is this second, stronger request that emerges in the systematic pursuit of definitions in the first section of the *Meno*.

It is against the background of this radical but skillfully concealed duality of the *what-is-it?* question that we can understand the ambiguous status of Meno's paradox and the ambivalence of Socrates' response. On the one hand, he qualifies the argument as eristic; on the other hand, he replies by invoking the mystic doctrine of immortality and rebirth, and by introducing the theory of

---

13. For a clear statement and defense of this strong reading, see Benson (1990a) 19–65.
14. This emerges most clearly when Meno defines virtue as "being able to rule over human beings." He must be reminded by Socrates to add "ruling justly" (*Meno* 73C 9–D 8).

recollection that will dominate the next section of the dialogue. But this ambivalence is profoundly puzzling. If Meno's argument is eristic, why does it deserve such a powerful response? I suggest that the distinction between the weak and strong versions of epistemic priority provides the clue needed to resolve this puzzle.

Meno asks: "How will you seek for something if you don't know at all what it is? Which of the things you don't know will you propose as object of your search? And even if you find it, how will you know that this is the thing which you did not know?" (*Meno* 80D). The argument will count as eristic or sophistical if it is seen to depend upon an equivocal use of "to know." On this reading the paradox can easily be dispelled once "knowing" is disambiguated. We need only know in a weak sense (be able to identify) a subject, about which knowledge in some fuller sense is lacking and needs to be sought for.[15] This is clearly the case for any topic of scientific research. And it is this weaker sense of "to know" that was suggested at the beginning of the dialogue by the comparison to knowing who Meno is.

On the other hand, the fact that Plato uses Meno's paradox to introduce the doctrine of recollection shows that he has in view the stronger conception of prior knowledge associated with the notion of explanatory essences. It is only because this "eristic" argument points to a deeper problem posed by the strong principle of epistemic priority, that Meno's paradox can justify the heavy artillery that Plato brings out to meet it.

Meno's paradox has to be taken seriously because it is a generalization of the kind of objection Geach has raised to the priority of definition.[16] If you must have essential knowledge of X, a full understanding of what-X-is, in order to know anything else about X, how will you acquire any knowledge at all? It will not help to ap-

---

15. This distinction between (a) knowing enough to identify a subject for research, and (b) achieving full scientific or explanatory knowledge of the same subject, will also disarm Socrates' paraphrase of the paradox: "You cannot investigate either what you know (for in that case there is no need for investigation) or what you don't know (for then you don't know what to look for)" (80E). The same ambiguity figures significantly in the *Charmides*, where Socrates asks how one can know what one is ignorant of. See below, pp. 198f. with n.25.

16. Of course Geach's fallacy is not the same as Meno's paradox, but both are entailed by the strong reading of the priority of definition. The connection has been recognized by Vlastos (1994) 78 and by Benson (1990b) 148.

peal to the concept of true belief (or opinion, *doxa*) introduced later in the dialogue, for belief can give only the weak sense of knowledge required for recognizing examples and identifying individuals. This might permit us to give an extensional account of any concept, a conjunction of necessary and sufficient conditions. (See below, §6.1.) It could not give us access to explanatory essences. No accumulation of true beliefs about virtue could provide us with the knowledge of *what-virtue-is*. It would seem that essences must be recognized directly or not at all.

Some passages in the *Meno* might lead the reader to believe that Plato admits the possibility of our epistemic bootstrapping ourselves up from true belief to knowledge. Thus the slave boy is said to have produced true beliefs that might eventually lead to accurate knowledge (85c–d). And Socrates later asserts that if true beliefs are fastened by a calculation of the reason (or "reasoning concerning the cause," αἰτίας λογισμῷ), they will become knowledge (98a 6). In both cases, however, the transition from true belief to knowledge is an instance of *recollection*, that is of recovering knowledge that was previously present, and is in some sense still "in the person" (85d 6). Metaphorically speaking, true beliefs represent the initial waking-up phase of knowledge that was asleep inside the soul.[17] Plato's thinking here is Eleatic in form: as Being cannot come from Not-being, so knowledge cannot come from what is not-knowledge. If knowledge of essences can ever be realized in actual cognition, that is because it was already present in some way in our soul.

On the strong principle of epistemic priority, then, we must know the essences of things in order to know anything at all. This is the requirement that the doctrine of recollection is introduced to satisfy, by reassuring us that we do in fact have such knowledge already. Recollection (together with the myth of the soul's preexistence as presented in the *Phaedrus*) can of course explain how the knowledge of essences is prior to the knowledge of other things,

---

17. For the notion that true belief represents knowledge that is asleep and needs to be awakened, see 85c 9 ("as in a dream") and 86a 7 ("aroused by questioning"). It is in this sense that the slave boy can be said to "have knowledge now" (85d 9); because "the truth concerning realities (*ta onta*) is always in the soul" (86b 1). As Scott (1987: 351) points out, recollection is proposed "as the solution to a problem about how we can transcend our opinions and achieve knowledge."

including their particular applications and exemplifications. But it can explain this fully *only* when recollection is completed with a theory of what is recollected, namely, essential forms. The prior knowledge of essences must be different in kind from ordinary knowledge, or the problem of how *that* knowledge was acquired will simply recur at the earlier stage. So the epistemic challenge raised implicitly by the priority principle in the *Laches*, and explicitly in the *Meno*, is not finally met until we get Recollection-with-the-Forms, in the *Phaedo*. The *Phaedo* makes clear that the doctrine of Forms and the doctrine of the transcendent psyche, as introduced in the *Meno*, belong together.[18]

Looking back from the *Phaedo* to the *Laches*, we can see that Plato's literary strategy is to introduce the epistemic version of the priority principle in a context where we can easily accept the weaker reading (as in the reference to knowing Meno, and in the initial statement in the *Laches*: "how can we give advice on inculcating something if we don't even know what we want to inculcate?"), and then press towards the stronger reading with Meno's paradox. Upon reflection, however, we see that the stronger reading of epistemic priority must already have been implicit in the *Laches*, since otherwise the generals' failure to give a definition of courage could not serve as a test of their credentials for competence, that is, for adequate knowledge in the field of moral education. To this extent, the search for definition in these dialogues, as a prerequisite for knowledge in the strong sense, serves directly to propound a problem for which the doctrine of Forms will supply the solution.

It should be clear that, in order to play the role for which they are cast in the *Meno*, the objects of recollection must be a priori concepts embedded in the human psyche at birth, concepts that represent the essences of objective reality in such a way as to make human experience and human learning possible.[19] Hence the full conception of recollection developed in the *Phaedo* and in the myth

---

18. *Phaedo* 76D–77A, where the reliance on the Forms in knowledge is invoked as a proof of preexistence: "the necessity is the same ... The existence of our souls before we were born is in the same case [i.e. has the same necessity] as the reality [of the Forms] which you were mentioning" (76E 8ff.). So implicitly at *Meno* 86B 1: "because the truth concerning *ta onta* is always in the soul."

19. Cf. *Meno* 81C 9: "all nature is akin, and our soul has learned all things."

of the *Phaedrus* is implicit here in the *Meno*. Furthermore, if the essences of the world of nature are available to a transcendent psyche, they must themselves be transcendent essences. And if the grasp of such essences is to make our experience of the world possible, then the sensible world itself must somehow be shaped by (or "participate in") these essences.

Thus the most fundamental features of Plato's metaphysics are all entailed by the doctrine of learning as recollection. But this doctrine in turn is explicitly motivated by the problems posed by the principle of epistemic priority for definitions, as asserted in the *Laches* and reinforced in the *Meno* by the paradox of inquiry. I see no reason to doubt that Plato had all of this in view when he chose to introduce this paradox at precisely this point in the *Meno*. We can only guess how far ahead he could see when he proposed the principle of epistemic priority in the *Laches*. As we have seen, the *Meno* points to many principles that it does not state. (Above, p. 64.) But the transcendental destiny of the soul, which is obscurely hinted at in the *Gorgias*, is here unequivocally asserted. In the *Meno* Plato thus reveals for the first time the otherworldly space in which his metaphysics, epistemology and, in the end, his psychology also will be located.

5. THE DEFINITION OF COURAGE

A dialogue like the *Laches* can be read at many levels. We have seen its concern with the epistemology of definition; in the next section we consider it as an exercise in the logic of definition, where the *Euthyphro* and the *Meno* are to count as its sequel. As an exploration of the concept of courage, the *Laches* raises a topic that is also pursued in the *Protagoras* and in *Republic* IV. Finally the dialogue can be seen as a personal elenchus of the two generals, testing them for an account of their own character and belief. Our concern now is with these last two topics: the account of courage given by the two generals. We will see how Plato's use of the aporetic form serves both to disclose and to conceal an understanding of the topic.

Laches is unused to philosophical discussion, and he does not immediately grasp what is meant when Socrates asks him what courage is. He answers: "That is not hard to say. If someone is willing to remain in formation to fight the enemy and not run

away, you may be sure he is courageous" (190E). Although Laches'
statement is true, it does not answer Socrates' question. He has
said what is courage, that is, what is a case of courage; he has not
said what courage is. So Socrates gives as an explanation the example of quickness. Just as courage can be found not only in standard hoplite formations but in the cavalry and in more complex
tactical maneuvers, and not only in war but in other forms of
danger as well, in confronting disease, poverty, political terrors,
and even in combat with pleasures and desires, so also quickness
can be found not only in running but in playing the lyre and in
speaking and in learning and in movements of the body. When
Socrates asks, what is quickness? he means to ask *what is the same in
all these cases?* And he offers as his sample definition: the capacity
(*dunamis*) to do many things in a short time. Analogously, what is
the capacity to be found alike in all the different cases of courage?

Having understood what is required, Laches now answers:
"a certain perseverance or steadfastness (*karteria tis*) of the soul"
(192B 9). This answer has the merit of locating courage not in any
particular type of behavior but in the psyche as a character trait,
which is where the virtues belong. The particular trait that Laches
has selected, however, is too broad: stubborn perseverance can
often be foolish and harmful, whereas courage must be something
admirable and beneficial. So Socrates reinterprets Laches' suggestion as "*intelligent* perseverance," and Laches acquiesces (192D).

Although Laches' emended definition "intelligent perseverance"
is now formally correct, specifying a character trait guided by intelligence or understanding (*phronēsis*), we need to know what kind
of intelligence: intelligence *in regard to what*? (192E 1). The rest of
the dialogue can be seen as an exploration of this problem. What
kind of knowledge or wisdom is required if sheer perseverance is
not to degenerate into blind stubbornness or, alternatively, to reflect merely prudential calculation? The counterexamples which
Socrates brings to bear, and which lead Laches to perplexity and
contradiction, are examples of confidence resulting from various
kinds of technical knowledge, where the person who faces danger
without such knowledge seems to exhibit more courage. Thus the
trained horseman who fights in the cavalry will be judged less
brave than the cavalryman who fights without training in horsemanship, and the man who dives into a well without special skill
will be thought braver than the skilled well-cleaner (193B–C). What

is intriguing about this argument is that the same two examples are used by Socrates in the *Protagoras* to make what seems to be the opposite point: the greater confidence exhibited by the trained cavalryman and the experienced well-diver serve as premises in an argument whose conclusion is that wisdom is courage (*Prot.* 350A–C). But the *Protagoras* argument is unsatisfactory; Protagoras attacks its logic, and Socrates immediately abandons it. What Protagoras points out is that the confidence of the untrained cavalryman and unskilled well-diver is not so much courage as madness (*Prot.* 350B 5), and this remark rejoins Socrates' conclusion at *Laches* 193C 9–D 4 that the same examples represent "foolish daring and endurance" rather than courage. What Laches has failed to see is precisely what Protagoras observes for the parallel cases: in some circumstances confidence is not a moral virtue, and hence not a mark of courage.

The elenchus of Laches leaves us with the question: what kind of knowledge is required to guarantee that daring and endurance will be courage rather than foolhardiness? The implied answer, thus far, is that it will not be a technical skill like horsemanship or archery; but that does not mean that it will not be a *technē* at all. The situation here is parallel to the implied conclusion of the *Hippias Minor*, that justice must be relevantly different from ordinary skills and trained capacities. And the question is the same: different in what way?

It is at this point that Nicias enters with a suggestion based upon what he has often heard Socrates say, namely "that each of us is good in those things where he is wise, bad in those where he is ignorant." Hence, says Nicias, courage must be a kind of wisdom (194D). When challenged, Nicias specifies: courage is "the knowledge of what is and is not to be feared (*ta deina kai tharralea*), in war and in everything else" (194E 11). Laches protests: the doctor and the farmer have this kind of knowledge without being brave. Nicias responds by rehearsing an argument used by Socrates in the *Gorgias*: the doctor does not know whether it is better for you to live or to die, and even the prophet who can foresee the future does not know what is best for you to undergo (195C–196A 3, paralleling *Gorgias* 511C–512B). Here we have an explicit contrast between technical competence and the special knowledge that is required for virtue, the knowledge that knows *what is best*.

Socrates proceeds to the elenchus of Nicias in two stages. First he cites the animals that are generally regarded as courageous, such as the lion and the wild boar: are they to be regarded as wise in these matters? Nicias answers skillfully by distinguishing here between courage and fearlessness; the latter but not the former can be possessed by animals, children, and foolish men and women.[20] It is the second stage of the elenchus that brings Nicias to grief. First he accepts the earlier assumption that courage is a part of virtue. Then Socrates gets him to agree (1) that fear is an expectation of future evil, and (2) that knowledge of a given subject matter should be the same for past, present, and future. From this it follows that anyone who has knowledge of future goods and ills must know about good and evil generally, regardless of time. Now this "knowledge of all things good and evil, and in all circumstances" would not be only a part of virtue, but *aretē* as a whole (199E). But since we were looking for a part of virtue, we have not succeeded in finding what courage is. And the philosophical discussion ends on this note of failure.

This conclusion is perplexing in several respects. In the first place, the formula proposed by Nicias and rejected in the end is practically identical with the definition of courage defended by Socrates in the *Protagoras*: "The wisdom concerning what is and is not to be feared (*deina*)" (*Prot.* 360D 4). Furthermore, since the wider formula into which Socrates in the *Laches* has converted this definition, "the knowledge of all things good and bad," is said by Socrates to fit virtue as a whole, the conclusion should be counted as a success rather than a failure. After all, our original need was to define *aretē*; we only chose courage because it was supposed to be easier (190C–D). Ironically, it has turned out that the effort to find the easier thing has "failed" because we found the harder thing instead. Finally, it has been pointed out by many commentators, beginning with Bonitz more than a century ago, that if we add Nicias' formula to Laches' definition as emended by Socrates, we have a perfectly respectable definition of courage: perseverance and toughness of soul guided by the knowledge of what is good and what is bad, what is and is not to be feared.[21] And this is not

---

20. Nicias thus makes essentially the same point about irrational daring that Protagoras makes in the passage just cited, *Prot.* 350C–351B 2. The point is echoed in *Meno* 88B 3–6 and in the definition of courage in *Republic* IV, 430B 6–9.

21. See Bonitz (1871) 413–42; O'Brien (1963) 131–47 and (1967) 114.

very different from the definition of courage that is actually given in *Republic* IV: the capacity to preserve a correct opinion about what is and is not to be feared, the dye in the soul that remains fixed despite the trials of pleasure and pain, fear and desire (429C–430B).[22]

Plato has thus composed the *Laches* in such a way that a thoughtful reader may see (1) that the knowledge of good and bad is put forward as a general account of virtue, and (2) that toughness of soul and a special application to what is and is not really fearful are the distinctive features of courage.[23] The apparently negative conclusion is intended as a challenge to the reader; not all is made clear, but the outlines of a solution are visible. And from a literary point of view, the distribution of different parts of this solution between the two generals is entirely in character. The blunt, pragmatic Laches recognizes the fact that courage is primarily a feature of character or temperament, whereas it is up to Nicias, who has intellectual pretensions, to propose the "Socratic" definition of virtue in terms of knowledge.[24] We are left with two questions: how is this account of courage related to that in the *Protagoras*? and how is it related to what has been called Socratic intellectualism, the purely cognitive account of moral virtue?

There are four distinct but interconnected parallels between the *Laches* and *Protagoras*: (1) the examples of the trained cavalryman and the skilled well-diver as questionable cases of courage (*Laches* 193B–C, *Prot.* 350A), (2) the definition of fear as anticipation of evil (*Laches* 198B 8, *Prot.* 358D 6), (3) the definition of courage as knowing what is and is not to be feared (*Laches* 194E 11, *Prot.* 360D 5), and (4) the distinction between courage and sheer daring or fearlessness (*Laches* 197A–B, *Prot.* 350B, 351A). On points 2 and 4 the two dialogues are in agreement, but topics 1 and 3 are treated quite differently. The examples under 1 are cited by Socrates in the *Laches* to show that expert knowledge may diminish rather

---

22. Most of the definitions of *Republic* IV specify right opinion rather than knowledge, because the concept of philosophic knowledge (and hence philosophic virtue based on knowledge) is not introduced until we meet the philosopher-king late in Book V.

23. *Karteria* as a component of courage is endorsed by Socrates himself at 194A 4.

24. On the match between the character of the generals and their position in the discussion see O'Brien (1963) and (1967) 114–17; Devereux (1977) 134f.

than augment one's claim to courage, whereas they are invoked by him in the *Protagoras* as part of an abortive argument designed to identify courage with wisdom. And this identification, which is proposed by Nicias but rejected by Socrates in the *Laches*, is adopted by Socrates himself in the *Protagoras*. What are we to make of these discrepancies?

In a detailed discussion of these passages, von Arnim was led to conclude that the *Protagoras* was earlier and that the *Laches* represented Plato's more mature treatment of courage.[25] But this chronological inference is unconvincing. For one thing, Protagoras immediately objects that the daring of those who take risks without the necessary competence exemplifies folly rather than bravery (*Prot.* 350B). This distinction would answer Socrates' argument at *Laches* 193B–C, but it is in fact introduced only later, and in a different context (*Laches* 197B). Thus Protagoras tells us directly what the reader of the *Laches* is expected to think out for himself. And Plato does not give up (though he will reformulate) the account of courage that is challenged in the *Laches* and defended in the *Protagoras*. Insight into what is and is not fearful remains part of the definition in *Republic* IV, as we have seen. The *Protagoras* has many peculiarities of its own, to be considered in a later chapter. The only one that concerns us here is the absence of any reference to the emotional or temperamental dimension of courage, the dimension represented by *karteria* in the *Laches*. For this neglect of the non-cognitive component is also a striking feature of Nicias' account of courage, which he claims to derive from Socrates.

Are we dealing here with the intellectualism of the historical Socrates, who is said by Aristotle to have defined the virtues as so many forms of knowledge? Many scholars have accepted this view as historical. In Chapter 3 I argued that although the close connection between knowledge and virtue must be historically Socratic, the presentation here of this view in the form of a *definition* is likely to be Plato's own work.

What is clear in any case is that, for the author of the *Laches* as

25. Von Arnim (1914) 24–34. A similar conclusion was argued by Vlastos (1994: 117) on the grounds that in the *Protagoras* Plato had not clearly seen the important distinction between moral wisdom and technical skill. Identifying Plato with Socrates, Vlastos has neglected the sharp distinction drawn in Protagoras' speech (*Prot.* 321D 4–5, 322B 5–7, C 5ff.; cf. 318E–319A and below, Chapter 8, pp. 215f.

for the perceptive reader, a purely cognitive account of courage is insufficient: what Laches calls *karteria*, "steadfastness," is an essential component.[26] But the final emphasis of the dialogue is on the epistemic conception, the knowledge of good and bad. This conception is inadequately represented by Nicias, who is a naive spokesman for a view he does not fully understand. The repeated reference to prophets in the elenchus of Nicias is almost certainly intended as a reminder of his disastrous mistake at Syracuse, where his superstitious fear of the evil omen from a lunar eclipse led to the total destruction of the Athenian army.[27]

The art of the general does not think it should be subservient to prophecy but rather to rule over it, on the grounds that it knows better what happens and what will happen in warfare. And the law commands not that the prophet rule the general but that the general rule the prophet. (198E–199A)

Socrates' reminder here confirms the need for wisdom, for knowing what is to be feared, as an essential component of true virtue. For this is just the wisdom that Nicias so conspicuously lacked at the crucial hour, and that is symbolized in the dialogue by his failure to defend the relevant thesis against Socrates' attack. It is in this way that the elenchus obliges the general to give an account of his own life.

6. ON THE LOGIC OF DEFINITION

It remains for us to consider the *Laches* as the introductory essay in a systematic study of the logic of definition, to be pursued in the *Euthyphro* and the *Meno*. Plato's treatment of definition is of course of interest for its own sake. But my concern here is above all to point out the continuity and cumulative quality of the exposition in these three dialogues, as an indication that they were planned as, and intended to be read as, an interlocking group. This is one of the more striking cases of expository continuity between the

---

26. See n.23 above. Hence some scholars who regard Nicias' view as faithfully Socratic find that Plato is here having second thoughts about the purely intellectualist account of virtue. See Santas (1971a), 196n. and Devereux (1977), 136 and 141.
27. Thucydides VII.50.4 with the sequel down to Nicias' death at VII.86. The connection is well made by O'Brien (1963).

threshold dialogues, comparable to the continuity in the discussion of courage (between the *Laches* and *Protagoras*) and in the priority of definition (between the *Laches* and the *Meno*, with echoes in the *Charmides, Protagoras, Lysis,* and *Republic* 1). Another nice example of thematic continuity between these dialogues is the set of fathers cited in the three passages on illustrious parents who fail to transmit *aretē* to their sons: Aristides and Thucydides, represented by their sons in the *Laches*; Pericles (also represented by his sons) in the *Protagoras* 319E–320A; all three of these plus Themistocles in the *Meno* (93C–94D). In each of these four separate cases of thematic continuity, it seems natural to regard the *Laches* as the initial member of the group (as it is natural in the first and fourth cases to regard the *Meno* as the final member).

My argument for this expository priority of the *Laches* will be implicit in the discussion of parallel passages, but let me make it explicit here. For the example of insignificant sons of famous fathers, as for the definition of courage, the treatment of this theme in the *Laches* is the most detailed and extensive, and also the most carefully motivated. (In the *Laches* it is the sons themselves who make the complaint and thus initiate the dialogue, which has courage as its main topic.) For the principle of priority of definition, the formula in the *Laches* is less explicitly epistemic and less generally formulated than in the *Meno* (and again, more elaborately introduced as a test for possession of the relevant *technē*). Coming now to the logic of definition, we see once again that the need for a definition is more carefully prepared by the preliminary conversation in the *Laches*. Furthermore, in this dialogue the only criteria applied are extensional (unlike the *Euthyphro* and the *Meno*); and technical terminology (such as *ousia, eidos,* and *idea*) is altogether lacking.

To speak of the logic of definition is slightly anachronistic, since the term "definition" (and still less the term "logic") is not yet a fixed concept for Plato, as it will be for Aristotle. Plato never uses Aristotle's word for definition (*horismos*); and the term he does occasionally employ for this notion, *horos*, preserves the flavor of its literal meaning "boundary-mark." What we call "defining" is for Plato "marking the boundaries" or "delimiting," *horizesthai*.[28]

28. *horizesthai* for drawing the boundaries of a definition occurs once in the *Laches* (194C 8), where Laches criticizes Nicias' attempts to define courage.

Although it is irresistibly convenient to speak of "the dialogues of definition," we need to bear in mind not only that we come upon the concept of definition here *in statu nascendi,* but above all that Plato's focus is not on the linguistic definiens as such but on its objective function in grasping an essence, in saying what-something-is.

6.1 Extensional relations

The brief exchange with Laches, occupying only two or three Stephanus pages (190D–192D), contains a brilliantly conceived introduction to the principle of co-extensivity for definiens and definiendum: the principle that a definition must specify both necessary and sufficient conditions for what is to be defined. Laches' first answer, in terms of hoplite combat, provided a sufficient but not a necessary condition for courage: it was too narrow. His second answer, in terms of moral toughness or perseverance (*karteria*), gives a necessary but not a sufficient condition: it includes too much. Socrates' proposed emendation "intelligent perseverance" has the correct form of a standard definition, locating the definiendum within a broader genus by means of a specific differentia. This is as far as Plato takes us in the *Laches* in developing the formal features of a definition. The issues of co-extensivity and genus–species relations will be treated more elaborately in the *Euthyphro* and *Meno,* to which we now turn.

When Euthyphro is asked to say what the pious is, he begins like Laches with an over-precise answer: "the pious is just what I am doing now, pursuing a wrongdoer, whether concerning murder or theft of sacred property or any misdeed of this kind" (5D 8). When Socrates insists upon a single rule to cover all the cases, Euthyphro immediately produces a more general formula: what is pleasing to the gods is pious, what is not pleasing is impious (6E 10). Co-extensivity, which was treated at length in the elenchus of Laches, is here swiftly and easily achieved. (This is, I suggest, to be read

---

Similarly at *Gorgias* 453A 7, and more systematically in the *Charmides* (163D 7, 173A 9, cf. *diorizomai* at 163E 11, *aphorizesthai* at 173E 9). But often the sense is "distinguish" rather than "define" (*Charm.* 171A 5, 9, *Euthyphro* 9C 7, D 5; cf. *Gorgias* 191C 1, 513D 5), sometimes with the sense of establishing a standard or criterion (cf. *horon horizesthai* at *Gorgias* 470B 10, to draw a line between what is better and worse; similarly 475A 3; *diorizesthai* 495A 1).

not simply as a mark of Euthyphro's intelligence, but rather as a sign of continuity of exposition. Plato sees no need to repeat himself.) The second definition will also be rejected, but not on extensional grounds; hence we postpone for the moment our consideration of it. A third attempt is thereupon initiated by Socrates himself, who suggests that everything pious is also just and then asks whether, on the other hand, everything just is also pious? Euthyphro does not understand the point, so it is carefully explained by the example of awe (*aidōs*) and fear (*deos*): "many people fear disease and poverty and many other things which they do not hold in awe ... Fear extends further (*epi pleon*) than awe. For awe is part of fear, just as odd is part of number" (12B–C). Similarly, where one finds the pious one also finds the just; "but the just is not always there, wherever the pious is. For the pious is part of the just" (12D 1–3). The extensional relationship between these two concepts, which in formal logic will be represented as class-inclusion, is here expressed in terms of whole and part. This corresponds to Aristotle's distinction between genus and species. When Socrates goes on to ask "what part of the just is the pious?" he is in effect asking for the specific difference that marks piety off from other forms of justice. And the rest of the *Euthyphro* is devoted to a more or less unsuccessful attempt to specify this differentia.

This discussion of species–genus relations in terms of part and whole, which was briefly introduced in the *Laches* (190C 8–9, 198A, 199E), and further developed in the passages just cited from the *Euthyphro,* is systematically carried forward in the *Meno.* In response to Meno's second definition of virtue, in terms of political rule, Socrates asks whether we should not add "rules justly, not unjustly." Meno agrees that virtue entails ruling justly, "because justice is virtue." Socrates then asks: "is it virtue, or a certain virtue (*aretē tis*)?" Like Euthyphro on the parallel occasion, Meno fails to understand the question, and Socrates must provide an explanation. (The interlocutor's need for a clearer explanation is Plato's standard device for marking an important new point.) "Take for example circularity. I would say it is a certain figure (*schēma ti*), not simply that it is figure. And the reason I would say this is that there are also other figures" (73E). Meno immediately catches on: "You are right, and I also say that there are other virtues besides justice." The other virtues (courage, temperance, and so on) are all referred to later as *parts* of virtue (78E 1, 79A 3ff.). So what looks at first like a distinction between the *is* of identity and the *is* of predication ("is virtue" as against "is a virtue") is interpreted again in terms of the extensional relation between a conceptual whole and its logical parts. What Socrates wants is an account of virtue as a whole (*kata holou* at 77A 6). And he insists that the principle of epistemic priority recognized earlier for definition applies here to the priority of whole to part: "Do you think anyone can know what some part of virtue is if he does not know virtue itself?" (79C 8). The principle of epistemic priority is here interpreted as a general rule for dialectical inquiry, that one cannot answer a question by reference to items that are still under investigation and not yet agreed upon (79D 3). The danger of an indefinite regress here will be obviated by the introduction soon afterwards of the method of hypothesis (86Eff.), which permits inquiry to proceed conditionally, on the basis of tentative solutions to logically prior problems.

6.2 *Requirements that go beyond co-extensivity*

Euthyphro's second definition, piety is what the gods approve, can in fact satisfy the criterion of co-extensivity. That is not immediately clear, because Euthyphro's previous remarks allow for the possibility of conflict between the gods. Now if the gods quarrel, they will not all like the same thing. If a given action is pleasing to some and hateful to others, it turns out to be both pious and impious according to Euthyphro's definition. To prevent the definition from issuing in contradiction, we must eliminate the possibility of disagreement among the gods. For Socrates this is not a problem, since he was unwilling to suppose that the gods quarrel with one another in the first place (6A 7). For Euthyphro this means that the definition applies only in cases where all the gods agree.[29] Within these limits, we have satisfied the extensional requirements on a definition: an action is pious if and only if the gods approve.

29. 9D. Note that Euthyphro's revised definition is compatible with Socrates' assumption of divine unanimity: "I would say that the pious is what all the gods love; and the opposite, what all the gods hate, is impious" (9E 1). Since the intermediate case, where the gods disagree, is not mentioned here, Plato's formulation has carefully bridged the theological gap between Socrates and Euthyphro.

Under these circumstances the method of counterexamples can no longer serve to refute the definition. Euthyphro's definition will nonetheless be rejected, and the reason given is as follows. "Euthyphro, it turns out that although you were asked what the pious is, you did not want to make clear its being (its *ousia* or is-ness), but you mentioned a property (*pathos*) of it, that the pious has this attribute of being loved by all the gods. But what it is, you have not yet said" (11A). This passage introduces into philosophy the notion of an essence, an *ousia*, as the content of a definition that goes beyond specifying necessary and sufficient conditions for the correct application of a predicate, and does so by stating *what the thing (truly, essentially) is*. In contrasting a logical proprium with an essence, Plato here draws a line between the condition of extensional equivalence, which Euthyphro's definition satisfies, and the criterion of intensional content or "meaning," which it does not. And Plato's notion of intensional content is made quite precise in the argument by which Euthyphro is refuted.

The preliminaries of this argument are obscured by some features of the Greek that cannot be lucidly translated into English.[30] But the point of the argument is perfectly clear. Euthyphro's definition is unsatisfactory because it is not explanatory: it does not specify *what makes pious deeds pious*. The crucial question is asked by Socrates at the very beginning: "Is the pious loved by the gods because it is pious, or is it pious because it is loved by the gods?" (10A 2). The novelty and importance of the question are then emphasized by Plato's usual literary device: the interlocutor does not understand what is being asked, and Socrates must give an elaborate clarification before posing the question again (at 10D). Now Euthyphro answers unhesitatingly that it is precisely *because it is pious* that what is pious is loved by the gods (10D 5). But it does not make sense to say that what is pious is loved by the gods

---

30. The logical distinction between the passive participle *phenomenon* and the finite verb *pheretai* at 10B 1 (with parallels in 10B–c) is impossible to render in English, since both are inevitably translated as "is carried." The same difficulty holds for translating the distinction between "is loved by the gods" (*phileitai*) and "god-beloved" (*theophiles*). Plato's point is that the action or attitude expressed by the finite verb (whether in active or passive form) is logically prior to, and explanatory of, the description of the result in participial or adjectival form (*philoumenon, theophiles*).

because it is god-beloved or *dear to the gods* (*theophiles*).[31] This failure
of substitution shows that Euthyphro's definition, although true
(and uniquely true) of piety, lacks the explanatory force of a *logos
tēs ousias*, a statement of what the thing is. The explanatory requirement, which is here made explicit, was hinted at earlier when
Socrates asked Euthyphro to specify "that very form (*eidos*) in virtue of which all pious things are pious" (ᾧ πάντα τὰ ὅσια ὅσιά
ἐστιν 6D 11).

By introducing this explanatory requirement on the statement
of an *ousia*, the *Euthyphro* moves decisively beyond the extensional
considerations applied in the *Laches*. When we turn to the *Meno*,
we find that all of the innovations of the *Euthyphro* have been assimilated, including the terms *eidos* and *ousia* for the object of definition (*Meno* 72B 1, C 7, D 8, E 5) as well as the explanatory condition (δι᾽ ὃ εἰσὶν ἀρεταί 72C 8). Socrates now directs our attention
to a different point: the requirement of unity for both definiens
and definiendum. When Meno offers him a definition in the form
of a list (the virtue of a man, the virtue of a woman, that of a
child, etc.), Socrates insists that he wants a single account for a
single nature or essence. This will be what is common to the different items on the list. So in the case of bees: "Do you say that
they are diverse and different from one another in being bees (τῷ
μελίττας εἶναι)? Or do they not differ in this respect (τούτῳ) but
in some other, such as in size or in beauty or the like?" To which
Meno replies: "They don't differ at all in the way they are bees
(ᾗ μέλιτται εἰσίν)" (72B). Thus the *qua*-terminology introduced in
Ion 540E is used here to indicate the notion of intensional content
("in virtue of being F") as a way of specifying the essence or common nature for diverse members of a single class.[32] So the various

---

31. My analysis of the argument at 10A–11A is essentially in agreement with that
of Cohen (1971) 165ff. Cohen's objection, that "because" in the argument
corresponds to two different relationships (a logical-semantic "because" in
one case, a reason for the gods' attitudes in the other case), is correct but irrelevant. The point is that in "it is god-beloved because the gods love it"
and in "they love it because it is pious," both instances of "because" are explanatory. On the other hand, "the gods love it because it is god-beloved" is
false, since the second clause offers no explanation.

32. So also the strength of a man and the strength of a woman "don't differ at
all with regard to being strength" (πρὸς τὸ ἰσχὺς εἶναι), *Meno* 72E 6. Similarly, πρὸς τὸ ἀρετὴ εἶναι 73A 1.

geometric figures – circle, square, and the like – do not differ from one another "qua figures": they are all the same "in regard to being figures."

This intensional unity is presented here as the reference or nominatum of a general term: "this thing of which 'figure' is the name" (74E 11). "Since you call these many things by one name ... even though they are opposite to one another, what is this that includes (*katechei*) the curved no less than the straight, which you name 'figure'?" (74D 5). The search for unity here is precisely the search that will culminate in the identification of a Form: "We are in the habit of positing some one form (*eidos*) in each case of many things to which we apply the same name" (*Rep.* x, 596A).

In the *Meno* Socrates offers three quite different examples of definition, only one of which is recommended as pointing in the direction of a genuine essence. The first example, defining figure as "the only thing that always follows on color" (75B 10), has the obvious defect of indicating an attribute (*pathos*) rather than the essence of figure. Even if we grant extensional equivalence in this case, the definition provides only a distinguishing mark or property: it does not tell us *what figure is*. The example that Meno prefers but Socrates regards as theatrical (*tragikē*) is the Empedoclean definition of color as "effluence from shapes that is commensurate with sight and perceptible" (76D 4). This definition is explanatory only if one accepts a particular mechanistic theory of vision.

The definition that Socrates prefers[33] is the second definition of figure, as the limit or boundary of a solid (76A). This locates the notion of figure within the larger framework of mathematical knowledge, and connects it with the three-dimensional structure of bodies in space. For Plato this represents a genuinely scientific account, in contrast to the pseudo-scientific formula derived from the physics of Empedocles.[34] Socrates' preference here for the mathematical definition anticipates his critique of Presocratic physics in the last section of the *Phaedo*.

---

33. 76E 7: the definition of figure is better than the definition of color. Some scholars take this to refer to the first definition of figure, which has been rejected on grounds of method (79D 2). But clearly it is the second, mathematical definition that is preferred. So rightly Sharples (1985) 137.
34. For the importance of mathematics in the *Meno*, see Vlastos (1991) ch. 4: "Elenchus and Mathematics."

6.3 The nature of the definiendum

The *Laches* does not have much to say about the status of a definiendum, in this case courage, beyond the suggestion that it is a
capacity (*dunamis*) like quickness, and that it is "the same in all the
cases," that is, in different kinds of danger, temptation, and the
like (191E, 192B 7). The *Euthyphro* says similarly that "the pious is
the same as itself in every action" (5D 1). But the *Euthyphro* goes on
to suggest that, since the essence is explanatory of the properties
things have, a knowledge of the essence may serve as criterion for
their correct description. Socrates asks Euthyphro: "Didn't you
say that it was in virtue of one form (μιᾷ ἰδέᾳ) that impious things
are impious and pious things pious? ... So explain to me what this
form itself (αὐτὴν τὴν ἰδέαν) is, in order that I can refer to it (εἰς
ἐκείνην ἀποβλέπων) and make use of it as a model (*paradeigma*), so
that whatever you or anyone else does that is like this (*toiouton*) I
will say is pious, and whatever is not like this I will say is not
pious" (6E; cf. *Meno* 72C 8 for "looking to the form" in answering
a *what-is-it?* question). Of all the references to forms or essences in
the dialogues of definition, this passage of the *Euthyphro* is richest
in terms and phrases that anticipate the full theory of Forms.

In Chapter 11 we will return to these essences and trace their
continuity with the Forms of the middle dialogues. For the moment I note only that this continuity is strongly marked by the terminology derived from the *what is X?* question. The term *ousia*,
which emerges here as a nominalization of this question (*Euthyphro*
11A 7, *Meno* 72B 1), becomes the word not only for "essence" but
also for the "reality" of the Forms (e.g. *Phaedo* 76D 9, 77A 2). And
of course Plato's most technical expression for Form and essence is
precisely the inversion of this same question: *to ho esti* (*hekaston*)
"the what-each-thing-is" (*Phaedo*, 75B 1, D 2, *Rep.* VI, 507B 7, etc.).

7. THE VIRTUES OF *APORIA*

If, as I claim, Plato has designed the *Laches*, *Euthyphro*, and *Meno* as
a cumulative lesson on the logic of definition, this lesson is lost on
Laches and Nicias, Euthyphro and Meno. Insofar as the lesson is
cumulative, it is addressed not by Socrates to his changing set of
interlocutors but by Plato to his readers, as it were over the heads
of the speakers in the dialogues. For only we the readers can fol-

low the development from one dialogue to another. I want now to point out that a similar meta-dialogical intention can be seen in the general comments on the benefits of *aporia* in the *Meno*. These comments serve to guide the reader in the interpretation of the aporetic dialogues as a group.

It is often assumed that these aporetic dialogues, being typically "Socratic," are among Plato's earliest works. I have suggested, on the contrary, that they all belong after the *Gorgias*. This would explain the tight thematic connections between the *Meno* and the aporetic dialogues, on the one hand, and between *Meno* and *Phaedo* on the other hand. Concerning the nature and teachability of virtue there are also strong ties between the aporetic dialogues and the constructive treatment of these topics in the *Republic*. In regard to literary form, we may recall that the three shortest dialogues – the *Crito, Ion,* and *Hippias Minor* – are all in simple mime form, with no dramatic prologue and no narrative introduction. These have some claim to be (with the *Apology*) Plato's earliest writings; but none of them has an aporetic conclusion. Nor is any dialogue by any other Socratic writer known to be aporetic. I suggest that the aporetic (and hence for many scholars typically "Socratic") dialogue is a new creation on Plato's part, marked by experimentation with new literary forms (such as the dramatic prologue and the narrative frame), in deliberate preparation for the more ambitious enterprise of the middle dialogues. Why Plato chose the aporetic form can be best understood if we attend to his own reflections in the *Meno* on the benefits of *aporia*.

I am not alone in suggesting that, in the lesson with the slave boy, Plato is offering a new interpretation of the Socratic elenchus.[35] The elenchus is presented here as a necessary preliminary to constructive philosophy, but as a preliminary only. Whereas in the *Gorgias* this method of elenchus, together with the *epagōgē* or argument from analogy, is used to defend positive theses against Polus and Callicles, and similar methods are used in support of paradoxical claims in the *Ion* and *Hippias Minor*, in the dialogues of definition the elenchus leads only to negative results. In these dialogues, as in the first part of the *Meno*, Socrates and his interlocutors prove unable to define the virtue in question. But, as we have seen in the geometry lesson (above, p. 99), this failure may

---

35. See in particular Benson (1990b) 130.

have educational value. To clear the mind of the illusion of knowledge is to prepare the way for further inquiry. In the *Meno* Socrates expressly draws the parallel between the slave boy's confusion
after two false answers and Meno's own state of mental numbing
once all his attempts at definition have been demolished: "Do you
see where he has got to in recollecting?" He was ignorant then as
now, but now that he has recognized his ignorance and fallen into
aporia, he is better off; for he now has a desire for knowledge that
he did not have before (*Meno* 84A–C).

Meno will not learn much from this lesson. But we the readers
are allowed to see that this is the function of *aporia* generally and
of the aporetic dialogues in particular: to eliminate the false belief
that these are simple matters, easily understood, and to instill a
desire for further inquiry. Hence the aporetic dialogues are all
also protreptic, urging us on to the practice of philosophy.

For the dialogues of definition, *aporia* reaches a climax when the
principle of epistemic priority issues in Meno's paradox. This is
the moment at which Plato has marked the shift from the negative,
purgative elenchus to the positive theory of recollection and the
constructive method of reasoning from hypothesis. In this respect
the *Meno* brings the aporetic mode to an end, and opens the way
to the middle dialogues.

Of course the content of the dialogues of definition is not
wholly negative and cathartic. We have traced a study of the logic
of definition in these dialogues, and we have seen how a reasonable definition of courage and a Socratic-Platonic definition of
virtue can be found partially expressed in the *Laches*. These are
positive clues for the alert reader. In the *Seventh Epistle* Plato says
that an attempt to write on the most important philosophical matters would not have a beneficial effect on the reader, "except for
those few who would be able to discover the truth themselves with
a few indications (*smikra endeixis*)" (341E). Indications of this kind
are scattered throughout Plato's works, particularly in the positive
hints within what seem to be merely aporetic dialogues.

8. POSTSCRIPT ON THE PRIORITY OF DEFINITION

The principle of epistemic priority is expressly affirmed in the *Laches* for the case of virtue and generalized in the *Meno* for any case:
If you do not know at all what X is, you cannot know anything

about X. As we have seen, there are allusions to, applications of, or variants on this principle in a number of other dialogues. The closest parallel is at the end of *Republic* I, where Socrates says "When I do not know what justice is, I will scarcely know whether it is really a virtue or not, and whether its possessor is happy or not" (354C). Here we have a direct application of the priority principle of the *Meno*. On the other hand, there is only an oblique allusion to such a principle in Socrates' joking remark at the end of the *Lysis* that he and the boys have made themselves ridiculous since, although they claim to be friends, "we were not yet able to discover what a friend is" (*Lysis* 223B 6). There is no suggestion here that, without a definition, they cannot *know* whether or not they are friends. It is simply reasonable to expect that if people are really friends, they should be able to find out what friendship is; just as it is natural to suppose that if Charmides is genuinely temperate, he should be able to say what temperance is (*Charmides* 159A). Such expectations may be disappointed; but they are certainly not fallacious in Geach's sense, since they make no claim to epistemic priority.

A closer parallel to the principle of priority occurs at the end of the *Charmides* (176A), when the namesake of the dialogue insists that he does not know whether or not he possesses temperance: "How could I know the thing concerning which even you [Socrates and Critias] were not able to discover what it is?" Here Charmides at any rate pretends to perceive their failure to define temperance as an obstacle to further knowledge on that subject.

At the end of the *Protagoras* Socrates refers to the principle in weaker form: a definition of virtue would be a sufficient, not a necessary condition for settling the controversial issue of teachability: "for I know that if it could be made clear what virtue is, we would see whether or not it is teachable" (361C). But the same principle in its strong form (as a necessary condition) is definitely implied in an early passage in the same dialogue, when Socrates and the young Hippocrates are discussing his desire to study with Protagoras. Hippocrates does not know what a sophist is (312E, 313C 1–2); so how can he know whether studying with him will be harmful or beneficial (314B)?

In the *Euthyphro* (with which Geach's charge of fallacy began) we have the quite reasonable claim that knowing the nature of piety will make it possible for us to decide disputed cases (6E): the definition is presented as a sufficient, not a necessary condition for judging examples.

The only text in the Platonic corpus where Socrates actually commits Geach's fallacy, by claiming that the knowledge of the definition (knowing what beauty is) is a prerequisite for judging examples (beautiful things) is the *Hippias Major*. The principle of epistemic priority is implied there at 286c–D and clearly stated at 304D–E, precisely in the form of the fallacy denounced by Geach.

Am I not ashamed to have the temerity to discuss beautiful practices, when I have been so clearly refuted on the subject of the beautiful (*to kalon*) and proved not even to know what this thing itself is? And my interrogator will say to me: "How will you know who has composed a beautiful discourse or done anything else beautiful, if you are ignorant of the beautiful?"

This only confirms my judgment, argued elsewhere on other grounds, that the *Hippias Major* was not composed by Plato. The author has borrowed this principle from the *Meno* and *Republic* and clumsily misapplied it here, apparently unaware of the problems involved. Plato is more cunning. He does not allow the issue of circularity latent in the principle of priority to come to light until he chooses to do so with Meno's paradox, which he dramatically presents in such a way as to provoke the great theoretical response of recollection.

In conclusion, I note that we cannot eliminate the priority principle from the "Socratic" dialogues proper, as has been suggested by Vlastos (1990 = 1994, 67ff.) and Beversluis (1987), who would restrict this principle to the three "transitional" or post-Socratic dialogues (*Meno, Lysis*, and *Hippias Major*). Quite apart from any question of chronology, this suggestion is incompatible with the assertion of epistemic priority for the *what-is-X?* question at *Laches* 190B, and with the clear allusions to this principle in the *Charmides* (176A) and *Protagoras* (312Eff.). For these three are typical examples of what Vlastos counts as elenctic, and hence fully Socratic dialogues.

CHAPTER 7

Charmides *and the search for beneficial knowledge*

I. A SURVEY OF THE *CHARMIDES*

The *Charmides* presents itself as a kind of companion piece to the *Laches*: an unsuccessful attempt to define temperance (*sōphrosunē*) matching the unsuccessful attempt to define courage in the *Laches*. In fact the two dialogues are very different from one another, and the *Charmides* poses many problems of its own.

A central thread connecting the *Charmides* with the other threshold dialogues is reflection on the parallel themes of knowledge in the strict sense, as *technē*, and virtue or moral excellence (*aretē*). The *Charmides* pays little attention to the topic of the teaching of virtue, which occupies center stage in the *Laches*, *Protagoras*, and *Meno*, as later in the *Republic*. The primary concern of the *Charmides* is to interpret temperance as a beneficial form of knowledge, the kind of knowledge that can make us "do well" (*eu prattein*) and lead a happy life. The chief peculiarity of the *Charmides* (aside from the choice of interlocutors) is its preoccupation with the ambiguous claim that temperance must be knowledge-of-knowledge or self-knowledge, not knowledge of anything else.

Since the course of the argument is a tortuous one, let me state in advance what I take the conclusion to be. As a positive sub-text in this overtly aporetic dialogue we find the following three claims: (1) that any kind of knowledge must be defined by reference to a definite subject matter, not defined reflexively by reference to itself; (2) that the most beneficial kind of knowledge will take as its object the good and the bad; and (3) that only if such knowledge is able to rule in a city, will everyone in the city be in a position to do his or her own proper work (*ergon*), so as to obtain a good life both for themselves and for the city as a whole. In short, if such knowledge is to be fully beneficial, it must exercise political power.

Thesis 1 develops a theme that is familiar also from the *Ion* and the *Gorgias*. Thesis 2 appears as an implicit conclusion in the *Laches*, but it is systematically developed here in the contrast with other, more technical kinds of knowledge in Socrates' dream. (See below, §7.) Thesis 3 prefigures the central claim of the *Republic*; it is partially paralleled by arguments in the *Lysis* and *Euthydemus*, as we shall see.

This dialogue has other distinctive features. The subtle analysis of reflexive and irreflexive concepts marks it as one of the most technical of all threshold dialogues. The complex conditional reasoning of 169A–175D bears some resemblance to the hypothetical method of the *Meno*. Such reasoning is paralleled in these dialogues only by the quasi-conditional argument from hedonism in the *Protagoras*. Finally, the critical distance from which this dialogue reflects on the Socratic interpretation of self-knowledge as knowledge of one's own and of others' ignorance suggests that the *Charmides* cannot be, what it is often taken to be, a typically "Socratic" dialogue.

2. THE FRAMEWORK OF THE DIALOGUE

The points of similarity between the *Charmides* and the *Laches* are so numerous that the two dialogues have frequently been regarded as a pair.[1] Both dialogues emphasize Socrates' influence on young men of distinguished families: he is already well known to them before the conversation begins (*Laches* 181A, *Charmides* 156A); and it ends in each case with the youths in question being entrusted to his care. Like the *Laches*, the *Charmides* opens with a reference to Socrates' military career; and the interlocutors in both works are famous figures from Athenian political history. In addition to these external parallels, there is a more substantial connection in philosophical theme: each dialogue attempts to define a particular virtue, and each also alludes to the possibility of explaining virtue in terms of the knowledge of good and evil.

Despite these parallels, the *Charmides* is peculiar in many respects. Whereas the *Laches* contains a straightforward attempt to define the virtue in question, the *Charmides* soon turns aside to pursue the concept of knowledge-of-knowledge. Furthermore, the

---

1. So Pohlenz (1913) 56.

interlocutors of the *Laches* are men of eminent respectability. Even Nicias, despite his catastrophic end, is said by Thucydides to have practiced throughout his life "what is ordinarily regarded as virtue" (VII.86.5). The two chief interlocutors of the *Charmides*, on the other hand, are associated with the darkest period in Athenian history, the tyranny of the Thirty. Both Critias and Charmides were counted among the Thirty, and Critias is described by Xenophon as "the greediest and most violent and most murderous of them all."[2] It seems exceedingly strange for Plato to have chosen such a companion to discuss with Socrates the topic of *sōphrosunē*, the virtue that typically implies restraint, modesty, and self-control!

The dramatic framework of this dialogue is constructed with unusual care. The *Charmides* may be Plato's first narrated dialogue. It is also one of the very few dialogues (other than those which refer to the trial and death of Socrates) to which Plato has assigned a precise fictive date, since it opens with a reference to the battle of Potidaea in 432 BC.[3] The choice of interlocutors probably explains this precision in dating: Plato wants to present Critias as a relatively young man who has not yet begun his sinister political career,[4] and to show Charmides as a modest teenager of unlimited promise.

But what explains the choice of interlocutors? Unlike Xenophon, who is eager to defend Socrates against the charge of having corrupted Critias and Alcibiades, Plato seems to go out of his way to

2. *Mem.* 1.2.12.
3. Thucydides 1.63. The dating of the *Charmides* is not only fictive but apparently fictitious as well, since Socrates cannot have returned to Athens shortly after the battle (as the dialogue claims at 153B 5). Plato has forgotten or simply ignored the fact that the battle of Potidaea occurred at the beginning rather than at the end of the long siege. For Socrates' presence there during the siege, see *Charmides* 156D and *Symposium* 219Eff. Compare Gomme (1945) 219.

    Aside from those dialogues that are dated by Socrates' trial and death, perhaps only the *Symposium* has a comparably precise date, given by Agathon's first victory in 416 BC. As in the *Charmides*, the motive for precise dating is connected with the biography of the interlocutors. Plato wants to present Alcibiades at the summit of his political career, a year before the Sicilian expedition and the scandal of the Hermae.
4. Although implicated in the desecration of the Hermae in 415 BC, Critias seems not to have been active in politics until after the oligarchic revolution of 411. See Ostwald (1986) 403, 428, 462–5. It is significant that Socrates is led personally to Critias by Chaerephon (153C 6), who was later to be found among the democratic exiles when Critias was in power (*Apology* 21A). The dialogue takes place in a happier, more harmonious social world.

depict Socrates on terms of intimate friendship with both men. Presumably that was in fact the case, but the fact itself does not explain Plato's literary motivation. His treatment of Alcibiades is much easier to understand, since the latter's friendship with Socrates was also a familiar theme in the writings of Antisthenes and Aeschines. But the focus on Critias and Charmides here, and on Socrates' close relationship to both, calls out for some explanation.

In the first place, Plato may have intended a deliberate counterpart to the *Laches*. There courage is analyzed by two brave generals who died fighting for their city; here *sōphrosunē* is discussed by two men whose later career showed that they conspicuously *lacked* this virtue, and who died fighting against their countrymen for their own personal power. There seems to be a quiet allusion to the tyrannical future of these men in their bantering reference to using force rather than persuasion on Socrates (176C–D; cf. 156A 3).

But perhaps the plainest clue points in a different direction, to Plato's pride in his own family. Charmides is introduced as son of Glaucon (154B 1), who is Plato's maternal grandfather. So Charmides is Plato's uncle, his mother's brother, and Critias is his mother's first cousin (and hence Charmides' guardian, *epitropos* 155A 6). When Socrates says that Charmides must have a naturally noble soul "since he belongs to your family" (154E 2), the family in question is Plato's.[5] The case is the same when Socrates compliments Charmides on the grounds that "no other Athenian could easily show a union of two such families as would be likely to produce better and finer offspring" (157E). The two families are, on the one hand, the family of Critias, Charmides, and Plato's mother, which was praised by many poets for being "outstanding in beauty and virtue and in what is called happiness"; on the other hand there is Charmides' uncle Pyrilampes, an associate of Pericles and

5. As Burnet recognized, "The opening scene of the *Charmides* is a glorification of the whole [family] connection ... [Plato's] dialogues are not only a memorial to Socrates, but also to the happier days of his own family." Burnet (1964) 169f.

The self-reference to Plato's family continues when Socrates tells Critias that the love of poetry and learning derives "from your kinship with Solon" (155A 3). See Witte (1970) 51, who emphasizes a possible parallel between Charmides and Plato himself. I doubt, however, that Plato means to correct the popular condemnation of the tyrant (as Witte suggests, p. 49). The character portrayal of Critias here shows signs of the vanity, ambition, and intellectual dishonesty that will lead to his moral downfall (162C, 169C 2–D 1).

Athenian ambassador to the Great King, who is said to have been as tall and handsome as any man at the Persian Court (157E–158A). But Pyrilampes is Plato's stepfather and his great-uncle. So the two families joined in such an auspicious union to produce Charmides are in fact the same two families that were joined in Plato's own household, first by the union between his maternal grand-parents and again by his mother's second marriage.[6]

We can only speculate as to what Plato's deep feelings were in regard to Critias and Charmides.[7] What we know from the text is that the choice of these interlocutors permits Plato to elaborate on the fame and distinction of his own family and its connections by marriage. (And when Critias reappears much later in the *Timaeus*, it is once again to emphasize Plato's ancestral connections with Solon; *Timaeus* 20D–21D.) To this extent, the presence of Critias and Charmides serves as a kind of personal signature, super-imposed upon the anonymity of the Socratic dialogue form, just as the presence of his two brothers as principal interlocutors imprints Plato's signature on the *Republic*. The conspicuous self-reference in the prologue to the *Charmides* suggests that this too must be a work in which Plato takes an unusually personal interest.

The dramatic framework is important in another respect. The portrait of Charmides as a gifted young nobleman is lovingly drawn, and the physical impact of his beauty on Socrates leads to one of the most vivid expressions of erotic emotion in Greek literature.

Then, my noble friend, I had a view of what lay inside his clothes and I was set on fire and no longer master of myself. And I thought how wise Cydias was in matters of love, who said in advising someone on the sub-ject of a handsome boy "to take care lest, like a fawn in front of a lion, he provide a meal for the beast." It seemed to me that I had fallen victim to a wild animal of this sort. (155D)

This episode prefigures the topic of the dialogue by exhibiting Socrates' subsequent success in regaining his self-control, whereas

6. See Davies (1971) 329f.
7. For some plausible insight into Plato's sympathy for the corrupted talent of men like Critias and Alcibiades, see Jaeger (1944) English tr. 267–71, compar-ing *Republic* VI, 494–6. The portrait of Charmides is particularly suggestive. The capacity for virtue may be inborn, as the aristocratic tradition believed, but how it develops will depend upon moral education, and in this case upon the baneful influence of Charmides' *epitropos*.

Critias is later shown to lose his self-restraint when his proposed
definition is subjected to ridicule (162c–d).

We should not miss the philosophic significance of Plato's depiction of the disruptive impact of sensual emotion upon Socrates
in his glimpse of Charmides' private parts, and the consequent
effort required for him to regain rational control (156d). Like the
emphasis on steadfastness (*karteria*) in the *Laches*, this dramatic presentation of the moral emotions stands in what seems to be a deliberate contrast with the "intellectualist" tendency in both dialogues to identify virtue with some form of knowledge. Whatever
the speakers in these two dialogues may imply, the author of the
Charmides and *Laches* is certainly attentive to the importance of the
emotions in any full account of the moral life.[8]

3. THE DEFINITION OF *SŌPHROSUNĒ*

The conversation with Charmides begins with two naive but serious attempts to define the virtue in question: first in terms of external behavior, "doing everything decorously and quietly" (159b),
and then in terms of moral feeling: *sōphrosunē* is "what makes one
feel bashful or ashamed; it is like shame or respect" (*aidōs*, 160e 4).
From the point of view of Greek moral consciousness, both suggestions are on the right track.[9] *Sōphrosunē* means many things, but
above all a sense of what is proper and fitting; hence it denotes
chastity in women and decency and self-restraint in men.

Charmides has just displayed the modesty that is appropriate
for a young man in the company of his elders, by blushing when
he was asked about his own *sōphrosunē* and avoiding anything that
might resemble self-praise (158c 5–d 6). His second answer in
terms of shame or modesty is thus an accurate reading of what he
sees in himself as temperance (to accept, from here on, the standard rendering of *sōphrosunē*). But just as in the conversation with

---

8. Note the reference to *epithumia*, desire for pleasure, *boulēsis* as desire for good,
and *erōs* as desire for the beautiful, at *Charmides* 167e. This elaborates the embryonic discussion of the moral emotions found in the *Gorgias*. Notice that the
hyper-intellectual account of temperance in the *Charmides* is exceptional. Plato
normally associates *sōphrosunē* with the control of pleasure and the appetites;
e.g. *Gorgias* 491d 10, *Phaedo* 68c, *Philebus* 45d–e, *Laws* IV, 710a

9. In the myth recounted by Protagoras, *aidōs* or shame corresponds to *sōphrosunē*
(*Prot.* 322c 2, 323a 2).

Laches on courage, so here too with Charmides on temperance, Socrates is less interested in constructing a satisfactory account of the virtue than in bringing his interlocutor to reflect critically on a concept he has heretofore taken for granted. So by means of an arbitrary quotation from Homer Socrates shows that shame is not necessarily a good thing, whereas it has been taken as agreed that temperance is both admirable (*kalon* 159C) and good (*agathon* 160E).[10]

Charmides' second definition is thus speedily dispatched. Socrates had treated his first proposal with more respect; the refutation there takes the form of a regular *epagōgē*, although it is equally superficial in regard to the substance of the matter.[11] The serious point in both cases is that neither external behavior nor subjective feeling provides a reliable basis for identifying a moral virtue like temperance. Both action and feeling may be misguided. What is needed is a correct sense of what is appropriate, and that entails some kind of knowledge or insight. To this extent the movement of the argument here will be the same as in the *Laches, Protagoras, Euthydemus,* and *Meno*: to bring to light the decisive role of knowledge or correct judgment in the exercise of virtue.

In this case, however, instead of proceeding directly to the concept of knowledge the discussion takes a more devious course, by way of a third definition that Charmides remembers having heard from someone else: temperance is "doing one's own thing," *ta heautou prattein* (161B 6). Readers of the *Republic* will recognize this as Plato's formula for justice, and the political implications of this passage will be discussed below in § 8. The immediate effect of introducing this third definition is to draw Critias into the conversation, since he is apparently its author and now becomes its defender; he will remain Socrates' interlocutor for the rest of the dialogue.

10. Something seems to be wrong with the text at 160E 11. The argument needs to show that σωφροσύνη is not only καλόν but also ἀγαθόν (160E 13), presumably because it makes men ἀγαθοί. Van der Ben (1985: 30) tries to find this argument in the received text. For an attempt to amend the text accordingly, see Bloch (1973) 65 n. 18.

11. Socrates' first refutation ignores Charmides' mention of *kosmiōs panta prattein*, "doing everything in a decorous manner" and limits the attack to the attribute of quietness (*hēsuchiotēs*), arbitrarily interpreted as slowness. Socrates' initial interpretation of "doing one's own thing" at 161D–162A is similarly perverse. (But for a more positive development of the notion of *sōphrosunē* as quietness and slowness, see *Statesman* 307Aff.)

The conversation with Critias begins with some rather sophistical wordplay on Critias' part concerning the difference between doing (*prattein*) and making (*poiein*), which results in a revised definition. Since what is one's own (*oikeia*) is good and beneficial, whereas what is alien (*allotria*) is bad and harmful, temperance is doing good things and not doing bad things (163E). This construal of the good as what is proper or one's own (*to oikeion*), which is closely connected with the notion of virtue as "doing what is one's own," is a conception that we will meet elsewhere in the dialogues, notably in the *Lysis* and *Symposium*.[12] But nothing more is made of it here.

It is at this point that Socrates introduces the question of knowledge. Must the temperate person know what he or she is doing? If someone does good things in ignorance, is that temperance (164B–c)? If the conversation were fully under Socrates' control, we can suppose that his next move might be to add knowledge to action: temperance would be knowing and doing what is good, knowing and avoiding what is bad. This would lead directly to a formula involving the knowledge of good and bad, like the definition that is suggested but formally abandoned at the end of the dialogue.

Critias, however, is not an interlocutor that Socrates can so easily control, and he bounds off in a new direction. Certainly not, says Critias, temperance is not acting in ignorance, and if this follows from anything I have said "I would gladly recognize my error rather than admit that a person who is self-ignorant can be temperate. For I claim that this is practically what temperance is, to know oneself" (164D). Critias then proceeds to expatiate on the significance of the Delphic inscription, "Know thyself," which he takes to be the god's command to those who enter his temple: "Be temperate!" So Socrates' question about acting in ignorance has, in effect, led Critias to replace his earlier definition "doing one's own thing, doing what belongs to oneself," with an entirely new formula: "knowing one's own self."[13]

12. See below, pp. 266 and 290f.
13. Critias' shift to τὸ γιγνώσκειν ἑαυτόν at 164D 4 was carefully prepared by Socrates' repeated use of the reflexive idiom ὁ ἰατρὸς οὐ γιγνώσκει ἑαυτὸν ὡς ἔπραξεν "the doctor does not recognize what he has himself done" at 164C 1, and similarly at 164C 6: ἀγνοεῖ δ' ἑαυτὸν ὅτι σωφρονεῖ "he doesn't know that he is being temperate," which Critias takes to mean "the person who is temperate does not know himself." (Compare Tuckey [1951] 23f.)

What is going on here? This is the first of several unexpected shifts of direction in this dialogue that make the *Charmides* one of the more puzzling of Plato's works. The search for moral knowledge, which is characteristic of so many threshold dialogues, here takes a reflexive turn to *self-knowledge* that loses all contact with the ordinary meaning of *sōphrosunē* and with Charmides' earlier attempts to define it.

The transition is made possible by the fact that the Delphic "Know thyself" admits two distinct readings: (1) know that you are a mortal and not a god, acknowledge your limitations and your place in the world, and (2) know your own ignorance, recognize that you lack wisdom. The first, more general reading corresponds to one traditional understanding of *sōphrosunē*, and this explains the enthusiasm with which Critias immediately endorses the new definition.[14] But the second, epistemic reading is more specifically Socratic; it corresponds exactly to the interpretation given by Socrates in the *Apology* of the oracle that declared no one wiser than he. In the remainder of the *Charmides* it is Socrates' strategy to impose this "Socratic" interpretation on Critias' Delphic formula. The formula itself is one that Plato in a later work will combine with "doing one's own thing" in a motto that sounds proverbial: "it was well said long ago that to know oneself and do what is one's own belongs to him alone who is temperate (*sōphrōn*)" (*Timaeus* 72A). In the *Charmides*, however, doing is almost forgotten; and from here on knowing will be the topic under discussion. In effect, temperance in the ordinary sense drops out of sight.

4. THE ELENCHUS OF CRITIAS AND THE CRITIQUE OF *EPAGŌGĒ*

Socrates begins by refusing to agree with Critias' proposal until they have investigated it, "because I myself do not know" (165B 8). This avowal of ignorance serves delicately to prepare us for the argument to come, which will focus on the Socratic undertaking to know "what one knows and what one does not know." First, however, the dialogue will survey the problems of reflexive knowledge.

Critias' abrupt shift to the new formula demonstrates his intellectual versatility, not to say slipperiness, and his lack of serious commitment to the earlier definition.

14. See Tuckey (1951) 9ff. and North (1966).

The elenchus of Critias' definition falls into three parts: 1. An initial exchange designed to clarify (and give a distinctively Socratic twist to) the concept of self-knowledge (165C–167A). 2. The question of possibility: can there be knowledge of knowledge? (167B–169D) 3. The question of utility: even if such knowledge is possible, how would it be beneficial? (171D–175E). Between parts 2 and 3 comes the philosophical center of the dialogue: the argument for the very limited content of knowledge of knowledge, even granting its possibility (169D–171C). It is at this point that the dialogue becomes most self-reflective: here Socrates himself examines the possibility of Socratic self-knowledge. Part 1 will be treated in this section, parts 2 and 3 in the sections that follow.

Socrates begins by asking what self-knowledge is knowledge *of*, and what product (*ergon*) does it provide?[15] Medicine provides health, house-building provides houses; what does self-knowledge produce? But Critias challenges the comparison: "Socrates, you are not proceeding correctly. These sciences are not similar to one another, but you are treating them as alike." (Here and in what follows, the plural *epistēmai* will for simplicity be rendered "sciences" rather than "kinds of knowledge.") Calculation and geometry do not provide a product, unlike house-building or weaving (165E).

We are reminded of a similar reference to calculation and geometry as non-productive sciences in the *Gorgias* (450D–457C). And again as in the *Gorgias*, Socrates asks next about the subject matter: although it has no product, calculation (*logistikē*) has a subject matter distinct from itself, the odd and the even; weight-measuring is concerned with the heavy and light. What is the distinct subject of the knowledge that is temperance? Again Critias challenges the assumption of uniformity on which Socrates' use of *epagōgē* is built: "You are looking for a similarity between temperance and the others. But this is just the point at which it differs from all the rest ... Temperance alone is knowledge both of the other sciences and of itself" (166B 7–C 3). And Critias accuses Socrates of foul play: he is seeking to refute his interlocutor rather than to clarify the topic.

---

15. Notice that Plato here supplements the principle of the *Ion* and *Gorgias*, that a *technē* is individuated by its subject matter, with the additional principle that to each capacity or competence corresponds a specific product or function (*ergon*). These two principles are combined and reformulated at *Rep.* v, 477D.

This gives Socrates one more opportunity to advertise his ignorance: his only motive in asking questions is the fear that he may,
unwittingly, think he knows something that he does not know
(166D 1). And so, when Critias restates his account of temperance
as "the only knowledge that knows both itself and all other sciences (*epistēmai*)," Socrates innocently asks: "and is it knowledge of
ignorance as well?" (166E 7).

Critias sees no problem in agreeing to this; and it is of course a
standing Socratic-Platonic assumption that the knowledge of opposites is one and the same.[16] In this case, however, the addition
of ignorance makes possible the crucial move to a Socratic interpretation of Critias' formula:

So the temperate person will be the only one to know himself and be
able to examine what he knows and what he does not; and he will be
similarly capable of inspecting others, to see what someone knows and
thinks he knows, if he does know anything, and what on the other hand
he thinks he knows but does not know. (167A)

And so we get the new reading for "to know oneself": to know
what you know and what you do not know.[17] Temperance is now
explicitly modeled on what Socrates in the *Apology* acknowledges
as his only claim to wisdom: the recognition of his own ignorance.

In the rest of the dialogue the discussion oscillates between this
personal reading of self-knowledge (knowing what you know and
what you do not) and the more abstract reading: "knowledge of
knowledge." In some contexts the abstract formula seems to function simply as a variant for the personal construction. Critias is
quite clear about this when he says: "when someone has beauty,
he is beautiful; when he has knowledge, he knows; and when he
has self-knowledge [literally, knowledge of itself] he knows himself" (169E). This means taking the abstract formula of *self-knowledge* (*epistēmē heautēs*) as if it were simply the nominalized transform
for *knowing oneself*, understood here Socratically as *knowing what one
knows*. And it is this Socratic reading of the personal form *knowing
oneself* that prevails throughout the later sections of the dialogue.

16. See, e.g. *Phaedo* 97D 5.
17. 157A 5–7. This final version of Critias' formula is greeted with the invocation
"the third (libation) to the saviour," i.e. to Zeus Soter, the first two versions
being (1) doing one's own as doing good things (163E 10), and (2) the Delphic
"know thyself" (164D 3-165A 1). Similarly Van der Ben (1985) 50.

But several passages analyze the concept of *knowledge of knowledge* in a way that does not lend itself to the conversion into personal form. And this ambiguity is one of the features that makes the *Charmides* such a puzzling work.[18]

Before proceeding to the second stage of the elenchus, we note two important methodological points made in this first part. In the first place Critias succeeds in blocking Socrates' use of *epagōgē* by twice challenging the tacit assumption of similarity on which the argument from analogy must rely. If this tactic had been available to Charmides earlier in the dialogue or to Laches in the dialogue named after him, they could have parried the moves by which Socrates refuted their definition. It is not simply that Critias is a more skillful dialectician, though of course he is. The point is that the author of the *Charmides* has now made the reader aware of the weakness of any argument from *epagōgē*, in its implicit assumption of relevant similarity between the cases cited and the item under dispute.[19] The reader may now expect greater rigor in the method of argumentation. And the second point responds in part to these expectations. Socrates carefully distinguishes two separate questions to be pursued in the elenchus: (1) is it possible for someone to know what he knows and what he does not know? and (2) if it is possible, what benefit will there be for us to have this knowledge? (167B, restated at 169B).[20] To the decline of confidence in the inductive argument from analogy corresponds greater care and flexibility in identifying the premises assumed in deductive reasoning.

5. THE POSSIBILITY OF KNOWLEDGE-OF-KNOWLEDGE (*CHARMIDES* 167B–169A)

The analysis of possibility divides into two parts, separated by the interlude at 169C–D where Critias is described as succumbing to the contagion of Socrates' *aporia*, like a man who begins to yawn

18. For various theories on the relationship between *knowing oneself* and *knowledge of knowledge*, see Tuckey (1951) 33–7 and 109ff., with commentators cited there.
19. Compare the criticism of this form of argument by Eucleides of Megara; above, p. 14.
20. We have again an anticipation of *Republic* v, where questions of possibility and benefit are systematically distinguished (452Eff., 456C, etc.) See below, pp. 204f.

when he sees another yawning. The first part analyzes the possibility of knowledge-of-knowledge taken abstractly, as part of a general theory of reflexive relations. The second part deals specifically with the concept of self-knowledge taken Socratically, as knowing what you know and what you do not know.

The general discussion of the possibility of knowledge-of-knowledge is philosophically the most technical stretch of the dialogue. We have here the first attempt at a systematic exploration of the logic of relative terms, with the aim of determining which relations can be reflexive, which not. Plato does not develop any general theory, but he raises a number of fundamental problems.

1. The first objection to the concept of a knowledge that takes as object only itself and other sciences is an *epagōgē* of the parallel concepts of perception, desire, and opinion. Socrates points out that each of these intentional states will take something distinct from itself as an object. Vision does not see itself without seeing color, hearing does not hear itself without hearing sound. Appetite (*epithumia*) is of pleasure; rational wanting (*boulēsis*) is of the good; *erōs* is of the beautiful. These perceptions and desires are all object-directed; and similarly for fear and opinion. Such parallels strongly suggest that the same must be true for knowledge. But now that the logical limitations of *epagōgē* have been pointed out, Socrates draws only a probable conclusion: "We cannot be sure there is no such thing, but it would be strange" if there were knowledge such that it had no content (*mathēma*) other than itself and other sciences (168A 6–11).

2. Consider correlatives. If A is by its very meaning (*dunamis*) related to B, as *greater* is to *lesser*, then if A is reflexive, i.e. is related to itself as it is related to B, then it must also have the nature (*ousia*) of B. For quantitative relations (other than equality) this is impossible. One thing cannot be both greater and smaller than itself, any more than it can be double or half of itself. By citing such examples Plato in effect recognizes the existence of irreflexive relations (168B 5–D 3, E 5–8).

3. In other cases the relation may be reflexive, but only if the first term has the nature of the second: if hearing has sound, it can hear itself; and if vision has color, it can see itself. But not otherwise.[21] Concerning these relations, and others such as self-moving

---

21. This is the problem discussed and resolved by Aristotle in *De Anima* III.2.

and self-heating, Socrates makes no decision: he only recognizes the magnitude of the problem: "It would take a great man[22] to draw these distinctions adequately in every case, and to determine whether anything has its relation (*dunamis*) to itself or only to something else, or whether some do and some do not; and, if there are some things which are self-related, whether knowledge is among them" (169A).

We have here the beginnings of a technical terminology for the theory of relations, a sample of professional philosophy even more advanced than the treatment of extensional relations in the *Euthyphro* and *Meno*, and a hint, perhaps, as in the second part of the *Parmenides*, of the kind of questions that specialists might be studying in the Academy.

At all events Socrates does not feel competent to decide such matters, and Critias is clearly out of his depth. So a new method of inquiry is needed. Let us *assume* that knowledge of knowledge is possible, not only in the abstract case (169D 3) but also concretely: that a person can have self-knowledge (169E 4–7). Does that mean that someone can know *what he knows and what he does not know*? This brings us back to the Socratic reading.

Before we follow this reading, however, we must take notice of the subtle innovation introduced into the mode of reasoning. What we have here is a kind of conditional argument that is comparable in principle to the method of hypothesis encountered in the *Meno*. (See Chapter 10 § 6.) Since we cannot solve a problem directly, we simplify it by making an assumption, that is, by accepting a proposition provisionally, with the intention of returning later to see whether the proposition conditionally assumed deserves to be accepted. So we take for granted, for the moment, that it is possible to have reflexive knowledge, including knowledge of self, in order to explore the implications of such an assumption. This is the first of a series of provisional assumptions that will be carefully tabulated at the conclusion of the dialogue (175B 4–D 2).

---

22. There is a parallel to the "great man" needed here to resolve the problem of reflexive properties in *Parmenides* 135A, where it would take "a man of much talent (πάνυ εὐφυής)" to unravel problems in the theory of Forms. I see this as a figure of speech rather than as a tasteless self-reference on Plato's part, as some commentators have proposed (*pace* Szlezák (1985) 138f., citing Witte and Bloch); cf. Erler (1987) 191f.

6. THE POSSIBILITY OF SOCRATIC SELF-KNOWLEDGE
(169E–171C)

Assuming that one can know oneself, does that mean that a person can know *what* he (or she) knows and *what* he does not know? Critias does not see the problem (170A), and Socrates is forced to explain, as so often when an important new idea is introduced. Knowledge of what one knows may be unproblematic, but what about knowledge of one's ignorance? (170A 3). The careful argument that follows is designed to show that second-order knowledge, the knowledge only of knowledge as Critias has defined it, would be empty and pointless without first-order knowledge, the mastery of a definite subject. For it is the subject matter that distinguishes one science from another, as medicine is knowledge of health and disease, and the political art (*politikē*) is knowledge of what is just.[23] So if the temperate man is possessed only of second-order knowledge, but denied first-order knowledge of a particular subject matter such as health or justice, he may perhaps know that he knows something. But he cannot possibly know *what* he knows or *what* he does not know, since he cannot distinguish one science from another. So we must give up the Socratic version of self-knowledge as knowing *what* one knows and *what* one is ignorant of (170C 9–D 2).

This conclusion has serious consequences for the Socratic enterprise of testing the wisdom of others. How can one distinguish a good doctor from a quack unless one knows some medicine oneself? Socrates rather generously admits that a second-order knowledge-of-knowledge might permit the examiner to recognize that a doctor knows something, but it would not permit him to determine what sort of knowledge the doctor has. So in general if temperance is knowledge-of-knowledge alone, it will not equip someone to distinguish experts from false pretenders in any field, unless the temperate person happens *also* to be an expert in that field himself (171C). According to this argument, Socrates' avowal of ignorance,

23. 170B 3. Note the echo of (or parallel to) *Gorgias* 464B 4–8, 510A 4, 521D 7, where *politikē technē* is knowledge of what is just, as medicine is knowledge of what is healthy.

Again taken for granted here is the principle of individuation for arts and sciences, familiar from the *Ion* and the *Gorgias*, alluded to earlier at *Charmides* 166A–B and formally restated at 171A 5–6.

repeated so conspicuously in what precedes, is problematic in two ways. How can he know what he is ignorant *of*? And how can he test any pretensions to knowledge unless he himself possesses the kind of expertise that is in question? If the argument here is correct, or if Plato thought it was, then there is serious trouble in store for Socrates' quest for wisdom as depicted in the *Apology*.[24]

How good is this argument? Or how good did Plato think it was? First of all, there is some doubt whether the notion of second-order knowledge without first-order content is defensible at all. Does it correspond to epistemology, perhaps, or to something like philosophy of science? The dialogue is repeatedly non-committal on this point (169A, D, 175B 6–7); this is apparently not the focal issue for Plato. But assuming the possibility of such second-order knowledge, the preceding argument must be evaluated with regard to four difference cases:

1. X knows that he possesses the knowledge of F (e.g. of medicine).
2. X knows that he does not possess the knowledge of F.
3. X knows that Y possesses the knowledge of F.
4. X knows that Y does not possess the knowledge of F.

The first case, knowledge of one's own first-order knowledge, is not paradoxical, and is implicitly allowed for in the argument at 170B 6–7. (See also 172B.) Plato is careful (at 170A 2–4) to distinguish this from the second case, which he explicitly represents as incoherent: "it is impossible to know somehow or other what one does not know at all" (175C 5).

Here we might suppose that Plato is exploiting, or is victim of, an ambiguity of reference of the type that we have analyzed in Chapter 6 §4. For I really can know *of* some subject F *that* I am ignorant of F. Thus without knowing quantum mechanics I can know enough *about* quantum mechanics to know that I am ignorant of it. Of course I must know *something* about it besides the name, or I could not be sure of my ignorance; I cannot be wholly

24. Plato's deliberate reference here to the Socratic elenchus as described in the *Apology* is guaranteed not only by the repeated claim to ignorance (165B 8, cf. 166D 2) but by the recurrence of the characteristically Socratic term for examining opinions, *exetasai* at 167A 2, 170D 5, 172B 6–7. Compare *Apology* 22D 6, 23C 4–5, 38A 5, 41B 5. So correctly Pohlenz (1913) 53f. See also Tuckey (1951) 66: "Socrates was invalidating his own claims, if the argument was sound."

ignorant of the subject. So the argument is not without a point even in this case. Knowing one's ignorance of subject F implies *some* first-order knowledge of F after all.[25] But it is above all to cases 3 and 4, to the Socratic enterprise of examining his interlocutors for their knowledge or ignorance, that the argument seems cogent. I cannot test the credentials of an alleged expert in quantum mechanics or computer science unless I know quite a lot about the subject in question. Of course I can rely on the judgment of others, i.e. of his peers. But that is not relevant either to the argument or to the Socratic enterprise as represented in the dialogues. By asking the generals in the *Laches* to say what courage is, Socrates is explicitly presenting this question as a test of their credentials as experts in virtue (*Laches* 189D 5–190C). This use of the *what-is-X?* question as a test of expert knowledge may be, as I have argued, a peculiarity of the Platonic Socrates. But there is no doubt that it is a development from the personal elenchus on questions of virtue that is characteristic of the historical Socrates.

It seems, then, that for cases 3 and 4 the argument is sound: one cannot test the credentials of others in regard to a subject in which the tester himself lacks expertise. If this conclusion is correct, or if Plato thought it was, the implications for Socratic self-knowledge are considerable. Before pursuing these implications, we need to consider two possible objections to the argument.

One objection will invoke the practice of the dialogues to deny the conclusion. What permits Socrates to refute Laches, Nicias, Euthyphro, and Meno (as well as Charmides and Critias) is not his mastery of the theory and teaching of virtue but his elenctic expertise: his skill in pursuing the consequences of an interlocutor's thesis and exposing the latent contradictions. The Socrates of these dialogues is an expert in the art of the elenchus, not in the knowledge of what virtue is or how it is produced. For the latter is precisely the kind of wisdom of which he consistently claims to be deprived.

I think that this objection fails to respond to the thesis of the argument, namely, that knowledge is essentially defined by its subject matter. In the relevant sense of *technē*, there is no such thing as

---

25. See the distinction drawn above (pp. 159ff.) between weak and strong senses of "to know." The weak sense is applicable here, but not to the cases that follow.

elenctic knowledge. There is only knowledge of medicine, knowledge of housebuilding, knowledge of good and bad, including knowledge of virtue. For an examiner to show that someone lacks expertise in any of these fields, the examiner himself (or herself) must possess the expertise in question. This obliges us to ask ourselves what is really going on in the aporetic dialogues, when Socrates exposes his interlocutors' ignorance. We cannot take for granted that something like elenctic expertise, the logical critique of knowledge claims, validates Socrates' performance in these dialogues. For that is precisely what the argument of *Charmides* 169E–171C calls into question.

A more promising objection relies on the fundamental distinction between moral knowledge and technical knowledge, a distinction that is implicit in the paradox of the *Hippias Minor* and developed at length in the *Gorgias* and the *Protagoras*.[26] For technical subjects such as medicine and quantum mechanics, it is true that only an expert can expose a bogus claim to expertise. But the analogy for knowledge of virtue fails precisely because of this fundamental discrepancy. As Protagoras will point out, the basic moral virtues are something that *everyone* must have, at least to a minimal degree. So everyone is at least a potential expert in the area of good and bad. Hence Socrates can rely on the interlocutor's intuitions, and on his own, to expose ignorance and confusion on matters of moral excellence, without any claim to special expertise.

This objection does more justice to what actually occurs in the dialogues. In effect, it takes account of the universal human moral sense that we have recognized in the *Gorgias* as the deep desire for the good. (See above, pp. 138–47.) But the *Gorgias* itself insists that this is a subject matter that requires a *technē*. And the *Laches*, like the *Charmides*, goes in search of the *technē* that corresponds to the knowledge of good and bad. So this objection fails to take account of the fact that the issue is one of knowledge. How can one *know* what someone else knows or does not know? Can one judge competence in a *technē* that one does not possess?

The historical Socrates never claimed to possess such a *technē*. But the Socrates of the *Charmides* is arguing that without a *technē* in virtue, one cannot expose anyone's ignorance in matters of good and bad, matters of virtue. One can only test one's own colleagues

26. See Chapter 8 §2.

(*homotechnoi*), those who are experts or alleged experts in the same field (171c 6).

What are the implications for the Socratic elenchus? One implication might be that, if Socrates can test his interlocutors for temperance, he must himself be temperate. But that is scarcely surprising; and it is in any case independently indicated by his behavior in the prologue, his self-control in response to Charmides' charms (155Dff.). The more significant implication is that Socrates cannot successfully test for knowledge in any subject in which he is himself ignorant. So his claim here and elsewhere to have only second-order wisdom, the knowledge of his own ignorance, cannot be taken at face value.

It is appropriate, then, to see the Socrates of the *Charmides* as reflecting critically on the Socrates of the *Apology*. Insofar as Socrates undertakes to expose the ignorance of others in a matter where he disavows knowledge, either the elenchus must be fraudulent or the disavowal must be ironical and in some sense insincere. The elenchus will be fraudulent if it relies only on dialectical tricks, on Socrates outwitting his interlocutors by extracting ambiguous premises to which they are not actually committed. (This is the method so deliciously depicted in the *Euthydemus*. One function of that dialogue is surely to make plain that Socratic dialectic, despite occasional lapses, is really not like that. See Chapter 10 § 8.) Insofar as the Socratic elenchus is a successful technique for revealing ignorance in the interlocutors, Socrates must himself possess the relevant sort of first-order knowledge. Or so the argument of *Charmides* 170A–171c clearly implies.

What is the knowledge that Socrates possesses and that his interlocutors generally lack? The final section of the dialogue provides us with the needed clue. If he successfully examines his fellow Athenians concerning virtue and the good life, Socrates must himself know something about human excellence and, more generally, something about what is good and what is bad. He must possess the kind of knowledge that is beneficial for human beings and that makes for a happy life.

In the *Apology* any claim to such knowledge remains hidden behind the ironic mask of ignorance. What the *Charmides* shows is that this ostensibly modest claim only to second-order wisdom, knowledge of one's ignorance, cannot be the whole story. The success of Socrates' elenchus (in the dialogues, at least, and perhaps in real life) presupposes his own possession of the relevant form of knowledge or expertise.

Surprisingly few commentators have recognized that this argument constitutes a serious critique of the Socratic avowal of ignorance. One recent writer who does recognize this sees Plato as here indicating the limitations of the Socratic elenchus as a philosophical method.[27] This may be correct in the sense that Plato is here systematically expanding his own repertory of argumentative techniques. But this need not be seen as an attempt on Plato's part to distance himself from the historical Socrates. It is an essential feature of the Socratic dialogue form, for Plato as for other Socratic authors, that the *persona* of Socrates enjoys an independent life, free from any historical or chronological limitations. So here it is Socrates "in person" who criticizes the Socratic avowal of ignorance.

By this device Plato is not so much criticizing Socrates as endowing him with the full prerogatives of the true (i.e. the Platonic) philosopher, who is here prepared to go beyond the negative elenchus and the argument from analogy in order to explore new techniques of analysis and argumentation. In this respect the critique of Socratic self-knowledge in the *Charmides* points in the same direction as the comments on *aporia* in the *Meno*. (See Chapter 6 §7.) The philosopher who (like Plato, and hence like the Platonic Socrates) wants to take an inquiry beyond the stage of *aporia* and ignorance to genuine, positive knowledge, must give up the avowal of ignorance and presume to be a *technikos*.

If I may hazard a guess as to Plato's own thoughts in the matter, I suggest that he ultimately regarded his own theory as providing the necessary foundation for the moral and intellectual stance of the historical Socrates. In this sense, Platonic metaphysics and epistemology can be seen as Plato's answer to the question: what kind of knowledge is logically required for the success of the Socratic elenchus described in the *Apology*? The critique of Socratic ignorance in the *Charmides* seems carefully designed to make clear that, for Plato, this is a question that requires an answer. The answer is not, of course, intended to imply that Socrates historically possessed such knowledge. Rather, Plato's own theory can be seen as his attempt to provide for the world, and for himself, a coherent

27. McKim (1985) 59–77.

account of what kind of knowledge would be required for full competence in the search for moral wisdom that Socrates had begun.

7. SOCRATES' DREAM: WHAT SORT OF KNOWLEDGE WILL BE BENEFICIAL?

As we know from the *Gorgias*, from the *Republic* and from the *Laws*, for Plato the theory of virtue is a topic not only in ethics but also in politics. The true art of politics, *politikē*, is the art of moral education, as the *Gorgias* insists. When virtue and education are discussed in the *Laches* and *Charmides*, the political theme remains in the background, but it is dramatically represented by the choice of interlocutors: the future tyrants in one case, the distinguished generals and the sons of even more distinguished statesmen in the other. Like the young Hippocrates in the *Protagoras*, what the fathers in the *Laches* want for their sons is a form of training that will prepare them to play an outstanding role in the affairs of the city. The polis, and the political life, is the natural habitat for *aretē*.

In the *Charmides* the political theme makes its first appearance when temperance is defined as "doing what is one's own" (161Bff.). We know that this will be Plato's formula for justice in the *Republic*. The first readers of the *Charmides* can scarcely have known this, but they too will be able to see that the formula has political implications: " 'Do you think that a city will be well governed by this law which commands each one to weave and wash his own cloak, to make his own shoes, and so forth?' ... 'I don't think so,' he replied. 'However,' I said, 'a city which is governed temperately will be governed well?' 'Of course' " (161E 11). This argument serves to *exclude*, by means of ridicule, the frivolous interpretation of "doing one's own thing" as a ban on the division of labor; and hence it is quite compatible with the passages in the *Republic* that employ the same phrase to impose just such a division (II, 369B–372A, IV, 433A–D).

From our point of view, this passage in the *Charmides* looks like a playful allusion to the doctrine of justice in the *Republic* (where the reference to weaver and shoemaker will recur, at II, 369Dff.). But given our conviction that the *Charmides* (like all dialogues in Group I) was written first, we can say that Plato is here toying with an idea that he will put to serious work in his major political dialogue. And more parallels to the *Republic* will emerge in a moment.

The political theme returns in the final section of the *Charmides*, after Socrates has shown that knowledge-of-knowledge as understood by Critias, without first-order subject matter, would only permit its possessor to recognize *that* he (or someone else) is or is not knowledgeable, but would not enable him to specify *what* it is that he knows or does not know.

What benefit then, Critias, would we get from temperance if it is of this sort? Now if, as we at first assumed, the temperate person knew what he knows and that he knows it, what he does not and that he does not, and if he were able to examine someone else in the same way, it would be enormously beneficial for us to be temperate. We who possessed temperance would live our lives infallibly, *and so would all the others who were ruled by us.* [At this point the reader may well remember that Socrates is speaking to a future tyrant.] ... The household managed by temperance would be well managed, the city would conduct its political affairs well, and so would everything else that is ruled by temperance. For error would be eliminated, correctness (*orthotēs*) would lead the way, those who live under such conditions would necessarily fare well in every action, and those who fare well would be happy ... This would be the great good of knowing what someone knows and what he does not know. (171D–172A)

This is the utopian picture of a society where something like the Socratic test for knowledge is in charge, delegating power only to experts in any given field, "and not allowing the people we rule over to engage in any activities except those which they can accomplish correctly (*orthōs*), namely, those where they have knowledge" (171E 3–5).

Again, we are reminded of the principle of specialization that structures the city of the *Republic*, a city where each class and each citizen is an expert in his or her own line of work, each one "doing his or her own thing." But in the *Charmides* this vision is rejected for two quite different reasons. In the first place Socrates has just argued that temperance as defined by Critias, as second-order knowledge without any first-order content, would not enable its possessor to test for expertise in any first-order field. So the political situation just described is impossible. But then Socrates goes on to argue that, even if it were possible, the resulting reign of experts would not be a great good for mankind (172D 7–173A 1). Here again the argumentation of the *Charmides* prefigures, in reverse, the theory of justice in the *Republic*, where Plato argues in Book v, first, that a given institution (education of women, community of wives) is possible, and second that it would be beneficial if established. Here the caricature version of the Platonic polis is shown to be (1) impossible and (2) of no great benefit even if achieved.[28]

The argument for this second claim is given in what Socrates announces as his dream (173A 7). The division of labor among experts would indeed produce solid results. If only competent doctors were allowed to practice, people would be healthier; if only genuine ship captains could sail, life at sea would be safer, and in general everything would be done skillfully (*technikōs*). But it is not clear that living and acting with knowledge (*epistēmōs*) will mean living well and happily (173D). To achieve that goal one particular kind of expertise is required, namely, the knowledge of what is good and bad (174B 10). This is the only knowledge whose function (*ergon*) it is to produce benefit (*ōphelia*, 175A). "Without this, we will lose the result that everything is done well and beneficially" (174C 9).

Socrates' dream is an extravagant thought, for which he offers some apology in advance: "You may think I am talking nonsense" (*lērein*, 173A 3). The point of absurdity lies in the suggestion that the knowledge of good and bad could be entirely *separate* from the choice of competent experts and the evaluation of good technical results in the various first-order fields. After all, health is a good thing, and so is survival at sea. The drastic nature of Plato's assumption here is a kind of thought-experiment, a device designed to isolate conceptually the dimension of unqualified goodness and desirability ("all things considered"), as instantiated in the goodness of a good life and the virtue of a healthy soul, in order to contrast this specifically moral knowledge with the technical norms of correctness and success.

The same point is made in a similar passage of the *Gorgias*, where it is pointed out that the ship captain does not know whether he has done well in preserving the lives of his passengers

---

28. The inverse relationship between the *Charmides* and the *Republic* (both on the interpretation of "doing one's own thing," and also on the pattern of argument that considers, first, whether a proposal is possible and then whether it would be beneficial) may be correlated with the fact that the interlocutors are Plato's close relatives in both cases. With his brothers we have constructive argument and positive theory; with the uncle and cousin no such progress is possible. This is the wrong side of Plato's family for any successful discussion of the beneficial organization of the city.

(511E–512A), and in the *Laches* where Nicias argues that doctors do not know when it is best for their patients to live or whether it would be better for them to die (195C–D). Plato does not mean to deny that life and health are, under most circumstances, to be counted among good things. But they are not unqualified goods. In the terminology of the *Gorgias* (467C–468C), such items are naturally good as means; their goodness will ultimately depends upon that of the ends "for the sake of which" they are employed. Hence the knowledge of health that the physician will possess is not the same as the knowledge of why and when health is good.

The distinction between the knowledge that produces "correctness" in Socrates' dream, and the beneficial knowledge that is lacking there, is a development in the *Charmides* of the distinction between technical skill and moral knowledge that we noticed in the preceding section, as well as an application of the distinction between ends and means in the *Gorgias*. What these passages have in view is a conception of knowledge of the good that can plausibly be identified with virtue, and that can be seen as indispensable both for the happiness of the individual and for the good management of the city. Hence the recurrence of the political theme.

As we have seen, the discussion of "doing one's own thing" in the *Charmides* offers us a kind of negative sketch of the division of labor that structures Plato's city in the *Republic*. Similarly, the critique in Socrates' dream of the utopian rule of knowledge shows that, for the desired result to be achieved, the rulers of the city must be masters not merely of epistemic caution in the Socratic manner, but of some positive knowledge of goodness, of the sort that the guardians of the *Republic* will be trained to acquire.

Socrates' dream thus serves to demarcate the beneficial knowledge that can count as virtue by a double contrast, distinguishing it on the one hand from craft knowledge or technical expertise, and insisting, on the other hand, that it must go beyond a Socratic recognition of ignorance in order to constitute positive knowledge of a definite subject matter: knowledge of what is good.

8. KNOWLEDGE, POWER, AND CORRECT USE

The theme of an essential connection between knowledge and political rule, highlighted in Socrates' dream, can be traced throughout the threshold dialogues. Thus in a charming conversation with the boy Lysis Socrates points out that Lysis' parents, who desire his happiness, nevertheless allow even servants to rule over him in those matters in which he lacks knowledge, but that "on the day when your father thinks you have better understanding (*beltion phronein*) than he does, he will entrust both himself and his property to you" (209c). The effect of such wisdom on Lysis' part will extend not only to his family but also to his neighbor and to the Athenians as a whole, who will entrust the affairs of the city to his care (209D). In the playful tone appropriate to the tender age of his interlocutor, Socrates pursues this thought to laughable extremes. The Persian King will allow Lysis to oversee the cooking and seasoning of the King's meat, and even to take care of the eyes of the King's son, if only he possesses the appropriate form of wisdom. "Greeks and barbarians, men and women, all will turn their affairs over to us, in those matters in which we become wise" (210A 9–B 2). Power, freedom, and benefit will all follow upon wisdom (210B–C).

Unlike Socrates' dream in the *Charmides*, this light-hearted passage in the *Lysis* does not specify the content of the knowledge that will make the boy "useful and good" (210D 2). But the concept of usefulness plays a key role in two closely parallel arguments from the *Meno* and the *Euthydemus*, the second of which will return us to the theme of political rule. Both arguments claim that knowledge or wisdom is the only guide to correct use (*orthē chrēsis*), and hence the only source of what is good and beneficial (*ōphelimon*). We will discuss these arguments in the next chapter, in the context of Socratic intellectualism. (See Chapter 8 §4.) Here we are concerned only with their common feature, and with the political application that follows in the *Euthydemus*.

What is distinctive of these two arguments is the claim that prima-facie goods such as health, or even temperance, justice and courage, are not good in themselves. They are beneficial only when guided and used correctly, under the leadership of knowledge or wisdom; but they can also be harmful when used incorrectly under the leadership of ignorance. Hence only knowledge is unqualifiedly good and beneficial (*Meno* 87E 5–89A 2; *Euthydemus* 280E–281E).

Like the passage cited earlier from the *Lysis*, the argument in the *Meno* does not specify what kind of knowledge it is that guarantees correct use. In the *Euthydemus*, however, this issue is squarely faced. Socrates concludes his first protreptic display with a challenge to the sophists: should the young Clinias seek to acquire every kind of knowledge, "or is there some one knowledge that he must get in order to live a happy life and be a good man? And if so, what knowledge is this?" (282E). We recognize, of course, the final question of the *Charmides* (173E–174D). The resemblance to the *Charmides* passage becomes even more striking when Socrates, in his second protreptic, reformulates the question as "what is the knowledge that will be of benefit (*ophelos*) to us?" (*Euthydemus* 288E–289B). The passage that follows is full of riddles, to be discussed later. Here we touch only on what is directly relevant to the question of the *Charmides*: what kind of knowledge will be beneficial?

After several unsuccessful attempts to answer this question, Socrates and his interlocutors hit upon the royal art as the form of knowledge most likely to procure happiness, since it alone knows how to use the products of the other arts (291B 5, C 9). The art of the king is here identified with the art of the statesman, the *politikē technē* (291C 4), which (as we know from the *Gorgias* and from *Charmides* 170B 1–3) has justice as its subject matter and the virtue of citizens as its product or *ergon*. But in the context of the *Euthydemus* that result is paradoxical. For our previous argument has concluded that the only good thing is knowledge or wisdom (281E). So if the royal art makes men wise and good, in what will they be wise? Not in carpentry and shoemaking? The royal art cannot have as its product something that is neither good nor bad. But if it is to procure something intrinsically good, "knowledge itself must only procure itself."[29] But what can such knowledge be good for? How will it be useful? Or shall we say that it serves to make other people good? But what will *they* be good for? And shall we say that they will make yet others good and useful, and these again yet others? We seem to have fallen into an infinite regress, and to have made no progress whatsoever towards identifying the knowledge that can make us happy (292D–E).

The *Euthydemus* offers no clue as to how the regress is to be bro-

---

29. "The clearest indication so far of the connection between the knowledge sought here [sc. in the *Euthydemus*] and the knowledge of knowledge proposed in the *Charmides*," Hawtrey (1981) 137f. The connection is recognized on other grounds by Tuckey (1951) 79.

ken. But in the Book VI of the *Republic* Socrates will begin to tell us about "the highest object of knowledge," the *megiston mathēma*: the Form of the Good, "by the use of which justice and the rest became useful and beneficial."

We do not know it adequately. And if we do not know this, even if we know all the rest, we get no benefit (*ophelos*), just as we get none from possessing something without the good. Or do you think there is any advantage to possessing great possessions, which are however not good? Or to know everything else except what is good, and still to know nothing good nor admirable? (*Rep.* VI, 505A–B)

What began in the *Laches* and *Charmides* and continued in the *Meno* and *Euthydemus* as a search for beneficial knowledge, knowledge of the correct use of instrumental goods, finds its climax here at the end of *Republic* VI, in an appeal to knowledge of the Good itself.

The doctrine of the Good in the *Republic* raises many problems of its own, but one thing is clear. In Plato's view it is the Good itself, the good as such, that must be the object for royal knowledge, for the art of the philosopher-kings.[30] And such knowledge will be useful precisely because, in the hands of the rulers, it will guide the right use of the workings and products of all the other arts, as it governs the whole society in the light of what is genuinely good, including the right use of those prima-facie goods, such as prosperity, freedom, and civic harmony, which were rejected in the argument of the *Euthydemus* as capable of being misused.[31] This is what lies behind the beneficial knowledge of good and bad in the *Charmides* and behind the royal art of the *Euthydemus*. Or perhaps we should say, this is what lies ahead. For, unless they have some privileged access to what may have been his oral instruction, the first readers of the *Charmides* and *Euthydemus* will not easily guess where Plato is bound. For readers of the dialogues all this will become clear only retrospectively, when they reach *Republic* VI. Here as often we see that, in the threshold dialogues, all roads lead to the *Republic*.

30. The connection of the regress of *Euthydemus* 292D–E with *Rep.* VI, 505B is recognized by Hawtrey (1981) 119.
31. *Euthydemus* 292B, referring back to 281A–D. Compare Aristotle's view of *politikē* as the master art which guides and uses all other sciences (*NE* 1.2, 1094a26ff.).

CHAPTER 8

Protagoras: *virtue as knowledge*

I. THE PLACE OF THE *PROTAGORAS* AMONG THE DIALOGUES

Among the seven works grouped together here as threshold dialogues, the *Protagoras* is clearly the literary masterpiece. It is the longest of the seven, roughly the same length as the *Symposium* and *Phaedo*. As an exemplar of Plato's dramatic art the *Protagoras* is rivaled only by the *Symposium* in the number and eminence of the speakers, the vividness of the dialogue, and the diversity of the action. Plato has taken pains to create here a brilliant picture of Athenian culture in the last years of the Periclean age, a half dozen years before his own birth, as backdrop for a full-scale treatment of the question raised by Socrates in the *Laches*: what is the proper goal of moral education, and how can this goal be achieved?

But if the *Protagoras* is one of the most brilliant of Plato's dialogues, it is also one of the most perplexing. There is, first of all, the question why Socrates' offers such an elaborate misinterpretation of Simonides' poem. This episode has often been an embarrassment to admirers of Socrates, since he seems here to be playing the part of the sophist rather than that of the philosopher. There is the much-discussed problem of Socrates' identification of pleasure and the good in the final argument, which is unlike what we find in any other dialogue. And there is also the strange denial of *akrasia* in the same argument: the denial of what we call weakness of will or yielding to temptation, acting against one's better judgment. Here Socrates seems to be denying obvious facts about human nature, and facts that were well known to Plato's audience since they had been emphasized by Euripides in two plays, *Medea* and *Hippolytus*, presented about the time of Plato's birth. Why does Plato make Socrates behave in such a paradoxical way?

To answer these questions we will have to engage in a detailed analysis of the final argument, where hedonism and *akrasia* make their appearance. First, however, we survey the dialogue as a whole and seek to clarify those themes which seem less problematic.

The *Protagoras* opens with a complex prologue, consisting of three parts: first, a frame dialogue in which Socrates reports the story to an unnamed interlocutor; then a preliminary conversation between Socrates and the young Hippocrates, who is passionately eager to study with Protagoras as the wisest man of his time; and finally the picturesque scene when Socrates and Hippocrates arrive in Callias' house, where the three sophists are being entertained. The ensuing conversation with Protagoras consists of four principal episodes, divided in the middle by an interlude in which Socrates threatens to leave but is prevailed upon to stay. Episode 1 begins with Protagoras' statement about the goals of his instruction (318E–319A), to which Socrates responds by his question whether virtue can be taught. Protagoras then presents his case for the teachability of virtue in what has become known as his Great Speech.[1] In Episode 2 Socrates shifts the question from teachability to the parts or species of virtue: how are the several virtues related to one another? In an inconclusive elenchus Socrates argues against Protagoras' common-sense attempt to distinguish the virtues from one another. Protagoras loses patience and Socrates consequently offers to abandon the conversation. After this interlude, Episode 3 opens with an almost comic reversal of roles. Protagoras accuses Socrates of accepting a contradiction in Simonides' poem on virtue; Socrates responds by some sophistical maneuvers which Protagoras refutes. We then have Socrates' long speech on the meaning of the poem, the formal counterpart to Protagoras' Great Speech in Episode 1. Finally in Episode 4 Socrates presents a sustained argument to prove that courage is a form of knowledge, using as premises first the hedonist identification of pleasure and the good, and then the explanation of *akrasia* as an error of judgment.

The position defended by Socrates in this final section of the *Protagoras* presents a challenge to my interpretation of the threshold dialogues as aporetic-proleptic introduction to the philosophy

1. Since Vlastos' classic Introduction to *Plato's Protagoras* (Ostwald–Vlastos, 1956).

of the middle works. It is widely believed that Socrates' identification of the virtues with wisdom and his apparent denial of *akrasia* are flatly incompatible with the tripartite psychology of the
Republic and with the large allowance made there for non-rational
motivation. This view of the *Protagoras* is the strongest support
from within the dialogues for the belief in a distinctively Socratic
period in Plato's thought. Hence this is a crucial issue, to which
we must return (below, §§ 4–8). First, however, it is important to
recall how centrally located the *Protagoras* is among the threshold
dialogues, and how close are the thematic links that connect it
both with the dialogues of definition and with the *Meno*.

While the *Laches*, *Charmides*, and *Euthyphro* are devoted to the virtues of courage, temperance, and piety taken severally, the *Protagoras* considers the relation of these virtues to one another and
raises the question of their unity.[2] As the *Protagoras* ends with Socrates insisting that they must know what virtue is before they can
decide whether it is teachable, so the *Meno* begins with Socrates'
repetition of this claim in response to Meno's question: "Can you
tell me, Socrates, is virtue teachable?" In thematic terms, the *Meno*
can be regarded as the direct sequel to the *Protagoras*. These five
dialogues thus constitute a formally unified group of interconnected discussions, where the theme of virtue is closely entwined
with the theme of *technē*, in a double sense. Is there an art of making men virtuous? And is virtue itself a kind of *technē*, a form of
knowledge or expertise?

2. *TECHNĒ* AND THE TEACHABILITY OF VIRTUE

The thematic unity of the *Protagoras* is provided by this persistent
concern with the nature of *aretē* and, to a secondary extent, with
the problem of its teachability. The question of an explicit definition ("What is virtue, after all?") does not arise until the very
end of the dialogue (360E 8, 361C 5); but the substance of this
question is present throughout, in the discussion of teachability (in
Episode 1), in the topic of unity (in Episodes 2 and 4), and even in
the discussion of Simonides' poem (in Episode 3).

The underlying assumption is that virtue is teachable if and only

2. For the detailed overlap between the *Laches* and *Protagoras* in discussion of
   courage, see Ch. 6 § 5.

if it is a *techne*, an art or expertise.[3] In fact the question whether virtue is a *techne* is often treated as equivalent to the question whether the *teaching* of virtue is a *techne*; the two questions are scarcely distinguished from one another. The basic conception seems to be that, as a discipline, a *techne* is constituted by a chain of teachers and learners who become teachers in turn. Thus Socrates' initial doubts as to whether Protagoras possesses the art (*techne, technema*, 319A 4 and 8) he claims to possess is reformulated as the question whether virtue is teachable (319A 10, 320B 5, C 1). And competence in this area is contrasted with other subjects that are recognized as areas of professional expertise (*en technei einai* 319C 8).

If education in virtue is an art, it is a *techne* of a special sort. It is both compared to, and contrasted with, training in one of the traditional arts and disciplines. Thus Protagoras can claim that, although he is the first to announce himself as a *sophistes*, a specialist in wisdom, the profession (*techne*) is in fact an old one, going back to Homer and Hesiod, and including not only poets but doctors, athletic trainers, and musicians (316D–E). These men, however, took refuge behind their technical specialties (*technai* 316E 5); Protagoras is the first to present himself openly as an educator (317B 4).

The term *techne* is crucially ambiguous here, since it designates both the new profession of the sophist and the more traditional arts of poetry, medicine, and the like. The same ambiguity is brought out when Socrates questions Hippocrates on his goal in studying with the sophist. If he were studying with Phidias it would be to become a sculptor, but he certainly does not wish to become a sophist by studying with Protagoras. It seems rather like studying with a schoolmaster or an athletic trainer. Such learning is not for professional purposes (*epi technei*) but for education (*epi paideiai*), as becomes a freeman and an amateur (312B). Hence in this case not every learner will become a teacher. (Contrast the situation for Antimoirus of Mende, who is studying with Protagoras professionally, *epi technei*, 315A 5.)

Considered in its historical context, this distinction between liberal and professional ("technical") education reflects the appearance of the sophists as the first professors of higher education.[4] In

3. With *episteme* instead of *techne*, this biconditional is implicitly asserted at *Prot.* 361B, explicitly at *Meno* 87C.
4. See Marrou (1950), Ch. V.

the context of this dialogue, however, the contrast is more narrowly focused. Whereas other teachers (such as Hippias) may force
their pupils back into the arts (*technai*), "teaching them calculation
and astronomy and geometry and music" (what later becomes the
quadrivium of the liberal arts), Protagoras will give them only
what they have come for: "good judgment (*euboulia*) in administer-
ing one's household and in directing the affairs of the city, so that
they will be most capable [or most powerful, *dunatōtatos*] in speaking and acting in the city's affairs" (318E). This is the conception
of *aretē* that Protagoras has to offer. And since he presents this as a
teachable skill or knowledge, such training can also be described
as a *technē*. "I think you mean the political art," says Socrates,
"and you undertake to make men good citizens." And Protagoras
concurs (319A).

Here again *technē* appears on both sides of the contrast. But
whereas the professional arts and crafts are well defined[5] and their
successful transmission is attested by an established tradition, the
new art of Protagoras is open to question, and its status as a
teachable *technē* will immediately be challenged.

First, however, we note that Socrates has described it by the
term used elsewhere for the art that improves the souls of the citizens (*Gorgias* 521D 7), which has justice as its subject matter (*Charmides* 170B 1–3), and which in the *Euthydemus* is identified with the
royal art, responsible for making people wise and good (291C 4):
the *politikē technē*. This terminology might lead us to expect a more
specifically Platonic conception of the "political art": namely,
moral-political wisdom understood as the knowledge of ultimate
ends, in contrast to the kind of instrumental competence that
guarantees technical success. (As we have seen, this is the contrast
emphasized in Socrates' dream at the end of the *Charmides*; above,
pp. 205f.) But although the reader of the *Protagoras* may be familiar with such a conception of the master *technē*, the true knowledge
of good and evil, the interlocutors in our dialogue have never
heard of it. Socrates is unwilling here to challenge directly Protagoras' assumption that everyone present knows what is meant by
being "most capable of speaking and acting in the affairs of the

5. Thus Aristotle (*Pol.* 1.4, 1253b25) contrasts the "definitely established arts"
(*hōrismenai technai*) with *oikonomia*, the art of household management, which is
part of Protagoras' new profession (*Prot.* 318E 6).

city," just as the fathers in the *Laches* can assume that everyone knows what is meant by an illustrious public career.

Traditional notions of political success are thus not called into question here, as they are in the *Gorgias*. The only note of criticism is sounded in the prologue, when Socrates describes the sophist as a salesman of groceries for the soul, who does not know whether his wares are harmful or beneficial (313C–314B). The young Hippocrates may not know what Socrates means by an expert (*epistēmōn*) who would have medical knowledge concerning the soul (313E 2–3), but the informed reader will recognize the doctrine of the *Crito* (47C–48A), more fully developed in the *Gorgias*, according to which the political *technikos* is precisely an expert in what is good for the soul. So when Socrates warns Hippocrates to take care for the health of his psyche, "which you regard as more precious than your body" (313A), this is a kind of signal to the reader on Plato's part, as it were over the head of Socrates' interlocutor. But this Socratic-Platonic conception of virtue as psychic health, the inner well-being of the person, is kept in the background here, to re-emerge only in a few hints in the exegesis of Simonides' poem in Episode 3.[6] Only in the prologue, then, together with these obscure allusions in the interpretation of Simonides, can we recognize the conception of virtue in the *Protagoras* as genuinely Socratic, in the sense defined by the "care of the soul" in the *Apology*, *Crito*, and *Gorgias*. In most of this dialogue, other notions of *aretē* will be explored.

Socrates is ultimately arguing here for a conception of virtue as knowledge or wisdom. Now since the terms for knowledge (*epistēmē*) and wisdom (*sophia*) are often interchangeable with that for art or craft (*technē*), the relationship between virtue and the arts or *technai* becomes a fundamental theme of the dialogue. We can see this in the myth with which Protagoras begins his Great Speech. Hermes asks Zeus whether the gift to mankind of Justice and Respect (*dikē* and *aidōs*), which will make it possible for them to have *politikē technē*, the art of living in cities (322B–C), should be distributed like the other *technai* to specialists, or to everyone. Zeus responds: "To everyone. Let them all have a share. For cities will

---

6. *Prot.* 345B 5 "the only misfortune (*kakē praxis*) is to be deprived of knowledge"; 345E 1 the wise men all believe that everyone who does bad and shameful things acts involuntarily (*akontes*).

not exist, if only a few share in this as in the other *technai*" (322D). And in the argument that concludes the same speech, Protagoras distinguishes virtue as the art in which there must be no laymen (327A 1). This skill is indispensable for social life, and therefore everyone eagerly teaches it to everyone (327B), unlike the other *technai* which fathers teach only to their sons (328A). This contrast is echoed in Episode 4, when Socrates introduces the calculus of pleasures and pains as "the salvation of our life," and compares it to the art of measuring magnitudes, and to arithmetic, the art of measuring odd and even numbers (356D–357A). So the correct choice of pleasures and pains (i.e. of goods and evils) is also a *technē* of measurement, a form of expert knowledge (*epistēmē*). "But just what art and knowledge this is, we will consider on another occasion" (357B).

Thus an analogy to the recognized arts and crafts is a constant feature of Plato's discussion of virtue and moral knowledge, in the *Protagoras* as in Plato's other works. But the emphasis here is upon the *difference* between practical wisdom and other types of expertise. By introducing the model of a hedonistic calculus, the *Protagoras* perhaps comes closer than any other dialogue to assimilating virtue and "the political art" to an ordinary *technē*. All the more important, then, for us to recognize the systematic care with which the author of this dialogue has, from the beginning, accentuated the differences.

3. THE UNITY OF VIRTUE

If there is one dominant theme in the *Protagoras*, that is the unity of the virtues in wisdom. This thesis is implicit in the elenctic arguments pressed by Socrates in Episode 2 and then explicit in the final refutation of Protagoras in Episode 4. But what is the status of this unified conception of virtue? And how is it related to the more conventional notions of justice and temperance that figure in Protagoras' major speech, and to the rather different notion of *aretē* that brings ambitious young men like Hippocrates to study with the sophist, out of a "desire to become famous in the city" (316c 1)?

The discussion of teaching virtue in Episode 1 thus opens with an ambiguity between the ordinary virtue of citizens and the extraordinary talent of outstanding political leaders. On the one hand Hippocrates is eager to learn from Protagoras the skill (*sophia*) that will make him a powerful speaker (312D), because, as Socrates points out, he has the means and natural gifts for a public career (316B 9). On the other hand something much more egalitarian is suggested by Socrates' comment to Protagoras: "You undertake to make men good citizens" (319A 4).

Socrates' question about the teachability of virtue tends to maintain this ambiguity. He begins by suggesting that the Athenians believe there are no experts in these matters. But then he goes on to cite the case of Pericles as an example of how "the wisest and best among the citizens" are unable to transmit their own *aretē* to their sons and relatives (319E). The implication seems to be that the difference between the *aretē* of a good citizen and that of a great statesman is only a matter of degree. It is precisely this assumption that makes possible Protagoras' reply. For his long and carefully constructed speech, beginning with the myth and ending with good empirical arguments, is calculated only to show that ordinary civic virtue is teachable. The sole allusion to his own more elitist pedagogy comes at the end: "everyone teaches virtue, as far as he can; only a few of us can give more advanced training and are better able to help someone become noble and good" (*kalos kai agathos*, 328A–B). This leaves the nature and goals of sophistic education entirely unexplored.

Protagoras does, however, give a very thoughtful account of moral education in the conventional sense. To a large extent Protagoras' argument anticipates Hume's theory of justice. The benefits of social cooperation and peaceful life in the city are impossible without justice and respect for others; hence society takes care to see that all its members are imbued with these qualities. This notion of virtue as social conditioning, as coming to accept and comply with the norms of one's society, does not have the moral depth of the Socratic notion of psychic health and the Socratic critique of the "unexamined life." But Protagoras does offer a solid defense for what Adkins has called the quiet or cooperative virtues of justice and temperance.[7] These are precisely the virtues that Plato in the *Republic* will assign to all the citizens, including

---

7. Adkins (1960) 6f. It is the cooperative virtues of justice and temperance (*aidōs*) that specify the content of what Protagoras in the myth refers to as *politikē technē*, the art of living in a civic community.

the lowest and most numerous of his three classes. In short, what Protagoras offers in the Great Speech of Episode 1 is a persuasive account of training in popular or "demotic" virtue,[8] the traditional training which Plato would replace by a purified curriculum of music and gymnastics in *Republic* II–III.

The discussion of virtue in the *Protagoras* is thus designed to skirt the problems raised by the tension between two quite different tendencies in the traditional notion of *aretē*, between a civic and cooperative conception of *aretē* and the more ambitious and competitive view. This is the tension that erupts in the confrontation between Socrates and Callicles in the *Gorgias* and again between Socrates and Thrasymachus in *Republic* I. But this potential conflict is carefully avoided in the *Protagoras*. Instead of raising any question of moral substance Socrates turns to what is apparently a quite different issue, barely alluded to in *Protagoras'* speech: the parts of virtue and their relation to one another.

What does Plato have in view by making Socrates argue here for the unity of the virtues in wisdom? For one thing, this does present a challenge to traditional views as interpreted in a reasonable way by Protagoras. Taking the virtues in their ordinary sense, most Greeks would agree with Protagoras that they can be possessed separately: that you can find people who are just but not wise (329E 6), and that many soldiers are "exceedingly brave but also very unjust, irreverent, ignorant and sensually unrestrained" (349D 6). Socrates' arguments for unity will mean taking these virtues in a non-standard sense, extending courage to include not only resistance to fears but also "being able to fight against appetites and pleasures" (*Laches* 191D), and taking *sōphrosunē* in its old etymological sense of practical wisdom or sound wits (as in the *Charmides*) rather than in the ordinary sense of self-control and moderation.[9] As the continuation of this topic in the *Phaedo* will

8. Most explicitly characterized in Plato's reference at *Phaedo* 82A 11 to "those who have practiced popular (*dēmotikē*) and civic (*politikē*) virtue, which they call temperance and justice, produced by habit and practice, without philosophy and rational understanding (*nous*)." Cf. *Rep.* VI, 500D 7: "temperance and justice and all of popular (*dēmotikē*) virtue."

9. Contrast *Phaedo* 68C 8: "what most people call temperance (*sōphrosunē*), not being upset by one's desires (*epithumiai*), but to pay no heed to them and keep them under proper control (*kosmiōs echein*)." Similarly in Agathon's speech: "*Sōphrosunē* is generally agreed to be rule over pleasures and desires" (*Symp.* 196C 4). See parallels above, Chapter 7, n.8.

make clear, the unity of the virtues in wisdom is in fact a new moral ideal, the theoretical counterpart to the portrait of Socrates that Plato is sketching in his dialogues, from the *Apology* and *Crito* to the *Symposium* and *Phaedo*. What is characteristic of the discussion both here in the *Protagoras* and also in the *Meno* (73E–75A) is that Plato's preparation for his new theory of virtue takes the form of a technical discussion of the problems of the one and the many.

As Plato says much later towards the end of his life, it is easy to say how the virtues are many but hard to say how they are one. For it is hard to see what is the same in them all, "what we say is one in courage and temperance and justice and in wisdom, rightly calling virtue by a single name" (*Laws* XII, 963D 4–7, 965D 1–3). The search for that unity begins here in Episode 2, with a preliminary delineation of the question and a formal elenchus of Protagoras' defence of plurality.

Both here and in the *Laws*, the problem is posed in terms of a relationship between name and nominatum. How does one name, "virtue," apply to what is also called by several different names? Socrates' question to Protagoras is this: assuming that virtue is one, as Protagoras has declared it to be (325A 2), what about justice and temperance and piety, which he has also referred to in his speech? Are these parts of the one thing which is virtue, or are these so many different names for a single thing? Protagoras answers that they are parts of a unity.

Consider for a moment the alternative that Protagoras has rejected: that there is no real difference between the virtues, but that *courage, temperance,* and *justice* are simply different names for the same thing. This is, in effect, the notion of referential synonymy, which Plato develops in the *Cratylus*.[10] As we have seen, a rather similar view was maintained by Plato's friend Eucleides of Megara. He or his followers, the Megarians, are said to claim that virtue (*aretē*)

---

10. *Cratylus* 393A–394C: *Hector* and *Astyanax* mean the same thing, namely ruler or king (394C 3). This concept of synonymy is also used in the final argument of the *Protagoras*, which turns upon the substitution of *good* and *pleasant* for one another (and likewise *bad* and *painful*) as two names for the same thing (355Bff). The notion of synonymy in play here has more to do with reference than with sense: the nominata in question are thought of as things (a ruler, a pleasure) rather than as concepts or "meanings." But the distinction is not sharply drawn.

is one but called by many names.[11] Since we do not have Eucleides' own words we do not know how close his view was to the one mentioned but apparently left undefended in the *Protagoras*. (Whether Socrates means after all to defend it will be discussed below.) The unmistakable resemblance nevertheless suggests that the problem of one thing/many names is likely to have been a subject of discussion between Plato and Eucleides. Our passage in the *Protagoras* is one of the first indications of Plato's inquiries into the theory of language. Similar inquiries are reflected in the *Meno* (where the converse problem is raised, how different virtues can all be called "virtues," and different figures truly described by the same name "figure"); they are more fully pursued in the *Cratylus*, and later in the *Sophist*.

Socrates' next question concerns the relation between the parts of virtue. Are they like the parts of the face, each with its own function or capacity (*dunamis*) different from the others? Or are they like the parts of gold, homogeneous with one another and with the whole?[12] Protagoras rejects the second alternative, which would assign to virtue the logically simpler unity of a mass concept like water, where the plurality of parts is so to speak accidental, with no internal principle of diversity other than spatial location and magnitude. On the contrary, says Protagoras, courage, temperance, and the rest will differ both in themselves and in their specific power, as the eye and ear differ in both structure and function.

Protagoras has accepted the analogy of different organs with different functions, but this leaves entirely open the question of unity. What do the virtues have in common? The parallel to parts of the face gives us no definite clue. The elenchus that follows turns upon the obscurity of the question, how can parts of a single whole have a generic nature in common while differing specifically from one another? In effect, Protagoras is impaled upon the horns of a spurious dilemma: either the individual virtues must be wholly

11. Above, p. 13.
12. Plato here gives a clear if somewhat crude characterization of what Aristotle will call a homoiomerous entity: a whole whose parts are the same in kind with one another and with the whole. What is crude here is the phrase "differing from one another and from the whole *only by being smaller and larger*" (392D 8). Of course the parts of gold can also differ in shape, location, duration, etc.

unlike one another, or they will be indistinguishable. The deeper problem of logical unity-in-diversity is left untouched. (It is explicitly raised, though again left unresolved, in the corresponding passage on word–thing relations in the *Meno*, 74D–E.)

The unity of virtue is never expressly defended by Socrates in the *Protagoras*; he only argues *against* the claims of plurality and diversity maintained by Protagoras. Hence the dialogue does not tell us in what way the unity of the virtues in wisdom is to be understood. Modern scholars have nevertheless followed the ancient Stoics in proposing various interpretations of the Socratic position.

One of the most influential contemporary accounts is offered by Terry Penner.[13] Penner argues persuasively against two interpretations that have been prominent in recent scholarship: (1) the weak view of identity which claims only that the virtues are inseparable from one another, so that anyone who has one virtue must have them all, and (2) the strong view of semantic identity or strict synonymy, that the names for the individual virtues (*justice, courage, wisdom*, etc.) all have the same meaning. Penner argues instead that in implying that these terms are "five names for a single thing" (349B 1–3; cf. 329D 1) Socrates intends to claim not that they are the same in sense or that the five words all mean the same thing (which seems clearly false) but rather that all five names have the same reference, that they all refer to a single thing. The term *bravery* in the question "what is bravery?" refers to "that psychological state which explains the fact that certain men do brave acts – what we might call a theoretical entity;" that is, "what it is in many psyches that makes them brave."[14] The thesis of the unity of the virtues is then the claim that it is the same psychic disposition or the same psychological motive-force that makes men brave and that makes them just and temperate and pious, as well as wise. The unity thesis is thus a substantive claim in moral psychology, a causal or explanatory account of virtuous action. This causal-explanatory principle is what the dialogues describe in terms of wisdom, that is, the knowledge of good and evil.

This is quite satisfactory as far as it goes, but it leaves unexplained (1) how, if at all, the various virtues differ from one

13. Penner (1973) 35–68.
14. *Ibid.* pp. 41, 57.

another, and (2) how the knowledge of good and evil can have the required motive-force so as to guarantee virtuous action.

In regard to the diversity of the virtues, I want to suggest that Plato in the *Protagoras* has deliberately left the thesis of unity indeterminate and open for further discussion. Even in the *Republic*, where the virtues are individually defined and their unity implied by the definition of justice, Plato insists upon the inadequacy of the account he has given.[15] And in the *Laws*, where he says that it is not so easy to see how the many virtues are one, he insists that the search for the one in the many in this case is a particularly good topic for training in philosophic thought.[16] That Plato has left the unity thesis of the *Protagoras* conceptually underdetermined will be clear if we cast a glance at the continuation of this discussion by Stoic philosophers who were consciously working in the Socratic tradition.

The founder of the Stoic school, Zeno, claimed that the virtues were all one, namely wisdom (*phronēsis*), but distinct in their operations. His followers disagreed as to how this distinctness was to be understood. Ariston of Chios held that courage, temperance, and the rest were strictly identical as far as their intrinsic nature was concerned; they were distinguished from one another *only* by their external relation to circumstance and application. Thus courage is wisdom applied to circumstances of danger, temperance is wisdom in circumstances of desire and pleasure, and so forth. But Chrysippus disagreed: for him the distinction was not merely one of external relations (*pros ti pōs echein*) but of intrinsic quality ("That the Virtues are Qualities, *poiai*" was the title of his book). According to Chrysippus the virtues are distinguished from one another by their primary focus or chief province (*kephalaia*), but they have a secondary concern with the content of the other virtues. Hence, although they are intrinsically different from one another, they are nevertheless inseparable: anyone who has one virtue must have them all, and every action that instantiates one of the virtues will instantiate them all.[17]

---

15. *Rep.* IV, 435D; VI, 504B, C9. Since justice requires that each part of the soul perform its proper task (441D–E, 443C–E), possessing justice will entail possession of the other virtues.
16. *Laws* XII, 963Dff.
17. See Schofield (1984) 83–95. I am indebted here to Schofield's article and to an oral presentation by D. Hutchinson. See Long and Sedley (1987) I, 377–84.

The subtlety of these Stoic distinctions illustrates how much room Plato has left for the analysis of unity among the virtues. But the Stoic doctrine also reminds us how "violently paradoxical" the unity thesis is.[18] For the Stoics the virtues could be possessed only by the Sage, *ho sophos*, who must be a flawless example of moral perfection. But the Stoics were not convinced that any human being could actually attain this status; exceptional moral individuals like Socrates showed only that "progress" towards this goal was possible.

For the Stoics, then, the unity of the virtues represents an absolute ideal, which every Stoic philosopher should aspire to approach as far as possible. For Plato, I suggest, the unity thesis also points to a rare and difficult ideal. The unity of the virtues will not be realized in ordinary cases of decent men and respectable citizens, like Nicias in the *Laches* or Cephalus in *Republic* I. The best we can hope for in most cases is the ordinary or demotic virtue described as slavish in the *Phaedo* and contrasted with the virtue of the true philosopher in *Republic* VI.[19] It is only in the case of the truly wise man, the philosopher-king of the *Republic*, that knowledge of the good will be strong enough to determine action in every case and guarantee virtue in practice. Much of the puzzlement of the *Protagoras* is due to the fact that it operates with two quite distinct notions of *aretē*: the ordinary conception of demotic virtue, available to the average citizen and taught in the ways described by Protagoras in his Great Speech; and the exceptional virtue of the true philosopher, as personified in Socrates. The latter notion of philosophic virtue is never explicitly recognized or thematized in this dialogue; yet it is only to the latter and not to the former that the unity thesis can plausibly apply.[20]

How can philosophic wisdom be so effective as a motive-force? This is not a question that can be answered on the basis of the *Protagoras*, which simply leaves us with the paradox. For an answer

---

18. Schofield (1984) 93: "such a violently paradoxical form of moral absolutism," referring to the Stoic theory of virtue.
19. Passages cited above, n.8. The same contrast is implied by the opposition between true virtue and its image in *Symp*. 212A 4–5.
20. There is a secondary application of the unity thesis to the guardians of *Republic* IV, since if they have psychic justice they will have all the virtues. (See above, n.15.) But in their case the unity cannot be furnished by wisdom, since they have only true belief, not philosophic knowledge of the good.

we must go to Plato's theory of desire and his doctrine of philosophic *erōs*, to be discussed in the next chapter.

4. THE PROBLEM OF SOCRATIC INTELLECTUALISM

In Chapters 5 and 6 we traced the gradual articulation in the threshold dialogues of a conception of moral-political knowledge as *epistēmē* or *technē* that prefigures the art of the philosopher-king. In the *Protagoras* we encounter two different conceptions of moral expertise, represented by Protagoras and Socrates respectively. I have suggested that Protagoras serves as spokesman for a vulgar or popular conception of *aretē*, whereas Socrates' thesis of the unity of virtue in wisdom must ultimately be understood by reference to the conception of philosophic virtue found in the central books of the *Republic*.

However, the psychological account offered by Socrates in Episode 4 seems to constitute an insurmountable obstacle to such a "unitarian" reading of the *Protagoras*. The identification of virtue with knowledge and the reinterpretation of *akrasia* as an intellectual mistake are difficult to reconcile with the theory of virtue and non-rational motivation in the *Republic*. These two moral psychologies are so radically different that the Socrates of the *Protagoras* appears to be a different philosopher – or at least, the spokesman for a different philosophy – from the Socrates of the *Republic*. So it is easy to see why Aristotle concluded that the views expressed in the *Protagoras* were those of the historical Socrates, and why so many ancient and modern authors have followed him in this assumption. Even if we put aside the question of the historical Socrates, there seems to be clear evidence of a development from one theory of moral psychology to a new and different theory. As Gregory Vlastos put it in a memorable phrase, for Socrates in the *Protagoras* "the intellect is all-powerful in its control of the springs of action; wrong conduct, he believes, can only be due to ignorance of the good." Vlastos goes on to show that such a view is decisively rejected in the *Republic* by the introduction of the tripartite model for the psyche, where passion and appetite are recognized as independent sources of motivation. The concept of moral virtue must accordingly be redefined. Thus courage, which in the *Protagoras* (360D) is "a cognitive achievement, an excellence of the rational soul," will become in the *Republic* "an emotional achievement, an excellence of the passionate soul" (IV, 442B–C).[21] This discrepancy provides the strongest textual evidence for the developmental view of Plato's work. If we are able to resolve this apparent incompatibility, we will have nullified the most important objection to our unitarian interpretation of the threshold dialogues.

First of all it will be well to situate the doctrine of the *Protagoras* within the wider context constituted by what is known as the intellectualist moral psychology of the other dialogues. This consists of two closely related themes: (1) a conception of virtue in terms of knowledge; knowledge is necessary and sufficient for correct action, so anyone who knows what is good will do what is good; and (2) the Socratic paradox that no one does evil voluntarily. These two views are logically connected by (3) the assumption that everyone wants what is good; if anyone does what is bad, that can only be by mistake. Hence virtue consists in a correct recognition of what is good. I will briefly review the evidence for these views in the dialogues of Group I.

The *Laches* and the *Charmides* both hint at a definition of virtue in terms of the knowledge of good and evil, but they do not develop this conception in any detail. The *Gorgias* argues that anyone who knows what is just will be a just person and act justly (460B); it refers repeatedly to a kind of expert knowledge (*technē*) that would know what is good and bad and be required for acting justly,[22] and it explicitly affirms that "no one wants (*boulomenos*) to act unjustly, but all who commit injustice do so involuntarily" (509E 5).

There is a similar argument in the *Meno* to show that no one wants bad things, that everyone wants what is good (77B–78B). Since virtue is nevertheless something exceptional, not shared by all, virtue will perhaps consist in the capacity to *provide* good things (78C 1). And a later argument in the *Meno* makes clear that what we need for happiness is not merely the possession but the correct use of good things. Hence virtue must be a kind of wisdom (*phronēsis*), understood as practical knowledge of the right use of what are prima facie goods, so as to guarantee that they will be truly good and beneficial, not harmful (87D–89A). A parallel argument

---

21. Vlastos (1988) 89–111. For similar views see Kraut and Penner in Kraut (1992) 5f. and 127f. respectively.
22. *Gorgias* 500A 6, B 3; 503D 1; 509E 1, 510A 4.

in the *Euthydemus* claims that wisdom is the only good, since it is both necessary and sufficient for happiness (281E–282A). What these last two arguments have in common is the assumption that the usual moral virtues, namely justice, temperance, and courage, are not good in themselves (*auta kath' auta*) but good only when correctly used, that is to say, when their use is guided by knowledge and wisdom. Both arguments conclude, in effect, for the decisive role of practical wisdom in the moral life, and thus provide more definite content for that knowledge of good and bad that is hinted at in the *Laches* and *Charmides* as a definition of virtue. This is the knowledge we must have to get what we really want: only good things.[23]

What does the *Protagoras* add to this account of virtue as practical knowledge? First of all, it provides in Episode 2 a set of elenctic arguments for identifying the individual virtues with one another and, ultimately, with wisdom (330D–333E). But these arguments are not allowed to reach their intended conclusion; and they are in any case less convincing than the protreptic arguments for virtue as knowledge just cited from the *Meno* and *Euthydemus*. The major contribution of the *Protagoras* is the constructive development in Episode 4 of a hedonist model for decision-making with the corresponding definition of choice in terms of measurement, so that any bad action will be seen as the result of a miscalculation. This is the most carefully worked out defence of the Socratic paradox in all of Plato's dialogues – the paradox which claims that no one does bad things voluntarily.

5. EVALUATING SOCRATIC INTELLECTUALISM

What are we to make of these claims, collected under the title of Socratic intellectualism? On a traditional reading, which goes back at least to Aristotle, these views represent a purely rationalist ac-

---

23. It appears, however, that the arguments of *Meno* 87D–89A and *Euthydemus* 278E–282A establish only the necessity, not the sufficiency, of wisdom for virtue and happiness. If wisdom is the knowledge of correct use, there must also be some (potentially) good resources for knowledge to use. Nothing in the *Meno* argument suggests that knowledge alone can provide such instrumental goods. But perhaps that is the point of the curious passage in the *Euthydemus* argument to show that, when wisdom is present, there is no further need of good fortune (*eutuchia*, 279C–280B).

count of human motivation and decision making; and they have been severely criticized from this point of view. Aristotle may not have been their first critic. It would seem that Plato himself, in introducing his tripartite analysis of motivation in *Republic* IV, presents his own psychological theory as an explicit correction of Socratic intellectualism.

We will return to this passage in *Republic* IV. But first we should seriously consider what is entailed by reading these arguments as a descriptive account of how human beings actually behave. We are immediately struck by the total disregard of emotional, affective, or otherwise non-rational factors in human motivation. The only emotive consideration in the relevant sections of the *Gorgias, Meno,* and *Euthydemus* is the desire for happiness or a desire for the good. And if we look closely at the corresponding arguments in the *Protagoras,* we see that desire is not even mentioned.[24] More exactly, emotive factors such as fear, anger, and love (*erōs*) are referred to only as part of the vulgar account of *akrasia* (352B 7f.) that is to be rejected. (So there is no question of the emotions not being noticed in the *Protagoras.* They are explicitly mentioned and then explained away.) In the *Protagoras* the very concept of desire is replaced by the notion of pleasure as an object to be pursued and a quantity to be maximized, so that questions of motivation can be formulated reductively in quasi-behaviorist language, as a matter of pursuit and avoidance. The *Protagoras* thus represents the extreme case of the general tendency of Socratic intellectualism to ignore the emotional and affective components of human psychology, or to reinterpret them in terms of a rational judgment as to what is good or bad.

From the historical point of view, it is natural to see the *Protagoras* in the context of a debate about the role of rational deliberation in human action that began, as we have seen, before Plato was born. In two tragedies, *Medea* and *Hippolytus* (produced in 431 and 428 BC), Euripides presents his heroine struggling with passions that her judgment tells her to resist or suppress. For Medea,

24. The deliberate absence of any reference to desire in the *Protagoras* model for action and choice is underscored by the fact that Socrates cites the distinction between the two words for desiring, *boulesthai* and *epithumein,* as an example of Prodicus' art of distinguishing near-synonyms (340A 8). Note the indirect implications for reductive hedonism of Prodicus' parallel distinction between two verbs for being pleased (*euphrainesthai* and *hēdesthai*) at 337C 2–3.

it is the anger and hatred for Jason that leads her to kill her children; for Phaedra it is her erotic passion for her stepson Hippolytus that is driving her to disaster. Now Euripides has made both of his heroines reflect publicly on this struggle, and on the limits of rational control. "My passion [or anger, *thumos*] is stronger than my decisions, passion which is cause of the greatest evils to mankind," says Medea (1079–80); and Phaedra echoes her sentiment (*Hippolytus* 377ff.). Bruno Snell has interpreted these passages as the expression of an on-going debate between Socrates and Euripides on the power of reason in human affairs.[25] Now about the views of the historical Socrates in 431 BC we are so poorly informed that there is no way of knowing whether or not Euripides is actually alluding to a Socratic opinion. (Snell was relying on evidence from the *Protagoras* and other fourth-century accounts of Socrates.) On the other hand, it is very likely that Plato has Medea and Phaedra in mind when he speaks of passion (*thumos*), pleasure, and *erōs* as factors that "most people" would invoke as prevailing over knowledge.[26]

The Socrates of the *Protagoras* seems precisely to be denying the psychological facts as Euripides has portrayed them, the power of the emotions to overcome reason. And that appears to be the very point on which Socrates and Protagoras find themselves in agreement. But the actual statement of this thesis needs to be carefully examined. What Socrates asks Protagoras to agree to is the following:

Do you think that knowledge is dragged about like a slave by all these other factors, or do you think it is something noble and capable of ruling a person? And if someone knows the good and the bad, he will not be overcome by anything so as to do other than what knowledge commands, but wisdom (*phronēsis*) is adequate to assist a person? (352C)

This passage admits both a descriptive and a normative or protreptic reading, depending upon how knowledge and wisdom are understood. A protreptic reading is suggested by the evaluative overtones of the denial that knowledge is a slave, the description of it as noble (*kalon*) and "such as to rule" (*hoion archein*), as well as by the reference to wisdom as "adequate to come to one's assis-

---

25. Snell (1953) 182; followed by Vlastos in Ostwald–Vlastos (1956) xliv.
26. *Prot.* 352B. Cf. *thumos* in *Medea* 1079; *eran* and pleasure in *Hippolytus* 347ff., 382ff.

tance" (*hikanēn boēthein*). And this normative perspective is reinforced by the nature of Protagoras' response: "It would be shameful (*aischron*) for me above all to deny that knowledge and wisdom (*sophia*) are the most powerful of all things human" (352D 1). Read normatively, these texts imply an appeal to cultivate moral knowledge and practical insight into the consequences of your action, in order to guarantee that you will not yield to mindless passion or impulse. (It is precisely practical insight of this sort that the sophist professes to teach. Hence it would be disgraceful for Protagoras "above all" to deny the power of reason.) Descriptively, the same passage can be read in two ways, the first of which is close in spirit to the normative reading just suggested. If knowledge is taken in a very strong sense, complete self-control can be seen as its inevitable consequence, and hence as a criterion for the possession of such knowledge. Knowledge so understood would correspond to philosophical virtue as depicted in Plato's portrait of Socrates, and developed theoretically both in the description of the philosopher-king in *Republic* VI and, later on, in the Stoic account of the sage. This is how Snell read the *Protagoras*.[27]

Gregory Vlastos, on the other hand, follows Aristotle in criticizing Socrates for neglecting the facts of human psychology, the power of irrational fears or momentary impulse.[28] This criticism assumes that Socrates is asserting the sovereignty of reason not only in the super-strong case of genuine knowledge of the good – the case just referred to as philosophic virtue – but that he means to claim that the intellect in general, rational judgment or mere belief, is "all-powerful in its control of the springs of action."

Such a thesis of omnipotent rationalism seems patently false: the audience of Euripides did not need to wait for modern depth psychology to discover the power of irrational forces in human motivation. And yet the text seems to make just that implausible claim:

If the pleasant is [the] good, no one either knowing or believing that something else is better than what he is doing, and possible for him to

27. Snell (1953) 182: "Socrates' demand is exacting, so exacting indeed that very few men will be able to carry it out. He asks them to place their passions and impulses completely under the control of the understanding."
28. Vlastos (1971a) 15f. The critique of Socratic intellectualism can be traced back as far as George Grote. For a survey of nineteenth- and twentieth-century scholarship on this issue see O'Brien (1958) 451–72.

do, still does this when something better is available. Nor is loss of self-control (τὸ ἥττω εἶναι αὐτοῦ) anything other than ignorance, nor self mastery (κρείττω ἑαυτοῦ) other than wisdom ... No one voluntarily (*hekōn*) pursues what is bad or what he thinks is bad, nor is this, as it seems, in human nature, to be willing (*ethelein*) to pursue what one thinks is bad rather than what is good. And when someone is obliged to choose between two evils, no one will choose the greater when the lesser is available. (*Prot.* 358B–D)

Construed as a model for rational decision-making, this is a brilliantly simple scheme, very much like the scheme that underlies rational choice theory in contemporary philosophy and social science.[29] As a descriptive account of ordinary human behavior, however, it is quite incredible.

What has happened here? In the passage just quoted the possibility of a protreptic or normative reading has been eliminated: the claim is now asserted as a fact of human nature. And the super-strong notion of knowledge, entailing philosophic virtue, is also excluded. Instead of knowledge and wisdom alone, as in the earlier passage (at 352C), Socrates speaks here of *believing* that something is better, or *thinking* that something is bad. (The verb is *oiesthai* at 358B 7, C 7, and D 1.) Thus he seems to be denying precisely what Medea and Phaedra assert: that other motivating forces can prevail over their better judgment.

To realize just how extraordinary this view is, we need only compare it with other statements of the paradox. The central thought in the passages we have surveyed from other dialogues is this: that a correct judgment concerning what is good and what is bad is the decisive factor in human life, the only guarantee that one will live a good and happy life. Virtue is precisely that form of knowledge or wisdom that provides correct judgment in every

29. For a contemporary version of the theory see Herrnstein (1990) 356–67. "We start with a paradox, which is that the economic theory of rational choice (also called optimal choice theory) accounts only poorly for actual behavior, yet it comes close to serving as the fundamental principle of the behavioral sciences. No other well articulated theory of behavior commands so large a following in so wide a range of disciplines" (p. 356). The theory holds "that the choices a person (or other animal) makes tend to maximize total utility," which Herrnstein identifies with "the modern concept of reinforcement in behavioral psychology." He concludes that the theory of rational choice "fails as a description of actual behavior, but it remains unequalled as a normative theory." (I owe this reference to Richard McNally.)

case. The paradoxes of the *Gorgias* and the *Meno*, which insist that everyone wants what is good and will do what is wrong only by mistake, do not consider (and hence do not exclude) the possibility that someone might act against their better judgment. For example, the first paradox of the *Gorgias* argues that many people, who do what they think best, do not do what they want, because their judgment is bad: that is, because they lack knowledge of the good (*Gorgias* 468c–d). Such paradoxes clearly have a normative-protreptic appeal. They are designed to provoke the interlocutor (and the reader) into reflecting on what it is that he or she really wants, on what it is that is truly good for them. For it appears obvious that people do in fact want bad things – things bad for them and things bad absolutely. In challenging these appearances, the paradoxes do not only serve to emphasize the importance of moral knowledge. According to the interpretation offered here (above, pp. 140ff.), they also aim to put Callicles and his like in touch with the healthy part of themselves, the part that really wants what Socrates and Plato understand by the good: in the first instance, a virtuous soul.

Now in these other statements of the paradox Plato is not at all concerned with people of good moral judgment who occasionally lose control and act contrary to their judgment. He is concerned instead with people like Callicles, Polus, and Thrasymachus who propound and defend *bad* moral judgments, or people like Meno, whose commitment to the right principles is inconsistent or insincere. The paradoxes are calculated to produce a shock effect, like the sting of elenctic refutation, not in order to strengthen someone's resolve in the face of temptation (as if the threat came from *akrasia*), but in order to bring the interlocutor (or the reader) into a fruitful state of self-doubt, the volitional equivalent of a recognition of one's ignorance, as a necessary condition for being able to move on, to achieve the volitional equivalent of knowledge or, at least, of true belief: a recognition of one's deep, half-conscious desire for what is good.

If that is true for the paradoxes generally, what light can it shed on this, the most provocative statement of all, the claim that no one ever acts against their judgment of what is best? Could this have been Socrates' own position? But it would not solve our problem even if we could be certain that the historical Socrates had actually talked this way. For we would still not know why he did so: because he had a naive belief in the omnipotence of reason? or because he wished to be provocative by defending paradoxes? or because he had a complex psychological view such as the Stoics later developed (under the inspiration of the *Protagoras*), according to which pathological emotions result from an intellectual error?[30] The question for us to answer, as readers of the *Protagoras*, is not what Socrates said or believed but why Plato puts this view into his mouth, and what role it plays in the larger argument of the dialogue.

To answer this question we will have to examine the text closely, to see how the rationalist thesis is qualified or clarified by its context. Before we do so, however, I think we can reassure ourselves that the author of the *Protagoras* does not himself mean to endorse the omnipotent rationalism of the passage in question. For example, the avoidance of any reference to desire in this connection must arouse our suspicions. We know that the author of the *Gorgias* is well aware of the diversity (and possible conflict) of desires: the desires (*epithumiai*) for pleasure celebrated by Callicles are quite different from, and potentially opposed to, the rational desire (*boulesthai*) for the good that Socrates pursues.[31] And this contrast is not limited to the *Gorgias*. As we have seen, the *Charmides* recognizes three kinds of desire, differentiated by their object: appetite (*epithumia*) for pleasure, wanting (*boulēsis*) for good, and sexual desire (*erōs*) for beauty (*Charm.* 167E). In the prologue to the *Charmides* Socrates is described as momentarily overwhelmed by his sensual response to the glimpse of what lies under Charmides' cloak (155 D–E). And, in a different key, the initial discussion of courage in the *Laches* is focused on the non-rational element of toughness or endurance (*karteria*). These are just a few indications of what we might in any case guess: that a great dramatist like Plato was as acutely aware as Euripides was of the role played by strong feeling and temperament in the lives of ordinary human beings.

30. In fact there seems no good reason to attribute intellectualism in this extreme form to the historical Socrates. The account of Socrates' denial of *akrasia* that we read in *NE* VII.2 is a literary reflection of our dialogue rather than a historical explanation of it. Xenophon's confused account seems equally dependent on the *Protagoras*. See the Appendix, p. 395.
31. See above, p. 141.

What is extraordinary about Socrates is that his emotional nature is so completely under rational control.[32] That is why Plato's portrayal of Socrates can serve as a model for philosophic virtue and, later, for the Stoic sage. But this conception of rational self-mastery points to an interpretation of the Socratic paradox not in terms of omnipotent rationalism for ordinary judgment or belief, but in terms of that super-strong sense of moral knowledge or wisdom as a condition that pervades the whole character. This is essentially the same ideal condition that Aristotle calls virtue in contrast to self-control (*enkrateia*), namely, a perfect union between practical wisdom (*phronēsis*) and moral character, which insures that a deliberate judgment as to what is best will always prevail in choice and action, without any opposition from non-rational feeling or desire. And that Aristotelian conception largely corresponds to the account of virtue as psychic harmony in the case of a philosopher-king in the *Republic*, where correct moral training is a pre-condition for philosophical understanding.

From other dialogues, then, we see that Plato is committed to the Socratic paradox in its normative or ideal form: *if* one had genuine knowledge of the good, one would never act badly. There is no evidence from outside the *Protagoras* that Plato is committed to the naive reading of the paradox as affirming the omnipotence of reason in ordinary human behavior. Now this more plausible, restricted reading is possible for one part of the passage in question, the claim that "self-mastery is nothing other than wisdom (*sophia*)" (358c 3). But three times in our text Socrates asserts that no one voluntarily (*hekōn, ethelein*) acts against their judgment (*oiesthai*) as to what is good. This amounts to a denial of *akrasia* as ordinarily understood. Why does Plato assign such an extreme position to Socrates?

32. Compare Socrates' remark in Phaedo's *Zopyrus* that the physiognomist who diagnosed him as a sensualist and a womanizer had correctly perceived his natural proclivities, but these had been overcome by rational training and philosophy. (Above, p. 11.) By depicting Socrates' strong reaction to Charmides' sensual beauty, Plato makes a similar point about the underlying tension between Socrates' emotional temperament and his moral character. So in the *Phaedrus* (256A 7–B 7) he gives an allegorical account of this successful outcome in the philosophic taming of the wild horse.

6. AN INTERPRETATION OF *PROTAGORAS*
358B–D IN ITS CONTEXT

The passage in question (which I shall refer to as the rationalist text) occurs at a crucial moment in one of the most intricate dialectical maneuvers in all of Plato's work. This final argument of the dialogue, which occupies most of Episode 4, is divided into three sections by the shift in interlocutors. Section I is the long Dialogue with the Many (353A–357E), in which Socrates coopts Protagoras as joint interrogator, with Protagoras authorized to answer questions in the name of the Many. The rationalist text belongs in a brief transitional passage, Section II (358A–E), addressed to all three sophists. In the concluding Section III (359A–360E) Protagoras is obliged to answer alone in defense of his thesis that wisdom is separate from courage, and he is finally brought to acknowledge defeat (360E).

The shift between three sets of interlocutors serves to structure both the logic and the rhetoric of the argument. The essential premisses are established in Section I, on the basis of what the Many would say. In Section II the conclusions reached in the preceding argument are accepted by all three sophists, and supplemented by a few apparently innocent propositions required for the final stage of the argument. The devastating conclusion is drawn in Section III in the exchange with Protagoras alone, isolated now both from the Many and from the other two sophists.

In Section I Socrates argues (with the concurrence of Protagoras) that although the Many believe that one's better judgment can be overcome by pleasure, their account of the matter is incoherent, since in the long run the Many have no criterion for what is good except the balance of pleasure over pain. Hence, by their own criteria, *akrasia* or "being overcome by pleasure" is really a mistake in measuring the long term balance between pleasures and pains.

In Section II our rationalist text is immediately preceded by two important moves: (1) the dramatically highlighted moment in which Socrates switches interlocutors, abandoning the Dialogue with the Many in order to gain the participation and assent of all three sophists, and (2) the relatively inconspicuous passage in which the three sophists accept a proposition that is not utilized until later in Section III, in the final exchange with Protagoras alone: "Are not all actions noble (*kalai*) that lead to a painless and pleasant life? And a noble act is good and beneficial?" (358B 4, preparing for 359E 6). We will see in a moment how this new proposition contributes to the final dénouement. But first we must identify the function of the rationalist text. Its role will be clearer if we begin with the refutation of Protagoras in Section III.

The final argument is presented by Socrates as a continuation of the line of reasoning begun in his first, abortive attempt to prove that courage is the same as wisdom, at the very beginning of Episode 4, at 349E.[33] This preliminary attempt was broken off (at 350cff.) by Protagoras' complaint that Socrates was distorting his concessions and reasoning invalidly. Socrates here recalls two agreements from this earlier exchange that Protagoras now reaffirms: that brave men are bold (*tharraleoi*), and that they are eager (*itai*) to confront and pursue what most people are afraid of (349E 2–3, recalled at 359B 8–C 4). But now it is impossible to say (as people generally would say) that cowards pursue what is safe, whereas brave men pursue what is fearful (*deina*). This has been ruled out by two concessions that were extracted from all three sophists in the transitional Section II. The two concessions are (1) that fear is an expectation of evil (358D), and (2) that no one pursues what they believe to be evil. Hence no one pursues what they believe to be fearful (358E 3–6, recalled at 359D 5). Proposition 2 is of course derived from our rationalist text, and its larger implications are recalled here in the context of the final argument: "since loss of self-control was found to be ignorance" (359D 6). It turns out that the decisive function of this rationalist doctrine that rules out *akrasia* is that it also rules out the ordinary understanding of courage and cowardice: "All men pursue what they regard as safe, both cowards and brave men, and in this respect they pursue the same goals" (359D 7). All this follows "if the previous arguments were rightly demonstrated" (359D 3–5), namely, the arguments derived from the rationalist doctrine that no one pursues what they believe to be evil.

Nevertheless, brave men are willing to go to war, cowards not. Why? At this point we get the new interpretation of courage that will assimilate it to wisdom. It is noble (*kalon*) to go to war (359E 5).

---

33. On this and on several points in what follows, I have profited from a discussion of this passage with John Cooper.

But we have agreed that if it is noble, it is also good. (This is where the inconspicuous premiss from Section II is put to work.) Hence cowards are unwilling to do something that is noble and good. But if it is noble and good, it is also pleasant (360A 3, recalling the hedonist identification of the good and the pleasant in the Dialogue with the Many, implicitly accepted by the sophists in Section II). This inference from good to pleasure serves to set up the decisive question: "Do cowards knowingly (*gignōskontes*) refuse to pursue what is more noble and better *and more pleasant*?" (360A 4). Protagoras recognizes that if we accept this, "we will violate our previous agreements." What acceptance of the implied statement would violate is precisely the rationalist premiss that everyone pursues what they take to be good. We can now add "and pleasant," on the strength of the hedonist identification. If the cowards knew that going to war was noble and good (and pleasant), they would be eager to go! They must be acting out of ignorance.

The appeal to hedonism here, to the good understood as the pleasant, is logically superfluous. The argument would go through quite smoothly on the basis of the rationalist premiss alone, in terms of pursuing good and avoiding evil, in conjunction with (1) the judgment that going to war is noble, and (2) the inference from noble to good. Hedonism is not stressed in this context, since it is intuitively not very plausible to claim that brave men readily go to war because they find it more pleasant than staying at home. But the hedonism is nevertheless recalled, since it provided the original basis for the metrical model for choice, which in turn supports the rationalist doctrine that cowards cannot knowingly avoid what is better. Strictly speaking, the hedonist premiss did logical work *only* in the Dialogue with the Many, by eliminating the ordinary understanding of *akrasia*. But it casts its shadow over the entire argument, since (as we shall see) the later stretches of the argument would collapse if *akrasia* were not eliminated.

Once Socrates has got Protagoras to grant that cowards are mistaken in their judgment as to the goodness or badness of going to war, he is home free. Courage can now be defined in terms of knowing what is and is not fearful, i.e., bad; cowardice will be the corresponding form of ignorance. Nearly all of the premisses for this argument are already established in the transitional Section II, in which all three sophists accept propositions (the goodness of pleasure, the link between the noble and the good, the rationalist calculus of good, the definition of fear as expectation of evil) that embody and extend the cognitive model for choice developed in the preceding Dialogue with the Many. Only two new premises need to be accepted by Protagoras for his final refutation in Section III: (1) the uncontroversial observation that brave men are willing to go to war, cowards not, and (2) the moral judgment that going to war is noble (*kalon*).

Since Socrates and Protagoras share the standard Greek view of the matter, the second proposition is also not controversial for them. Hence, in terms of the strategy of the argument, Protagoras is now left without any path of escape. But it is not only a dialectical trap that has been sprung; Socrates has changed the terms of the debate. Because of the link previously established between the noble and the good, this proposition that going to war is noble has the crucial effect of introducing moral values into what might otherwise seem a value-free calculus of utilities, with good and bad interpreted quite narrowly in terms of perceived advantage and disadvantage. (Socrates had earlier prevented Protagoras from appealing to moral considerations as represented by *ta kala*, "things honorable," at 351C 1. The significance of this early move becomes apparent only now, in the final stage of the argument.)[34] In fact the identification of *good* and *bad* with pleasure and pain in the Dialogue with the Many imposes the subjective, prudential interpretation of the good as what I perceive to be in my interest, as distinct from a normative understanding of good as what is morally right or impersonally best. But the addition of *to kalon* in Section II allows the final argument to re-establish contact with the moral-social perspective within which courage can be found both admirable and good. And it is this introduction of *to kalon* that explains how Socrates is able to perform the sleight-of-hand trick by which courage and cowardice are transformed into wisdom and ignorance.

---

34. Protagoras had attempted to introduce the dimension of social-moral approval into the initial discussion of hedonism, by objecting that a pleasant life was good "on condition that one takes pleasure in honorable things (*ta kala*)" (351C 1). But this effort to limit the hedonistic account of the good is brushed aside by Socrates, who will insist (and get Protagoras to agree) that the many have no ultimate criterion to appeal to other than pleasure and pain. Consideration of *to kalon* is reintroduced only after the Dialogue with the Many is concluded, at 358B 5 and 359E 5ff.

I think we may see this careful maneuver, in which moral considerations are at first excluded and then at the last moment reintroduced, as reflecting Plato's awareness that one cannot get from
hedonism to morality as ordinarily understood without invoking a
fundamentally different standard for moral approval and disap-
proval. But if this is correct, we are free to see both the hedonism
of Section I and the omnipotent rationalism built upon it in Section II as asserted here not for their own sake but instrumentally,
for the sake of the Socratic conclusions to be derived in Section
III.[35]

How does this understanding of the argument affect the status
of the rationalist text? The denial of *akrasia* contained in this text
now appears as a cunning stratagem designed to serve the more
fundamental purpose of the argument, namely, to equate virtue
with knowledge, vice with ignorance, and thus establish the Socratic paradox and demonstrate the unity of the virtues. As Socrates said earlier, in response to Protagoras' impatient question why
they should bother with the vulgar view of *akrasia* in the first
place, "I think this is useful for finding out how courage is related
to the other parts of virtue" (353B 1–3). The unity of the virtues in
wisdom is the underlying theme of the entire dialogue, from the
moment that Socrates first raises the question of how the parts of
virtue are related to one another. And it is the rationalist account
of *akrasia*, with the corresponding reduction of fear to a purely
cognitive state, the expectation of evil, that permits Socrates to
dismiss the usual understanding of courage in order to identify it
(and, by implication, all the other virtues) with wisdom, that is to
say, with the knowledge of what is good and what is bad.

Turning now to the antecedents of the rationalist text in Section
I, in the Dialogue with the Many, we see that this intellectualist
doctrine depends upon hedonism in two respects. First of all, it is
the identification of the good with the pleasant that rules out as
incoherent the usual account of *akrasia* as "being overcome by
pleasure." (The argument here, at 355A–356A, depends upon the
substitution of "pleasant" and "good" for one another, which is
only justified if the two terms are logically equivalent.) And if this
ordinary account of *akrasia* had not been rejected, it would be easy

35. This is essentially the view of Zeyl (1980) 250–69 as far as hedonism is con-
    cerned; but he is inclined to count the denial of *akrasia* among the Socratic
    conclusions.

to say that "no one pursues a lesser good or a greater evil, *except when they are overcome by pleasure.*" But to allow such an exception would be to undermine the rationalist text, on which the final argument depends. In order to equate cowardice with ignorance, Socrates must eliminate *akrasia* and reduce fear to a judgment of future evil. For otherwise the interlocutor could always claim that the coward knows what is noble and good but is overcome by fear.[36]

Socrates' model for rational choice in terms of measurement and calculation rests upon the assumption that we have only two commensurable values, one positive and one negative, in terms of which all decisions are to be made. In principle, of course, we could substitute other concepts such as satisfaction, desirability, reinforcement or utility for pleasure (and correspondingly for pain) without any change in the model. But the result would be less intuitive. We are appealing here to the Many; and the Many prefer to speak in terms of pleasure and pain.

Ultimately, then, the whole argument against *akrasia* in the Dialogue with the Many depends upon the identification of the good with the pleasant. Socrates is quite clear on this point. He says explicitly "all of the proofs depend upon this" (354E 7); and he repeatedly reminds us that he is relying on the inability of the Many to recognize any criterion of good and bad in the long run other than overall pleasure and pain (353E 6, 354B 7, D 8, 355A 1–5). Hence, although the Many are initially unwilling to identify the pleasant and the good (351C 3), they end by having no other choice. In this respect the hedonism of the *Protagoras* is after all the popular view.

Now, curiously enough, it is not Socrates who proposed this hedonist thesis. He began by suggesting only that pleasure as such is good, pain as such bad (351C 4–6, E 1–3).[37] This leaves open the possibility that there are other goods than pleasure: for example, honor. It is Protagoras who misunderstands him to be asserting an identity thesis, which Protagoras himself is reluctant to accept

---

36. For a parallel development of the argument against "overcome by pleasure" to cover the case of "overcome by fear," see Santas (1971b) 284–6.

37. This seems to me the natural reading of καθ' ὃ ἡδέα ἐστίν, ... ἀγαθά, καθ' ὃ ἀνιαρά, κακά at 351C 4–6 (and similarly at E 1–2). For a stronger interpretation which construes Socrates as proposing hedonism from the start, see Zeyl (1980) 252–4. Plato never denies that harmless pleasures are good. See *Rep.* II, 357B 7, *Philebus* 63E 2–7, 66C 4–6.

(351E 5). Socrates argues only that *the many* must recognize this identity, since in the long run they can find no other criterion (no *telos* or final outcome) for distinguishing good and bad. He then exploits the hedonism of the many against their notion of being overcome by pleasure (355Aff.). So Socrates' argument here has the overall structure of an elenchus, refuting the thesis of the many from premisses they accept. By adopting the general view of the many on good and bad, he can show that their special view on *akrasia* is absurd, just as he will later show that the popular conception of courage and cowardice is incompatible with their general view, once *akrasia* has been eliminated.

Socrates himself never agrees to the identification of the good with the pleasant *in propria persona*. When he turns from the many to the three sophists at the beginning of Section II, he propounds the thesis in an ambiguous form: "You agree, then, that the pleasant is good, the painful bad" (358A 5, and so again at B 6: "if then, the pleasant is good ... "). The sophists naturally understand this as an identity, since that is how the thesis had functioned in the preceding arguments of Section I. But Socrates has committed himself only to the weaker view, that pleasure as such is a good thing, and that being pleasant is to that extent – qua being pleasant – being good. And this view is of course too weak to support the rationalist thesis that follows. If we do not have an identity, the substitution of "pleasant" for "good" (and conversely) cannot be made, and the argument against *akrasia* collapses. The perceptive reader will again be attentive to this gap between the moderate view proposed by Socrates and the unrestricted hedonism finally accepted by the many. Such a reader will recognize that the argument against *akrasia* and in support of omnipotent rationalism, depending as it does on the hedonist assumption, is throughout an argument *ad populum*.

That is not the only subtle clue in this context to suggest that Socrates is here arguing tongue in cheek. The acceptance by all three sophists of the popular view is secured by a rhetorical ploy that has perhaps not been adequately appreciated by the commentators.[38] In concluding the Dialogue with the Many at the end

38. For an honorable exception see Zeyl (1980) 268 n.37, who also cites O'Brien (1967: 138) on 357E: "This is more than an ironical aside in an otherwise straightforward exposition: it is rather a clue that Socrates is not being straightforward at all."

of Section I, and immediately before turning to the three sophists, Socrates remarks that, since being overcome by pleasure has proved to be the greatest form of ignorance, and since teachers such as Protagoras, Prodicus, and Hippias claim to be able to cure such ignorance, the many are making a great mistake by refusing to spend their money on education for themselves and their children (357E). It is not then so surprising that, when Socrates immediately afterwards asks the sophists whether what he says is true, they all three enthusiastically concur (358A 4). At this point the attentive reader will recall that a quite different view of the value of sophistic teaching was suggested by Socrates to Hippocrates in the prologue (313A–314B). And such a reader may well be suspicious of the bait the sophists are so eagerly swallowing. Plato has thus put us on guard against the ensuing exchange with the three sophists in Section II (358A–E). But it is precisely in this passage that the rationalist account of human nature is established, together with the other key premises for the final argument against Protagoras.

We saw earlier that the evidence from other dialogues indicates that Plato was no more committed to omnipotent rationalism than he was to the hedonist equation of pleasure with the good. We have now found a series of signposts carefully placed in the text, in such a way that they seem designed to alert the reader that Socrates is engaged in an elaborate set of tactical moves, so that not everything he says can be taken at face value. It may be useful to tabulate here the clues we have noticed.

1. The refusal to allow Protagoras to introduce social-moral considerations (*ta kala*) before the Dialogue with the Many (see above, n.34); whereas Socrates himself will do so surreptitiously *after* that dialogue has been concluded.

2. The careful refusal on Socrates' part to *assert* the identity of pleasure and the good, while exploiting this identity in the rejection of *akrasia*, once Protagoras has introduced it for consideration.

3. Repeated emphasis on the fact that this identity is established only by the inability of the many to specify any standard for good other than pleasure. (This correlates with the fact that *to kalon*, the principle of moral-social approval, has been excluded from the discussion of the good throughout the Dialogue with the Many.) The hedonistic premiss is thus supported *only* from the viewpoint of the many.

4. The avoidance, within the Dialogue with the Many, of any

reference to the hedonistic calculus in terms of virtue (though it is recognized as "the salvation of our life"); and the added qualification that we have not yet specified what *kind* of knowledge the measuring art must be (357B 5).

5. The device by which the agreement of the sophists is obtained to the results of the Dialogue with the Many – by appealing, so to speak, to their pocketbook.

6. Finally, the ambiguous position of pleasure in the final discussion of courage. Moral approval of courage is first expressed by *kalon* ("admirable"), which then entails "good", which then entails "pleasant." The conception of virtue as such is thus *inserted* into the hedonist calculation; the preference for courage over cowardice is neither derived from the calculus nor justified by it, *except* as a result of this external consideration in terms of moral approval.

(The limitations of the argument in the *Protagoras* as a defence of Socratic morality will be further discussed in § 8.)

Accordingly, we have abundant hints and clues from the last argument of the *Protagoras* that much of Socrates' reasoning here is manipulative and insincere. But why has Plato made Socrates seem so perverse? I suggest that Socrates is here deluding the sophists with a rationalist theory of choice, just as he has deluded them with Laconic philosophy in the interpretation of Simonides' poem, and that the motivation in both cases is the same: to establish the paradox that no one is voluntarily bad, and hence that deliberately bad actions are always motivated by a false view of the good. This result was insinuated in the poetic episode[39] and is now deductively argued for on the basis of the hedonist premiss and the rational model for decision. The author of the dialogue is committed to the truth of the paradox.[40] He is no more committed to the hedonism and the rationalist decision theory than he is to the virtuoso misinterpretation of Simonides' poem. The former, like the latter, is a device contrived for presenting the paradox, and in this case presenting it as the necessary consequence of certain popular assumptions about human motivation.

If we thus avoid a naive reading of this extremely subtle argu-

---

39. See above, n.6.
40. And he remained committed. Cf. *Rep.* IX, 589C 6: the enemy of justice is not voluntarily mistaken (*ou gar hekōn hamartanei*); and quotations from the *Timaeus* and *Laws* in § 9 below, with *Soph.* 228C, 230A; *Philebus* 22B.

ment, we see that neither Plato nor Socrates in the *Protagoras* is guilty of ignoring obvious facts of human behavior or denying the complexity of motivation that is conceptualized for the first time in the psychological theory of the *Republic*. The author of the *Protagoras* is playing with a simple model of rational decision theory as a hint of deeper thoughts to come, concerning the *technē* that is knowledge of good and evil.

7. PLATO'S "REVISION" OF SOCRATIC INTELLECTUALISM

The apparent discrepancy between the intellectualism of the *Protagoras* and the moral psychology of the *Republic* is troublesome only if the former is interpreted as a descriptive account of ordinary human action and motivation. If, on the other hand, the notion of knowledge as sufficient for virtue is construed as a normative ideal, applicable only in the case of philosophic virtue as represented by Socrates, then there is no problem in reconciling this with the psychology of the *Republic*, where a similar ideal prevails. And if the denial of *akrasia* is understood not as a thesis to which Socrates (or Plato) is committed, but as a dialectical device for bringing the many and the sophists to accept the Socratic paradox and the unity of the virtues in knowledge, then again there is no conflict with the *Republic*.

It will be objected, however, that Plato himself recognizes such a conflict, since he explicitly forswears Socratic intellectualism in *Republic* IV. On the developmental account, this marks the point at which Plato decisively abandons his earlier, Socratic psychology. Hence we must examine this passage closely.

In order to establish the difference between the rational and non-rational parts of the soul, Socrates insists that thirst as such is the desire for drink alone, not for good drink. To this claim he foresees the following objection:

Watch out lest someone take us by surprise and disturb the argument, claiming that no one desires (*epithumei*) drink but good drink, and not food but good food. For everyone desires good things (*ta agatha*). If thirst is a desire (*epithumia*), it will be the desire for good drink or something else good, and so for the other desires. (IV, 438A)

This is a "Socratic" objection, which the new Socrates must refute. For the psychology of the *Republic* depends upon the assumption that "the soul of a thirsty person, to the extent that it is thirsty, wants (*bouletai*) nothing other than to drink" (439A 9). Hence not every occurrent desire, every episode of wanting or craving, can be or involve a judgment as to what is good. In *Republic* IV it is clear that Plato does not endorse the medieval axiom: *quidquid appetitur, appetitur sub ratione boni*, "everything that is desired, is desired under the aspect of good."[41] He recognizes the reality of brute desires, independent of any judgment as to what is good or beneficial.

Nevertheless, neither here nor elsewhere does Plato deny the general thesis maintained by the objector, namely, that *everyone desires good things*. This thesis is, in effect, a quotation from the *Meno* (77C 1, 78B 5). And we have found the same view articulated in the *Gorgias*: "When people act, they do all their actions for the sake of what is good (*heneka tou agathou*), for it is only good things that we want (*boulometha*)" (468B–C). Now this view is not given up in the *Republic* but forcefully reasserted: the good is "that which every soul pursues, and it is for the sake of this (*toutou heneka*) that it performs all its actions" (VI, 505D 11). So Plato maintains that the desire for good is universal in two respects: everyone has such a desire; and the good is the aim of every voluntary action. Everyone desires good things, because everyone has a rational principle, the *logistikon*, the capacity to calculate benefit and harm. And in the claim that the soul aims at the good in every action we recognize, in effect, the Socratic paradox. According to this paradox, failure to aim at the good will make the action *involuntary*, and hence not a proper act.[42]

What Plato rejects in *Republic* IV is not the thesis that everyone desires good things, but a different proposition that might easily be confused with this, namely, that every desire as such is a desire for something good or for something perceived as good. (This is a

41. I take the axiom to refer to desire construed opaquely or *de dictu*, and thus to claim that all desire conceives its object as good. The same thesis may be construed transparently (*de re*) as claiming that natural desires such as thirst aim at objects that are in fact normally beneficial, such as drink. If the axiom is so construed, Plato need not reject it; but I also see no evidence that he affirms it.

42. Another way to put the paradox is to say that true desire is always transparent or *de re*: what we really want is in every case what is actually (not what is apparently) good. (See *Rep*. VI, 505D 5–9.) Desire understood opaquely, as in the tyrant's desire for power by criminal means, will for Plato represent an error of judgment, a failure to recognize what one really wants.

third and different kind of universality.) But is the Socrates of the *Gorgias, Meno,* and *Protagoras* committed to this second proposition? Only in that case would we have evidence for a radical change in Plato's view.

Now the *Gorgias* will not help here, since the desires (*epithumiai*) that Callicles would develop and gratify to their maximum (491Eff.) are notoriously indifferent to whether or not their objects are intrinsically good. For Callicles happiness means pleasure or the satisfaction of desire, regardless of its object. A similar notion of desire not necessarily directed toward an object judged to be good is implied by the passage from the *Charmides* cited in §5, where *epithumia* for pleasure is distinguished from *boulēsis* of good. This distinction would be pointless if all desires were desires for something good.

The situation in the *Meno* is more complex. The relevant argument claims that no one desires bad things, because they do not want to be harmed: when they seem to desire bad things, it is in the mistaken belief that these are good (*Meno* 77B–78B). This leaves entirely open the possibility that some objects of desire are neutral, neither good nor bad; and so that not every desire is a desire for something perceived as good. The proposition rejected in *Republic* IV might *seem* to follow from the argument in the *Meno*. But in fact that argument (if it goes through at all) still goes through smoothly if the proposition in question is denied. For the conclusion that no one desires bad things neither entails nor presupposes that every desire is for something good. A whole range of desires may be neutral with regard to judgments concerning what is good, as long as no desire is for something (perceived as) bad. The fact that the *Meno* ignores neutral desires does not mean that it denies their existence.[43]

---

43. The only text that might be construed as ruling out good-independent desires is some slightly inconsistent language in the means–ends analysis of *Gorgias* 467C–468C, where Socrates first *denies* that we desire the means to a desired end (467D 7 and 468B 9), but then says we want such means only if they are beneficial (468C 4ff.). The verb for wanting here is *boulesthai*, not *epithumein*; and in the *Gorgias* that makes a difference. Hence it would be a mistake to interpret this text as a general denial of brute or value-neutral desires. The *epithumiai* endorsed by Callicles at 491Eff. are conceived precisely in this way, as urges or drives spontaneously experienced and uncritically endorsed. For the notion that a desire such as thirst can be beneficial, harmful or neither, see *Lysis* 221B 1ff.

What about the *Protagoras*? Like the *Meno*, it ignores the possibility of value-neutral or good-independent desires, and it does so all the more easily since it ignores the concept of desire altogether. Still, it might seem that the behavioral equivalent of the rejected proposition is entailed by the claim that "no one knowing or believing that something else is better than what he is doing, nevertheless does this when something better is available" (358B 7ff.). This does imply that, whenever an evaluation in terms of good–better or bad–worse is applied to a choice between actions, the agent will always choose the better or the less bad.[44] But is there anything in the text to imply that the good–bad calculus will come into play every time one acts? The rejected proposition (that every desire is a desire for something good) cannot be asserted in the *Protagoras*, because in this dialogue Socrates avoids the language of desire. And the behavioral parallel to this proposition would be: that every action is pursued for the sake of the good. But this is precisely *not* a thesis that Plato will give up, as the quotation above from *Republic* VI, 505D makes clear. The Socratic paradox entails that every voluntary action will aim at the good, or at the perceived good. But it does not entail the rejected proposition about desire. Hence Plato can and will remain loyal to the paradox[45] after his explicit recognition of non-rational, value-neutral desires in *Republic* IV.

When they are carefully examined, then, the texts that form the dossier for Socratic intellectualism are seen neither to contain nor to entail the proposition that every desire aims at something good. Since no such position is defended in these dialogues, there is no earlier moral psychology that the later psychology must refute or reject. When we look closely, we see that the intellectualist texts in question can refer only to *rational* desire for something recognized as good or advantageous. But nowhere does Socrates claim that

---

44. If rational judgment concerning the good is applied to an action, the judgment will always be acted on: it is in this sense that the rationalist text does deny the reality of *akrasia*. According to that text, if there are brute, unreflective desires, they will never prevail against one's better judgment, although they might prevail if one behaved quite thoughtlessly. According to the doctrine of *Gorgias* 468B–C and *Rep.* VI, 505D, such thoughtless behavior could scarcely count as a (voluntary) action, since all actions are performed "for the sake of the good."

45. See n.40 above.

reason is the only force in the psyche, and hence that all desires are rational. These texts make no general claims about the psyche at all; and so they do not provide us with a moral psychology different from that of the *Republic*. What they offer instead is a sketch of rational choice theory: a blueprint for the *logistikon*, not for the psyche as a whole.[46]

8. THE DEFENSE OF THE SOCRATIC PARADOX

We have interpreted both hedonism and the denial of *akrasia* as dialectical devices designed to provide a persuasive defense of the Socratic paradox that no one is voluntarily bad but that vice in general, and cowardice in particular, is due to ignorance. Now what the *Protagoras* gives is a very limited, if very elegant, defense of this paradox. To make this point clear, it will be convenient to distinguish between moral and prudential versions of the paradox.[47]

The moral version interprets *good* and *evil* in terms of right and wrong and asserts that no one does wrong (*adikein*) voluntarily. The prudential version takes *good* and *evil* to mean advantageous and disadvantageous, and claims only that no one willingly and knowingly acts against their own best interest. The moral paradox follows from the prudential paradox if one adds the Socratic premiss (S) *It is never in one's interest to act unjustly (adikein).*[48] In order to justify

46. As far as I can see, the only text before the *Republic* to attempt even an embryonic distinction between parts of the soul is the reference in the *Gorgias* (493A 3, B 1) to "this [part] of the psyche where the *epithumiai* are." In the *Symposium* we have a mention of the whole range of psychic phenomena (207E: "temperaments [*tropoi*], characters [*ēthē*], opinions, desires [*epithumiai*], pleasures, pains, fears"), but no model for the psyche. In the *Phaedo*, where the tripartite psychology is twice prefigured (68C 1–3, 82C 3–8), the psyche is generally identified with the rational-cognitive principle, while the non-rational desires are assigned to the body (66C 6–D 1). Strictly speaking, there is no Platonic theory of the psyche before the *Republic*.

The bipartite psychology that was adumbrated in the *Gorgias* is finally spelled out in the *Phaedrus*, in the theory of motivation offered in Socrates' first speech (237Dff.). There we can recognize it as a simplified, less technical version of the tripartite psychology presented in the *Republic* and reflected later in the *Phaedrus*, in the psychological allegory of Socrates' second speech (246Aff.). It is essentially the same simplified, reason–emotion dualism that is utilized by Aristotle in the bipartite (rational/non-rational) psychology of *NE* I.13.

47. Following Santas (1964) 147–64.

48. For this premiss see *Crito* 49A, *Gorgias* 469B 8, C 2, 470E 9–11.

S, Plato must appeal to the conception of virtue as the good or healthy condition of the psyche, as he does in the *Gorgias* and at length in the *Republic*. But it is often a strategic advantage to keep premiss S out of sight, so as to defend the paradox in its less controversial, prudential form.

That is what we find in the *Protagoras*, where the hedonist premiss guarantees that good will be understood throughout in terms of the advantage of the agent as subjectively perceived. (The moral dimension is introduced only at the end, as we have seen, where the notion of the admirable is added to the notion of good, thus mixing together judgments of moral approval with judgments of personal advantage.) It is of course part of Plato's larger strategy to show that virtues such as justice and courage are not only good and admirable but also good-for-the-agent. In the end, and in the larger view, the prudential reading will always collapse into the moral view. But it is part of the cunning of these dialogues for Socrates on occasion to present the prudential version as if it were autonomous. This has encouraged some interpreters to characterize Socrates, or even Plato, as an ethical egoist.[49]

The distinction between the two readings is clearest in the *Gorgias*, where the paradox is most fully stated. In the debate with Polus Socrates will defend the paradox in its stronger, moral form. But he moves one step at a time. And the first step (down to *Gorgias* 468E) can be read as establishing only the prudential paradox. For here Socrates argues that persons who are ignorant of the good may do what they think best and yet not do what they want. It is because Polus takes "good" and "bad" to refer to the agent's advantage that he can unhesitatingly agree to the premises: that we all want what is good and beneficial, and that it is for the sake of

49. Most recently Penner in Kraut (1992) 135 and 155, n.23 (following many others, including Grote). The terminology can be misleading. There is a sense in which the moral philosophy of Plato (and presumably of Socrates as well) is egoistic, as is that of Aristotle and the Stoics. They all take for granted that the goal or *telos* of practical reason is a good life for the person who deliberates. However, if egoism is taken to imply a lack of respect for the welfare of others, none of these philosophies is egoistic. Since in the Socratic tradition virtue is an essential ("sovereign") component of the good life, there is no room for a conflict between morality and self interest correctly understood. That is why for Plato no one is voluntarily unjust. (After writing this note, I see that the point about egoism has been fully and lucidly developed by Annas [1993: 223–6].)

good things that we perform all our actions (468A–C). It follows
that anyone who (by mistake) does what is bad does not do what
they want (*bouletai*, 468D). Polus is perplexed by this result, but not
outraged. He becomes openly contemptuous only in the next
stage, when Socrates introduces the equivalent of proposition S in
the assertion that acting unjustly (*adikein*) is the greatest of evils
(469B 8), and adds to this the claim that Polus and everyone else
actually agree with him (474B). It is clear from the course of the
argument here that the prudential reading is only a preliminary
tactical move, designed to appeal to a wider audience and to a
hostile interlocutor like Polus, who is not prepared to accept the
Socratic moral position represented by proposition S.

The parallel argument in the *Meno* is more condensed and more
cunning. The moral implications are clearly indicated by references to justice, piety, and temperance in the context (78D; cf.
73A–C); and the argument is actually a response to Meno's suggestion that virtue be defined in terms of a desire (*epithumein*) for noble
things (*ta kala*, 77B 4). But Socrates immediately replaces "noble"
with "good" (*agatha*) and presents the argument in such a way as
to admit the prudential reading throughout. Thus he gets Meno
to conclude that "no one wants (*bouletai*) what is bad" (78B 1), because bad things are harmful (*blabera*), and no one wants to be
harmed. Anyone who desires (*epithumein*) bad things does so in the
belief that they are good and beneficial (*ōphelein*). So in reality,
everyone wants good things (78B 5).[50]

There are familiar problems with the logic of this argument that
need not concern us here.[51] What is noteworthy is that both in the
Gorgias and in the *Meno* the paradox is formulated in terms of *desire*
for the good; and it is in this form that the doctrine is recalled in
Republic IV. As we have seen, however, the *Protagoras* replaces the
notion of desire with a more strictly behavioral reference to pursuit
(*ienai epi*) of the good, avoidance of evil. How are we to explain
this striking *absence* of any reference to desire in the rationalist

50. Whereas in the *Gorgias* and *Charmides* Plato draws a terminological distinction
between *boulēsis* and *epithumia* that prefigures Aristotle's contrast between rational desire and appetite, in the *Meno* Plato alternates between *epithumein*
and *boulesthai* without any noticeable difference in meaning. So in the *Protagoras* this verbal distinction is treated as typical of the pedantry of Prodicus
(340A 8).

51. See the discussion above, p. 140.

account of action in the *Protagoras*? Probably this represents a deliberate precaution on the part of an author who is acutely aware of the diversity and potential conflict between desires. Any allusion to such diversity would make the omnipotent rationalism of *Protagoras* 358B–D seem less persuasive. The final argument of this dialogue relies upon a simplistic model for calculating benefits that must ignore desire, just as it ignores the emotions in general.

We may recall that a progression from the prudential to the moral reading of the paradox is suggested, but not developed, in the introduction of *to kalon* and the dimension of moral approval in the last stage of the argument (*Prot.* 359E–360B). As we have noted, the genuine Socratic position on justice and the health of the soul is never mentioned in the *Protagoras*, although there is a reminder of these concerns in the opening conversation with Hippocrates, where the sophist is described as a kind of merchant of groceries for the soul (313cff.). And there is a hint of Plato's own view in the notion that wisdom unites the parts of virtue. But if we want to know what the author of the *Protagoras* really thought of Socrates' arguments here, we can perhaps do no better than turn to the *Phaedo*:

I am afraid this is not the right exchange in regard to virtue, to exchange pleasures for pleasures, pains for pains, fear for fear, the greater for the less, like coins; but rather this is the only right coin: wisdom (*phronēsis*), against which all the rest should be exchanged. And when this is present there is real courage and temperance and justice and, in sum, true virtue, in the company of wisdom, regardless whether pleasures and pains and all the rest of this kind of thing are added or subtracted. But if they are exchanged for one another in separation from wisdom, I fear that virtue of that kind is a mere semblance (*skiagraphia*) and really slavish virtue, which has nothing sound or truthful in it. (69A–D)

The *Phaedo* goes on to expound a conception of wisdom directed to the Forms that has no parallel in the threshold dialogues. And commentators who regard Socratic intellectualism as a distinct stage in Plato's philosophical development may be inclined to recognize the *Phaedo* text as marking a change of mind on his part.[52]

---

52. So, for example, Irwin (1977) 161f. I am not convinced by the attempt of Gosling and Taylor (1982: 88–91) to deny the reference to the *Protagoras* in the exchanges of "pleasures for pleasures, pains for pains, fear for fear, the greater for the less, like coins" at *Phaedo* 69A.

But although there is a clear progression in philosophical exposition in the *Phaedo*, I see no evidence of any break with an earlier point of view. Thus the contrast between apparent or slavish virtue without wisdom, and true virtue determined by wisdom, is clearly prepared in the two arguments on right use cited above from the *Meno* and *Euthydemus* (pp. 225f.).

The conception of virtue based upon the hedonistic calculus in the *Phaedo* text is recognizably that of the *Protagoras*. So if Plato in the *Protagoras* is unwilling to speak of *aretē* in connection with this model, but uses instead euphemisms like "the salvation of our life" (356D 3, E 8, 357A 6),[53] that is likely to reflect his recognition that the prudential scheme developed in that dialogue represents only a deficient, popular or "slavish" conception of *aretē*, based upon the vulgar identification of the good with the pleasant. But he explicitly leaves the way open for a richer notion of wisdom to be developed elsewhere. For our present purposes, says Socrates, "it is enough (to establish) that it is knowledge. What kind of *technē* and knowledge it is, we will consider on another occasion" (357B 5). If we read this statement retrospectively, in the light of Plato's later work, we realize that the occasion in question was in fact provided by the *Phaedo* and the *Republic*. The conception of wisdom as a *metrētikē technē*, an art of measurement, in the *Protagoras* is thus a partial but deliberate foreshadowing of the stronger, metaphysically grounded notion of *phronēsis* we find in the *Phaedo*.

Why then does Plato bother to give us such an elaborate piece of argumentation for such an inadequate account of wisdom and virtue? First of all, as we have seen, the calculus model for practical knowledge in the *Protagoras* provides a brilliant (if not entirely satisfactory) defense of the Socratic paradox by confirming it even at what might seem to some critics its weakest point, in the denial of *akrasia*.[54] In this perspective, the argument is a real *tour de force*. But the final section of the *Protagoras* gives us more than a defense of the paradox. It provides a schematic account of practical wisdom,

---

53. The refusal to mention *aretē* in this connection is most striking at the very end of the Dialogue with the Many, where the clause "on the grounds that it is not teachable" (357E 6) clearly refers to virtue, although the word for virtue has not been pronounced.

54. Plato, it seems, never draws the Aristotelian distinction between *akrasia* and vice, so this is not really his problem. Like vice, genuinely akratic action will be involuntary. See below, §9.

defined by a preliminary sketch of its content, the good. From the *Laches* and *Charmides* we have hints of a conception of virtue as knowledge concerning good and evil; in the *Meno* and *Euthydemus* virtue is further specified as knowledge of the right use of prima-facie goods. But these formulae give us little more than promissory notes. What, after all, is right use? And what is the good?

The *Protagoras* represents Plato's only attempt to deal directly with these issues in the threshold dialogues, without the richer resources of the *Symposium* and *Phaedo*. Plato has chosen to explore here the connections between knowledge and the good in the context of a debate on moral education between Socrates and Protagoras that is, I suggest, to be read in the light of his own educational project.

Both Antisthenes and Isocrates, Plato's chief educational rivals, could, like Protagoras, pay lip service to the central importance of knowledge or wisdom (*phronēsis, sophia*) for a good and successful life.[55] Neither of them, however, was in a position to specify with any precision the scope and content of such supremely beneficial knowledge. It is one of Plato's principal goals in the threshold and middle dialogues to do just this: first, to show the decisive role of knowledge in the good life, and then to give a theoretical account of the object of such knowledge.

Knowledge being defined by its content, the knowledge that is to be beneficial must be specified by a clarification of the notion of good. This clarification is pursued in two stages, the first of which is represented here in the *Protagoras*, where Socrates is articulating the view of "the many." This will give us only a popular conception of the good. For the second, more philosophic stage in Plato's account of the good we must look to the *Lysis* and to the theory of love to be discussed in the next chapter. The final section of the *Protagoras* is best understood as Plato's first step towards a progressive clarification of this notion of the good as the object of beneficial knowledge. That explains why it contains the most substantial piece of constructive argument in any dialogue before the *Phaedo*.

What we have in the *Protagoras* is of course only a schematic model for knowledge of the good, based upon the "vulgar" iden-

---

55. For Antisthenes see above p. 7. For Isocrates see Eucken (1983) with reference to Marrou (1950) 121–36 and Jaeger (1944) English tr. 46–155.

tification of the good with the pleasant. But this model is not entirely misleading. Pleasure *does* represent the good in one crucial respect, as an object of universal desire and pursuit.[56] And reason will remain for Plato a power of calculation, a *logistikon*. After all, the hedonistic calculus is not a bad model for ordinary prudence. And prudence in turn is a kind of image, an inferior likeness for what wisdom will mean for Plato.[57]

9. EPILOGUE ON *AKRASIA* IN PLATO

Since we do not know what went on between Socrates and Euripides in the fifth century, for the history of philosophy the discussion of *akrasia* begins with the *Protagoras*. It was taken up then by Aristotle, whose discussion of voluntary action in *Eudemian Ethics* II.7–8 is largely dominated by problems connected with *akrasia*: is action voluntary when done in accordance with rational desire (*boulēsis*) against appetite (*epithumia*)? or conversely? And is yielding to temptation a matter of compulsion (*bia*)? "Therefore there is a great deal of dispute about the *enkratēs* and the *akratēs*" (*EE* II.8, 1224a31). And in the *Nicomachean Ethics* VII (= *EE* VI) Aristotle devotes ten long chapters to the analysis of this phenomenon and its varieties. He takes it for granted that there is an important distinction to be drawn between *akrasia* and vice: the akratic person is one who knows an action to be morally bad but does it nevertheless because of passion (*pathos*), whereas the vicious person does not recognize what he does as bad (*NE* VII.1, 1145b12).

Among contemporary philosophers also the issue of *akrasia* has been a fruitful topic for discussion in moral psychology. We can mention, as two among many, the classic papers by Donald Davidson (1980), and Gary Watson (1977). Watson takes Plato as his

---

56. Compare *Philebus* 20D 8: "every subject that recognizes the good goes in pursuit and hunts it down, wanting to catch and possess it"; but a life without pleasure is not choiceworthy (21E).

57. Note the return of the hedonistic calculus in the popular morality of Plato's prologue to his law code in *Laws* V, 733A–D. It is "pleasure and pains and desires (*epithumiai*)" that represent "what is naturally most human" in the domain of motivation (732E 4). So also *Laws* II, 663B 4: "No one would willingly be persuaded to perform an action unless the consequences involve more pleasure than pain." For the primary importance of pleasure and pain in the psychology of the *Laws* (where they first enter as "two foolish counselors" in Book I, 644C 6), see Stalley (1983) 59–70.

point of reference, and identifies "socratism" as the best-known denial of akratic behavior.

In the face of this millennial tradition deriving from Plato's *Protagoras*, it may seem paradoxical to suggest that Plato himself had relatively little interest in the phenomena of acting against one's better judgment, and that he systematically ignores the distinction between *akrasia* and vice. Yet this seems in fact to be the case. Plato's primary interest, in the *Protagoras* as elsewhere, is in the deep meaning of the Socratic paradox that no one does evil voluntarily, because what everyone really wants is the good. Actions done out of ignorance of the good are thereby counted as involuntary. Behavior against one's judgment as to what is best will (it seems) scarcely count as an action at all; such behavior may either be ignored or assimilated to ignorance. For if one's grip on the good, or the apparent good, is so weak as not to prevail in action, it cannot count as knowledge and is scarcely better than ignorance.

Such is, I take it, Plato's view not only in the *Protagoras* but in the *Republic* as well. In the *Protagoras* he makes Socrates deny such behavior (in despite of common sense and common experience), because this is the decisive move in an elaborate dialectical "revision" of the notion of courage. As we have seen, Socrates' account of courage (as knowledge of what is and is not to be feared) would collapse if the interlocutor could reply: the coward often knows that he should not run away, but he is simply overcome by fear. The deep point is that a person would not even be touched by fear, or at any rate would have no inclination to yield to it, if he or she truly *understood* that death in battle was preferable to life with dishonor.[58] But this deep point cannot be effectively made in a dialectical exchange with Protagoras as representative for the many. So instead a formally equivalent but more superficial version of the same point is made by establishing the definition of courage in terms of knowledge of what is fearful, on the basis of the denial of *akrasia*.

In the *Republic* Plato does not deny *akrasia*. On the contrary, he gives a clear example of it in the story of Leontius, who is de-

58. For this super-strong concept of moral knowledge, which presupposes emotional self-control, compare John McDowell's notion of virtue as *silencing* other motivation. See McDowell (1980) 370.

scribed as in conflict over the urge to gaze on corpses, but is finally "overpowered by the desire" (IV, 440A). So, says Socrates, "we observe in many other cases, when desires (*epithumiai*) compel someone [to act] against reasonable judgment (*logismos*), that the person scolds himself and is angry with the compelling part in himself; it is as if two parts were in conflict (*stasiazontoin*)" (440B). This is unmistakably a description of *akrasia*. But it is conceptually identical with the account of psychic *stasis* that is characterized as "injustice and depravity (*akolasia*) and cowardice and ignorance and, in short, all vice," when one part of the soul revolts, so that the soul is ruled by a part that ought to be subservient (444B).

Despite the fact that the tripartite psychology gives Plato the theoretical resources for a distinction between *akrasia* and vice, his description of non-virtuous individuals in Books VIII–IX draws no such distinction and takes no account of cases such as Leontius. In effect, Plato in the *Republic* gives two alternative versions of the psychology of vice. In Book IV vice is represented as *stasis* or conflict between the parts of the soul. If the lower appetites revolt against reason and prevail (*kratein*), the resulting condition of vice is indistinguishable from *akrasia*. (Thus at IV, 430E 6 *sōphrosunē* is defined as *enkrateia* of pleasures and appetites, while at 431A 7–B 2 *akolasia* is described as loss of self-control, being ἥττων ἑαυτοῦ). In the later books, however, the non-virtuous types are described not as situations of psychic revolt but rather as established, post-revolutionary regimes, with the lower principle comfortably seated on the throne of the soul. In these contexts Plato tends to represent the victory of the lower parts as a distortion rather than as an overthrow of reason: the person does not act against his better judgment because that judgment itself has been perverted. (See *Rep.* VIII, 553D 1–4 and the texts cited below, Chapter 9 §5.) Aside from the Leontius passage, Plato in the *Republic* avoids describing a situation where someone can judge correctly but act badly nevertheless. His concern is not with moral weakness but with alternative principles that can rule in the psyche. Perhaps he neglects cases of weakness because such cases might seem to tell against his claim that vice is never voluntary.

In his later work, however, Plato finds ways to reaffirm the paradox while at the same time giving full recognition to the reality of moral weakness or loss of self-control. He now divides vice into two kinds, corresponding to the difference in treatment between

Book IV and Books VIII–IX. Thus in *Timaeus* 86B he recognizes two kinds of psychic disorder, both of them characterized as folly (*anoia*), but distinguished as ignorance (*amathia*) and madness (*mania*). The former is attributed to bad social influence and inadequate education; the latter is due to corporeal imbalances producing excessive pleasures or pains. So that "in almost all cases of failure to overcome pleasures (*akrateia hēdonōn*) it is a mistake to make it a reproach, in the belief that people are voluntarily bad. For no one is voluntarily bad, but it is because of some bad condition of the body and growing up without education that a bad person becomes bad; but these states are hateful to everyone and voluntarily accepted by no one" (86D–E).

In the prologue to the law code of *Laws* V the same distinction is mentioned in conjunction with the same paradox, but the category of madness is apparently replaced by *akrasia*. "It is clear that every depraved person is, by necessity, involuntarily depraved (*akolastos*). For the mass of mankind live an intemperate life because of ignorance (*amathia*) or lack of self-control (*akrateia*) or both" (734B). In the *Laws* the phenomenon of *akrasia* is described on at least three different occasions (III, 689A 1–C 3, hating what seems noble, loving what is judged base and unjust; IX, 875A 1–C 3, weakness of human nature under great temptation; X, 902A 6–B 2, acting against one's better judgment as characteristic of the *phaulotatoi* of human beings). It is above all in the context of a situation of unlimited political power that Plato acknowledges that intellectual insight alone is not sufficient for virtuous action (IX, 875A–C; cf. III, 691C 5–D 4 and IV, 713C 6–8).

Even in the more popular, less explicitly theoretical discussion of the *Laws*, where the need for emotional rather than intellectual training tends to predominate, the loss of control over the emotions (*akrateia*) is seen as a source of vice, not as an alternative to it. As with Leontius in the *Republic*, so more extensively in the *Laws*: Plato is perfectly willing to recognize the phenomenology of *akrasia*, but (as far as I can see) he will never draw a theoretical line between *akrasia* and vice. *Akrasia* is merely the extreme example of a failure to harmonize the emotions with reason, precisely the kind of vice (*ponēria, kakia*) that the *Sophist* defines in terms of disease and conflict (*stasis*), in contrast to an intellectual failure to perceive the good (*Sophist* 228A–E).

For further discussion of *akrasia* see Stalley (1983) 50–4 and Bobonich (1994) 3–36. Stalley (p. 52) concludes that for Plato "acts done through weakness of will are not genuinely voluntary," just as vice in general is involuntary. Similarly Bobonich (p. 18, n.33): "all strict akratic and near akratic action is unwilling."

CHAPTER 9

The object of love

I. ERŌS AND PHILIA

No philosopher has had more to say about love than Plato. From the literary point of view his interest in the subject – or shall we say his passion – was favored by the fact that *erōs* was independently established as a central theme in the tradition of Socratic literature. But in strictly philosophical terms the importance of this subject in Plato's thought is greater than is commonly realized. I shall argue that Plato's theory of *erōs* provides an essential link between his moral psychology and his metaphysical doctrine of Forms. So it is for good reason that Plato selects the discussion of *erōs* in the *Symposium* as the occasion for announcing to the world the new conception of reality represented by the Forms. From the point of view of ingressive exposition, we can see the *Symposium* as providing a transitional moment between the inconclusive treatment of virtue, knowledge, and education in the aporetic dialogues, and the great constructive theories of the *Phaedo* and *Republic*.

To avoid misunderstanding, we must qualify the sense in which Plato develops a theory of love. First of all, the Greeks have two terms corresponding to "love" in English or *amour* in French: *erōs* and *philia*, which are quite different in meaning from one another. Plato's theory is almost exclusively concerned with *erōs*. Furthermore, Plato's account of *erōs* is developed less for its own sake than for further philosophical purposes, which are moral and metaphysical. We are principally concerned here with this broader function of the theory. But first we need to take account of the contrast between *erōs* and *philia*.

The noun *erōs* and its verb *eran* properly denote sexual passion, whereas *philia* and *philein* describe milder forms of affection.[1] Hence *philia* is generally translated as "friendship" rather than "love." The distribution of interest between Plato and Aristotle on these two themes is instructive. Aristotle devoted three books of his *Ethics*[2] to the topic of *philia* or friendship, with scarcely a word about *erōs*, which he once refers to as "an excess of *philia*."[3] Aristotle either regarded *erōs* as an unimportant topic for philosophy, or felt that enough had been said on the subject by Plato and others. Plato composed two major dialogues on the theme of *erōs*, whereas he discusses *philia* in the shorter, aporetic *Lysis*. Even in the *Lysis* the conversation on friendship is set within a narrative frame that depicts an erotic infatuation of the youth Hippothales for the boy Lysis; and the discussion of *philia* is itself oriented in the direction of *erōs*, as we shall see.

In devoting so much attention to *philia*, Aristotle may be seen as undertaking to complete a job that Plato had left undone. It has often been remarked that Aristotle's discussion of friendship does in fact take as its point of departure the *aporiai* propounded by Plato in the *Lysis*. But whereas Aristotle is genuinely concerned to give an adequate account of the phenomena of interpersonal friendship and affection, it would be a mistake to interpret Plato as embarking on a comparable account of *erōs*.

As several recent authors have pointed out, Plato does not attempt to construct a comprehensive philosophy of love.[4] Plato is concerned with *erōs* as the strongest form of desire. But it is not desire in general that counts as *erōs*. For Plato, *erōs* is desire of what is beautiful (*to kalon*); and what is beautiful is closely akin to what is good (*agathon*). We shall have more to say about the nature of this kinship. I will argue that the theory of *erōs* formulated in the *Symposium*, and prefigured in the *Lysis*, is a direct development and transformation of the doctrine of the *Gorgias* and *Meno* that everyone desires the good. When the good appears as the beautiful, desire takes the form of *erōs*.

---

1. On the meaning of *erōs* and *philia*, see the studies of Dover and Vlastos cited in Halperin (1985) 163 with n.15.
2. *EE* VIII, *NE* VIII–IX.
3. *NE* IX.10, 1171a11. For further details see "Aristotle on Erotic Love" in Price (1989) 236–49.
4. See Halperin (1985) and Ferrari in Kraut (1992) 248ff.

It might seem that the erotic passion for the beautiful is ambivalent in a way that the desire for good is not. To take a striking example, the criminal despotic passion in the tyrant's soul in *Republic* IX is also called *erōs* (573A–575A). But the criminal desires can rule in a soul only by corrupting the rational part, the *logistikon*, so that it accepts as the good (or, in the case of *erōs*, as the good-and-beautiful) whatever these lawless desires propose as their object. (See an illustration of such corruption below, p. 278.) So in the *Phaedrus* the dark horse of lust can achieve its goal only with the consent of the charioteer, reason.

Of course in the tripartite model for the psyche the theory of desire becomes more complex. We begin with the *Symposium*, where the conception of *erōs* is simpler and more closely tied to a desire for the good. I shall argue that the erotic urge driving the philosopher up the ladder of love is fundamentally identical with the universal desire for the good that appears in the *Gorgias* and *Meno* as a clue to the Socratic paradox. (See Chapter 8 § 8.) The specification of this desire for the good as *erōs* reflects the fact that the sexual passion aroused by a beautiful person is the most common and most elementary form in which an intense desire for the good-and-beautiful is experienced. As the *Phaedrus* puts it, Beauty is the only Form with clear visual images. But the response to such images can assume many different shapes. Plato's use of the term *erōs* to designate the dominant passion in the tyrannical psyche is a reminder that the same psychic principle which, when properly guided, can lead one to philosophy can also, when totally misguided, direct a life of plunder and brutality.

Because *erōs*, as the most potent form of desire, can play this decisive role in fixing the goal of a human life, it is of much greater philosophical significance for Plato than the concept of *philia*.[5] Furthermore, the concept of *erōs* has a logical or structural feature that makes it more appropriate as the instrument for formulating a Platonic account of love. The experience of *erōs* can be (and in Greek depiction often is) asymmetric, whereas friendship is properly reciprocal. Since Plato is constructing a theory of desire (and ultimately, of *rational* desire), *erōs* serves his purpose in a way

5. Although the sexual connotations of ἔρως are central and typical, the broader usage for non-sexual desire is old and well established, e.g. in the Homeric formula "when they had put away their ἔρος for meat and drink" (*Il.* 1.469, and often).

that *philia* does not. For example, the term *philos*, "friend," means both "fond (of)" and "dear (to)"; and this active–passive ambiguity is exploited by Plato in several of the dialectical *aporiai* of the *Lysis*. But such reciprocity is secondary or accidental in the case of *erōs*. In the conventional Greek view of boy-love, the *paidika* or object of erotic passion is not expected to feel passion in return. When Plato in the *Phaedrus* wishes to introduce the notion of erotic reciprocity, he is obliged to invent a new concept, *anterōs*, "*erōs* in return," which is cunningly explained as the result of the beloved seeing his own reflection in the lover's eyes (*Phaedrus* 255C–D). Taken alone, *erōs* (unlike *philia*) points only in one direction.

This asymmetric structure of *erōs* fits the relation between the human psyche and the good-and-beautiful. Not only in the case of the Forms, but in the desire for many other good and beautiful things, the notion of reciprocity would be entirely inappropriate. Hence Plato's "theory of love" is necessarily a theory of *erōs*, not of *philia*.

In such a theory, the object of desire is only initially or instrumentally a person. Reciprocal relations between persons would have to be treated in an account of *philia*, which Plato did not develop. If this distinction is clearly kept in view, many criticisms of Plato's theory are seen to be misconceived. In the *Symposium*, it is clear, the account of *erōs* offered by Diotima does not claim to be an account of friendship or affection between persons.[6]

2. ERŌS AND DESIRE

Although Plato's discussion of *erōs* (in the *Symposium* and *Phaedrus* as well as in the prologue to the *Lysis*) unquestionably deals with cases of being in love, the doctrine of the *Symposium* is best understood as a theory of (rational) desire rather than as a theory of love. This is clear from the very first formulation of the theory, in Socrates' interrogation of Agathon. "Does *erōs* desire (*epithumei*)

---

6. The situation in the *Phaedrus* is more complex. There philosophical *erōs* is again primarily directed to the Forms, by way of recollection, but Plato's account includes recognition (and repression) of carnal desire, on the one hand, and the possibility and desirability of genuine *philia* on the other hand (256A–E). And, of course, Plato will also use the terminology of *philos* and *philein* when referring to a relationship whose logical structure corresponds to *erōs*.

that of which it is *erōs*, or not?" (*Symp.* 200A 2). The answer is of course that it does, and what follows is precisely the famous analysis of desire as deficiency or lack (200A–E), which dominates the entire theory.

It will be useful to say a word here about the vocabulary of desire in Plato. The word for desire in the passage just mentioned is *epithumia*, and that is Plato's most general term. In *Republic* IX, each part of the soul is said to have its own *epithumia* and its own pleasure (580D). But *epithumia* can also be used more narrowly for appetitive desires, as when thirst is said to be *epithumia* only for drink in *Republic* IV (437D–E). Plato thus lacks or avoids the systematic terminology that we find in Aristotle.

Aristotle has a generic term for desire, *orexis*, under which he recognizes three species: *boulēsis* (sometimes mistranslated as "wish"), a rational desire for what is good or what is judged to be good; *thumos*, self-assertive feelings connected with anger, pride, and the desire to strike back; and *epithumia*, appetite or desire for pleasure. Now Aristotle's tripartition of desire and two out of his three names for the parts are directly based upon Plato's tripartite psychology in the *Republic*. Aristotle never defends this classification of desires; he seems simply to take it for granted, as an analysis accepted in the Academy.

Plato, by contrast, has no generic term other than *epithumia*; the word *orexis* never occurs in his writings. The two ordinary words for wanting or desiring, *boulesthai* and *epithumein*, are most often used by him interchangeably. These two words have of course different semantic nuances, reflecting on the one hand the etymological connections with *thumos*, "anger," "passion," "emotional impulse," and on the other hand with *boulē*, "council," and *bouleuesthai* "to deliberate." There are passages in Plato where this lexical contrast is respected.[7] One context in the *Charmides* (167E) suggests a tendency to fix this distinction terminologically, as Aristotle will later do. And so in the *Republic* the term *epithumētikon* designates the appetitive part of the soul. But such is Plato's horror of fixed terminology that he not only systematically varies his usage of the two words but makes fun of Prodicus for "distinguishing *boulesthai* and *epithumein* as not being the same" (*Protagoras* 340B 1).

7. See above, pp. 141f. and 232, for the distinction between *epithumein* and *boulesthai* in the *Gorgias*.

Hence Plato expresses the generic concept of desire not by any single term but by free movement back and forth between a number of different expressions, including *epithumein, boulesthai*, and *eran*.[8]

We see, then, that although the author of the *Gorgias* and *Charmides* is well aware of the possibility of a terminological distinction of the Aristotelian type, between *epithumia* as sensual appetite and *boulēsis* as rational desire, the author of the *Meno, Lysis*, and *Symposium* (who is of course the same) has decided to ignore this linguistic contrast and treat these words as more or less interchangeable. Why? Is there more at stake here than the avoidance of a rigid terminology?

I suggest that there is an important philosophical motive in Plato's decision to meld the various desire-words into a conceptual unity. And that is the intention to create a theory of desire that will (until he introduces the tripartite complications of *Republic* IV) focus *exclusively* on the *rational desire for the good*, precisely that desire which underlies the Socratic paradox. This is the rational desire that Aristotle calls *boulēsis*. But in Plato's scheme *boulēsis* has a more powerful role to play. It is this universal human desire for the good, conceived now as the good-and-beautiful, that becomes *erōs* in the ladder of love in the *Symposium*. In its final, metaphysical form, the *erōs* of the *Symposium* reappears in the *Phaedo* as the philosopher's love affair with wisdom and truth, and in the central books of the *Republic* as erotic attachment to the Forms, ultimately to the Form of the Good. The universal desire for the good that is central to Socratic intellectualism is thereby not rejected but deepened, reconstrued as *erōs*, and fully integrated into Plato's mature metaphysics and psychology.

We will misconstrue the theory of the *Symposium* and the arguments of the *Gorgias* and *Meno* if we imagine that in claiming that no one desires bad things but that all action aims at the good, Plato (or Socrates) is attempting to offer a general account of human motivation, which he implausibly reduces to a judgment concerning what is good. As we have seen in the last chapter, only the cunning argument of *Protagoras* 351ff. makes such general claims,

---

8. Parallel use of *epithumein* and *boulesthai* in *Meno* 77B–78B; *epithumein, eran*, and *philein* in *Lysis* 221B 7–E 4; *epithumein, boulesthai*, and *eran* in *Symp.* 200A 3–201B 2, *eran* and *boulesthai* ibid. 204D 5–205B 2.

for its own very special purposes. In dialogues before the *Republic*, Plato offers no general account of moral psychology. On the contrary, his discussion of desire is systematically *limited* to rational desire for the good, since that is the fundamental thought underlying the Socratic paradox. Thus the *psuchē* in the *Phaedo* is essentially the rational principle; what the *Republic* identifies as non-rational parts of the soul belong in the *Phaedo* to the body. And so the theory of *erōs* in the *Symposium* is ultimately a theory of rational desire for the good understood as the good-and-beautiful.

There is an obvious rhetorical advantage in using the term *erōs* in this way to designate the full power of rational desire. And there is also a philosophical justification for this conceptual fusion of reason and passion in Plato's theory. For a rational agent, reason and desire must come together in any decision to act. Any intense desire that is, upon reflection, not rejected will provoke or imply a judgment that the desired object is good. More on this below in §5.

3. FROM THE *LYSIS* TO THE *SYMPOSIUM*

In the *Lysis* we can see Plato carefully assembling the various pieces out of which he will construct his theory of *erōs*. So I deal briefly with the dialogue here, and more fully in §6. We have already noted that, although the *Lysis* is overtly concerned with the theme of friendship illustrated by the relationship between the two boys, Lysis and Menexenus, the topic of *erōs* is presented in the prologue by an elaborate lesson in courtship administered to Hippothales by Socrates, who describes himself as recipient of a divine gift of discernment in matters erotic (204C 1). A sharp contrast is drawn between the asymmetric pattern of *erōs* in Hippothales' case and the symmetry of friendship between the two boys. For Lysis and Menexenus are alike in age, beauty, noble birth, and willingness to talk to Socrates. Now as lover (*erastēs*) Hippothales would like to be on friendly terms (*prosphilēs*, 206C 3) with his beloved Lysis. But in fact he is afraid to provoke hostility by his courtship (207B 7). And this emotional asymmetry is underscored again at the end of the dialogue, when Socrates argues that a genuine lover deserves to receive affection (*phileisthai*) in return from his beloved. At this point the two boys are deeply embarrassed, while Hippothales is ecstatic (222A–B 2). We recall that an erotic advance is not supposed to be reciprocated; when courted, a boy is expected to show indifference, even annoyance.[9] Friendship between peers, on the other hand, is nothing if not reciprocal.

The *Lysis* is thus carefully staged as a conversation on friendship set within the frame of an erotic courtship. The asymmetric pattern of *erōs* becomes increasingly predominant in the second half of the dialogue; and that is no accident. It is precisely by the development of this asymmetric model that the *Lysis* prepares the way for the theory of *erōs* presented in the *Symposium*.

The shift from friendship to *erōs* begins with the introduction of desire (*epithumein*), first at 215E 4 (the dry desires the moist, the cold desires the hot), and then systematically from 217C 1 and E 8, with the introduction of the asymmetric model: what is neither good nor bad desires what is good, because of the presence of what is bad. This curious shift follows four sets of aporetic arguments concerned exclusively with *philia*, which have ended only in perplexity. We were unable to say, when A loves (*philein*) B, whether it is A or B that is properly the friend (*philos*); and we are equally unable to say whether friendship is between likes or between unlikes. It is to avoid the antinomies that seem to plague the conception of *philia* between both likes and unlikes (e.g., between good and good, bad and bad, or good and bad) that the notion of the neutral subject, what is neither-good-nor-bad, is finally introduced (216C–E).

For an unprepared reader of the *Lysis*, it is at first difficult to see the point of this neutral subject, something that is neither good nor bad. Clarification comes with two examples, the second of which applies the asymmetric pattern to philosophy. Just as the neutral body desires the good of medicine because of the evil of disease, so likewise in the case of cognition: the neutral subjects are people who are neither so good as to be wise, nor so bad as to be hopelessly ignorant by believing that they know what they do not know. It is these cognitive in-betweens who can become lovers of wisdom and pursue philosophy (218A–B).

In the *Lysis* Plato thus gives us a brief glimpse of the erotic model for philosophy that is taken up by Diotima in the *Symposium*. In the allegorical introduction to her lesson of love, Diotima will describe Eros as a philosopher whose position lies between wisdom

---

9. Dover (1978) 85 and *passim*.

and ignorance, since he not only lacks wisdom but is conscious of his lack (*Symp.* 203D–204A; cf. 202A). No more is said about philosophy in the *Lysis*, but other components of the erotic theory of the *Symposium* are tentatively presented here, in the bewildering twists and turns of the argument about *philia*. An analysis of this argument is given below, in § 6. Here I simply list the points at which the *Lysis* hints at or prefigures important elements in the theory of the *Symposium*.

1. The lover-of-wisdom (*philo-sophos*) as neither wise nor ignorant (218A–B; cf. *Symp.* 204A).
2. Love as desire (*epithumia*) for the good (217C 1, E7; cf. *Symp.* 204E–205A).
3. The good interchangeable with the beautiful (*kalon*) as object of love (216D 2; cf. *Symp.* 204E).
4. Desire as lack or deficiency (221D 7–E 3; cf. *Symp.* 200A–E).
5. The good understood as what is akin (*oikeion*) (221E–222D; cf. *Symp.* 205E).
6. The primary dear object (*prōton philon*) for the sake of which everything else is dear (219D, 220B, D 8; cf. *Symp.* 210E 6, 211C 2).
7. What is *truly* dear, in contrast to mere images (*eidōla*) (219D 3–4; cf. *Symp.* 212A 4–6).

In addition to these parallels, which bear directly on the theory of *erōs*, the *Lysis* also anticipates two technical features of the full-blown doctrine of Forms.[10]

No reader who comes to the *Lysis* without knowledge of the doctrine expounded in the *Symposium* could understand what is implied by "the primary dear, for the sake of which everything else is dear." Nor could such a reader grasp the importance of the brief reference to desire as deficiency, or to the beautiful as dear (216C 6) and as a property of the good. This crucial connection

10. The specific terminology for the Forms as essences, "that which [truly, essentially] is F," introduced explicitly at *Phaedo* 74D 6 as αὐτὸ τὸ ὅ ἐστιν (cf. 75B 1, D 2, 78D 3, etc.) is anticipated at *Lysis* 219C 7 ἐκεῖνο ὅ ἐστιν πρῶτον φίλον, and also at *Symp.* 211C 8 αὐτὸ ὅ ἐστιν καλόν. (See on this Kahn 1981 107ff.) The other technical anticipation in the *Lysis* is further developed not in the *Symposium* but only in the *Phaedo*. Things other than the Primary Dear are said to be dear for the sake of something else "which is truly dear", whereas they are only dear in words (*rhēmati*, 220B 1). This is a rough prefiguring of the doctrine of *epōnumia*, that things are derivatively named after the Form they participate in (*Phaedo* 102B, 103B 8).

between the good and the beautiful is tossed out by Socrates ("I say that the good is beautiful," 216D 2) at a moment when he claims to be giddy with *aporia*, and does not know what he means himself. Plato thus presents us with a series of enigmatic hints that form a kind of puzzle for the uninitiated reader to decipher, but that become completely intelligible when interpreted from the perspective of Socrates' speech in the *Symposium*. For there again the beautiful will be equated with the good as object of desire (204E), thus establishing the fundamental identity between *erōs* as desire for the beautiful and the more general human desire for happiness and the good.

The informed reader can thus discover Diotima's theory of *erōs* as a kind of sub-text in the *Lysis*. And by positing the need for a first principle (*archē*) as a final end or goal "for the sake of which everything else is dear," as the only thing that is *truly* and non-derivatively dear, the *Lysis* points the way not only to the Beautiful itself in the *Symposium*, but also to the Form of the Good in the *Republic*.

4. THE GOOD AS THE BEAUTIFUL

The adjectives *agathos* and *kalos* often entail one another, but they are never exactly equivalent. Hence the common Greek phrase for a gentleman or a fine person, *kalos kàgathos*, is not a tautology. In classical usage *kalos* has a wide range of meanings, and much of this does overlap with uses of *agathos*. (In Modern Greek, and in some late scholia, *kalos* has actually replaced *agathos* as the normal word for "good.") But there are two respects in which *kalos* is distinctive: it signifies physical beauty, on the one hand, and moral-social approval on the other. Hence *kalos*, but not *agathos*, can often be translated as "beautiful," and in other circumstances as "admirable" or "honorable." As we saw in the last chapter, Plato is careful to use only *agathon* when stating the Socratic paradox in its non-moral or prudential form, where *agathon* can be understood as good-for-the-agent. The term *kalon*, on the other hand, is introduced to mark what is socially approved as distinct from what is personally advantageous, for example as in the definition of courage as a virtue (*Protagoras* 359Eff.; see above, Chapter 8 §5). It is precisely the potential discrepancy between what is good-for-the-agent and what is socially admirable that leads Polus to insist that, although doing injustice may be more dishonorable (less *kalon*) than suffering injustice, it is not worse, i.e. not worse-for-the-agent (*Gorgias* 474C).

When *to kalon* is regarded as the object of *erōs*, however, it is not moral excellence but visual beauty that is primarily intended. "The characteristics by virtue of which a person is *kalos* are usually visual," as Dover reports.[11] And so in the myth of the *Phaedrus* it is by sight, "the sharpest of the bodily senses," that we apprehend the likeness here of transcendent Beauty, and of that Form alone (250D). Consequently, the first step in the pedagogy of *erōs* is for a young person to fall in love with a beautiful body – just as Socrates, who was no longer so young, was momentarily overwhelmed by the physical beauty of Charmides. What is new in the theory of the *Symposium*, and first announced in the mythic tale told by Aristophanes, is the idea that the emotional storm of physical passion aroused by such beauty contains within itself a metaphysical element, that is to say, an aspiration that transcends the limit of the human condition and that cannot possibly be satisfied in the way that hunger and thirst can be satisfied.[12] In terms of the psychology developed in the *Republic*, the phenomenon of falling in love involves not only the physical desire of *epithumia* or lust, but also a metaphysical element that properly belongs to the rational principle that desires what is good, that is to say, what is good-and-beautiful.

Thus Plato discovered the metaphysical dimension in *erōs* that was inherited by medieval mysticism (as in Dante's transfiguration of Beatrice) as well as by modern romanticism (as in Goethe's vision of the Eternal Feminine "that draws us upward"). But what is specifically Platonic is more than the connection between beauty and sex, on the one hand, and transcendental aspiration on the other. According to the doctrine of the *Symposium*, the *kalon* that is object of *erōs* is triply determined. It is identified first with the good, as defined by the prudential and moral versions of the Socratic paradox (that everyone desires what is good); secondly, with

11. Dover (1974) 69.
12. This distinction between appetite and desire is elegantly drawn by Halperin (1985: 169f.), who points out that Plato has prepared the reader for Diotima's theory of *erōs* by "embedding her premises" symbolically in Aristophanes' myth, thus providing "the non-philosophical reader with a basis in ordinary human experience for initiation into the mysteries of Platonic erotics."

various mortal forms of immortality that complement (though they it do not replace) the immortal destiny of the soul as described in the *Meno*; and finally, with the new realm of reality defined by the theory of Forms. These three dimensions of Platonic *erōs* are presented here as successive stages in the educational program proposed by Diotima.

Diotima's lesson begins by defining *erōs* quite generally as the desire for happiness, understood as the possession of what is good-and-beautiful (204D–E, 205D). Hence in this first stage *erōs* taken generically is identified with that universal desire for good things that the Socratic paradox attributes to every human being. But the erotic context of Diotima's exposition gives this claim an entirely new twist. We move then to the second, more specifically erotic stage of the pedagogy (from 206B). The attraction of a beautiful body inspires more than the desire of possession. What the lover aspires to is creativity: birth in beauty, both of the body and of the soul.[13] The engendering of offspring is the mortal form of immortality. So at the biological level, in an immortality that is shared by the animals, the creative element of *erōs* expresses itself in reproduction. But this second stage also includes higher forms of personal transcendence: in noble deeds that secure undying fame, in great poetry and creative art, and (Plato's highest category for this-worldly achievement) in legislation and the organization of virtuous cities. These are all presented as extensions of the biological urge to survive death by leaving behind something of oneself. "Such is the manner by which what is mortal shares in immortality; but what is immortal shares in a different way" (208B 2). Agathon's dinner party is not an appropriate occasion for expounding that more other-worldly conception of immortality which is announced in the *Meno* and developed in the *Phaedo*.[14]

The situation becomes more complex when, towards the end of the second stage, we consider the erotic pursuit of immortality in the form of undying fame for *aretē* (in 209Aff.). Here we find a certain tension in Diotima's account between a conception of love and virtue that is general enough to apply to different aspects of Greek culture, including the conceptions expressed by the other

13. For this distinction between generic and specific *erōs* see Santas (1988) 32ff.
14. For the adaptation of doctrine to audience on this point, see above, pp. 68–70 and below, pp. 344f.

speakers in the *Symposium*, and a more specifically Platonic view of
the cultivation of virtue, as a springboard for the ascent described
in the final mysteries, the *telea* and *epoptika* of 210Aff. The notion
that the lover is inspired to produce "discourse (*logoi*) on virtue
and on what a good man should be and what practices he should
engage in" (209B 8ff.) seems at first sight compatible with the view
of pederastic love expressed in Pausanias' speech, according to
which the older lover undertakes to educate his younger beloved.

But we have not yet reached the final mysteries. In the end,
Diotima's conception of moral and intellectual birth in beauty
turns out to be something rather different, much more like the
discourse in which Socrates exhorts his interlocutors to examine
their lives and ennoble their souls. For it is not the conversation of
Pausanias but only the Socratic *logoi*, as we find them recorded in
Plato's dialogues, that can move the learner on to the third and
final stage of erotic pedagogy, as "discourses that improve the
young" (210C 1–3) in the relevant respect, discourses that permit
both the speaker and auditor[15] to comprehend the moral beauty of
practices and laws (C 3–6), and thence to proceed to the intellectual beauty of the sciences (C 6ff.), after which, beholding the
great sea of beauty, he will generate "many beautiful *logoi* and
thoughts in unstinting love of wisdom (*philosophia*)" (210D).

It is natural to recognize in these philosophical *logoi* an implicit
reference to Socrates' flirtatious conversations with handsome men
like Meno, as well as reference to the protreptic speeches Socrates
loves to address to much-admired youths like Charmides and
Clinias (in the *Euthydemus*) or to beautiful boys like Lysis and Menexenus. For it is not the mundane conception of *philosophia* cultivated by Isocrates or expounded by Xenophon, but only the conception of philosophy gradually unfolded in Plato's dialogues, that
can raise the lover to the level needed for the next and final step.
It is only when he has been enlightened by the vision of intel-

---

15. There seems to be some incoherence at *Symp.* 210C 3. How can the production of educational *logoi* serve to force *the speaker* to behold moral beauty?
Should not ἵνα ἀναγκασθῇ θεάσασθαι refer to *the auditor* of such discourse?
The parallel at *Phaedrus* 252E–253A suggests that the two cases will tend to be
similar to one another. For alternation in *Symp.* 210A–D between references to
teacher and learner cf. Dover (1980) 155.

lectual beauty and by the practice of philosophical discussion that he is able to catch a glimpse of the ultimate science, which is knowledge of the ultimate beauty (210Dff.). The rational and metaphysical component in erotic desire has now found its home. In this way, the beatific vision of the Form of Beauty is presented as culmination for the educational enterprise that began with the aporetic and protreptic *logoi* of the earlier dialogues.

I am suggesting that we read the final section of Diotima's speech as Plato's self-interpretation of the philosophical and pedagogical intention of his earlier work. The ladder of love is here the path that leads from the Socratic elenchus to the doctrine of Forms, from the universal desire for what is good to the transcendent vision of what is uniquely Beautiful. In the final analysis, for Plato the Good and the Beautiful will be interchangeable. Or perhaps we can say with Ferrari and the Neoplatonists that "the beautiful is thought of as the quality by which the good shines and shows itself to us."[16] Beauty reveals the Good in its most accessible form. So it is appropriate that we are introduced here in the *Symposium* to the notion of an ascent to the vision of the Beautiful, before we encounter in the *Republic* the prisoners who must climb out of the sensory Cave to behold the Good shining as the noetic Sun. There too, I suggest, we can properly see the prisoners' release from the shadows as one more Platonic reflection on the pedagogical course he has been trying to depict in the dialogues and provoke in the reader.

5. PHILOSOPHIC *ERŌS* AND THE UNITY OF VIRTUE

The philosophic lover who reaches the summit of the erotic ladder, and who gazes on divine Beauty with the appropriate organ (namely with his intellect, *nous*), will "engender not images of virtue, since he is not in contact with an image, but true virtue, since he is in contact with what is true" (212A). As the commentators have seen, this implies a contrast between the true virtue of the successful philosopher (and of his companion as well, if the latter

16. Ferrari in Kraut (1992) 260. Compare Plotinus' conclusion that "the nature of the good holds the beautiful before itself as a screen (*probeblēmenon*)" (*Ennead* 1.6.9).

manages to reach the top) and more ordinary forms of virtue generated at a lower level.[17]

This distinction between the true virtue of a philosopher and
other, more popular forms of virtue is more explicitly drawn in
the *Phaedo* and *Republic*, as we have noticed.[18] But the distinction as
such is not new. The *Meno* concludes with a contrast between virtue based upon knowledge and that which relies upon true opinion. And I have argued that the thesis of the unity of virtue as
proposed in the *Protagoras* properly applies only to the ideal case
of philosophic virtue (above, pp. 223f.). For such a unity cannot
plausibly hold for the virtues of the average citizen, as represented
by justice and temperance in Protagoras' Great Speech, the virtues that are taught to everyone by everyone. We have seen that
the unity thesis implies the notion of a special psychic state called
wisdom (*phronēsis*), a psychic state that will command not only the
intellectual insight but also the motive-force to make a person just
and brave and temperate as well as wise. Of course the *Protagoras*
does not describe such a state. So it leaves unanswered the central
question of Socratic intellectualism: namely, how wisdom as the
knowledge of good and evil, the art of beneficial use, can have the
necessary psychological force to overcome the emotional or affective obstacles to right action. How can the intellect exercise complete control over the springs of action, so that knowing what is
good guarantees doing what is good?

Plato's answer to this question is complex. The first part of an
answer consists in the recognition of a need for the pre-theoretical
training of character. Such a need is taken for granted in the account of traditional moral education, for children and for adults,
that is given in Protagoras' Great Speech. Education of this type
is able to produce the ordinary civic virtues of honesty and self-
restraint, the *dikē* and *aidōs* without which the city cannot exist.
And this need for basic moral training is more elaborately recognized in Books II–III of the *Republic*, where musical education in
particular is designed to bring harmony into young souls, so that
they will habitually and spontaneously reject what is disgraceful
(*aischra*) without yet knowing the rational account (*logos*) of right

17. See *Symp.* 209A and E 2–3 for virtue at lower levels, with the comments of
    Price (1989) 51 and those of Rettig: the images of virtue at 212A are *Tügenden
    zweiten Grades* (quoted by Bury (1909) 132).
18. See the texts cited above, p. 218, n.8.

and wrong. (See especially *Rep.* III, 401B–402A.) Whatever the historical Socrates may have thought, the author of the *Protagoras* knows as well as the author of the *Republic* that pre-theoretical moral training is an indispensable prerequisite for good moral character and civic virtue. As the *Republic* will explain, the appetites and competitive instincts must be trained in order for right opinion to prevail in the soul.

But there is a great gap separating ordinary civic virtue, or its Platonic variant in *Republic* IV, from the philosophical ideal implicit in the concept of the unity of virtue in wisdom. And it is to fill this gap that the theory of philosophical *erōs* will be required.

For Plato, and for Socrates as Plato represents him, the commitment to philosophy is conceived as something comparable to a religious conversion, the turning of the soul from the shadows to the light. This involves a radical restructuring of the personality in its values and priorities, the kind of psychic transformation which the mystics of the East call enlightenment. Rationalist though he is, Socrates plays a role among his followers like that of a Zen master or an Indian guru. Nowhere is that clearer than in the *Symposium*, where the first narrator, Apollodorus, is a recent convert to philosophy and a daily companion of Socrates, who regards everyone he meets as a miserable human being, except Socrates. In particular Apollodorus pities his rich businessmen friends, "because you think you are doing something important, when you are really doing nothing" (*Symp.* 173C). The emotional climax of the dialogue comes when Alcibiades describes the impact Socrates has on him. He is agitated and as it were possessed by Socrates' words, even when these are repeated by someone else: "When I hear him, my heart leaps ... and tears pour from my eyes at his words, and I see many others doing the same thing." Alcibiades is so moved by Socrates' exhortation to the philosophic life that he feels that life is not worth living in the slavish condition in which he finds himself (215D–216A).

How are we to account for this effect on individuals as different from one another as Apollodorus and Alcibiades, Antisthenes and Aristippus?[19] Plato's explanation, as I understand it, lies in positing a deep, half-conscious desire for the good in every human soul, a desire that is ultimately identical with rationality as such, but

19. For the story of Aristippus' conversion to philosophy, see above, p. 16, n.30.

that can be experienced as *erōs*. If all were able to grasp the nature of the good as Plato conceives it, no one would pursue any other goal. Most of us, however, live in the cave of greed and sensuality, in the pursuit of wealth or honor or power. Only the true philosopher can recognize the goal of everyone's deepest desire, that for the sake of which all other things are dear, and can pursue it with some hope of success. The unity of virtue points to the total transformation of the personality that must occur if such a pursuit is to be successful.

The doctrine of philosophical *erōs* is designed to explain how such a transformation can take place. How can one pass beyond ordinary civic virtue, as fashioned by good social training, to the kind of effortless self-mastery exhibited in Plato's portrayal of Socrates? Plato's explanation here has two aspects. The first aspect is the direct impact of the vision of the Forms upon those who are able to behold them. (Seeing in this connection is simply a metaphor for intellectual contact.) The second aspect is the reorientation of desire on the part of those who pursue and enjoy the vision. Plato's theory describes both aspects in the ideal case: the philosophic lover of the *Symposium*, the liberated philosopher of the *Phaedo*, and the philosopher-king of the *Republic*. I submit that we have in these dialogues not three different doctrines but three context-dependent perspectives on a single psychological theory.

The enormous gratification that comes to the philosopher from intellectual contact with the Forms is described by Plato in passages too numerous to quote. As we have seen, the *Symposium* says that "there, if anywhere, is the life worth living for a human being, beholding the Beautiful itself. And if you ever see it, you will not rank it with the things that impress you so much now: gold and garments and handsome boys and youths" (211D). The *Phaedo* speaks in similarly erotic terms: the life-long lover (*erastēs*) of wisdom should be ready to die, just as other men have been willing to die for their wives or beloved ones (68A–B; cf. 65C 9, 66B 7, 66E 2–3, 67B 9). But it is in Book VI of the *Republic* that the erotic language is pushed to its limit in the description of contact with the Forms. The philosopher (who has from the beginning been introduced as a lover: *Rep.* V, 464C 8–475C) is here said to pursue reality and not to be dulled or desist from his passion (*erōs*) until he grasps the nature of each essential being (*autou ho estin hekastou*) by the kindred part of his soul, "by which he approaches and joins in intercourse with the really Real, thus engendering intelligence (*nous*) and truth, and he comes to have knowledge and truly to live and be nourished, and thus to be relieved of the pangs [of love], but not before" (*Rep.* VI, 490B).

As with religious mystics down through the ages, Plato's experience of intellectual contact with his transcendent Entities is so powerful that only the language of sexual union seems adequate to give it expression. The relevant psychic organ for contact with the Forms is of course the rational principle of thought or intellect. But the nature of these Beings is such as to have a profound influence not only on the intellect but also on the emotions, and on the moral character of the person who has this experience.[20]

Such a person will not be inclined to direct his gaze below, on the quarrels and hatred of mankind. On the contrary, continues Socrates, since such a one "looks towards things orderly and forever immutable, and beholds them neither committing injustice nor suffering injustice from one another, but disposed in good order and according to reason, will he not imitate and come to resemble that thing whose company he so enjoys? ... Keeping company with what is divine and orderly, he becomes himself orderly and divine, as far as that is possible for a human being" (*Rep.* VI, 500C–D).

The consequence of love is assimilation to the beloved. As a result of his access to such a noble model, the philosopher-king will be able not only to shape the city in the image of the Forms, but also to shape himself. Since the Forms are paradigms of justice and goodness, the philosopher will himself become just and good. He (or she) will thus "establish in the characters of human beings, both privately and publicly," what they see in the divine model, and hence become skillful artisans "of temperance and justice and popular virtue as a whole" (500D).

The direct moral impact of the vision of the Forms is thus the same process of imitation or resemblance that is described in the famous passage in the *Theaetetus*, where the only escape from the evils of this world is said to be ὁμοίωσις θεῷ: "assimilation to

---

20. Conversely, a certain harmony of character is a prerequisite for full intellectual initiation (*Rep.* VI, 486B 11, 496B 2; *Ep.* VII, 344A). That is why the future philosophers must be trained in music and gymnastics, so that when *logos* comes, they will receive it gladly as belonging to them (*di' oikeiotēta*), *Rep.* III, 402A 3.

the divine as far as possible. And assimilation is to become just
and pious with wisdom (*phronēsis*)" (176B).

On the other hand, the indirect moral influence of ascent to the
Forms is described in terms of the rechanneling of desire.

When a person's desires incline strongly in one direction, we know that
they will thereby be weaker in other directions, like a stream of water
directed off into one channel. So when someone's desires have set to flow
towards learning and the like, they will be concerned with the pleasures
of the soul itself by itself and will abandon the pleasures of the body, if
he is truly a lover of wisdom (*philo-sophos*). (*Rep.* VI, 485D)

The very same hydraulic image was used by Freud in his account
of sublimation. Now Freud was happy to acknowledge Plato's
view of *erōs* in the *Symposium* as a precursor for his own theory of
sexuality.[21] The Freudian parallel, when applied to the passage
just quoted, suggests that we might interpret Platonic *erōs* as a
common pool of motivational energy, to be distributed between
Plato's three parts of the psyche in such a way that more for one
means less for another.

Attractive as it may be, this Freudian analogy is unsatisfactory
both as an interpretation of the *Republic* passage and as an account
of *erōs* in the *Symposium*. Unless the hydraulic image is carefully
interpreted, the comparison to Freud will distort our picture of
Plato's theory. The notion implied by the theory of sublimation,
of object-neutral desires leaving the channel of bodily pleasure to
direct themselves towards learning, is strictly incompatible with
the psychology of the *Republic*, according to which each part of the
soul has (or is) its own distinctive desire, defined by the object in
each case: the love of knowledge, the desire for victory and honor,
and the various appetites that compose the *epithumētikon* (IX, 580D–
581C). The desires of the *epithumētikon* cannot be transferred to a
more noble object; they are defined by what they are the desire
for. Hence we must beware of a too literal reading of the text on
rechanneling. The analogy to irrigation leads Plato to write as if it
were the same *epithumiai* that are diverted from one channel to another. However, if we are to remain true to Plato's conception of
desire as individuated by its proper object, we must understand
that "desires inclining strongly in one direction" means that a certain type of desire is strengthened by erotic reinforcement; whereas

21. See the passage cited in Santas (1988) 154ff.

"they abandon the pleasures of the body" means that the corresponding appetites have been devalued, deprived of the erotic charge, and hence weakened. What one values most is what one practices and pursues, and this becomes stronger; what one values less is consequently neglected and diminished. The process referred to by the image of rechanneling in the *Republic* is in fact the very same phenomenon that is described in more mechanical terms in the *Timaeus*, where the role of desire is replaced by the notion of a proper motion for each part of the psyche.

> There dwell in us three distinct forms of soul, each having its own motions. Accordingly, we may say now as briefly as possible that whichever of these lives in idleness and inactivity with respect to its proper motions will necessarily become the weakest, while the one in constant exercise will be strongest. (*Timaeus* 89E, translated after Cornford)

Returning to the more cognitive psychology of the *Republic*, we see that it is only the desire of the *logistikon*, the rational desire for truth and for what is good and beneficial, that is flexible enough to be misdirected and attached by mistake to the goals of sensual gratification or political glory and power. (The *thumoeides* or honor-loving part is flexible in a derivative sense, since it will tend to be influenced by whatever reason accepts as good.) Taken literally, the simile of rechanneling can refer only to the misplaced desire for the good-and-beautiful that needs to be redirected to its proper object.[22] This turning to knowledge and reality is what it means for the desires to be focused on "the pleasure of the soul itself by itself" (485D 11, an echo of *Phaedo* 65C 7, 66A 1-2, E 1, where the psyche is the rational soul).

This essentially rational and cognitive interpretation of rechanneling in the *Republic* can be confirmed by the account of *erōs* in the *Symposium*.[23] The text explicitly defines *erōs* as a special case of the universal human desire for good things (205A, D). As we have seen, the universal rational desire for the good implied by the Socratic paradox is essentially identical with Aristotle's *boulēsis* and

---

22. In the context of the hydraulic image at VI, 485 the rational principle is said to take as its object knowledge and reality. But a later passage in Book VI (508E 3) tells us that these are both derivative from the Good.

23. I am arguing here for a view that has often been disputed, namely, that the monistic account of *erōs* in the *Symposium* is compatible with the tripartite psychology of the *Republic*, and that both are consistent with the psychology of the *Phaedo*.

Plato's *logistikon*. Far from being an undifferentiated pool of psychic energy that is neutral in regard to its goal, Platonic *erōs* is simply the most intense form of that profound desire for good (and ultimately for *the* Good) which animates every human soul. This desire is capable of being misdirected, but it has a built-in targeting device trained on what is naturally good, dear (*philon*), and desirable. According to Plato, what happens to the philosopher as he moves up the ladder of love, and what is expressed in *Republic* VI as a rechanneling of desire, is first and foremost the redirection of *rational* desire, our desire for what is good-and-beautiful, away from misguided targeting and onto its own proper object. The intellect plays the decisive role in this process, but its judgment as to what is good and beautiful carries with it the powerful erotic charge expressed in the hydraulic image of rechanneling. Animal appetite (*epithumia*) will remain fixed on attractive bodies. But the metaphysical yearning that is characteristic of erotic desire will be transferred upward as a consequence of greater intellectual insight.

We can see the reverse process taking place when reason is said to be enslaved by the lower parts of the soul. What this means is most vividly portrayed in Plato's account of the oligarchic personality in *Republic* VIII. In this case the throne of the psyche is occupied by the appetitive and money-loving principle:

The rational (*logistikon*) and spirited (*thumoeides*) parts are forced to sit at its feet, one on either side, having been made its slaves. It allows the former to investigate or calculate nothing except how to make more money from less, and it allows the latter to admire and honor only wealth and wealthy people. (VIII, 553 D)

For reason to be enslaved is thus for the rational principle to accept a notion of the good that is imposed by a different psychic principle, that is, for the good to be identified with the object of desire for a lower part of the soul. That is what it means for the lower principle to rule.[24] A non-virtuous action is not *simply* the result of an error of judgment on reason's part. But it will always

24. It will be useful to distinguish two senses of psychic rule. In what Klosko has called "normative rule," a psychic principle is said to rule if its proper object of desire (wealth, honor, sensual pleasure, etc.) is accepted by reason as determining the content of the good. (When reason rules in this sense, the good is determined by right opinion or philosophic knowledge.) In another sense (which is roughly what Klosko calls "direct rule") reason exercises

involve such an error if the agent acts voluntarily (*hekōn*), for that means that the rational part has consented.

It is by perverting our judgment as to what is good and desirable that the lower psychic principles can succeed in using reason for their own ends in the deviant lives of *Republic* VIII–IX. That is what lies behind the talk of enslaving reason. It is not by brute force – as the metaphors of combat and the allegory of the bad horse in the *Phaedrus* myth might suggest – but by persuasion, seduction and habituation that the psychic powers of the *Republic* act on one another. The *Phaedrus* also speaks of debate and "agreement" between the opposing parts of the soul.[25] In the *Phaedo*, where the psyche represents reason alone, its bondage to the body (which corresponds to the non-rational parts of the soul in the *Republic*) is described as follows:

When one feels intense pleasure or pain concerning an object, one is forced to regard this thing as outstandingly clear and true, although it is not ... Each pleasure and pain is like a nail which clasps and rivets the [rational] soul to the body and makes it corporeal, so that it takes for real (*alēthē*) whatever the body declares to be so. (83c–D)

Unless it is enlightened by philosophy, reason is obliged to live in the cognitive darkness of the cave constructed by the sensual appetites or by *thumos*, by ambition and competition for honor. One's ontology is determined by one's favorite pursuits. Hence in most human lives metaphysical desire is focused on the wrong object. Conversely, with rational enlightenment comes the rechanneling of desire: bodily pleasures will be less powerfully attractive once the philosophic lover has directed his (or her) metaphysical *erōs* on its proper target.

What the *Phaedo* construes in the ascetic mode as liberation from the sensory realm of the body, the *Symposium* describes in more positive terms as the education of desire, the redirection of *erōs* from bodily to moral beauty. A skillful erotic guide will use the initial triggering effect of sexual attraction (like the triggering effect

executive control in all action that is not incontinent, i.e. reason determines what action best serves the end determined by normative rule. This is simply the instrumental function of reason as potentially slave of the passions in Hume's sense. Plato's theory is primarily concerned with psychic rule in the first (normative) sense. Compare Klosko (1988) 341–56, with a slightly different version in Klosko (1986) 69ff.

25. For *homologia* between bad horse and charioteer see *Phaedrus* 254B 3, D 1.

of sense-perception in the *Phaedo*'s account of recollection) in order to get the lover to see his desired object *as beautiful*, and hence as an exemplar of a desirable principle that is to be found elsewhere as well. If we interpret the phenomena of the *Symposium* in terms of the conceptual framework of the tripartite psychology, we see that what is affected by this first step is not sensual appetite as such (which as the desire for sexual gratification belongs essentially to the *epithumētikon*) but the cognitive component, *to the extent that it represents the rational principle*, temporarily trapped in the attachment to a lovely body as something judged to be good and real, and hence as the object of misplaced *rational* desire.

What happens in the course of erotic initiation is that this rational element is directed "upwards," and first to the recognition of beauty as "one and the same" in all bodies. This cognitive shift will result in the devaluation and hence weakening of sensual fixation on a single body (210B 5–6). The process continues in a recognition of "beauty in soul as more precious than that in body" (210B 6–7): again it is the cognitive reevaluation that is the key to the upward movement.[26]

The rechanneling of desire from physical lust to metaphysical passion thus takes place by an essentially epistemic process, by altering the description under which the object is initially desired. This means converting the lover's attention from a view of the world as consisting of individual bodies to a vision of the incorporeal principles from which this phenomenal world derives whatever beauty and rational structure it possesses. This cognitive redirection requires just the sort of dialectical exercise that is described in *Republic* VI–VII, so that the initiate may come to see the beautiful images precisely as *images* of a higher Beauty. Like the conversion of the "eye of the soul" in the *Republic*, the education of *erōs* in the *Symposium* is essentially a cognitive enterprise, the liberation of *rational* desire from attachment to an inadequate object and its redirection to its proper goal, "the true knowledge which is knowledge of Beauty itself" (211C 7). What the *Symposium* makes clear is what is only partially indicated by the description of rechanneling in the *Republic*: that the process of enlightenment for reason is really one and the same as the process of reeducation for the desires. For the excessive strength of non-rational passion in less-

26. Compare Moravcsik (1971) 285–302.

than-virtuous characters, like the *erōs* that dominates in the soul of
the tyrant, is largely due to the complicity of *rational* desire, which
has accepted a distorted vision of the good and thus brings with it
the extraordinary impulse that Plato calls *erōs*.

Such is the theory by which Plato explained to himself, and to
the world, both the phenomenon of Socrates' life and death and
the inner meaning of the Socratic paradox, that no one does evil
knowingly but only out of ignorance of the good. How Socrates
himself construed this doctrine, we cannot know. He may well
have relied on more supernatural support for his own moral and
intellectual position, as the importance of the divine sign and repeated references to dreams strongly suggest. We know of nothing
of that sort for Plato. The life and teachings of Socrates left Plato
with a puzzle, for which he had to find a purely rational solution.
The doctrine of Forms and the theory of *erōs* are the result.

The theory shows that the knowledge which is or guarantees
virtue is a very scarce commodity, even if it is in a sense needed
and desired by everyone. Hence the educational scheme and political structure of the *Republic* are designed to protect and nurture
the rare natures that are properly gifted, while at the same time
maximizing lower levels of virtue for the citizen body at large.
Outside of such a system, philosophic virtue will occur only as a
providential accident, as it were by divine dispensation (*theia moira*:
Rep. VI, 492A 5, E 5, 493A 2). But the theory of *erōs* in the *Symposium*
and the philosophical religion of the *Phaedo* are there to reassure
us that philosophy can sometimes achieve such success without the
ideal social and educational conditions of the *Republic*. And such a
possibility must exist, if Socrates (and Plato himself, and anyone
else of this quality) is to count as an example of genuine virtue.

6. A PROLEPTIC READING OF THE *LYSIS*

The *Lysis* is one of the more perplexing dialogues, and its interpretation has been the subject of endless controversy. In this case I
think the puzzles are all soluble. Their solution is particularly relevant to my thesis for the interpretation of the threshold dialogues. For it shows how carefully Plato has planted hints and anticipations of his mature doctrine of *erōs* in this ostensibly juvenile
exercise in Socratic ignorance and *aporia*.

I divide the analysis of the argument into ten stages. The first four are concerned with *philia* proper, that is, with friendship and family affection. The last six stages are oriented towards the asymmetric pattern of *erōs* that is more fully developed in the *Symposium*.

1. (207D–210D) The opening conversation with Lysis has the true Socratic form of a moral elenchus, designed to bring the interlocutor to an awareness of his ignorance and his need for knowledge. Socrates' line of questioning leads to the conclusion that Lysis' power and ability to do what he wants will directly depend upon his acquiring knowledge and wisdom. The reasoning develops a familiar theme on the subject of beneficial knowledge, but it ends with a surprising result. If knowledge makes us beneficial, ignorance makes us useless. But who will love us if we are useless? No one, not even our own parents, says Socrates; and Lysis fails to object to this conclusion (210C 5–D 6). Now this passage began with Socrates and Lysis agreeing that his parents love him very much (207D), and there was no suggestion at that point that their love was based upon his usefulness. They simply want to make him happy, as good parents normally do (207D 7). There is, strictly speaking, no contradiction between the beginning and the end of this conversation with Lysis. But there is enough dissonance here for us to be suspicious of the sudden insistence that love must be based upon utility.[27] This unexpected claim will meet us again, as the key premiss in a dubious argument in stage 3.

2. (212A–213D) The theme of friendship and affection (*philia*), which was only touched on in the first section, becomes the central topic in the first conversation with Menexenus. Socrates' opening question is: "When one person loves (*philei*) another, which one becomes the friend (*philos*) of which? The one who loves (*philos*) of the one loved (*philoumenos*), or the one loved of him who loves, or does it make a difference?" Menexenus answers that it makes no difference; his model, like ours, is of friendship reciprocated. But

27. Our doubts will be reinforced at 212E 6–213A 3, where newborn babies are said to be particularly dear to their parents. I do not think that *Lysis* 210C–D, 213E, etc. can be read as a straightforward endorsement of the view that friendship must be based on utility. (So Vlastos, 1973: 6–9). See rather D. B. Robinson (1986) 69, n.15: "It is as erroneous to believe that Socrates really thought that Lysis' parents did not love him, insofar as he was useless, as to believe that the Persian king would ever have trusted him with his empire."

Socrates is out to make trouble, and he does so by deliberately shifting from *philia* to *erōs*. What if the loved one is indifferent or even hostile? Doesn't this happen, for example, between a lover (*erastēs*) and his beloved (*paidika*)? Menexenus agrees, with becoming conviction ("Yes, absolutely!" 212C 3). So it seems that in un-reciprocated love, no one is a friend (*philos*)? But this leads to new problems. How can one be a lover of horses, of wine, or of wis-dom (*philosophos*),[28] unless horses, wine, and wisdom can love us in return (212D)?

The *aporiai* in this section are mostly verbal, and they trade on the syntactic ambiguity between active and passive uses of *philos*. Socrates first takes the term passively to mean "loved by" or "dear to" (212E 6), and then actively to mean "loving," "fond of" (213B 5ff.). But instead of the clarification that might result from a simple disambiguation, he introduces new confusions by drawing a paral-lel inference for the opposite term *echthros*, "enemy."

The appearance of paradox or contradiction here is entirely due to passive–active ambiguities. There is no reason to suppose that Plato was confused. The surefootedness with which, after explicitly drawing the distinction, he nevertheless exploits these ambiguities, suggests that he knows perfectly well what he is up to. It is a chal-lenge to us, the readers, to pick our way through the traps he has set.

3. (213E–215B) The same is true of the next section, where Lysis is again interlocutor. Here Socrates, following the poets, "our fa-thers and leaders in wisdom," proposes that friendship must be between likes, and then finds reason to reject this principle. (We may remember from the *Ion* and *Protagoras* a somewhat different appreciation of the wisdom of poets.) The objection to the like-to-like principle (the principle that is in fact exemplified in the friend-ship of Lysis and Menexenus) falls into two distinct parts. First it is pointed out that bad people cannot engage in true friendship with their likes, or with anyone else. This is a constant theme in Plato,[29] and is presumably to be taken seriously here. That leaves us with

---

28. Note how the casual play here on the etymology of *philosophos* prepares us for the more explicit presentation of philosophy as a form of love, at 218A.
29. Price (1989: 5) cites as parallels *Gorgias* 509E 3–6, *Phaedrus* 255B 1–2, *Rep.* I, 351C 7–352D 2. Similarly Xenophon, *Mem.* II.6.10–20.

only half of the like-to-like proposal: that the good will be friends
with others who are good (214c 6).

Here we have reached a positive result, support for which can
be abundantly documented from other Platonic texts.[30] Friendship
between the good is also the model for perfect friendship in Aristotle. Why is it not accepted here? Socrates offers two objections,
both of them relying upon the suspect principle that love must be
based on utility: (1) Insofar as the two friends are *alike*, they cannot
render one another services that each could not render himself or
herself. (2) Insofar as the two are both *good*, they must be self-sufficient, and hence have no need of one another. The first objection
has no independent force; if it is to prove anything, it must pre-
suppose what the second objection asserts: that good friends will
be self-sufficient. (If the good were not self-sufficient, it is easy to
imagine that they could be of service to one another. Scratching
one another's back is only the most trivial example.) Now the com-
patibility between self-sufficiency and genuine friendship is a serious issue; and it evokes from Aristotle the elaborate theory of the
friend as another self, in *NE* ix.9. Plato may well have seen the
problem as one he had inherited from the Socratic tradition,
where the self-sufficiency of the sage seems to have been an accepted principle.[31] Plato does not pursue the question further. The
point of introducing it into the present context must be to make us
question once again whether love and friendship are always based
on utility.[32] If this assumption leads to the conclusion that good
people cannot be friends with one another, there must be something wrong with the assumption.

4. (215C–216B) Having given up the Homeric principle of like-
to-like, we now follow Hesiod in exploring the possibility that likes
will be rivals and enemies but that opposites will be friends. As an

---

30. *Phaedrus* 255B 2, *Laws* VIII, 837 A–D, etc.
31. For Antisthenes on self-sufficiency see above, p. 7, with echoes in Xenophon,
    e.g. *Mem.* 1.6.10: (Socrates speaking) "I believe that to lack nothing is divine,
    to lack as little as possible is the closest thing to the divine."
32. Is there perhaps, here again, a Socratic (or Antisthenic) precedent that Plato
    is calling into question? For friends as useful possessions see Xen. *Mem.*
    II.5.1–5, 6.1 and *passim*, esp. 6.16: "can useless people make useful (*ophelimoi*)
    friends?" Guthrie (1975: 145, referring back to 1969: 462–7) takes "Socrates'
    insistence on usefulness as the criterion of value or goodness" as historical.

account of friendship this is not to be taken seriously, and it is easily answered by objections both verbal (if we take *friend* and *enemy* as a pair of opposites, how can there be friendship between these two?) and substantial (how can the just person be friend to the unjust, or the good person to the bad?). The principle of opposite-to-opposite seems to have been brought in simply for the sake of symmetry, as a complement to like-to-like. In fact, however, it hints at the conception of *erōs* as desire for what one lacks ("Each thing desires its opposite ... For the dry desires the moist, the cold desires the hot ... Each one is nourished by its opposite," 215E). And the examples from natural philosophy point to the cosmic dimensions of *erōs*, familiar from Empedocles and developed at length by Eryximachus in the *Symposium*.

5. *(216C–E)* At this point the principle of reciprocity is abandoned (since like–like and opposite–opposite pairs have both been eliminated), and Socrates introduces the asymmetric model that serves as a basis for the rest of the discussion. He suggests that what is neither good nor bad may become friend (with *philos* taken actively = fond) of what is good.[33] This is, in effect, the model for philosophical *erōs*, as will be made plain in the next section. For the moment, however, nothing is plain. The interlocutor cannot understand this new formula, and Socrates confesses himself dizzy with *aporia* (216C 5). His first hint of clarity is to recognize the beautiful (*to kalon*) as the object of love, as equivalent to "what is good" (*to agathon*) in the formula just proposed. "For I say that the good is beautiful" (216D 2). But for the moment Socrates neglects this hint and proceeds to give an abstract defense of the formula. Assuming a division of everything into what is good, bad, and neither,[34] he points out that all pairs involving only good and/or bad have been ruled out by the argument so far. Taking, therefore, the neutral as the necessary first term, he shows that it can be *philon* only with the good. (Nothing can be friend to the bad, and if neutral were friend of neutral we would have like-to-like again, which was disqualified in section 3.)

33. The asymmetric pattern was suggested earlier, in the poor man's reliance on the rich and the sick man's on the doctor (at 215D); but it is fully formulated for the first time at 216C.

34. *Lysis* 216D, paralleling *Gorgias* 466E. Cf. also *Meno* 87Eff. and *Euthyd.* 280Eff.

6. *(217A–218C 3)* This asymmetric model for love is now made plausible by two examples. (1) The body, which is neither good nor bad, is (because of disease which is bad) friendly towards medicine which is good and beneficial (217A–B). And (2) philosophers, who are neither wise (good) nor foolish (bad), are lovers of wisdom (something good), because of the evil of ignorance (218A–B). So, says Socrates, summing up this first positive result, "we have discovered what the friend or lover (*philon* taken actively) is and what it is fond of."[35] "Both in the soul and in the body and everywhere, what is neither bad nor good is friend of the good, because of the presence of something bad" (218B 7–C 2).

The causal factor of evil introduced here will be discarded in what follows (in section 8), but its temporary appearance is the occasion for making an important distinction between two kinds of causal presence. If whiteness is present to blond hair in the form of white powder, the hair appears to be white but is not really so. However, when whiteness is present in old age, then the hair becomes "such as the thing present is, white from the presence of whiteness" (219D 8). This stronger notion of causation-by-presence is used without any explanation in the *Gorgias*,[36] and it reappears in the *Phaedo* as one possible account of participation in the Forms (*Phaedo* 100D 5). Here it is carefully explained in order to be excluded from the new formula: the philosopher is not to be made evil by the presence of ignorance (217A–218A).

This brief exposure to Plato's erotic model for philosophy is not further developed in the *Lysis*. We will, however, find here two concepts that play an essential role in the later theory: "for the sake of something" (*heneka tou*) and desire, *epithumia*.

7. *(218C 5-220B)* At the most intense moment of dialectical drama in the dialogue, the notion of "for the sake of something" (familiar also from the *Gorgias* and from *Laches* 185D–E) is introduced into this discussion, in order to prepare the recognition of a *prōton philon*, a primary object of love, for the sake of which everything else is said to be dear. But the new step is preceded by an outburst

35. Reading ἐξηυρήκαμεν ὅ ἐστιν τὸ φίλον καὶ οὗ (not οὔ), with Sedley (1989) 108.
36. See *Gorgias* 497E 1–3, 498D, 506D. Cf. *Euthyd.* 301A–B.

of doubt and suspicion in regard to the formula reached in the preceding stages. "Watch out!" cries Socrates, "we may be the victims of imposter arguments (*logoi alazones*, 218D 2)." The first move towards correcting whatever error has been committed consists precisely in introducing the *heneka tou* and expanding the previous formula as follows: "What is neither good nor bad is fond (*philon*) of what is good because of what is bad and hostile, for the sake of what is good and dear (*philon*, 219A 6)."[37]

But this formula may still be deceptive (219B 9). We say that medicine is dear for the sake of health; so will not health also be dear? But if dear, then dear for the sake of something? Namely, something dear? And then will that not also be dear for the sake of something else?

So will we not necessarily wear ourselves out by proceeding in this way, or reach some starting-point (*archē*) which will no longer refer to something else that is dear; but we will come to *that which is the primary dear* (*ekeino ho estin prōton philon*), for the sake of which we say that all other things are dear? (219C)

This, says Socrates, is what I meant to warn you about. We may be deceived by all those other things that we said were dear for its sake: "they are like images (*eidōla*) of it, but that primary thing is what is truly dear."[38] Socrates then gives two examples of instrumental means, valued or desired not for their own sake but for the cause they serve.

Is it not the same for what is dear? Whenever we say things are dear to us for the sake of something else dear, we turn out to be saying it [sc. dear] merely in words (*rhēmati*); what is really dear turns out to be that thing itself, in which all these so-called friendships (*philiai*) terminate. So what is truly dear is not dear for the sake of something dear.

Here one of the earliest regress arguments in the history of philosophy serves to articulate the concept of an intrinsic good, what

37. Note that *philon* is first construed actively in this formula at 219B 1–2 and then immediately thereafter passively, presumably not by chance. The same reversal occurs redoubled (twice active, then twice passive) in the even more perplexing reformulation at 219D 3, according to Burnet's text.
38. Omitting Burnet's comma after τὸ πρῶτον in 219D 4 and taking ὃ ὡς ἀληθῶς ἐστι φίλον as predicate clause with ἐκεῖνο τὸ πρῶτον as subject of the copula ᾖ.

is dear and desirable for its own sake, as an end and not as a means.[39] The identify of this primary dear, the one thing that is truly dear, is not immediately specified. The parallel regress argument in *NE* 1.2 has led some commentators to think here of happiness (*eudaimonia*) as the highest good, but there is nothing in the text to justify this interpretation. For Plato it is the good alone, the good as such (with its substitute or equivalent *to kalon*, the beautiful) which is of value for its own sake and the source of value for everything else.[40]

The deception against which Socrates warned turns out to be twofold. The first error is the one just exposed: to regard as true objects of love and value anything except the primary good itself. On the contrary, other things are dear only "for the sake of the good." The second error will be corrected in the next section.

8. (220B 6–221D 6) Can the good be loved "because of what is bad"? This phrase (*dia to kakon*) must be eliminated from the formula proposed in section 6. The phrase implies not only that what is good could be caused by its opposite,[41] but also that the good is desirable only because of its utility, "as a remedy for what is bad" (220D 3), and that in itself it is of no use "for its own sake" (220D 6–7). This is one more *reductio* against the utilitarian assumption, one more unacceptable result that follows from the principle that only what is useful to someone else can be dear.

For it is the primary dear that is in question here (220D 8), the one thing that is intrinsically dear. All other things are said to be instrumentally dear, dear for the sake of something else. Could

---

39. There is a close parallel at *Gorgias* 467–8, as D. B. Robinson (1986: 75) points out. But the uniqueness of the primary good is not asserted in the *Gorgias*. Of course the regress argument does not prove uniqueness. It is simply assumed here that there is one *philon* in which all *philiai* terminate (220B 2, D 8). The thesis of unity will be developed elsewhere. See below, pp. 348ff.

40. At 220B 7, immediately after the introduction of the *prōton philon*, it is recalled that "the good is *philon*" (from 219B 2 "for the sake of the good and dear"). The point was first made at 216C 6–D 2: "The *kalon* is dear ... And I say that the good is *kalon*." There is nothing about happiness as dear or object of desire in the *Lysis*. For an implied interpretation in terms of happiness see Vlastos (1991) 117 n.49; cf. Irwin (1977) 52, and now (1995) 54.

41. For the rule that opposites cannot be causes of one another see *Rep.* I, 335D: II, 379B–C, and the transmission theory of causation discussed below, pp. 333f.

what is truly dear (τὸ τῷ ὄντι φίλον) be loved because of its opposite, something bad? In the absence of anything bad, would the
truly dear cease to be dear (220E 5)?

We are flirting here with the notion of the final end or ultimate
good. How are we to get a grip on this notion of something intrinsically dear or desirable? Socrates proposes a thought experiment. Suppose evil were to disappear. Would desire also disappear? Socrates now laughs at his own thought experiment: "The
question is ridiculous ... Who knows?" (221A). What we do know
is that thirst, hunger, and desires (*epithumiai*) in general are not always harmful; they are sometimes beneficial, sometimes neutral. If
all evils were to disappear, at least neutral desires would still be
left.[42] And the object of these desires will be dear (*phila*). So the
cause (*aitia*) of something being dear is not the bad after all. It is
desire (*philein*) and being loved (*phileisthai*) (221D). The formula
proposed in section 6 turns out to be a pile of nonsense, or so
Socrates now claims (221D 5).

Socrates has been mischievous more than once in this dialogue,
however, and we must look again to see what is left of the formula
so badly maligned. It ran as follows: "What is neither good nor
bad becomes friend of what is good because of the presence of
what is bad" (217B 5, 218C 1). The causal explanation of the last
clause has now been replaced by the introduction of desire.[43] Furthermore, the regress of section 7 has been interpreted to show
that nothing is *really* an object of *philein* except the primary dear,
the intrinsic good. Other things are only called dear; they are not
valued for their own sake. But with these corrections, the formula
still stands: What is neither good nor bad loves and desires what is

---

42. Beneficial desires (221A 7–B 2) could be left as well, but Plato limits himself
here to the weaker assumption of neutral desires.
43. So correctly von Arnim (1914) 55. But von Arnim believes that the causal role
assigned here to desire is in fact incompatible with the objectivity of the
good as intrinsically desirable, and he sees the argument of *Euthyphro* 9Eff.
(that the gods love the pious because it is pious, not that it is pious because
they love it) as a correction of the doctrine implied here (*ibid*. pp. 56ff.). On
this point I think von Arnim is mistaken. The causality of desire is not invoked in the *Lysis* to explain why the good is good, and hence desirable, but
only to explain why it is *dear*, i.e. actually desired: it is *aitia tou philein te kai
phileisthai* (221D 1). There is no incompatibility between the objectivity of
good and the subjectivity of desire. That is precisely why desire must be enlightened by reason to focus on its proper object.

good. And philosophy is the form of love in which the good is understood as wisdom.

Here we have the implicit positive conclusion of the *Lysis*, which (together with the notion of the primary dear as the good and *kalon*) directly prepares for Diotima's doctrine of *erōs*. But this positive conclusion is buried under Socrates' final aporetic flourishes. In this respect the end of the *Lysis* resembles that of the *Laches* and *Charmides*, where we catch a glimpse of a positive conclusion that is then whisked out of sight by some final perversity or opacity on the part of Socrates. In this case the concluding maneuvers focus on two concepts that we meet again in the *Symposium*: desire (*epithumia*) and what is one's own or akin (*to oikeion*).

After the thought experiment of section 8 on the disappearance of evil, desire (which was a subordinate theme in sections 4 and 6)[44] comes to occupy a central place in the discussion, parallel to the notions of friendship and love. The concept of *erōs*, so prominent in the prologue, now reappears to prepare for the dramatic dénouement, in the argument about the appropriateness of loving genuine lovers in return that delights the lover Hippothales and disconcerts the two boys in the next section. But above all *erōs* serves here to unify the analysis by directly connecting desire with *philia*.[45] The return of *erōs* acknowledges the fact that the asymmetric model of love has replaced the reciprocity of friendship as the basic frame of reference for the discussion.

9. (221D 6–222B 2) In this brief section, besides the erotic play between Hippothales and the boys, Plato develops two thoughts that will play a part in Diotima's theory: that desire as such implies a lack (221D 7), and that what one lacks is *to oikeion*, what naturally belongs to one.[46]

10. (222B 3–D 8) This last stage in the conversation (before the negative summary and conclusion at 222E) explores the notion of

---

44. See 215E 4, 217C 1, E 8–9.
45. See the link between *epithumein*, *eran*, and *philein* at 221B 7, and the parallelism between *erōs*, *philia*, and *epithumia* at 221E 4.
46. The term *oikeioi* "relatives," "kinfolk" appeared earlier as a parallel for *philoi* (*Lysis* 210B–D). Compare *Charmides* 163C 5–D 3, where *ta oikeia* are construed as "what belongs to a person" (in the phrase "doing one's own thing") and identified with good things (*agatha*).

the kindred (*to oikeion*) as a new designation for the object of love. Is the *oikeion* the same as what is alike (*to homoion*)? But then it implies friendship as like-to-like, a principle we rejected earlier ... on grounds of inutility.[47] Or is the kindred the same as the good (222C 4, D 5)? That would bring us back to the case of true friendship: the good is friend only to the good. Of course we *thought* we had excluded that too, but on inadequate grounds.[48]

So the conversation with Lysis and Menexenus ends in this brief return to the theme of reciprocity that fits their own situation, after most of the conceptual analysis has been directed towards the quite different notion of *erōs* as love for a unique and primordial object of desire, the good as the *prōton philon*.

47. The like-to-like principle was rejected as useless in the case of good-to-good. The other like-to-like case, of bad-to-bad, was excluded on better grounds and is excluded again here, at 222D 1–4.

48. As von Arnim (1914: 62) observed, ᾠόμεθα at 222D 7 is a pointer (*Fingerzeig*) on Plato's part to indicate "that this proposition was not really but only apparently refuted."

CHAPTER 10

The emergence of dialectic

1. TRANSITION TO DIALECTIC AND THE FORMS

At this point our study undergoes a change of pace as well as a change in theme. Instead of moral psychology and the theory of virtue we turn now to the more technical heartland of Platonic philosophy: the concept of dialectic and the theory of Forms. This means moving also from the threshold dialogues to the *Phaedo* and *Republic*. It is Plato's own argument that has led us in this direction. In the last three chapters we have been following a line of thought that connects the beneficial knowledge of good and evil (as introduced in the *Laches* and *Charmides*) with the twin Socratic paradoxes familiar from the *Gorgias*, *Protagoras*, and *Meno*: that no one does evil voluntarily and that the moral virtues are somehow unified in wisdom or knowledge. But the problem remains: how can knowledge of the good guarantee right action? I have argued that Plato's conception of *erōs*, as a passionate desire for the good-and-beautiful, is the essential key to a Platonic understanding of these paradoxes. No one does evil willingly because our most fundamental passion is a desire for the good, a desire understood transparently or *de re* as a desire for what is truly good, and not merely a pursuit of what we happen to think is good. (This distinction is explicitly drawn by Plato in *Rep.* VI, 505D 5–9.) If we in fact pursue a goal or activity which is not really good, that can only be out of ignorance.

The task of philosophy, then, is to lead us to knowledge of the good. But, according to Plato, genuine enlightenment in this domain can come only from an intellectual grasp of fundamental realities, and this in turn requires an arduous training. The training and the method of approach is what Plato calls dialectic. The realities themselves, the ultimate object of both knowledge and desire, are what we refer to as the Forms. In this chapter we survey Plato's discussion of dialectic. In the next chapter we turn to the Forms.

What I propose is not a new analysis of Plato's epistemology and metaphysics, but something more modest: a reading of the texts that does full justice to Plato's cunning as a writer, and to his artistic use of the Socratic dialogue form as a device for articulating his vision of knowledge and reality. In focusing attention on the literary techniques by means of which Plato presents his philosophic thought, I hope to bring to light systematic elements of unity and continuity that the developmental approach to these dialogues tends to obscure. In this chapter I explore the various forms of linkage between different accounts of the concept of dialectic and the method of hypothesis. In Chapter 11 I do the same for the doctrine of Forms.

As we saw in Chapter 2 (pp. 6of.), the theme of dialectic provides one of the more striking examples of Plato's technique of proleptic exposition in dialogues before the *Republic*, that is, in dialogues of stylistic Group I. For the *Republic* is the very first dialogue in which Plato tells us what he means by dialectic. There are nevertheless unmistakable allusions to this topic in three earlier dialogues, namely in the *Meno, Euthydemus*, and *Cratylus*. Read retrospectively, from the vantage point of the *Republic*, these passages are fully intelligible; read in their immediate context at least two of these texts must seem enigmatic. For only in the *Republic* do we learn that "dialectic" has been chosen as the official designation for the highest kind of philosophical knowledge, the knowledge that is identical with, or indispensable for, the art required of the statesman: the *politikē technē* of the *Gorgias* and the royal art of the *Euthydemus*. And it is only from this point of view that the relevant passages in the *Euthydemus* and *Cratylus* can be understood.

There is a similar but more complex progression in the different contexts that refer to the method of hypothesis: first in the *Meno*, then in the *Phaedo*, and finally in the *Republic*. We will see that in the *Meno* and *Phaedo* the method of hypothesis is not only described but tacitly put to work, in long stretches of both dialogues. One function of these elaborate exercises in hypothetical method in the two earlier dialogues must be, by stimulating an interest in philosophical method, to prepare the reader for an understanding of what might otherwise be the quite unexpected account of dialectic in the Divided Line at the end of *Republic* VI.

Since it is in the central books of the *Republic* that dialectic is most fully described, we begin with this description, to be supplemented then in § 3 by references to dialectic in later dialogues, before returning in §§ 5–7 to trace the emergence of dialectic and the method of hypothesis in the earlier works. In § 8 we will look more closely at the *Euthydemus*, since this is the threshold dialogue most explicitly concerned with dialectic as a method of question and answer.

Finally, in view of the momentous career of the term "dialectic" after Plato – in Aristotle and the Stoics in antiquity, in medieval logic, and in modern times as used by Kant, Hegel, and Marx – it will be revealing to see (in § 9) how rare and restrained is the original use of this term by Plato, its inventor.

2. DIALECTIC IN THE *REPUBLIC*

We begin, then, with the Divided Line at the end of *Republic* VI. This is a line cut in four proportional sections, corresponding to four levels of cognition. The two top segments represent the intelligible domain (*to noēton*), that is, the range of truth and reality accessible to reason or intellect (*nous*), rather than to vision or sense perception. Of these two segments the lower corresponds to mathematical knowledge, the higher to knowledge of Forms. The relationship between these two levels poses one of the more vexed problems for any interpretation of Plato's theory of knowledge. I simply report here what we find in the text.

The conception of mathematics assigned to the lower of these two sections is relatively unproblematic. Plato represents mathematics as a partially or provisionally axiomatized system of deduction, where the axioms take the form of assumptions or "hypotheses" from which proofs and constructions can begin. For example, the geometers and number theorists

lay down as their hypotheses (*hypothemenoi*) the odd and the even and the geometric figures and three kinds of angles and the like for each branch of the subject (*methodos*). They take these assumptions as known, and they see no need to give an account (*didonai logon*) of them either to themselves or to others, as being plain to everyone. But starting from these they proceed through the rest and reach their conclusion in a consistent manner (*homologoumenōs*) [They make use of visible diagrams, but what they are thinking about is something else:] the square itself and the diagonal itself, not the ones they draw ... They seek to see those things themselves (*auta ekeina*) which one can only see in thought (*dianoia*). (VI, 510C–D).

By leading from the visible to the invisible, from the sensible to the intelligible, mathematical studies prepare the mind for the grasp of higher truths. But in order to reach the highest level of knowledge, the philosopher must overcome certain limitations imposed by the methods of mathematics. First, he (or she) must avoid the use of visual aids or diagrams and operate with intelligible concepts only. And secondly he must take nothing for granted: he must regard his hypotheses only as provisional assumptions, which he will be prepared in due course to criticize, to clarify or justify ("give an account of"), and if necessary abandon. At least that is one natural interpretation of the claim that dialectic will "remove" or "destroy" (*anairousa*) the hypotheses, whereas the mathematician is limited by the fact that he leaves them untouched (*akinētoi*) (VII, 533C).

By the highest segment of the intelligible I mean what rational discourse itself (*autos ho logos*) grasps by the power of dialectic (*dialegesthai*), taking the hypotheses not as starting-points (*archai*) but truly as hypotheses, like steps and departures (*hormai*), in order to proceed up to the non-hypothetical, reaching the starting-point of everything (*hē tou pantos archē*) so that, while grasping this and holding fast to what is connected to this, such discourse may thus descend to a conclusion, making no use at all of anything sensible, but using Forms alone, proceeding through them to Forms and concluding in Forms. (511B 3–C 2)

Just as mathematics makes use of visible models and diagrams in order to think clearly and consistently about intelligible structures, so dialectic makes use of mathematics itself as a conceptual model to achieve a knowledge of Forms. Exactly how this is to be done, Socrates will not say: only dialectic itself could show this, and only to someone who has been properly trained (VII, 533A 8).

We can only speculate as to how Plato understands the process by which dialectic can "rise above" the assumptions of mathematics (511A 6) and give an account of them, how it can proceed through Forms alone and reach the ultimate Form of the Good, the universal First Principle or starting-point for everything. Plato gives us only a few hints. The preparatory studies will culminate in the examination of connections and kinship between the various branches of mathematical science (VII, 531C 9–D 4, 537C): only the one who can see things together is a dialectician (*ho sunoptikos dia-lektikos*, 537C 7). So it is mathematics seen as a unified system, seen "synoptically," that serves as a conceptual model for dialectic.[1] But specialists in mathematics alone are not dialecticians, because they are not "able to give and receive an account (*logos*)" (VII, 531D 9–E 5). Only dialectic can proceed "through discourse (*logos*) without sense-perception towards what-each-thing-itself-is (*ep' auto to ho estin hekaston*) and not give up before it grasps what-good-itself-is (*auto ho estin agathon*) by means of intellection (*noēsis*) itself" (532A 6–B 1).

We have here Plato's most technical designation for Forms or essences (what-a-thing-itself-is), to be discussed in the next chapter. We note only that the dialectician is one who can exact an account of these essences, and can give such an account both to himself and to others (534B 3–5). So anyone who knows the Form of the Good must be able "to define[2] it in discourse by distinguishing it from all other things" and to defend this account "by passing through all tests (*elenchoi*) as in battle, eager to test it (*elenchein*) according to truth and what-is (*ousia*) rather than according to opinion and what-seems (*doxa*)" (534B 8–C 3). The future guardians must be so educated as to be able "to ask and answer questions in the most scientific way" (534D 9). Thus at the very moment when the new account of dialectic as copingstone of the higher studies reaches its climax (534E), Plato returns at least verbally to the more modest marks of Socratic argumentation: elenchus and question-and-answer – precisely those marks that recall the pattern of philosophic conversation from which dialectic takes its name.

3. DIALECTIC AFTER THE *REPUBLIC*

A brief survey of Plato's references to dialectic in dialogues later than the *Republic* will give us a more rounded picture of what it is whose emergence we want to trace in the earlier works.

1. I am indebted here, and on several other points in this chapter, to comments from Dr. Vassilis Karasmanis of the Polytechneion in Athens. See his unpublished Oxford dissertation, "The Hypothetical Method in Plato's Middle Dialogues" (1987).
2. *diorizesthai*, literally "to mark off the boundaries," "to distinguish." See Chapter 6, n.28 and the next note here.

It is perhaps the *Parmenides* that offers us the best specimen of what Plato's guardians might experience in their five years of dialectical training. The dialogue contains only one explicit reference to dialectic, in a final comment on the objections Parmenides has raised against the theory of Forms. If, says Parmenides, because of such difficulties someone gives up the theory, and "will not even distinguish[3] some form (*eidos*) for each one thing, he will have nowhere to direct his thought, if he does not allow that there is one form (*idea*) the same forever for each of the things that are real (*ta onta*), and in that case he will utterly destroy the power of dialectic (*dialegesthai*)" (*Parm.* 135B 5–c 2). So the possibility of dialectic, that is to say, of rational philosophic thought and discourse, is conditional upon the assumption of eternal, invariant Forms. As readers of Kant, we may see here the hint of a transcendental argument for the existence of Forms.

Socrates is unable to deal with Parmenides' objections because of his youth and his lack of philosophical preparation. Like the guardians of the *Republic*, Socrates will be able "adequately to see the truth" only after prolonged and rigorous training (136c 5; cf. 135D 6). The rest of the *Parmenides* illustrates what this training would be like, by an elaborate series of exercises in the method of hypothesis.

These exercises differ from the description of hypothesis in the *Republic* in two respects. First, the subjects hypothesized are not special mathematical concepts but highly general Forms, primarily the One and the Many. But Parmenides also mentions Similarity, Dissimilarity, Motion, Rest, Generation and Corruption, Being and Not-Being as possible subjects for hypothesis. And in the second place, Parmenides proposes that an affirmative hypothesis, "if *p*," should regularly be balanced by the corresponding negative hypothesis, "if not-*p*." "For example, concerning this hypothesis which Zeno laid down, *If there are many (things)*, one should consider what must follow both for the Many in regard to themselves and in regard to the One, and for the One in regard to itself and to the Many. And again, *If there are not many (things)*, we should once more consider what will follow ... " (*Parm.* 126A). This may be an example of what the *Republic* calls "removing" or "destroying" an hypothesis. How this will permit the student to rise above all

---

3. *horietai* "marks off," "determines," "defines."

assumptions to reach the unconditional Form of the Good is not explained. Perhaps Plato thought no explanation possible beyond the statement of the *Seventh Epistle*: after much hard work over a long time, "in friendly tests or refutations (*elenchoi*), using questions and answers without hostility, if one stretches human capacity to the utmost, the light of wisdom (*phronēsis*) and intelligence (*nous*) will shine on each subject" (*Ep.* VII, 344B).

In dialogues later than the *Parmenides* the method of hypothesis is apparently never mentioned again. Instead, dialectic is represented by a quite different form of inquiry, the method of Division or *dihairesis*. This method is best described in the *Phaedrus*, in a passage that we will consider in a moment. But it is a remarkable fact that this "later" conception of dialectic is actually mentioned in the *Republic* before the central discussion that we have cited from Books VI–VII.

This first reference to dialectic occurs not in an explicit discussion of philosophic method but as an aside in Socrates' response to an objection in Book V. He has famously proposed that women should have the same education and the same political responsibilities as men. The objection (raised by Socrates himself) claims that there is a contradiction between this egalitarian proposal and the Platonic principle of specialization: that different natures should have different tasks. Do not men and women have different natures?

In responding to this objection, Socrates complains that he and his interlocutors have unintentionally slipped from dialectic (*dialegesthai, dialektos*) into its opposite, antilogic (*antilogia*) or eristic (*erizein*), the pursuit of contradiction for its own sake, "because of an inability to consider the subject by dividing it into kinds (*kat' eidē diairoumenoi*), but pursuing a merely verbal opposition to what has been said" (454A). (The point is that the objection fails to consider *in what respects* men and women differ in nature, and whether that difference is relevant to the tasks assigned.) This passage is all the more interesting in that it is not thematically connected with the central account of dialectic in the *Republic*, but it looks both backwards and forwards: backwards to the contrast between dialectic and eristic that we will find in the *Meno, Euthydemus*, and *Phaedo*,[4] and forward to the conception of dialectic as Division (*dihairesis*)

---

4. We find this contrast again in *Rep.* VII, 539A–C, but not as part of the central account of dialectic.

according to kinds that is conspicuous in the *Phaedrus* and later dialogues but otherwise scarcely noticed in the *Republic*.[5]

The principal discussion of dialectic in Book VII makes no reference to Division; it emphasizes instead the correlative process of Synopsis or seeing things together. It is in the *Phaedrus* that Plato first describes these two complementary operations in their connection with one another. On the one hand, we must be able to "bring into one form (*idea*) things scattered apart in many ways and see them together, in order by defining (*horizomenos*) each thing to make clear what one wants to talk about" (*Phaedrus* 265D). But we must also "be able to cut things into kinds (*kat' eidē*) according to their natural joints, and not try to break them where there is no [natural] part, in the manner of a bad butcher" (265E).

I myself [says Socrates] am a lover of these divisions and collections, in order to be able to speak and to think. And if I believe someone else is capable of seeing how things are naturally grouped into One and Many, I follow "behind in his footsteps as in those of a god." And until now I call those who are able to do this dialecticians (*dialektikoi*), whether rightly or not, god knows. (266B)

This new definition of dialectic in terms of Collection and Division[6] is then approved by Socrates' interlocutor (266C 7). And it is this characterization which regularly serves as a basis for later references to dialectic, with significant variations, in the *Sophist* (253D), *Statesman* (285A–287A) and *Philebus* (16C–17A).

It would take us too far afield to examine these later variations in all their diversity. I note only a few points of continuity. Although there is no longer any reference to the method of hypothesis, the central position of unity and plurality in these later accounts is prefigured by the role of the One and the Many as hypotheses in the dialectical exercises of the *Parmenides*. (The central role of *sunopsis* and conceptual unification, noted above from *Republic* VII, is also maintained in the latest relevant text, the implicit reference

5. There may well be some play on the active sense of the verb *dialegō* "to select," "separate," brought out in this context by the parallel use of *diaireisthai* "to divide," and by the unique occurrence of *dialektos* here in the sense of "dialectic." For the natural association of meaning between the active verb and the notion of "dividing by kinds," see the text of Xenophon, *Mem.* IV.5.11, *dialegontas kata genē*, cited above, pp. 76f.

6. New at least by the emphasis on Division, and hence the need for a new defence of the term ("I call those ... *dialektikoi*," echoing *Rep.* VII, 532B 4, cited below, p. 327). At the same time Socrates insists that this is *not* an innovation!

to dialectic in *Laws* xii, 965B–C.) Furthermore, the key terms for the theory of Forms, *eidos* and *idea*, regularly reappear in later characterizations of dialectic,[7] although it is not always clear whether the Forms in question are the same as those of the *Republic* and the *Parmenides*. In the *Statesman*, however, it is emphasized that dialectic has as its concern "incorporeal entities, the greatest and finest of things," accessible not to sense-perception but to *logos* alone (286A). And in the *Philebus*, in what is probably the latest explicit mention of dialectic in the Platonic corpus, "the power of dialectic (*dialegesthai*)" is described as "by far the truest knowledge" because it deals with "being (*to on*) and what is truly real (*ontōs*) and by nature the same forever" (*Philebus* 58A), in an unmistakable echo of the ontological language of the *Phaedo* and *Republic*.

If it is true, then, to say with Richard Robinson that by dialectic Plato generally meant "the ideal method, *whatever that may be*," it is misleading to suggest that at different stages of his life Plato applied this honorific title to "whatever seemed to him at the moment the most hopeful procedure."[8] There is more consistency here than might at first appear. The fact that the dialogues refer to the method of hypothesis from the *Meno* to the *Parmenides* and not later tells us nothing of Plato's practice in oral discussion. And since the *Republic* describes dialectic *both* in terms of division (and synopsis) as well as in terms of hypothesis, it is not at all clear that the two procedures belong to different stages of his life. What is true is that *references* to the two procedures predominate at different periods of his written work. But in both cases – for hypothesis from the *Phaedo* to the *Parmenides*, for dialectic as Division in the passages just cited from the *Statesman* and *Philebus* – it is always the same supersensible, unchanging reality that dialectic takes as its object.

4. THE ORIGINS OF DIALECTIC

Having seen what Plato made of the concept of dialectic in the *Republic* and beyond, we must now turn back to trace the emer-

7. E.g. *Phaedrus* 265D 3 (*idea*), E 1 and 4 (*eidos*), 266A 3 (*eidos*), 273E 1 (*kat' eidē diaireisthai*), 2 (*idea*); *Sophist* 253D 1 (*eidos*), 5 (*idea*); *Statesman* 285A 4 (*kat' eidē diaireisthai*); *Philebus* 16D 1 and 7 (*idea*); *Laws* xii, 965C 2 (*idea*).
8. Richard Robinson (1953) 70: Robinson rightly recognizes, however, that the subject matter of dialectic was "in one sense always the same ... throughout Plato's life"; namely, it seeks "unchanging essences" (70f.)

gence of this conception in his earlier writings. And here our topic is really twofold. There is, first of all, Plato's explicit reference or implicit allusion to dialectic as the method of philosophy. Such reference is normally marked by an emphatic use of the verb *dialegesthai* or one of its cognates, but occasionally by a term like *hypothesis* that figures prominently in the central theory of the *Republic*. In this sense reflection on dialectic is limited to a small number of passages in six or seven dialogues from Group I. But there is, on the other hand, the actual *practice* of dialectic in the broad sense, as Socrates' manner of carrying on a philosophical conversation. And evidence for this is found in every argument in every dialogue. So if the development of the theory of dialectic, by explicit reflection, is a limited topic that we can trace with some completeness in the next section, the development of dialectic as the actual practice of the dialogues is an enormous subject, which we can barely touch on here.

Assuming, as we may reasonably do, that the term "dialectic" was originally chosen by Plato because of the paradigmatic role of Socratic conversation in his own conception of philosophy, there is no need to consider here the possibility that dialectic may in some sense be older than Socrates. Thus Aristotle is reported to have regarded Zeno of Elea as the inventor of dialectic.[9] Protagoras and other sophists may have trained their students to argue both sides of a given question, as indicated in the collection of arguments known as the *Dissoi Logoi*.[10] (This would explain why they were accused of "making the weaker argument the stronger," as in making a bad case prevail in court.) Plato's dialogues also suggest that some kind of question-and-answer technique was a form of virtuosity in which sophists like Hippias, Gorgias, and Protagoras claimed to excel.[11] All of these developments may have provided the background for Socrates' actual practice. But such developments do not concern us here. Our topic is not the intellectual history of the fifth century but the appearance of dialectic in Plato's writings.

---

9. D.L. VII.57, IX.25. Cf. Richard Robinson (1953) 91f. Aristotle was presumably influenced by Plato's treatment of Zeno in the *Phaedrus* (261D) and *Parmenides* (127Dff.).

10. DK 90, translation in Sprague (1972) 279–93. Cf. Guthrie (1969) 316–19. New text, translation and commentary in T. M. Robinson (1979).

11. *Hippias Minor* 363C–D, *Gorgias* 447C 5–8, D 6–448A 3, 449C 7–8; *Protagoras* 334E 4–335A 3.

The one historical question that we can neither avoid nor, unfortunately, resolve is the personal contribution of Socrates. How much of what we find in the dialogues did Plato actually owe to Socrates? As I have argued in Chapter 3, the literary evidence for Socrates' philosophy is so late and unhistorical that we cannot really answer this question with any confidence.[12]

What evidence we do have suggests that Socrates' practice of the elenchus was something much more personal and unsystematic than what we find in Plato's dialogues. This is reflected in the *Apology*, both in the cross-examination of Meletus and in Socrates' own statement: "If one of you claims to be concerned about wisdom and truth and virtue, I will not let him go, but I will question him and examine him and test him, and if he does not seem to me to possess virtue, but claims that he does, I will reproach him" (*Apology* 29E). So Nicias in the *Laches* warns that anyone who engages in conversation with Socrates, regardless of the question originally under discussion, will ultimately find himself obliged "to give an account of himself, what sort of life he is now living and how he has lived in the past" (*Laches* 187E–188A). From such indications as these, as well as from the paradigmatic elenchus depicted in Aeschines' *Alcibiades* (above, pp. 20f.), we may conclude that it was not so much the refutation of a thesis by formal contradiction that Socrates pursued, but rather the more pragmatic contradiction between what the interlocutor claims to believe and the life he actually leads.

5. REFERENCE TO DIALECTIC IN DIALOGUES EARLIER THAN THE *REPUBLIC*

We turn now to the explicit discussion of dialectic in the early dialogues, that is to say, in the dialogues of stylistic Group I. As we have mentioned, the emergence of the concept of dialectic is signaled either by a philosophically marked use of the verb *dialegesthai* and its cognates or by a discussion of the method of hypothesis. In this section we look at examples of the first kind; the method of hypothesis will be considered in §§ 6 and 7.

12. There is no reason to doubt that Socrates was a master of the art of philosophical conversation by question and answer, as illustrated in the dialogues. But there is every reason to doubt that Socratic practice had the rule-governed form sometimes attributed to the elenchus. See Kahn (1992) 251–6.

There are six dialogues earlier than the *Republic* in which *dialegesthai* and related forms are used with a special force. These passages fall into three groups, distinguished both by form and content. In the first group, comprising the *Hippias Minor, Gorgias*, and *Protagoras*, only the verbal forms occur, and the contrast is between Socratic conversational technique and the sophists' preference for speechmaking. In the second group, represented by a single text in the *Meno*, the adverbial form *dialektikōteron* ("more conversationally") appears, and the contrast is not with rhetoric but with eristic, as in the first reference to dialectic in the *Republic* (v, 454A cited above, p. 298). In the third group, in the *Euthydemus* and *Cratylus* (as in *Republic* vii and often in later dialogues) we have the adjective *dialektikos*, "skilled in (philosophical) conversation," in other words "dialectician." Thus the three groups span the gap between a perfectly idiomatic use of the verb "to converse" and the semi-technical terminology of the central books of the *Republic*.

Group A In the *Apology* and elsewhere Socrates often refers to his conversations by using the verb *dialegesthai*, with no suggestion that this word carries any special philosophical weight.[13] In the *Hippias Minor* we find what is probably the earliest methodologically marked use of *dialegesthai* for the technique of question and answer, in contrast to the sophist's preference for oratory. Hippias has proposed a competition between set speeches on a controversial topic (369c 6–8). Socrates says he will not profit from a long speech, but he could be cured of his ignorance by answers to his questions (373A). He appeals to his host, Eudikos, to request Hippias to answer him: "for you have urged me to converse (*dialegesthai*) with Hippias," not to listen to his speeches (373A 6–7).[14]

This same contrast is more systematically drawn in the *Gorgias* and *Protagoras*. Thus Socrates has come to converse (*dialegesthai*) with Gorgias and ask him questions, rather than to listen to his display speech (*epideixis, Gorgias* 447B–E). When Polus is asked to say what art Gorgias professes, he praises it instead of answering what it is (448E). His error shows that "he has studied what is called rhetoric rather than *dialegesthai*" (448D 9); if he had practiced the art

13. E.g. *Apology* 19D (*bis*), 21C, 33A, 41C.
14. For an indication that the pointed use of *dialegesthai* for Socratic questioning is pre-Platonic (and hence genuinely Socratic) see the text of Antisthenes in *SSR* v A 187, line 17 (cited above, Chapter 4, p. 123).

of conversation, he would have answered the question as asked.[15]
The two techniques are contrasted not only with respect to length
of replies (Socrates requests *brachulogia* rather than *makrologia* at
449C 5; cf. 461D 6) but above all with respect to the mode of proof
and refutation (*elenchus*). No matter how many witnesses Polus may
call to testify against him, "such a refutation is worth nothing as to
the truth" (471E 7), since they may all be giving false testimony.
Socrates is not good at counting votes. He will be satisfied only "if
I can call you yourself as the single witness who agrees with what I
say" (472B 6).

One aspect of this contrast between *dialegesthai* and oratory is to
distinguish Plato's conception of philosophical discourse from that
of Isocrates, who was fond of using the term *philosophia* for his
own type of training. Now Plato is quite willing to compete as a
speechwriter. We have only to recall the *Apology* and the Funeral
Oration in the *Menexenus*, not to mention the series of speeches in
the *Symposium* and *Phaedrus*. But although Plato can beat Isocrates
at his own game, his focus on *dialegesthai* as the method of question-and-answer is designed to make clear that oratory and the
lecture format are not the appropriate vehicle for serious philosophical inquiry.

The same opposition is pursued throughout the *Protagoras*. Socrates reminds Protagoras that the latter claims to be an expert in
question-and-answer as well as in speechmaking (329B), in short
answers (*brachulogia* again) as well as in long (334E 4–335A 3). It is
by insisting on this claim to double competence that Alcibiades is
able to force the sophist to bend to Socrates' demand, at the critical moment when Socrates offers to leave rather than listen to
long speeches. "Socrates yields to Protagoras in lengthy speechmaking (*makrologia*), but I would be surprised if he yielded to anyone in ability to converse (*dialegesthai*) and in knowing how to give
and receive a rational account (*logos*)," says Alcibiades (336B 8–C 2).
This last formula will remain as the distinctive mark of a dialecti-

---

15. This is the rule of good method, to specify what one is talking about before
    judging it good or bad (463C). (See above, Chapter 6 §3.) The passage at
    Gorgias 448D seems to be the only example before the *Republic* where *dia-
    legesthai* or its cognates is directly connected with the search for a definition.
    However, the emphasis there is probably on skill in question-and-answer
    rather than on the *what-is-X?* question itself.

cian: the capacity to defend a thesis rationally, or to exact such a defence, by means of question and answer.[16]

Group B The examples considered so far all make use of the verb, most often in infinitival form (*dialegesthai*). In *Meno* 75D we find what may well be the first occurrence in Greek of the nominal stem *dialektik-* that will (in the *Republic*) provide dialectic with its name. The contrast here is not with rhetoric but with eristic, that is to say, not with speechmaking but with a different mode of argumentation by question-and-answer. Here (and in several examples in later dialogues where dialectic is contrasted with eristic)[17] *dialegesthai* represents a constructive, cooperative form of conversation as opposed to quarrelsome competition.

Eristic is the pursuit of refutation for its own sake, as a kind of sport. Meno has complained that Socrates' definition of figure (*schēma*) makes use of the notion of color. "But what if someone says he has no knowledge of color and is just as much at a loss about that as about figure, what kind of answer do you think you have given him?" Socrates responds:

A true answer. And if the questioner is one of these clever, competitive eristics, I would say to him: "I have answered. If what I say is not correct, it is your task to call me to account (*lambanein logon*) and refute me (*elenchein*)." But if people want to have a conversation (*dialegesthai*) with one another like you and me who are friends, one must answer more gently and more conversationally (*dialektikōteron*). More conversationally is, I think, not only to answer truly but also by means of what the interlocutor[18] agrees that he knows. (*Meno* 75C 8–D 7)

Here the notion of conversing in the Socratic manner is given a much more precise structure. Socrates proceeds to get Meno to agree that he understands and accepts all the terms that will be used in Socrates' new definition of figure (75D 7–76A 3). We have as it were the sketch of a primitive axiomatization, relative to what the interlocutor will accept as known. Thus Socrates prepares an

---

16. For parallels to *dialegesthai* understood as *logon dounai kai dexasthai* see *Rep.* VII, 531E (cited above, p. 296); *Prot.* 336D 1, 338E 5, 339A 3 (and cf. 348A, B 5ff.); *Charm.* 165B 3, *Laches* 187C 2, D 2, 10.

17. *Rep.* V, 454A–B, *Phil.* 17A 4; cf. *Soph.* 231E 1–5; *Rep.* VII, 537E–539C.

18. The text here has ὁ ἐρωτώμενος "the answerer," but it should probably be ὁ ἐρωτῶν "the questioner." See Bluck's note *ad loc*. The sense is clear.

explicitly mathematical definition, characterizing figure as the limit of a solid body, by securing from Meno a preliminary acceptance of the undefined but familiar terms that will appear in the definition. By a similar procedure elsewhere, Socrates often begins an argument by getting the interlocutor to agree to certain basic terms or commitments.[19]

In the text quoted from the *Meno* (75C–D) there is an emphasis on epistemic order: the project of definition seems to require a movement from the familiar to the less familiar, from the known to the unknown. But, as we have seen in Chapter 6, this leads to Meno's paradox about looking for what you do not know, and the response to Meno's paradox is recollection. Recollection explains how the search for an unknown definition is possible in principle, but we have still not found any definition for virtue. So Socrates introduces as a substitute the method of hypothesis: if virtue is such-and-such, then it is teachable; if not, then something else follows. Since this method is essential for the later conception of dialectic, we return to the *Meno* in the next section.

Group C   From the same stem as the adverbial form just quoted from the *Meno*, in the *Cratylus* and the *Euthydemus* we find the adjective *dialektikos* for people who are skilled in the art of philosophical conversation. The literal meaning of the adjective thus remains in contact with the idiomatic usage of the verb. But the role of *dialektikoi* in these two dialogues involves large doses of new Platonic doctrine.

The *Cratylus* passage might have been designed to introduce the term *dialektikos* for the first time, since its appearance is prepared by a careful *epagōgē*. The dialectician will figure here as the user of words, and hence as the proper judge of whether the maker of words, the namegiver, has done his job well. This notion is introduced as follows (390B). "Who will know whether the carpenter

---

19. For parallels to τελευτὴν καλεῖς τι and ἐπίπεδον καλεῖς τι; at *Meno* 75E 1 and 76A 1, see *Meno* 88A 7 σωφροσυνη τι καλεῖς; *Prot.* 332A 4 ἀφροσυνην τι καλεῖς; *Gorgias* 495C 3 ἐπιστήμην που καλεῖς τι; etc. (For equivalent formulae see also *Prot.* 330C 1 ἡ δικαιοσύνη πρᾶγμά τί ἐστιν ἢ οὐδὲν πρᾶγμα; 332C 3 ἔστι τι καλόν; C 5 ἔστι τι ἀγαθόν;). The gambit is parodied by Euthydemus at *Euthyd.* 276A 3 καλεῖς δέ τινας διδασκάλους ἢ οὔ; (as Hawtrey notes, *ad loc.*).

who makes a shuttle has put the appropriate form (*eidos*) in whatever wood he uses?" Answer: the weaver who uses the shuttle. And so the lyre-player will be the best judge of the lyre-maker's work, and the ship captain of the shipbuilder's. Who then will best know how to judge the namegiver's work, to see whether he has put the appropriate form of word (*to tou onomatos eidos*) in whatever syllables he uses, "both here and among the barbarians? Isn't this the person who will use the product, namely the one who knows how to ask and answer questions?" "Yes." "But don't you call someone who knows how to ask and answer questions "one skilled in conversation' (*dialektikos*)?" "Yes, I do" (390C; cf. 390A 5).[20]

This passage cunningly connects the familiar Socratic technique of question-and-answer with a new assignment: to judge whether the words of any language have their natural form, by "looking to what is the name by nature for each thing" (390E 2), the natural name or the appropriate form. This is the form which a competent namegiver must know how to put "into the sounds and syllables, by looking to that what-name-itself-is (*pros auto ekeino ho estin onoma*, 389D 5–7)." Here, for the first time (and the only time in the dialogues of stylistic Group I) the *dialektikos* is conceived as someone who must have access to the Forms – to the Form of Name in general as well as to the Form corresponding to any particular name – in order successfully to exercise his conversational skills.

The Forms of the *Cratylus* are in some respects just like those of the *Phaedo* and the *Republic*. In particular, the technical designation for a Form is exactly the same here as there: "What-that-thing-itself-is," *auto ekeino ho estin*. In other respects the doctrine of the *Cratylus* is rather deviant; it will be discussed later in Chapter 11 §8.

Our last example comes from one of the most peculiar dialogues in Group I, the *Euthydemus*. This dialogue has a *mise en scène* in the Lyceum gymnasium that is reminiscent of the *Charmides* and *Lysis*, and a narrative frame that is more like the *Phaedo* than the *Protagoras* (since Socrates' auditor, Crito, repeatedly intervenes in the discussion). In regard to content there are so many connections

---

20. This passage is echoed in a light-hearted way later in the *Cratylus*, in the etymology of ἥρως at 398D 7, where *dialektikoi* are named next to wise men and orators as "good at asking questions (ἐρωτᾶν)."

with the *Meno* that the latest commentator on the *Euthydemus* suggests that these two dialogues were written as a pair.[21] And the style is unmistakably that of Group I.[22]

Since, then, there is every indication that the *Euthydemus* was written before the *Republic*, we have here the most striking case of proleptic reference in any early dialogue. For the mention of *hoi dialektikoi* at *Euthydemus* 290c can only be understood as an allusion to the relationship between mathematics and dialectic described in *Republic* VI–VII. The young Clinias, suddenly and mysteriously endowed with supernatural wisdom, is explaining why the generals' art cannot be the knowledge that guarantees happiness, because it is a form of hunting. Generals hand over their conquests to statesmen, who know how to make use of them, just as hunters and fishermen must hand over their catch to cooks.

And again geometers and astronomers and arithmeticians, they are hunters too. For they are not makers of diagrams, each of these experts, but they discover truths about reality (*ta onta*). Now since they don't know how to make use of their discoveries themselves but only how to hunt, I suppose that those of them who are not absolutely foolish hand their findings over to the *dialektikoi* to make use of. (*Euthyd.* 290c)

The *Euthydemus* is full of puzzles, but none more puzzling than this. This cryptic reference to the superiority of dialectic over mathematics must imply the epistemology of the Divided Line and, even more precisely, the curriculum of the guardians in *Republic* VII, where we meet the three branches of mathematics mentioned in this text.

This is the only semi-technical reference to dialectic in the *Euthydemus*. But the entire dialogue is concerned with the art of *dialegesthai* in the sense of *Meno* 75D, Socratic conversational technique as opposed to eristic refutation-chasing. Hence we will return to the *Euthydemus* in § 8, and find that it contains many other allusions to later Platonic doctrine.

For a reader unfamiliar with the doctrine expounded in the *Re-*

---

21. Hawtrey (1981) 8–10.
22. See, for example, the figures from Ritter quoted by Brandwood (1990) 66 and 72: out of forty-three features of Plato's late style, the *Euthydemus* has only four, the same number as the *Protagoras*. (*Republic* I has nine late features; the other books of the *Republic* range from thirteen to twenty-two; the *Theaetetus* has twenty-five, the *Phaedrus* twenty-one.)

public, this reference to dialectic at 290C can only seem baffling. What is the intended effect? My guess is that this passage is designed as a provocative hint of things to come. It thus serves a protreptic function not unlike what we have noted for the use of *aporia* in Chapter 6 §7.

6. HYPOTHESIS IN THE *MENO*

In the passage on the Divided Line in *Republic* VI, it is the use made of hypotheses that distinguishes dialectic from mathematics. The method of hypothesis is introduced for the first time in the *Meno*; it reappears in the *Phaedo* and in the *Parmenides* as well. We will consider in the next section the extent to which one can find any unified conception underlying these four accounts.

The notion of hypothesis in the *Meno*, which Plato claims to have borrowed from the mathematicians, provides us with the earliest known theoretical account of deductive inference. Examples of deduction are of course to be found in all the dialogues. Deductive arguments must have been a familiar procedure in mathematics; they can be documented in philosophy since the time of Parmenides and Zeno. Hence it comes as no surprise to find that Plato's early dialogues are in possession of a terminology for premisses as "what has been agreed upon" or accepted by the interlocutor (*ta hōmologēmena*),[23] for the consequence or conclusion as "what follows from the argument" (*ta sumbainonta ek tou logou*),[24] for drawing or "calculating" the consequences (*sullogizesthai*),[25] and for contradiction as "saying what is opposite to oneself" (*enantia legein heautōi*).[26] (Whether there is a precise term for logical consistency is a problem to be discussed below.) The early dialogues also employ the term *hupothesis* for the position or thesis that the interlocutor seeks to

---

23. The notion of "premiss" emerges naturally from the contextually specified sense of "what we have agreed upon," e.g. at *Gorgias* 477C 7 *ek tōn hōmologēmenōn* (cf. *Hippias Minor* 368E 3 *ek tōn hōmologēmenōn emoi te kai soi*), 479B 4 *ek tōn nun hēmin hōmologēmenōn*. So at 480B 3 *ta homologēmata*. Compare *Prot.* 332D 1, etc.

24. *Hippias Minor* 369A 5. *Gorgias* 479C 5, etc.

25. *Gorgias* 479C 5, 498E 10. Cf. *sumbibazō* at *Hippias Minor* 369D 5, *analogizesthai* at *Prot.* 332D 1. The conclusion is thought of as binding, and if a contradiction ensues one must resolve it by releasing or untying one of the premisses (*lusai* at *Gorgias* 509A 2, *Prot.* 333A 1, 6).

26. *Ap.* 27A 4, *Hippias Minor* 371A 6, *Laches* 196B 4, etc.

defend.[27] But the *Meno* is the first text, to my knowledge, to distinguish sharply and clearly between the truth of the premiss and the validity of the inference. It is in this sense that Plato's method of hypothesis initiates the theory of deductive inference.

Plato begins by citing an example of what we might call a conditional proof in mathematics, though he describes it as a problem in geometrical construction. Can a given triangular area be inscribed in a given circle? Answer: I do not know; but I can answer conditionally, on the basis of an assumption (*ex hupotheseōs*, 86E 3–4). If the area can satisfy a specified condition, one thing follows. If it cannot satisfy this condition, a different consequence follows (*allo ti sumbainein*, 87A 6). We can deal in the same way with the teachability of virtue. I do not know whether it is teachable or not. But I can specify a condition such that, if virtue satisfies this condition, it is teachable; if not, not. What is the condition? "If virtue is some kind of knowledge, it is clear that it is teachable" (87C 5). Here the protasis specifies the *hupothesis*, the apodosis tells us what follows if the condition is satisfied. Note that the apodosis does not follow immediately from the *hupothesis* (virtue is knowledge) but from this in conjunction with another premiss that has just been specified: "knowledge alone is teachable" (87C 2).

The fact that the connection between condition and consequence is formulated here, and again at 89C 3 and D 3, as a conditional sentence (of the form "if *p*, then *q*") has led some commentators to suppose that the *hupothesis* in question is the entire "if ... then ..." construction, rather than the protasis alone.[28] But this interpretation fails to take account of the mathematical example, which clearly distinguishes the condition from the consequence, but *links the two* by an "if ... then ..." formula: if the area is such and such, then it follows that such-and-such (87A). In the *hupothesis* about virtue the same connection is expressed by the same conditional form: "if virtue is knowledge, then *it is clear that* it is teachable," (87C 5), where the phrase "it is clear that" (*dēlon hoti*) is an

27. *Euthyphro* 11C 5, *Gorgias* 454C 4; so also *Phaedo* 94B 1. Compare the discussion of the verbs *tithēmi* and *hupotithemai* in Richard Robinson (1953) 93–7.
28. Richard Robinson in the first edition of *Plato's Earlier Dialectic* (1941) 122f. And so still Crombie (1963) II, 533 and Bostock (1986). Robinson corrected this error in his second edition (Richard Robinson, 1953: 116f.) in response to the criticism of Cherniss and Friedländer; followed by Bluck (1961) 86 with n.4.

expression for the logical consequence that connects the two clauses, just as "it follows that" (*sumbainei*) does in the mathematical example. Here the conditional form ("if ... then ...") does not specify a single proposition (as our familiarity with the sentential calculus might lead us to suppose), and hence it cannot refer to the *hupothesis* alone. This conditional form is precisely Plato's formula for the deductive link between two propositions, between the hypothesis and the consequence.[29]

As far as I can see, Plato has no word for the validity of an inference. But he clearly distinguishes here between (A) the question whether the conclusion "virtue is teachable" is conditionally true, i.e. whether it follows from the hypothesis, and (B) the question whether the hypothesis is true. The two questions are treated quite differently. Question A is decided immediately in the affirmative (87c 5–10). Question B is subject to debate for the remainder of the dialogue. First we are given an argument for the truth of the hypothesis (87c–89a 5). Socrates then expresses doubt about this view, while reaffirming the truth of the conditional (89d 3–5), i.e. reasserting his positive answer to A. There follows an interesting indirect argument against the hypothesis.

1. If virtue is knowledge, then it is teachable.
2. If virtue is teachable, there must be teachers of virtue.
3. But there are no teachers of virtue.
4. Hence virtue is not teachable, and therefore not knowledge.

From the point of view of logical form, this is a nice example of *modus tollens* correctly used to "destroy" or "remove" an hypothesis by denying its consequences: (1) p implies q, (2) q implies r, but (3) Not r, therefore (4) Not q, and hence (5) Not p. In terms of the theory of dialectic in *Republic* vi, this would be one way to get beyond an hypothesis, by removing it.[30]

29. The inferential value of the conditional form is even clearer in the *Parmenides* examples of hypothesis, e.g. 136a: "concerning this *hupothesis* which Zeno posited, if there are Many, what must follow ...," 137b 3 "Shall I begin with my own *hupothesis*, positing concerning the One itself, whether there is One or there is not One (*eite ... eite ...*), what must follow?"

30. My *modus tollens* reconstruction of the negative argument is meant to be suggestive rather than historical. A more Platonic reading of this passage would construe the existence of teachers as a prior hypothesis, as in the mathematical example: if there are teachers of virtue, then it is teachable; if not, not. (This follows a suggestion from Vassilis Karasmanis.)

Of course this particular argument in the *Meno* is not above suspicion, because of an ambiguity in proposition 2. What the subsequent discussion with Anytus and Meno shows is that there are
no generally recognized teachers of virtue (90A–96c). This does not
prove that teachers of virtue are non-existent, much less impossible. Even if there were really no teachers of virtue to be found,
that would only mean that virtue cannot be taught under present
circumstances, not that it is unteachable. (The Greek *didakton* is
conveniently ambiguous between "taught" and "teachable.") And
Plato ends the dialogue by a significant hint that a genuine teacher
might be found, who would be like Teresias among the dead, a
case of true virtue among the shades (100A).

Despite this half-hidden fallacy, the *modus tollens* argument against
the hypothesis serves usefully to introduce the distinction between
virtue based on knowledge and virtue based on true opinion. Thus
the positive branch of the argument which affirms the hypothesis
(that virtue is knowledge) and the negative branch which denies
this proposition both lead to truth. There are indeed two kinds of
virtue, as we have seen.[31] And in the *Republic* Plato will propose
two kinds of education (one in music and gymnastics, one in mathematics and dialectic) designed to produce them both.

Let us look again at the positive branch, where the hypothesis is
affirmed. We have a short and easy argument that derives the
conclusion "virtue is teachable" from the hypothesis. We then
have the more lengthy argument in support of the hypothesis that
virtue is knowledge. This begins with a more general premiss,
"that virtue is something good," which is expressly labeled an *hupothesis* (87D 3). So our hypothesis about virtue as knowledge is to
be supported by invoking a more fundamental assumption about
the essential nature of virtue, prefiguring what the *Phaedo* will call
a "higher" hypothesis. Here again our conclusion is not an immediate inference from the new hypothesis. We need as an additional premiss "that there is nothing good apart from knowledge"
(87D 4ff.). This proposition requires an extended argument, beginning from the premiss "that good things are beneficial" (87E 2). It is
surely significant that all three higher premisses contain the term
good, which thus provides the basis for "giving an account" of our
original hypothesis. Hence we have prefigured here, in the first

31. See above, p. 218, n.8, and pp. 271ff.

explicit illustration of the method of hypothesis, not only the method of supporting a hypothesis by appealing to a higher hypothesis, as in the *Phaedo*, but also the ultimate dialectical appeal to an understanding of what is Good, as in the *Republic*. These future developments are all implicit here in the text of the *Meno*, like the tightly packed petals of a Japanese flower that will unfold in water.

Looking back on our observations on hypothesis in the *Meno* we see that nearly half of the dialogue, from the introduction of the method of hypothesis at 86E down to the end of the dialogue at 100B, constitutes one long exercise in this method, an exercise in which Socrates argues both from the affirmation and for the denial of the hypothesis, as well as arguing in defense of the hypothesis itself. We will find a certain parallel in the *Parmenides* to the affirmative and negative branches of the method as used in the *Meno*. But first we consider the account of hypothesis in the *Phaedo*, which includes a theoretical description of the method practiced in the *Meno*.

7. HYPOTHESIS IN THE *PHAEDO* AND BEYOND

The *Phaedo* does not refer to dialectic as such. But what it says about "the art of argument" (*hē peri tous logous technē*) at 90B, the art which is contrasted with antilogic or arguments that aim at contradiction (*antilogikoi logoi*), is rightly regarded as equivalent to a mention of dialectic. And when Socrates comes to give an account of his own method of argument (*logoi*) at 99Eff. the concept of *hupothesis* plays a central role. Here Plato develops in a new way the distinction first drawn in the *Meno* between the questions labeled A and B above: between what follows from the hypothesis and whether the hypothesis itself is true. First you examine what results from the hypothesis (*ta ap' ekeinēs hormēthenta*) to see whether they accord with one another or not (*ei allēlois sumphōnei ē diaphōnei*, 101D 5). But the justification of the hypothesis itself is another matter. Only the lovers of antilogic (*hoi antilogikoi*) will mix up the discussion of the starting-point (*archē*) with the discussion of what results from it (*ta hormēmena*). If you are a philosopher who wants to discover truths (*ta onta*), you must keep this distinction clear (101E).

The interpretation of this text in the *Phaedo* is vexed at several points, which we will discuss after surveying the larger context. We consider first what this section of the *Phaedo* has to say about the downward path, the method of hypothesis proper as first described in the *Meno*. I begin, says Socrates, "by laying down (*hupothemenos*) in each case the *logos* which I judge to be the soundest. And whatever seems to accord (*sumphōnein*) with this I posit as true ... whatever does not, I posit as not true" (100A). For the notion of soundest or strongest *logos* here (*errōmenestatos*), we can compare Simmias' earlier remark that, on very difficult topics like immortality, where it may not be possible to have definite knowledge in this life, we must nevertheless not shrink from testing claims (*elenchein*) in every way, so that, if we cannot discover how things really are, "we take the best and most irrefutable of human *logoi* and accept the risk of sailing through life on this as on the raft of Odysseus" (85C–D).

The raft that Socrates has chosen in the *Phaedo*, the fundamental *hupothesis* which is designated as such only at 100B but which has in fact served as the basis for Socrates' position throughout the dialogue, is the doctrine of Forms. Socrates' first argument, his *apologia* for being willing to die, begins with the claim, "we say there is something just itself? and also something beautiful and good?" (65D). A bit later in the dialogue the doctrine of recollection again connects the soul with the eternal Forms. "If there is what we are always talking about, something beautiful and good and all this kind of being (*ousia*) ... necessarily then, just as these things exist (or are real, *estin*), so our soul must also exist even before we are born" (76D 7ff.). And when the objection is made that if the soul is a harmony it must perish with the body, Socrates points out that this view of the soul is incompatible with recollection and that Simmias must choose between them (92C). The choice is easy, because the harmony doctrine has been accepted without any proof (*apodeixis*), on the basis of plausibility only (*eikota*); whereas the doctrine of recollection has been carefully established by "an *hupothesis* that is worthy of being accepted," namely, the necessary connection between the soul and the Forms (92D). The use of the term *hupothesis* here may be seen as proleptic for the passage at 100B, where Socrates explicitly introduces the Forms as his hypothesis.

The logic of Simmias' response at 92D is that *since* the harmony doctrine is incompatible with recollection, and *since* recollection has been established on the basis of the most fundamental hypothesis, the doctrine of Forms, therefore the harmony doctrine must be rejected: it is "out of tune" with recollection (*ou sunōidos* 92C 8; cf. *pōs sunāisetai?* 92C 3). This rejection thus illustrates the negative branch of the downward path: "what does not accord (*sumphōnein*) with the hypothesis, I posit as false" (100A 6). The argument from Forms to recollection, on the other hand, like the final argument from Forms to immortality, illustrates the positive branch of the method: "what seems to me to accord with it, I posit as true" (100A 5). Thus the bulk of the *Phaedo*, like the last half of the *Meno*, is a systematic exercise in the method of hypothesis, with the difference that here the *hupothesis* is provided by the doctrine of Forms.

The notion of "according" (*sumphōnein*) employed at 100A in the passages just cited (and again at 101D, to be discussed in a moment) has been the principal subject of dispute among interpreters.[32] If logical consistency is at stake, it makes sense to reject what conflicts with the hypothesis but it would be madness to accept as true everything that was consistent with it. (For most hypotheses, and for many substitution instances of *p*, both *p* and not-*p* will be consistent with a given hypothesis.) On the other hand, if we take *sumphōnein* to mean "follow from" or "is entailed by," then it is reasonable to accept what follows from the hypothesis but unreasonable to count as false whatever does *not* follow. (Again, in many cases neither *p* nor not-*p* will follow from a particular hypothesis.) It is clear that, if Plato has a reasonable method in view, what he means by "accord" is stronger than logical consistency and weaker than logical entailment.

The difficulty here is created, I suggest, by imposing our own notion of deduction on Plato's text. When I claimed above that Plato's method of hypothesis initiates the theory of deductive inference, the notion of deduction was taken somewhat loosely. Plato's conception of inference does not have the formal precision of

---

32. See Richard Robinson (1953) 126–36 and further literature in Gallop (1975) 178, Bostock (1986) 166ff.

For parallels to the musical metaphor of accord see *Gorgias* 457E 2 *sumphōna*, 461A 2 *sunāidein*, 482B 6–C 2 *diaphōnein, asumphōna*; *Prot.* 333A 7–8 *ou sunāidousin, sunāidoien*. Cf. also *Crat.* 436C 4–E 1 *sumphōnein*.

Aristotle's syllogistic. He has a clear notion of logical contradiction,[33] and a definite notion of logical consequence as "what follows from the argument" (*sumbainein ek tou logou*). But the verb in question, *sumbainein*, means simply "to happen" or "to result," and Plato never draws a sharp distinction between such logical "results" (*sumbainonta*) and results in general. And in any case it is not the relatively precise terminology of consistency or consequence that is employed here. The expression "to accord with" (*sumphōnein, sunāidein*) is not equivalent to either of these.

Instead of speaking of what follows (*sumbainein*) Plato refers here to *ta hormēthenta*, "what has proceeded" from the hypothesis, or "the sequel." For a writer as careful as Plato, this choice of vocabulary must be significant. I suggest that the term for consequence is deliberately avoided, because Plato is here presenting the method of hypothesis as more flexible and also more fruitful than logical inference. The method functions not simply by drawing a linear chain of deductions but by building up a complex theory or constructing a model. Whatever is incompatible with some basic feature of the model, as specified in the *hupothesis*, will be "out of tune" (*diaphōnein*) or fail to accord. But the positive relationship of "being in accord" (*sumphōnein, sunāidein*) is not mere consistency. It means fitting into the structure, bearing some positive relationship to the model by enriching or expanding it in some way.

On the interpretation proposed here, being "out of tune" may simply mean logical incompatibility. But "sounding together" or "being in accord" (*sumphōnein*) means making some constructive contribution, as notes in a melody or voices in a chorus. The hypothesis of the Forms at *Phaedo* 100B is after all not a single prop-

---

33. In addition to passages of the form cited above in n.26 (*enantia legein heautōi*), see also *Gorgias* 495A 5: Callicles chooses his answer "so that what I say may not be inconsistent (*anomologoumenōs*)," *Prot.* 358E 4 "it is impossible from what has been agreed (*ta hōmologēmena*)" (similarly 360E 4), 360A 6 "If we agree to this, we will destroy our previous agreements (*homologiai*)." So the mathematical method, using only the test of consistency, concludes *homologoumenōs* (*Rep.* VI, 510D 2) and produces only *homologia*, not knowledge (*Rep.* VII, 533C 5).

For Plato's most formal statement of the principle of non-contradiction (as non-contrariety), see *Rep.* IV, 436B–437A. For a somewhat caricatured version of the principle at *Euthydemus* 293C 7–D 6, in terms of negation (Socrates is knowing and not knowing) rather than contrariety, see below, n.44.

osition (unlike the hypothesis of *Meno* 87B–C) but an explanatory theory. The doctrine of recollection and the immortality of the soul are not presented as logical consequences of the assertion that the Forms exist. The epistemology of recollection and the concept of the eternal psyche have their place in a larger philosophical scheme of things, whose most fundamental component is the ontology of Forms. The requirement that the other posits must "accord" with one another as well as with the hypothesis is equivalent here to saying that Plato's epistemology and psychology must not only be consistent with his ontology but must fit together with it in a unified philosophical structure.

Because the various developments (*to hormēthenta, ta hōrmēmena*) from the hypothesis are not simply deductions, it makes sense for Plato to say that we must consider "whether they accord with one another or are in discord" (101D 5). Robinson thought this meant "that the consequences of an hypothesis can be inconsistent one with another," and he argued that this need not be a logical absurdity, because a single hypothesis "may have conflicting consequences on our standing assumptions, that is, when combined with some of our paramount beliefs."[34] This is correct, and it accurately describes the method pursued in the *Meno*, where the conclusion "virtue is teachable" is derived from the hypothesis "virtue is knowledge" together with the standing belief that only knowledge is teachable (*Meno* 87C 2–9; above, p. 310). But just as the hypothesis of *Phaedo* 100B is more than a single proposition, so (I am arguing) the notion of what is derived from the hypothesis is looser and richer here than the notion of consequence in the *Meno*. It is more like the notion of theory construction in mathematics or physics.

So far we have been following the downward path in the *Phaedo*, beginning with acceptance of the hypothesis. But Socrates also considers what it would mean "to give an account of the hypothesis itself" – the thing which, in the *Republic*, mathematicians never

---

34. Richard Robinson (1953) 131, 133. Similarly Bostock (1986) 169. I do not think, however, that Plato means this as a test of the hypothesis, so that if the *hormēthenta* disagree with one another "the hypothesis should be rejected" (Bostock, *ibid.*). This is a test of whether we are deriving a coherent theory, not whether the starting-point was correct. The issue of justifying the hypothesis is postponed at 101D 3, and taken up only at D 6: "But when you are obliged to give an account of the hypothesis itself ..."

do but which is the proper task for the dialectician. When you are challenged here,[35] says Socrates, "you will give an account in the same way, positing another hypothesis which seems the best of those higher up, until you come to something adequate" (*hikanon ti*, 101E 1).

We are naturally tempted to think in this connection of the Good, the non-hypothetical first principle of dialectic in the *Republic*. And such a temptation is reinforced by Socrates' reference in the next clause to the hypothesis as an *archē*, a starting-point or first principle. But if it is true that there is a common pattern for the upper path in the *Phaedo* and in the *Republic*, it is also true that there are important differences. The hypotheses mentioned in the *Republic* are the starting-points for mathematics; here the hypothesis is the doctrine of Forms. And there is no hint in the *Phaedo* of a more powerful method of reaching beyond hypotheses, as in the *Republic* account of dialectic.

The statement about resorting to higher hypotheses in order to defend a starting-point is a quite general principle in Plato's logic of justification. In mathematics this principle will mean to work back from specific problems and theorems to more general theses and axioms. In Plato's own exposition this procedure of resorting to "higher" hypotheses is best illustrated not by anything in the *Phaedo*[36] but by the argument in which Socrates establishes his hypothesis (that virtue is knowledge) in *Meno* 87D–89A, as we have seen. The pattern of justification is the same, although the application is quite different. In the *Phaedo* the Forms are introduced as the strongest *logos* Socrates can find (100A 4). In the *Meno* the hypothesis is needed because we have not found a definition of

35. The verb *echoito* at 101D 3 must mean "cling to," not "attack": "If someone sticks to the hypothesis," i.e. wants to discuss this rather than the results to be derived from it, you must leave him alone for the time being. There are, as in the *Meno* passage, two stages in the method: building on the hypothesis, giving an account of it. Just as in the *Meno* an eristic will fail to distinguish the truth of the hypothesis from the question of what follows from it, so here the confusion will lie in muddling together a defense of the hypothesis with the use of it to develop a theory. There is only one test mentioned for the hypothesis: whether it can be supported by "something higher." But there are two tests for theory components: whether they accord with the hypothesis (100A), and whether they accord with one another (101D 5). Compare Blank (1986) 154.

36. Although most of the arguments for immortality in the *Phaedo* do rely on "higher assumptions," namely on the Forms.

virtue. (And to this extent the method of hypothesis is in both contexts a second-best, a *deuteros plous*, as Socrates says at *Phaedo* 99C 9.) The hypothesis of the *Meno* is immediately regarded as in need of support; and Socrates will later argue persuasively against it. The hypothesis of the Forms in the *Phaedo* is not subjected to doubt, and it is not clear what higher hypothesis could be invoked to support it. (Unless, that is, we are prepared to think of the Good, the non-hypothetical *archē*, as the "adequate something," the *hikanon ti* of *Phaedo* 101E 1 . . .)

Still, Socrates will conclude by insisting that "the primary hypotheses" must also be considered further, even if they seem trustworthy. "And if you examine them adequately, I think, you will follow the argument, as far as it is possible for a human being to follow it. And if this becomes plain, you will seek no farther" (*Phaedo* 107B). It is hard to see what these first hypotheses could be other than the Forms. Socrates' call here to investigate the primary hypotheses is answered in a later dialogue by Parmenides' systematic critique of the theory of Forms.

The *Parmenides* is the last dialogue in which the method of hypothesis is mentioned, and the one in which it is most fully worked out. I do not intend to venture onto the treacherous terrain of an exegesis of the *Parmenides*.[37] I would only recall that the complex dialectical exercise which occupies most of the dialogue is expressly limited to Forms, to "those entities which one might best grasp in *logos* [not in sense perception] and consider to be Forms" (*Parmenides* 135E 3). And this exercise is systematically structured by the balance between a positive and a negative branch, first affirming the One (and later the Many) and then denying the same hypothesis.

Formally speaking, then, the *Parmenides* "removes" each hypothesis in a way that recalls the *Meno*, by favorably considering its denial. And in the *Parmenides*, as in the *Phaedo*, the hypotheses consist in positing Forms. In the *Meno*, on the other hand, there is no mention of Forms as the goal of the method, but hypothesis is introduced as a substitute for the account of what-virtue-is, for the statement of the *eidos* of virtue, which they have not been able to give. In none of these dialogues, then, is the account quite the same as in the *Republic*, where the method of hypothesis is associated with

37. See now Meinwald (1991).

mathematics, and dialectic comes on the scene only when the philosopher rises above hypotheses to the non-hypothetical principle and operates exclusively with Forms (*Rep.* VI, 511B–C).

These differences might be thought to show that Plato has not one but four different methods of hypothesis. On the other hand, we have traced many lines of continuity between the diverse expositions of the method in the *Meno*, *Phaedo*, *Republic*, and *Parmenides*. I want to suggest that the unmistakable differences between these four accounts are to be seen not as changes in Plato's theory but (like the accounts of *erōs* discussed in the last chapter) as different perspectives on a single theory, differences in what he finds appropriate to say about the method in the context of a particular dialogue. But if the differences are undeniable, where can we find unity? What makes these four separate accounts into a single theory?

For Plato it can only be the unity of content or subject matter that makes a theory one. The intellectual operations that Plato has in view are the same in the four dialogues: positing an assumption, deriving results that fit together, and justifying, removing or otherwise "giving an account" of the assumption. It is the clear recognition both of the distinctness and also of the interdependence between these three operations, and the ultimate directedness of all three towards an understanding of intelligible Forms or essences, that gives Plato's theory of hypothesis its underlying unity, as a central constituent of his conception of dialectic.

A unified theory for Plato, then, does not mean a fixed doctrine that can receive some single, definitive formulation. In doctrine as in terminology, Plato abhors fixed formulae. Language, above all written language (as we shall see in Chapter 12), is unable adequately to render the subtlety and complexity of the subject matter that a philosopher needs to understand. So the theory of hypothesis, like any theory, must be an exercise in unity and plurality. We must be able to see that ultimately it is the same thing we are talking about in every case, namely, exploring the logical connections and distinctions between concepts, even though the description we give will be different each time. As Plato suggests in the *Laws*, seeing plurality is often easy but seeing unity is hard (XII, 963D). Hence most scholarly accounts of hypothesis and dialectic in Plato emphasize the differences, as for example between the method of hypothesis and the method of Division. But Plato's dialectician must be someone who can see things together in their connectedness: he must be *sunoptikos* (*Rep.* VII, 537C). And dialectical success lies in getting the details right, in identifying the precise middle terms between generic unity and disjointed plurality (*ta mesa, Philebus* 17A). What I suggest, then, is a multiply unitarian view of Platonic dialectic, a flexible unity recognized by a process of Collection and Division, respecting the radical diversity of perspective between dialogues without losing sight of the underlying unity of content. In all of its different manifestations, both in the later and in the earlier versions, dialectic is concerned with operations of the intellect in the investigation of eternal essences, as exhibited in the disciplined controversial technique of question and answer.

8. DIALECTIC, ELENCHUS, AND ERISTIC: THE *EUTHYDEMUS*

As noted in §5, the *Euthydemus* contains the most advanced reference to dialectic of any dialogue in Group I, since it alludes unmistakably, if enigmatically, to the subordination of mathematics to dialectic. Now the *Euthydemus* is a problematic dialogue in many respects, but one thing about it is perfectly clear. Plato's composition of this dialogue is intimately connected with his literary reflections on the theory of dialectic. This is indicated not only by the striking reference to *hoi dialektikoi* in the passage just mentioned (290C) but equally by the ambiguous way in which Socrates refers to the eristic virtuosity of the two brothers, Euthydemus and Dionysodorus. On the one hand he describes their art quite frankly as "doing combat in argument, and refuting whatever is said, whether true or false" (272A 8), and he recognizes that most people would be more ashamed to refute someone by such arguments than to be refuted by them (303D 4). But at the same time he claims to be in love with their wisdom (272B 10, at the very moment of describing it as eristic), he wants to become their pupil and urges Crito to do the same (272B, D), and he addresses them as if they were divine beings (273E 6).

The irony often seems a bit thick. We begin to understand its point when we notice that Socrates refers to the two sophists as experts in the *technē* of *dialegesthai*,[38] the art of philosophical con-

---

38. *Euthydemus* 295E 2; cf. 288A 5, 301C 3–5, 303E 5.

versation in which he is only a layman.[39] And we understand the irony more fully when we realize that the performance of the two brothers is in many respects a mimicry and caricature of Socrates' argumentative technique, as displayed in Plato's dialogues.[40]

As most commentators have recognized, it must be Plato's intention here to emphasize the profound difference, despite the superficial resemblance, between dialectic as he conceives it and presents it in the dialogues, on the one hand, and the sophistic art of refutation by question-and-answer on the other hand.[41] This contrast is underscored by the mysterious reference to dialecticians as superior to mathematicians, and illustrated by assigning to Socrates a sustained protreptic argument, which nevertheless maintains the external form of question-and-answer. At a moment in his own literary work when Plato is shifting from the negative elenchus, as deployed in the *Lysis* and the dialogues of definition, to the positive construction of philosophical theories and the use of the hypothetical method (as exhibited in the latter parts of the *Meno*, in the *Symposium*, and in the *Phaedo*), Plato seems to be encouraging our critical reevaluation of primarily negative forms of argumentation. In the *Meno* he makes clear that the paralyzing sting of *aporia* is only a necessary first step. In the *Euthydemus* he composes a new kind of dialogue, in which all the destructive tendencies of the elenchus are pilloried by comic exaggeration.

There is much more to the *Euthydemus* than this, of course, and more than we can do justice to here. In one perspective we have a treatise on education, in which the pursuit of philosophy is defended against its rivals and its unworthy practitioners.[42] The protreptic to philosophy, which is implicit in nearly all of the dialogues in Group I, becomes most explicit in the *Euthydemus*, where philosophy in Plato's sense – as illustrated in the genuine art of *dialegesthai*, in the *Gorgias*, the *Phaedo*, or the *Republic* – is carefully distinguished from alternative practices, both rhetorical and eris-

39. *Ibid.* 278D 5–7, 282D 6–8.
40. See in particular 276A 3 with Hawtrey's note; Platonic parallels in n.19 above. Other "Socratic" features at 285E 7 and 295A 4. For recognition of the parallels, Hawtrey (1981: 62) refers to Guthrie (1975), 275 and also to Sidgwick (1872).
41. So already Sidgwick (1872) 296: "It is just this difference [between Socrates and the eristics] which is dramatically exhibited in the *Euthydemus*, with much broad drollery of caricature."
42. See Hawtrey (1981) 19.

tic, with which it might be confused. That is the point of the contrast between Socrates' protreptic arguments and the refutations practiced by the two sophists – and the point also of the defense of philosophy that includes an attack on Isocrates and Antisthenes (as we shall see in a moment).

So on the one hand the *Euthydemus* can be read as a statement on educational practices. On the other hand we have, in the sophisms of the brothers and in Socrates' response to them, a series of allusions to major concepts and doctrines in Plato's later work, beginning with recollection,[43] but extending to an explicit statement of the principle of non-contradiction,[44] various deep ambiguities in the interpretation of *to be* (predicative, existential, veridical),[45] including the confusion between Difference and Negation which the *Sophist* will expose,[46] an elaborate parallel to the *peritropē* or self-refutation argument used against Protagoras in the *Theaetetus*,[47] and, above all, a complex allusion to the classical theory of Forms. Thus in sophism 18 Dionysodorus obliges Socrates to distinguish between many beautiful things and "the beautiful itself," and he then ridicules Socrates' attempt to explain the connection between them in terms of the presence of beauty in the many beautiful things (301A). It is no surprise, then, to find Socrates relying on self-predication ("is not the beautiful beautiful, and the ugly ugly?") in his attempt to confound the sophists by imitating their technique (301B). Quite apart from the chronological problems raised by what seems to be (and is, I think, truly) such a massive prolepsis of ideas to be developed in the *Phaedo, Republic,*

---

43. 294E 6–11, 296C 8–D 4. See Hawtrey (1981) 155, with references to Friedländer and Keulen.

44. 293C 7–D 6. Cf. 293B 9: "Euthydemus' version of the law of noncontradiction," Hawtrey (1981) 142.

45. Sophism 3 (according to the numbering of Bonitz, retained by Hawtrey) at 283C–D turns on copula-existence ambiguity of *einai*. Sophism 4 (283E 7–284A 8) on the impossibility of falsehood, turns on the veridical and the locative-existential, as does sophism 7 (285D 7ff.), the impossibility of contradicting what someone says.

46. Sophism 11 (298A 1–B 3) turns on an equivocation between Negation and Difference that is treated at length in the *Sophist*. Also possibly pointing to the *Sophist* is sophism 8, the pun on *noein* ("mean" and "think") that insists that there is no thinking (*noein*) without soul (287D 7–E 1). Cf *Sophist* 249A.

47. The *logos* that overturns itself (*anatrepōn autos hauton*) at 286C 4ff. is the impossibility of falsehood, and it is attributed to Protagoras (286C 2). Hawtrey (1981: 109) recognizes the parallel to the *Theaetetus*.

Theaetetus, and *Sophist*, we have the more immediate problem of internal exegesis. Why should a dialogue that focuses on the contrast between eristic refutations and philosophical dialectic contain such an abundant set of allusions to major aspects of Plato's own work, allusions that can be fully understood only by readers familiar with these other dialogues or with oral discussion of the same themes?

What we have in the *Euthydemus* is one of the more obvious examples of a Platonic dialogue written at different levels of meaning, accessible to different sets of readers. At the simplest level, the *Euthydemus* is a warning. Watch out! The method of question-and-answer can be abused.[48] Don't confuse the Socratic elenchus, which in the *Meno* represents the preamble and prerequisite to constructive learning, with the unscrupulous art of refutation played as a game. That is why Socrates keeps insisting that the verbal fallacies exploited by the brothers are only a playful introduction and that they will soon turn serious. For the Platonic Socrates, *aporia* is only the first step. So the first elenchus of Lysis serves, like the protreptic of the *Euthydemus*, to make the interlocutor ready and eager to learn. Even if, in a dialogue like the *Lysis*, Socrates' quasi-sophistical arguments seem often to lead to confusion rather than to clarity, the negative appearance lies only on the surface of the dialogue, as the deeper continuities between the *Lysis* and the *Symposium* have shown. (See above, Chapter 9 §§3 and 6.) So the most basic message of the *Euthydemus* is to look to the positive protreptic rather than to the tricky refutations for the true meaning of Socratic dialectic.

In addition, for readers concerned with the educational scene in contemporary Athens, the scarcely veiled polemic with Isocrates[49] and the implicit attack on Antisthenes,[50] taken together with the final appeal to Crito to distinguish between philosophy itself and its alleged practitioners, will clearly identify the *Euthydemus* as Plato's public declaration in defense of his own conception of philosophy as the proper form of moral and intellectual education.[51]

---

48. Compare *Rep.* VII, 537D–539C on the dangers of *dialegesthai* degenerating into *antilogia*.
49. *Euthydemus* 304D 4–306D 1 (cf. on *logopoios* at 289C 6–290A 6). See Hawtrey (1981) 30 and 190–5; Guthrie (1975), 283.
50. 285D 7–286B 6, with Hawtrey (1981) 24f. and 105f.
51. So rightly Hawtrey (1981) 19.

For readers who are already engaged in philosophy, the *Euthydemus* provides a kind of handbook of fallacies, with the analysis of what goes wrong left as homework. And at the highest level, for those readers who have some acquaintance with Platonic thought about recollection, dialectic, the Forms, and the logic of being, the allusion to these concepts will serve as a reminder of the actual content of philosophical education. Plato makes use of the frame dialogue between Socrates and Crito, both in the middle and at the end of the narrated dialogue, like the parabasis in an Aristophanic comedy, to speak as it were directly to the readers. These remarks aim to reassure us, not only that what the brothers practice is not the dialectic that presides over mathematics (290c), but also that genuine philosophy is a royal art, the best form of knowledge, even if the content of such knowledge cannot be fully specified within the confines of this dialogue (292c–e). For that we must look to the central books of the *Republic* and to the Form of the Good.

As we have seen at the end of Chapter 7, Socrates' second protreptic ends with a regress that can be resolved only when the content of the royal art is identified as the highest object of knowledge, the *megiston mathēma* of *Republic* VI, which lies beyond mathematics and can be reached only by dialectic. Seen in the light of what we know from the *Republic*, the enigmatic reference to dialectic in the second Socratic interlude of the *Euthydemus*, and the immediately following regress about knowledge and the good as objects of the royal art, are both recognizable as tantalizing hints of the conception of knowledge and reality that will determine the training program for Plato's philosopher-kings. The *Euthydemus* is a brilliant piece of comic writing designed to clear the air of fog and *aporia* and to prepare for the most lucid moment of Plato's career as a writer, the moment of the middle dialogues and the systematic account of dialectic.

9. THE NAME OF DIALECTIC

The ancients regarded the word *dialektikē* as Plato's coinage, and they were doubtless right,[52] since we can see the term taking shape

---

52. D.L. III.24. The parallel and priority of the term *rhetorikē* are clearly implied at *Gorgias* 448D 9, cited above, p. 303. For a full philological study see Müri (1944) 152–68.

before our eyes in *Republic* VII. In Book VI, however, when dialectic is introduced as the highest segment of the Divided Line, only the ordinary infinitive form of the verb is used. The method by which the philosopher can rise above the hypotheses of mathematics is described as the power (*dunamis*) and science (*epistēmē*) of *dialegesthai* (511B 4, C 5).

How is the reader supposed to know that *dialegesthai* here means more than "to converse" or "carry on a conversation"?[53] Is Plato's new, semi-technical use of *dialegesthai* to be understood here solely from the philosophical context in which it is embedded? That would be possible, but it is in fact not necessary. As we have seen, both the verb and its cognate noun *dialektos* (our word "dialect") occur in a philosophically marked use in Book V, before the discussion of dialectic in Books VI–VII. The contrast there is between *dialegesthai* and eristic disputation (454A; see above, p. 298). This echoes a contrast that was suggested in the *Meno* (75C–D) and developed implicitly throughout the *Euthydemus*. So a reader (who may or may not be familiar with the *Meno* and *Euthydemus*) will recognize in the notion of *dialegesthai* mentioned in *Republic* V, and characterized there as the ability to draw relevant distinctions by "dividing according to kinds," a reference to Plato's own conception of serious philosophical discourse. Such a reader is prepared, then, to give *dialegesthai* its new, more potent meaning when it reappears in the context of the Divided Line at the end of Book VI.

In the Divided Line passage only the ordinary verbal form *dialegesthai* occurs, although the thought conveyed is no longer that of the ordinary verb. Similarly loaded uses of the verb occur at the beginning of the discussion of the mathematical curriculum in Book VII, where numerical puzzles are said to provoke philosophical conversation, when the right questions are asked: for example, "What kind of numbers are you talking about (*dialegesthe*)?" (526A 2; cf. 525D 6–8). But the central discussion of dialectic begins with the introduction of the adjectival form *dialektikoi* at 531D 9 (echoing *Euthydemus* 290C): mathematicians are not "dialecticians," that is, not conversationally skilled in asking the right questions and giving the right kind of account (*logos*).

The method of dialectic is the principal topic under discussion

---

53. This, the normal sense of the verb, appears only a few pages later, at 515B 4, for the conversation between prisoners in the cave.

in these crucial pages of Book VII, and it is referred to repeatedly, first by the articular infinitive (*to dialegesthai* at 532A 2, 6), and then by the feminine adjective that will provide the canonical name for dialectic: "Do you not call this movement [to intelligible Forms] dialectical, *dialektikē*?" (532B 4).[54] Here we can finally say that *dialektikē* (like the preceding occurrence of *dialegesthai*) is being used as a technical term, that is, as the expression for a philosophical conception that can no longer be rendered by the ordinary sense of "conversational" or even "skilled in the art of conversation."

This new technical sense of *dialektikē*, as meaning roughly "(the art) of philosophical analysis and explanation by means of discussion," is also required for four more instances of the feminine form in the pages that follow. In two cases (and in two cases only) this form stands alone as a grammatical substantive: "we have placed dialectic (*hē dialektikē*) as a copingstone over the sciences" (534E 3); and mathematical sciences "must be studied as a preliminary to *dialektikē*" (536D 6).[55] Although the masculine form *dialektikos* for "dialectician," "expert in (philosophical) conversation" is quite common both in the *Republic* and elsewhere in Plato,[56] the feminine adjective *dialektikē* for the method itself, after this cluster of five occurrences in *Republic* VII, appears only twice again in all of Plato's works.[57] And the use of this form as an independent substantive, the name for dialectic that is commonplace in Aristotle and in the later philosophical literature down to our own time, disappears entirely from the pages of Plato after the two instances just cited from *Republic* VII (534E 3, 536D 6).

It seemed worth dwelling on these linguistic details at some length, because they represent a paradigm for Plato's use of philosophical language. They show us both how carefully Plato can

54. The feminine adjective *dialektikē* appears here in grammatical agreement with *poreia* ("movement," "transition"), but it can also be read as the independent substantive "dialectic." The substantival use is created by simply omitting the noun with which the adjective would agree, e.g. *technē* ("art") or *epistēmē* ("science"). This is what happens at 534E 3 and 536D 6 (cited in the text), and nowhere else in Plato's work.
55. The other two, purely adjectival uses are *dialektikē methodos* at 533C 7 and *dialektikē phusis* at 537C 6.
56. See examples cited above from *Cratylus* 390C 11 (echoed at 398D 7), *Euthydemus* 290C 5 and *Phaedrus* 266C 1.
57. For the dialectical art (*technē*) at *Phaedrus* 276E 5 and the dialectical science (*epistēmē*) at *Sophist* 253D 2.

prepare his readers for the more specialized meaning of a new technical term, and also how utterly he can abandon this terminology once its immediate purpose has been served.[58]

58. Compare Adam's comment (1902: II, 141) on *Rep.* VII, 533D 7 (there is no quarrel about names for people who are investigating such great topics): "Plato constantly reminds us that he has no fixed terminology, and the ancients were well aware of this fact, though modern interpreters of Plato too often forget it."

CHAPTER II

The presentation of the Forms

I. WHAT IS PLATO'S THEORY OF FORMS?

It would be difficult to overstate the importance of the concept of Forms in Plato's work. As the distinctive object of philosophical knowledge, the Forms in the *Republic* provide the criterion for distinguishing philosophers from non-philosophers. The Forms play this central role in Plato's epistemology precisely because they constitute the basic entities in his ontology. Furthermore, as source of value and ultimate object of desire, the Forms are equally fundamental in Plato's moral psychology, as we have seen in Chapter 9. In ethics and political theory they provide a *paradeigma*, a pattern to be imitated in the moral life as well as in the construction and government of the best city. In theology also the Forms are paradigmatic, since it is by their relationship to the Forms that the gods themselves are divine (*Phaedrus* 249c). In the *Cratylus* and the *Sophist* the Forms provide the basis for a theory of language; in the *Timaeus* they constitute the framework for Plato's cosmology and philosophy of nature. In the *Symposium* and *Phaedrus* the Form of Beauty functions as a principle for esthetics and above all for an account of love, including an account of that privileged form of *erōs* that constitutes the life in philosophy. No doctrine in the history of philosophy has been more ambitious, and few have been so influential.

Nevertheless, the status of this doctrine in Plato's work is problematic in more than one respect. In the first place the classic doctrine of Forms, as developed in the *Phaedo* and *Republic*, is subjected to rigorous criticism by Plato himself in the *Parmenides*; and the objections raised against it there are never directly answered. The Forms have practically disappeared from Plato's attempt to define knowledge in the *Theaetetus*, and when they reappear in the

329

Sophist, Philebus, and *Timaeus,* it is not clear to what extent the conception of the Forms is actually the same. A further problem is precisely one of identity: is there a single theory that is formulated in the *Symposium, Phaedo, Cratylus, Republic,* and *Phaedrus,* to mention only the dialogues of Plato's "middle" period in which the classic doctrine of Forms is to be found? The statements of this doctrine are so diverse and so programmatic that it is hard to know whether we can properly reconstruct a single coherent theory underlying all of these formulations. As one recent author put it, the presentation of the doctrine of Forms in these dialogues is "underdetermined" and "insufficiently developed."[1] There are similar questions to be raised about Plato's statements on the Forms in later dialogues, such as the *Sophist* and *Timaeus.* So from one point of view it looks as if Plato had several different doctrines; and yet no single presentation is detailed enough to count as a fully formulated theory.

We must deal further with this question in the next chapter, when we consider Plato's views on the limits of writing philosophy. My discussion here will focus on the middle dialogues, before the critique of the *Parmenides.* And I refer in the usual way to Plato's doctrine or theory of Forms, without confronting as yet the deeper question of what status these various formulations possess within Plato's conception of philosophy. My own assumption is that there is a single underlying *vision of reality* for which Plato has invented a series of different literary expressions, each of which is tailored to the needs and concerns of the particular dialogue in which it appears. If we bear in mind the etymology of *theōria* as a way of viewing or beholding the world, there seems no question but that Plato has expressed a coherent *theōria.* Whether these diverse formulations can be brought together in a fully explicit theory, understood as a systematically connected set of propositions, and whether Plato himself would have regarded such a reconstruction as a valid philosophical enterprise, are not questions that I attempt to answer in this chapter.

I do call attention, however, to the fact that Plato in the *Phaedo* explicitly refers to the Forms as a hypothesis or assumption (100B, 101D), and that in general he does not provide arguments in defense of this assumption. Perhaps his only direct argument for the existence of Forms is in *Timaeus* 51D–E, where the reality of the

---

1. Meinwald in Kraut (1992) 390, 393.

Forms is said to be required for the distinction between rational knowledge (*nous*) and true opinion. At *Phaedo* 74B–C there is an argument for the non-identity of Forms and sensible things on the grounds that the latter do, and the former do not, have diverse perspectival appearances. (If both arguments are fully spelled out, they may be seen as two versions of the same argument, since for Plato perspectival appearance and *doxa*, opinion, turn out to be coextensive.) And at the end of the *Cratylus* it is argued, against the doctrine of universal flux, that without some element of stability and invariance in things there could be neither knowledge nor referential language; and it is clearly implied that such invariance must be derived from the Forms. In general, however, Plato's arguments proceed *from* the Forms, not *to* them. The doctrine of Forms functions as the necessary and sufficient assumption on the basis of which the philosopher can organize his thinking and live his life, like the best human *logos* that Simmias in the *Phaedo* compared to the rough vessel of Odysseus: "one must take the risk of sailing through life with it as on a raft" (85C–D). In Plato's portrayal, the life and the theory reinforce one another. If, as we shall see, Diotima's account of philosophical *erōs* directed to the Form of Beauty serves to make intelligible to us Socrates' character and behavior as reported in the *Symposium*, in the *Phaedo* the rhetorical support seems to bear in the opposite direction, from character to theory. It is the noble courage and argumentative mastery of Socrates in the face of death that give credibility to the transcendental conception of the soul and its grounding in the reality of the Forms.

In the end, however, Plato is a committed rationalist, and no assumption is immune to criticism. We have seen that Socrates concludes the philosophical discussion in the *Phaedo* with his suggestion that "the primary hypotheses" will need further investigation (107B). And it is precisely the hypothesis of Forms that is in fact the object of scrutiny in the *Parmenides*. There must be few parallels in the history of philosophy to the spectacle of such pitiless criticism levelled by an author against his own theory, with no attempt at defense or reply. It would take an extraordinary talent, says Plato's Parmenides, to be able not only to discover the truth in these matters but to explain it adequately to someone else (*Parm.* 135B). Yet this is precisely what is required of the true philosopher: "to define the Form of the Good in argument (*logos*) and to pass through all tests and refutations as in a battle ... and emerge from all this with one's doctrine (*logos*) undefeated" (*Rep.* VI, 534B–C).

Such a defense of the theory is to be given in person-to-person argument and inquiry.[2] What we have in the dialogues is something else: the gradual, partial, and diversified exposition of a complex view. In this chapter I am concerned to plot the stages in Plato's exposition of the classical doctrine of Forms, and to focus attention on the subtle echoes and variations by which he pursues both continuity and diversity in this exposition. Above all I want to emphasize the practical and normative aspect of the theory as a moral ideal, the glimpse of a nobler reality that makes a life worth living, rather than as a logical solution to some set of strictly philosophical problems. I want to show how the doctrine that culminates in the vision of the Good is deeply rooted in the Socratic moral life and in the search for beneficial knowledge that we have traced in the *Charmides*, *Lysis*, and *Euthydemus*, the search for a kind of knowledge that is good for us because it is or produces virtue.

But first we consider some of the linguistic resources out of which Plato's theory is constructed.

2. RAW MATERIAL FOR THE THEORY OF FORMS

I list here four features of Greek thought and idiom, at least three of which are not specifically Platonic, that make Plato's way of presenting the doctrine of Forms by means of expressions like "the Beautiful" or "the Equal" seem more natural in Greek than in English.

(1) Platonism with a small "p." This is a way of referring to properties or characteristics in a form that we might regard as abstract, by a noun like "beauty" or "equality" or by the corresponding adjective treated as a noun ("the beautiful" or "the equal"),[3] and regarding these items as logically or causally more funda-

---

2. Cf. *Epistle* VII, 344B, where however the tone is less combative: "from the tests of friendly refutations (*elenchoi*), in the exchange of questions and answers without hostility (*phthonoi*)," the light of understanding bursts forth.

3. In Plato's usage the two linguistic forms are often interchangeable. Thus in the *Symposium* Plato prefers *to kalon* ("the beautiful) for the Form of Beauty (210Eff.), but immediately before this he alternates between *kallos* ("beauty") and *to kalon* (210C–D). In *Phaedo* 74C *isotēs* ("equality") is used as equivalent to *auto to ison* ("the Equal itself").

mental than the corresponding concrete instance, expressed by a descriptive use of the same adjective. Thus it seems natural in Greek to regard a concept like *beauty* (or *the beautiful*) not as an abstraction from, but as logically prior to, the corresponding adjectival descriptions: *beautiful face* or *beautiful body*. For example, in the *Protagoras* both Socrates and Protagoras can take for granted that temperate actions are due to temperance (*sōphrosunē*) and foolish actions are due to folly (*aphrosunē*; *Prot.* 332B–C, D–E). So Meno accepts without hesitation the claim that just action requires justice (*dikaiosunē*) on the part of the agent (*Meno* 73B 1–5), and that it is by the possession of virtue (*aretē*) that men become good (*agathoi*).

This conceptual priority of the abstract form corresponds to the semantic relation that Aristotle calls paronymy: *brave* is derived from *bravery*, *literate* (*grammatikos*) from *literacy* (*grammatikē*). This derivation holds not at the level of linguistic morphology (for in Greek as in English the adjectival form is often simpler than the corresponding noun) but at the level of psychological or moral explanation: a person becomes brave by in fact possessing bravery. I call this "platonism" because it spontaneously treats as a causal or explanatory factor an item we moderns might classify as an abstract universal. For these items are not only designated by an abstract linguistic form or nominalization; they are also abstract in not being direct objects of sense perception.

(2) Self-predication. A well-known passage in the *Protagoras* presents two examples of what in later dialogues has become known as self-predication: "Justice itself is just," and "Nothing else could be pious, unless piety itself were pious" (330C 4, D 8). The point being made here is not (as some critics have supposed) that the character trait is confused with the person characterized, but that it is precisely *because* the character trait is of this particular sort that persons who have it are similarly qualified.

(3) The two conceptions just described, "platonism" and self-predication, are connected by what is sometimes called the transmission theory of causation. This is the assumption that an effect must resemble its cause in the relevant respect, since the cause could not give what it does not have. Thus only fire, or something with the heat of fire, can make other things hot, just as only a teacher with understanding of the subject matter can make others understand. The principle is neatly expressed by Agathon in Plato's *Symposium*: "What one does not have or know, one can neither

give nor teach to another" (196E). Agathon is not enunciating a philosophical theory; he is speaking from the point of view of Greek common sense. The same principle is everywhere taken for granted in Plato and Aristotle, for example at *Rep.* I, 335C–D: "it is not the work (*ergon*) of dryness to make things moist, but the opposite." The stellar use of this principle in Plato is the claim that, since the gods are good, they can be the cause only of good effects, never of bad ones (*Rep.* II, 379B–C).[4] A nice pre-Platonic example is the argument reported by Aristotle (fr. 199 Rose) to explain the Pythagorean view that "the One must share in the nature of both odd and even." Why? Because "when it is added to an even number it makes it odd, but added to an odd number it makes it even; which it could not do if it did not share in both natures."

Note that self-predication follows trivially from the transmission theory for any property posited by the "platonism" mentioned above: if virtue makes men good, it must itself be good. That is in effect what is claimed at *Prot.* 330D 8: "nothing else could be pious, if piety itself were not pious."

(4) Participation as a metaphor for properties or attributes. The idiomatic use of the verb *metechein* "to share in," "to partake of," can apply metaphorically to the possession of qualities as well as more literally to participating in a group activity or receiving portions or shares in a distribution. A philosophical example is provided by the Pythagorean reference just quoted from Aristotle fr. 199 (sharing in the nature of odd and even), but there is nothing specifically Pythagorean about the idiom. Anaxagoras declares that "other things have a share (*moiran metechei*) of all things"; only *nous* is unmixed, because "if it were mixed with anything, it would share in (*meteichen an*) all things" (fr. 12). Such philosophical metaphors will be taken over by Plato when he speaks of participating in a Form. But these metaphors did not originate in philosophy. Pindar speaks of "not sharing (with someone else) in boldness," οὔ οἱ μετέχω θράσεος, *Pythian* 2.83), and Herodotus uses such phrases as "sharing in military prowess" (*alkēs metechein*, IX.18.3). Plato also makes frequent use of this metaphor in contexts that have nothing to do with the Forms: "sharing in a sense of shame and justice"

4. For Aristotelian examples see *Phys.* II.7, 198a26f. (with Ross' note); *Met.* α.1,993b24, Θ.8, 1049b24–9.

(*Prot.* 322D), sharing in courage (*Laches* 193E 2), sharing in immortality (*Symp.* 208B).[5]

The conjunction of these four ways of speaking and thinking about properties such as the virtues does not constitute a theory of Forms in any sense. Three out of four of these features are common to Aristotle, who rejected Plato's theory. (Aristotle seems to avoid the formula for self-predication, perhaps because he associates it too closely with Platonic teaching.) These simply provide part of the pre-theoretical raw material out of which Plato will construct his theory. And the same is true for the two terms for "form": *eidos* and *idea*, which are well attested in early prose with the meanings "physical appearance," "bodily form," "shape," "structure," "kind of thing." The pre-Platonic usage of these terms has been fully studied, and there is no need to return to the subject here.[6]

3. THE DEFINITIONAL SEARCH FOR ESSENCES

The first trace of a distinctly Platonic conception in this area is found in the dialogues of definition, in particular in the *Laches*, *Euthyphro*, and *Meno*. It is traditional to recognize in such dialogues "the seeds of the theory of Ideas," as Ross puts it.[7] On the developmental view, these dialogues represent an early stage in Plato's thinking, when he was led by Socrates' pursuit of definitions "to recognize the existence of universals as a distinct class of entity." However, Ross goes on to insist that even in the *Meno* "it is still the immanence of the Ideas in particulars that is insisted on."[8] R. E. Allen has similarly described Plato's "earlier theory of Forms," in which Forms are conceived as "universals, standards,

---

5. The converse metaphor for a quality or state "being present in" a subject (παρεῖναι), likewise familiar from fifth-century poetry (φόβος in Aeschylus, θαῦμα in Sophocles, cited in LSJ s.v. πάρειμι II), is frequently used by Plato, sometimes freely (*Gorgias* 497E 1, 498D 2–E 1; *Laches* 190B 5, E 1; *Charmides* 158E 7, 150A 2, 160D 7, 161A 9), but elsewhere more cautiously: *Lysis* 217D, *Euthydemus* 301A, *Phaedo* 100D 5.

6. For a survey of the literature on *eidos* and *idea* see Ross (1951) 13–16. Ross rightly remarks that "What was original was not the use of the words, but the status he [Plato] assigned to the things for which the words stood" (p. 14).

7. Ross (1951) 11.

8. *Ibid.* 14, 18.

and essences," each one "the same in all its instances, and something its instances have."[9] But this traditional account of the early doctrine in terms of immanent forms or universals is seriously misleading. In the first place, the very notion of immanent universals is, for familiar reasons, philosophically problematic: how can an item be one and self-identical, and yet located in many places at the same time? Furthermore, to speak of universals, particulars, and instances is to resort to a vocabulary much more technical and theory-laden than anything we actually find in Plato's text. In effect, the traditional view follows Aristotle in assigning an over-specific doctrine to Socrates (or early Plato) on the basis of an inaccurate reading of the texts.

The only thing resembling a technical term in these dialogues is the word *ousia* or "essence," and that is simply the nominalized form of the *ti esti* question, the *what-it-is-ness* that the *what-is-it?* question is asking about. What Socrates insists upon is the unity and identity of such an essence for all the items rightly called by the same name or (as we would say) described by the same predicate. The answer to the question "What is courage?" must specify something that is the same in resisting not only fear but also pleasure and pain and other difficulties, "the same in all these cases" (*Laches* 191E 10, 192B 6). In such phrases the preposition "in" is used idiomatically not to *localize* the essence but to generalize its application. It is, I suggest, a grave misinterpretation to take the preposition "in" in such a context as indicating immanence, just as it would be a mistake to take the verb "have" as indicating literal possession in the phrase "one and the same form (*eidos*) which all the virtues have, as a result of which they are virtues" (*Meno* 72C 7). That the "in" here does not indicate the location or immanent presence of the essence in particular instances is shown first of all by the fact that the "cases" in question in the dialogues of definition are never particular individuals, but always general types of cases.[10] And the avoidance of any strictly locative sense for "in" is made unmistakable by Plato's deliberately vary-

---

9. Allen in Vlastos (1971a) 319–34.
10. Interpreters who read immanence into the dialogues of definition may have been encouraged by Plato's usage in *Phaedo* 102B–103B, where immanence seems to be implied for the "opposites in us" by contrast with the opposites themselves. (And in the *Phaedo* passage the subjects are individual persons, not types of cases.) However, in the *Phaedo* Plato clearly regards the notion of

ing his choice of preposition. "In all these cases" at *Laches* 192B 6 is immediately paraphrased by *dia pantōn* "through all of them" at 192C 1. And in the *Meno* we find not only *dia pantōn* again (at 74A 9) but also *kata pantōn* "applying to all of them" (at 73D 1 and 74B 1) and *epi pasin toutois taùton* "the same for all of them" (at 75A 4–8).

Plato has thus left carefully indeterminate the nature of his essences and their relation to more specific cases or particular instances. What we are told about essences in the dialogues of definition is simply that (1) they are one and the same for all the cases to which they apply (for all the cases that "have" them); (2) they are explanatory of their cases: e.g., knowing what virtue is will permit you to know why courage is a virtue, and hence to "give an account" of the common nature or character that distinguishes virtues from non-virtues; (3) knowledge of any specific essence is logically prior to knowledge of other properties for the same subject (e.g., you cannot know whether virtue is teachable unless you know what virtue is), and (4) the *Euthyphro* adds that knowing what piety is will give you a model (*paradeigma*) for judging whether or not a specific type of action is pious. What we have in these four conditions is a more precise version of the pre-Platonic "transmission theory" of causal explanation described above in §2, with the notion of cause supplied now by the notion of essence as specified by the *what-is-X?* question. But the metaphysical status of such essences is left unspecified; and nothing whatsoever is said about their epistemic status, beyond the claim that knowledge of them is necessary or useful for other kinds of knowledge.

The four conditions just mentioned can be satisfied equally well by Aristotelian essences or Platonic Forms.[11] We know, of course, which interpretation Plato himself preferred. And when he comes in the *Phaedo* to specify the metaphysical and epistemic status of his Forms, he takes pains to remind the careful reader that these are the *same* essences that are under discussion in the dialogues of definition. He does so in two ways. First of all, the three examples

"presence" for the Forms as problematic (100D 5). Compare note 5, above, and the discussion in §6 below.

11. Condition 3, the epistemic priority of essences, holds for Aristotle if knowledge is taken in the strictest sense, since then it follows from (2), the explanatory priority. Neither condition (2) nor (3) holds for modern theories of universals, which satisfy only condition (1). So it is quite misleading to interpret Plato's definitional essences as a theory of universals.

he mentions to generalize the doctrine at *Phaedo* 65D ("I speak ... concerning the *ousia* of all of them, what each one truly is"), are precisely the same three forms that figure as examples of *eidos* at the beginning of the definitional discussion at *Meno* 72D: size, health, and strength.[12] And secondly, in the *Phaedo* he not only uses a version of the *what-is-it?* question as the proper term for essential Forms (*to ho esti*, the "what-it-is" at 74D 6, 75B 1, 75D 2, 78D 4, and 92D 9); he also refers repeatedly to the transcendent Forms as "that very *ousia* of whose being (*einai*) we give an account in questions and answers" (78D 1, echoing 75D 2–3). In this formula the verb "to be" (*einai*) represents the "is" of the *what-is-it?* question. And giving an account (*logos*) in questions and answers clearly refers to discussions of essence in the *Meno* and the dialogues of definition. These passages in the *Phaedo* illustrate Plato's constant technique of deliberate intertextuality or cross-reference between apparently autonomous dialogues, just as the first mention of recollection in the same work contains an implicit reference to the *Meno* (*Phaedo* 73A–B).

The author of the *Phaedo*, then, carefully marks the continuity between the metaphysical Forms of this dialogue and the metaphysically indeterminate essences of the *Meno* and the *Euthyphro*, just as he marks the continuity between the two accounts of recollection. Even a loyal proponent of the developmental hypothesis must recognize this retrospective continuity. But such a proponent may object that hindsight does not entail foresight, and retrospective continuity does not entail proleptic composition. The fact that Plato, when he reaches the position of the *Phaedo*, can look back and note the continuity with his earlier work, does not mean that when he composed the *Laches*, *Euthyphro*, and *Meno*, he had any intention of developing the theory of essences in the direction defined by the middle dialogues. Or so the developmental interpretation may argue.

Since we cannot read Plato's mind at the moment when he composed the dialogues of definition, we cannot refute the developmental claim of an earlier stage of Socratic immanence or metaphysical indecision on Plato's part. We can only call attention to the systematic way in which the earlier dialogues leave the status of definitional essences underdetermined. And we can recall the

---

12. I owe this observation to David Sedley.

argument presented in Chapter 6 § 3 to show that a transcendental status for the Forms is logically implied by the use of recollection to resolve Meno's paradox. In my opinion the links between the *Meno* and later works are too close and too numerous (essences, recollection, hypothesis, knowledge versus true opinion)[13] for us plausibly to suppose that the former dialogue was *not* composed with the basic doctrines of the *Phaedo* in view. The author of the *Meno* clearly knows where he is going. Now the terminology for essences in the *Euthyphro* anticipates that in the *Meno*, just as the priority of definition in the *Laches* prepares the way for this principle in the *Meno*. And, as argued in Chapter 6 § 5, the *Laches–Euthyphro–Meno* trio is best read together as a well-planned essay on definition. In my opinion, this network of connections is most naturally accounted for by our assumption that the dialogues of definition were, from the beginning, designed to be the first stage in an ingressive exposition of the very same philosophy that is more fully articulated in the middle dialogues.

If this is correct, what we have to explain is not Plato's development but his deliberate silence. Why in the dialogues of definition does he give no hint of the metaphysics and epistemology of the Forms? We have already discussed this question from several points of view (above, pp. 65ff. and 178–80). For a fuller understanding of Plato's reticence we turn now to the *Symposium*, where (if we imagine ourselves in the position of Agathon's guests) we get our first, unexpected revelation of a transcendent Form.

We cannot of course know whether the *Symposium* or the *Phaedo* was composed first, or whether (as seems likely) they were planned as a pair. But from the dramatic and rhetorical point of view, the *Symposium* is certainly designed to be read first. For in the *Phaedo* the metaphysical conception of Forms is taken for granted from the beginning of the dialogue, confidently expounded by Socrates and unhesitatingly accepted as a general theory by all the interlocutors. But in the *Symposium* this same conception is only briefly presented in the final section of a single speech, as a total surprise, and as a deep mystery to which even Socrates can perhaps not be initiated. If we have read the *Phaedo* first, we must temporarily

13. The contrast between knowledge and true opinion is not as conspicuous in the *Phaedo* as are the other three anticipations noted from the *Meno* (essences, recollection, and hypothesis). But it reappears at *Symposium* 202A and prepares for the new use of *doxa* in *Republic* V–VI.

suppress this knowledge in order to enter into the drama of Diotima's revelation. I want to suggest that Plato has planned the *Symposium* as the general reader's introduction to the doctrine of Forms, in much the same way as he has planned the *Laches* as a general introduction to the dialogues of definition.

4. THE REVELATION OF FORM IN THE *SYMPOSIUM*

The narrative of the *Symposium* opens with Socrates, on his way to Agathon's dinner party, inviting Aristodemus, our narrator, to join him. But when Aristodemus arrives at the party, he is surprised to find that he has left Socrates behind. Socrates, it turns out, is standing outside the neighbor's doorway and does not respond when called. The host wants to insist, but Aristodemus says to leave him alone. "This is a habit of his. He sometimes stands still wherever he happens to be. I think he will come soon" (175B). In fact Socrates arrives only when dinner is half over, and Agathon jokes with him about the wise thought he has completed while standing outside.

The reader is reminded of this opening episode much later, in Alcibiades' speech near the close of the dialogue, when Alcibiades reports how Socrates, on campaign at Potidaea, stood for a day and a night pursuing some train of thought (220C–D).

In neither of these episodes are we told what Socrates was thinking about. And of course Plato did not know.[14] But within the context of this dialogue the only line of thought that Socrates actually reports is the lesson of love attributed to Diotima, culminating in the beatific vision of the Beautiful itself. From the point of view of the dramatic structure of the *Symposium*, the doctrine of metaphysical Form is presented as a revelation designed to explain what Socrates is really in love with: where his thoughts are directed in these repeated episodes of personal detachment from his surroundings. In this perspective Diotima's theory of love enables the reader to understand the ease and serenity with which Socrates can resist Alcibiades' attempt at seduction. Alcibiades' praise of Socrates, which follows almost immediately upon Diotima's instruction, begins by comparing Socrates to the statues of satyrs

---

14. I assume that Socrates' fits of abstraction were historical, or at least legendary, not invented by Plato. But Plato would be entirely free in his treatment of the narrative. Agathon's dinner party is presumably a fiction; and the Potidaea episode, if historical, occurred four or five years before Plato's birth.

which, when one opens them up, display images of the gods within. By artful juxtaposition, then, Plato has arranged for us to construe Diotima's revelation as a hint of the divine images hidden inside of Socrates. The philosophical account of love, with its climax in the Form of the Beautiful, has as its literary function within this dialogue to make the phenomenon of Socrates intelligible to us, to make us see how he can be both an insider and an outsider at this elite gathering, both present and absent, the ugly lover of handsome young men who is in fact the object of erotic fascination for the younger men around him. Despite his urbane eloquence and apparent sensuality, his physical endurance and capacity for strong drink, Socrates turns out to be a figure not quite of this world. His true values are elsewhere, and the metaphysical doctrine of Beauty itself, *auto to kalon*, is introduced to suggest what such values might be:

There, if anywhere, life is worth living for a human being, beholding the Beautiful itself. If you ever see it, it will not seem to you to be comparable to gold and garments and pretty boys and youths ... What would it be like to see the Beautiful itself, pure, unstained, unsullied, not full of human flesh and colors and other mortal trash, but to catch a glimpse of the unique and single-formed divine Beauty itself? Do you think it would be a bad life for a person to gaze on such an object? (211D–E)

Modern scholarship has tended to follow Aristotle in construing Plato's theory of Forms as a solution to the logical problem of universal terms or concepts, a pioneering study in the theory of predication, the first recognition of a distinction between objects and properties, or, more generally, as a contribution to the theory of knowledge and reality. Thus Zeller sums up his introduction to the subject with the observation that, for Plato, without the Forms there could be "neither true knowledge nor true being."[15] And Cherniss has shown how the theory of Forms can be seen as a single hypothesis designed to account for phenomena in the diverse areas of ethics, epistemology, and ontology.[16] I do not intend to deny the fundamental importance of these concerns for Plato. But I want rather to suggest that the *Symposium* offers a different perspective on the function of the doctrine of Forms.

Plato has chosen Agathon's dinner party, a worldly gathering of poets and other non-philosophers, as the occasion for dropping his

15. Zeller (1889) 652, summing up 643ff.
16. Cherniss in Vlastos (1971b) 16–27.

metaphysical vision like a bombshell into the public domain. He has composed this, his most brilliant literary work, as a vehicle for presenting his doctrine of Forms to the world, in the context of a theory of love that represents this extraordinary conception of reality as a matter of passionate concern, not solely for philosophers but for everyone who wants a life worth living and a satisfaction for his or her deepest desires. By connecting the ascent to Beauty first with erotic passion and then with a general desire for happiness and immortality, Diotima presents Plato's doctrine as something that successful poets like Agathon and Aristophanes must also find significant, something that explains why Alcibiades can still see Socrates as offering him a nobler life than the career of political success he is actually engaged in. In short it is not as a theoretical solution to specifically philosophical problems that Plato has chosen to present his doctrine of Form in the *Symposium*, but as a practical ideal, of vital importance for every human being's conception of what makes life meaningful.

Let us look now at the final stage, the *telea* and *epoptika*, in Diotima's revelation.

One who has contemplated beautiful things rightly and in the right order will come then to the goal and completion (*telos*) of his erotic pursuits and suddenly catch sight of something marvelously beautiful in its nature, that very thing for the sake of which all his previous labors were undertaken:

> first, it forever *is*, and neither comes to be or perishes,
> nor does it augment or diminish,
> being not in one respect beautiful, in another respect ugly,
> nor beautiful at one time, not beautiful at another time,
> nor beautiful in one comparison, ugly in another,
> nor beautiful here, ugly there,
> being beautiful for some, ugly for others;

nor will the beautiful appear to him like a face or hands or anything else in which body has a share, nor like any discourse (*logos*) or knowledge (*episteme*); nor is it anywhere in something else, as in a living thing or in earth or in heaven or in anything else;

but itself by itself with itself it is eternally uniform, while all other beautiful things share in it in such a way that, as they come to be and perish, it becomes neither more nor less nor suffers any change. (210E–211B)

The ontology of the Forms is presented here in a maximally dense description focused on a single object, the Beautiful itself. Plato's rhythmic use of the *via negativa* for denying all perspectivism, imperfection, and relativity to the beloved object resonates with the tones of Parmenides' hymn to Being, that unchanging Entity which "remains the same in the same, and lies by itself" (B.8, 29). Thus Plato's term "uniform" (*monoeides*) recalls Parmenides' *mounogenes*, "alone of its kind" (B.8, 4).[17] But although the one Beautiful "that is forever" is the supreme object of knowledge and desire, Plato (unlike Parmenides) does not deny the reality of the many beautiful things, which come into being by sharing (*metechein*) in its beauty (211B 2).

The metaphor of sharing, which later seems to harden into a semi-technical notion of "participation" (*methexis*), appears twice in this passage; but the first occurrence is a purely idiomatic, even poetic phrase about "things in which body has a share" (211A 7). Neither of Plato's standard terms for Form (*eidos, idea*) is employed in this context. The closest thing to a technical expression in Diotima's account of the Form of Beauty is an inconspicuous anticipation of what will become (in the *Phaedo* and *Republic*) the most official designation for a Form, the "what-it-is" (*to ho esti*). Thus a few lines after the passage just quoted, in Diotima's summary of the program of erotic training, she says that it terminates in the study that is (*ho estin*) of nothing else but that Beautiful itself, so that the initiate "finally comes to know what beautiful is" (*ho esti kalon*, 211C 8). The second *ho esti* clause, which appears here so unobtrusively, prefigures (or echoes) the standard formula of the *Phaedo* and later dialogues.[18]

Socrates' audience in the *Symposium* contains no philosophic interlocutors; even Socrates himself is only reporting what he has heard. So this dazzling, momentary disclosure of the heart of Plato's metaphysics is left here without commentary or exegesis. That is the task of the *Phaedo* and *Republic*, where the various strands in Diotima's web will be teased apart and further unwound.

---

17. For a direct Platonic echo of Parmenides' term μουνογενές see *Timaeus* 30B 3.
18. Note that in the *Phaedo* also the distinctive relative-interrogative clause first appears in the same idiomatic construction after a verb "to know" at 74B 2. Probably the earliest occurrence of the marked relative clause with *esti* is at *Lysis* 219C 7: ἐπ᾽ ἐκεῖνο ὅ ἐστιν πρῶτον φίλον "to that which *is* primary dear," precisely in the passage that anticipates the Form of Good and/or Beautiful. See above, p. 266, n.10, and below §5.6.

Before following up these doctrinal developments, we may pause for a moment to notice the artistic connections that join the *Symposium* and the *Phaedo* in a dramatic diptych: Socrates in the midst of life; Socrates confronting his own death. The various contrasts between the two works are personified in the two deities who preside over each occasion: Dionysus in the *Symposium*; Apollo in the *Phaedo*. The cast of interlocutors is likewise entirely different. Like the *Protagoras* (which has an overlapping set of participants), the *Symposium* illustrates Socrates' preeminent position among the cultural elite of Athenian society; whereas the *Phaedo* depicts him in the smaller circle of his most intimate associates. And each dialogue is adapted to its respective audience. Thus the *Symposium* consists largely of rhetorical speeches, while the *Phaedo* deploys a series of intricate philosophical arguments.

Despite these contrasts, the two dialogues are closely connected at many levels: by their complex portrayal of Socrates' character, by the presentation of the doctrine of Forms, and by the conception of philosophy as a form of *erōs*. Also common to the two works is the implied link between character and theory. Just as Socrates' easy self-mastery in the face of physical hardships and sexual temptation is somehow explained by the lesson in metaphysical love he learned from Diotima, so his supreme serenity in the face of death is grounded in a new statement of the same doctrine of *erōs*. What is the philosopher in love with, if not with wisdom and the knowledge of reality?[19] And that is precisely why Socrates, at the beginning of the *Phaedo*, can assert his readiness for death. The body is a hindrance to intellectual activity. Hence the separation from the body at death offers the philosopher his best hope of more adequate access to the desired object. In this way the Forms are, from the outset, linked to the destiny of the soul.

In expounding the thesis of immortality in the *Phaedo* Socrates appeals to the Orphic-Pythagorean conception of the transmigrating psyche, a conception familiar to us from the *Meno* but never mentioned in the *Symposium*. The figure of Diotima is no doubt designed to remind us of those wise priests and priestesses who teach transmigration in the *Meno*. But Plato will not allow his priestess to mention such a wild doctrine here, where it might provoke smiles

19. The metaphor of the philosopher's love affair with Truth and Being dominates Socrates' opening *apologia*, from *Phaedo* 65B to 69D.

of incredulity from the worldly guests at Agathon's party. It is left for the more intimate and more philosophical setting of the *Phaedo* to bring together the transcendental metaphysics revealed in the *Symposium* with the otherworldly psychology outlined in the *Meno*.[20]

But first we follow the lines that lead from Diotima's teaching to the metaphysical doctrines of the *Phaedo* and *Republic*.

5. UNWINDING THE THREADS OF DIOTIMA'S REVELATION

Packed into Diotima's brief account of the ladder of love are nearly all the major themes of the doctrine of Forms (with the exception, already noted, of the immortal psyche and its epistemic link to the Forms in recollection). We take these themes one by one.

5.1 Being versus Becoming

The traditional Greek contrast between divinity and mortality was transmuted by Parmenides into the metaphysical distinction between eternal, unchanging Being and the realm of Becoming, a realm that includes not only coming-to-be and passing-away but all forms of change. The theological origins of this contrast are often invoked by Plato, when he describes the realm of Being as "immortal" or "divine" (*Symp.* 211E 3, *Phaedo* 79D 2, 80A, 84A 8, etc. cf. *Sophist* 254B 1, *Statesman* 269D 6). But metaphysical eternity is of course a stricter concept than the deathlessness of the gods. In the *Timaeus* Plato will insist that eternal Being is not only changeless but timeless as well (*Tim.* 37D–38A, echoing Parmenides B.8, 5 and 20). More frequently, however, the dialogues define "what is forever" (*to on aei*) in terms of fixity and invariance. The *Symposium* expresses the changelessness of the Beautiful itself by denying that it ever comes to be or perishes, grows larger or smaller, is beautiful at one time but not at another (211A 1–3); no matter what happens to its participants, the Form itself is unaffected (211B 5). In the *Phaedo* we encounter Plato's standard

---

20. The neglect of this relationship between doctrine and audience has left many scholars perplexed over the fact that the full doctrine of immortality is not expounded in the *Symposium*. Has Plato changed his mind again? The standard *Meno–Phaedo* view is, however, alluded to at 208B 4 (ἀθάνατον δὲ ἄλλη) and 212A 7 (ἀθανάτῳ καὶ ἐκείνῳ).

expression for invariance: *aei kata taùta kai hosautōs echei* "forever constant and in the same state" (78c 6, D 6, and *passim*). It is this formula for eternal Being that recurs in the *Republic* (VI, 479A 2, E 7) and in later dialogues as well (*Statesman* 269D 5, *Philebus* 59C 4; cf. *Timaeus* 28A 2, 38B 3). The contrasting phrase for Becoming is *allot' allōs (echomena) kai mēdepote kata taùta* "differently disposed at different times and never in the same state" (*Phaedo* 78c 6). The inconstancy of Becoming is also expressed by picturesque metaphors such as "rolling around" (*kulindetai, Rep.* V, 479D 4), "wandering" (*ibid.* 479D 9 *planēton*; cf. VI, 485B 2), and "flowing" (*rhein, Phaedo* 87D 9; cf. *Cratylus* 402A 9, 411C 4, and *passim*). As it were by homoeopathic effect, the flux in things often causes the soul itself to wander or become dizzy.[21]

5.2 Being versus Appearance

By "appearance" here I mean not only what is directly expressed by the verb *phainesthai*, "to appear, become visible," and its cognates such as *phantazesthai* (at *Symp.* 211A 5). I also include under appearance all forms of perspectivism and relativism, as in the denials that the Beautiful itself is "beautiful in one way, ugly in another; beautiful in one comparison, ugly in another; beautiful here, ugly there; beautiful for some, ugly for others" (*Symp.* 211A 2–5). It is precisely the freedom from such perspectival appearance that distinguishes the Equal itself from equal sticks and stones in the *Phaedo*: "Don't sticks and stones, while remaining the same, sometimes appear (*phainetai*) equal to one person and not to another?[22] ... But the Equals themselves have never appeared to you unequal, or Equality inequality?" (*Phaedo* 74B–C). The *Phaedo* can al-

---

21. For the soul's wandering and dizziness, see *Phaedo* 79C 6–9. The *Cratylus* suggests that the theorists of flux have projected their own confusion onto the world (411B–C, 439C, 440C–D). Cf. *Phaedo* 90C.

22. At *Phaedo* 74B 8–9, ἐνίοτε ... τῷ μὲν ἴσα φαίνεται, τῷ δὲ οὔ can be read either as "sometimes seems equal to one person but not to another" or as "sometimes seems equal in one respect but not in another." The construction is thus ambiguous between τῇ μὲν ... τῇ δέ and τισὶ μὲν ... τισὶ δέ at *Symposium* 211A 2–5. I suspect the ambiguity may be deliberate, intended to suggest three different modes of perspectivism by a single formula: temporal, aspectual, and observer-relative.

lude so briefly to the perspectival/non-perspectival opposition, because it is spelled out more fully in the *via negativa* of Diotima's revelation. (This is an instructive example of the way these two dialogues are designed to supplement one another.)

The same point is made, again in the language of appearance, in the first discussion of the Forms in *Republic* v: "Is there any of these many beautiful things that will not appear (*phanēsetai*) ugly? And of just things that will not appear unjust? and of pious things not impious?" (479A). This occurs in a context where the concept of *doxa* ("opinion") has been introduced as a general faculty of perspectival cognition or "seeming." Since *doxa* has been located in between knowledge and ignorance, its object (appearance, in the broad sense specified above) must be situated between complete Being and blank non-entity. In this context in *Republic* v the objects of *doxa* are specified as things that both are and are not F, for many values of F; whereas the corresponding Form is wholly and purely F. This distinction between perspectival and non-perspectival entities corresponds exactly to our contrast between Becoming and Being; but in the *Republic* this version of the antithesis is reserved for later. (The Being-Becoming contrast will be introduced towards the end of the next book, at VI, 508D, briefly prepared at 485B 2.) In Book V the realm of Becoming is characterized simply by the ambiguity of appearance, the lack of fixed character. By focusing here on the epistemic division between Knowledge and Opinion/Appearance (*doxa*), Plato is preparing his readers for what will be the first cut in the Divided Line at a later stage of the exposition (510A 9; cf. VII, 534A 1–3).

This complex conception of *doxa* in the *Republic* as the faculty for perspectival judgment, or judgments of appearance, is largely absent from the *Symposium* and *Phaedo*, which barely allude to it.[23] Diotima's revelation generally ignores epistemology, and the *Phaedo* operates with the simpler distinction between reason and sense perception.

---

23. As noted above, true *doxa* appears at *Symposium* 202A. At *Phaedo* 84A 8 the reality of the Forms is said to be ἀδόξαστον "not an object of *doxa*"; cf. δοκεῖν at 81B 4, δοξάζουσαν at 83D 6. For *doxa* as (deceptive) visible appearance, see Socrates' remark to Alcibiades at *Symp*. 218E 6: "You try to get the truth of what is beautiful in exchange for the appearance (*doxa*), like gold in exchange for brass!"

5.3 One versus Many

The problem of locating unity in plurality dominates the search for essences in the *Laches*, *Euthyphro*, and *Meno*: as a contrast between different kinds of courage and what is the same in all of them, between many pious actions and the single nature of piety, between the various parts of virtue and virtue as a single whole. "Stop making many out of one," complains Socrates to Meno (77A 7). This is a problem that will fascinate Plato all his life. In the last book of the *Laws* he challenges us "to look towards a single form (*idea*) from things that are many and dissimilar" (*Laws* XII, 965C); and his so-called Unwritten Doctrines take as their fundamental principles Unity and indeterminate Duality. It is precisely this theme of unity in plurality that ties the metaphysical Forms most closely to the dialogues of definition. In the *Symposium* and *Phaedo*, where the concern for definition is not essential to the discussion, the topic of unity is not emphasized. It is nevertheless acknowledged in both these works by repeated mention of the attribute *monoeides*, singleness of Form or uniformity (*Symp.* 211B 1, E 4; *Phaedo* 78D 5, 80B 2). In the *Republic* the theme of unity becomes central again, and it serves explicitly to introduce the doctrine of Forms in Book V: "Since beautiful is opposite to ugly, they are two ... And since they are two, each of them is one." "But by their joining (*koinōnia*) with actions and bodies and with one another,[24] they become visible (*phantazomena*) everywhere and each of them appears as many" (V, 475E–476A). The contrast between many beautiful and many good things, on the one hand, and the Beautiful itself and Good itself, on the other hand – the principle of One over Many – serves also to reintroduce the Forms at the end of Book VI. "Thus concerning all things which we then posited as many, we now again posit each according to a single form (*idea*), assuming that it is a unity, and call it 'what each really is' (*ho esti hekaston*)" (VI, 507B). Thus in the central books of the *Republic* the definitional unities of the *Meno* and *Euthyphro* make their return; but they are specified now as examples of the eternal, non-per-

24. I take ἀλλήλων κοινωνία at V, 476A 6 to refer to co-instantiation of Forms in sensibles rather than to participation of Forms in one another. The latter notion appears nowhere before the *Sophist*, where it marks a radical break in the terminology of participation. It is very unlikely that this major innovation would be introduced here by such an indefinite formulation.

spectival Being defined by Diotima, and as objects of the new epistemology to be described in a moment.

5.4 *Separation?*

According to Aristotle, what distinguishes Platonic Forms from their "Socratic" predecessors is their separation from sensible matter, or, in more modern terms, from their particular instantiations. It has perhaps not been sufficiently recognized that this term "separation" (*chōrismos*) characterizes the theory from an unfriendly point of view. The term is borrowed by Aristotle from Plato's own critique of the doctrine in the *Parmenides*.[25]

Of course the notion of separation corresponds to something that is really there in Plato's texts. As a first approximation, let us call it the ontological independence of the Forms from their sensible instances.[26] Such independence is everywhere implied by the radical distinction between Being and Becoming; it is more fully spelled out by Diotima's claim that, as beautiful things come to be and perish, the Beautiful itself is in no way affected. The independent existence of the Form is further expressed in the denial that it is located *in* anything else, neither in heaven nor earth, neither in a body nor in discourse (*logos*) nor in knowledge. To these negative statements of independence corresponds the positive claim that the Form exists "itself by itself with itself, eternally uniform" (*Symp.* 211B 1).

The reality of the Forms is thus free from any type of immanence, including immanence in human thought or discourse. Later Platonists will have recourse to an Aristotelian conception in order to construe the Forms as Ideas in a divine mind. But that is certainly not Plato's view. On the contrary, the Forms are ontologically prior to everything else. As the *Phaedrus* (249C 6) tells us, it is precisely by its relation to the Forms that a god is divine (*Phaedrus* 249C 6). The paradeigmatic Forms of the *Timaeus* are clearly presupposed by the action of the Demiurge, who takes them as his model for world creation, just as the philosopher-king of the *Republic* takes them as model for the just ordering of the city. (For

25. For χωρίς in the *Parmenides* see 129D 7 (once in Socrates' statement), 130B 2–D 1 (five times in Parmenides' restatements), then again in objections (131B 1–2, 5).
26. For discussion of separation for the Forms, see Fine (1984), Vlastos (1987), and Fine (1993).

more on "separation" and immanence in the final section of the *Phaedo*, see pp. 357f. below.)

5.5 Participation

We have seen in Diotima's account a single use of the metaphor for beautiful things "sharing" (*metechein*) in the Form of Beauty (*Symp.* 211B 2). This sharing or participation will become a standard term occasionally used by Plato, but regularly used by Aristotle and later Platonists, for the ontological dependence of sensible beings upon the Forms. The term *metechei* recurs in the last and fullest statement of the doctrine in the *Phaedo* (100C 5), where the repeated use of the aorist form *metaschein* gives rise to the rare term *metaschesis* for "participation" (101C 5, apparently the only occurrence of this word in Greek). The same metaphor with a different verb occurs once more in the *Phaedo*, in a summary reference to "the Forms (*eidē*) and the things that partake of them (*metalambanonta*)" (102B 2). But the *Phaedo* itself makes clear that this relation is left undefined: "Nothing makes a thing beautiful other than the presence of (*parousia*) or sharing in (*koinōnia*) that Beautiful itself, or whatever the relationship to it may be.[27] I don't insist upon this, but only that it is by the Beautiful that all beautiful things are beautiful" (100D 4).

The terminology of participation is so commonly employed by Aristotle and later authors in reference to Plato's theory that it comes as a surprise to notice how infrequently this metaphor appears in Plato's own statements of the relation of sensibles to Forms, outside of the passages just quoted from *Phaedo* 100–2. In the *Republic* it apparently occurs only once in this sense,[28] in what might almost be regarded as a quotation from the *Symposium*: the philosopher alone is "able to see both the Beautiful itself and the

---

27. (I follow recent editors in retaining the MS reading at 100D 6.) As we have seen, Plato plays with the notion of "presence" for the Forms in two other dialogues of Group I: the quibble on *paresti* at *Euthydemus* 300E–301A is implicitly disambiguated at *Lysis* 217C–E.

28. There is a parallel to *metechein* in the notion of "communion" (*koinōnia*) with Forms at *Rep.* v, 476A 7. At v, 472C 2 *metechein* for a man's sharing in justice may be regarded as an anticipation of the relationship to Forms, which appears a few pages later.

things that share in it (*metechonta*)," and to distinguish them from one another (v, 476D 1–3). The terminology of participation does not appear again until the theory is restated for the purpose of criticism in the *Parmenides*, where it is used systematically (*metalambanein* 129A 3ff. *metechonta* 129B 3ff. and *passim*). After the *Parmenides* this metaphor is never used again by Plato for the sensible–Form relation. (The significance of this change will be discussed below, pp. 357f.) By contrast, in the *Sophist* the terminology of participation is transferred to the relations between Forms. Instead of participation, the terminology of imagery and imitation predominates in the *Republic* for sensible–Form relations; and (outside of the *Parmenides*) this is the only terminology employed in later dialogues.[29] We can recognize one anticipation of this later usage in Diotima's speech.

5.6 Image and imitation

The lover who has seen the Form will engender "not images (*eidōla*) of virtue, since he has not been in contact with an image, but true virtue, since he was in contact with the truth" (*Symp.* 212A 4). This is Diotima's only hint of what is destined to become a major theme. In the *Republic* the Line and the Cave allegory make systematic use of the notion of images (*eidōla, eikones*) and likeness (ὁμοιωθέν, μιμηθέντα) for the lower levels of reality and cognition. The *Phaedrus* continues this terminology (250Aff.), which is later echoed in the *Statesman* (285E–286A 1) and regularly employed in the *Timaeus*. What the passage quoted from the *Symposium* shows is that, from early on, Plato had in reserve the image-vocabulary as an alternative to participation, an alternative that has the advantage of avoiding the gross physical connotations of the notions of "sharing in" and "partaking of."

There is one other dialogue from the pre-*Republic* group where Plato makes use of this very term "image" (*eidōlon*) in order to contrast a likeness with the real thing. As we have seen in Chapter 9, in the *Lysis* Socrates develops a regress from the principle that one thing is dear for the sake of a second dear thing, which in turn is

29. The significance of this important change in Plato's terminology was pointed out by Fujisawa (1974). Notice that at *Timaeus* 51A 7–B 1 μεταλαμβάνον has its normal metaphorical value (exactly as μετέχειν does at 51E 5), and it does *not* refer to the relation between sensibles and Forms.

dear for the sake of a third, and so on. And he breaks the regress by the notion of an intrinsic good, good for its own sake: the "primary dear" (*prōton philon*), for the sake of which all other things are said to be dear. These other so-called dear things are compared to images (*eidōla*), "whereas it is the primary dear that is *truly* dear" (*Lysis* 219D). This parallel to Diotima's mention of images follows in the *Lysis* immediately after another important piece of terminology that is common to this dialogue and the *Symposium*: the *ho esti* phrase that will eventually serve as the official designation for the Forms. If we are to avoid the regress, says Socrates, "we must reach some principle or starting-point (*archē*) that will no longer refer us to another dear thing, but we will come to that which is primary dear (*ekeino ho estin prōton philon*)." (*Lysis* 219C. Compare *auto ho esti kalon*, "what itself is Beautiful," in Diotima's speech at *Symposium* 211C 9.) Like the image–reality contrast, the *ho esti* formula is thus introduced inconspicuously in both *Lysis* and *Symposium*, as an anticipation of things to come.

The *Lysis* passage reminds us that the contrast between a Form and its image, alluded to in Diotima's peroration, prefigures another major theme of the *Phaedo* and the *Republic*: the defectiveness of the many beautiful things in comparison with the Beautiful itself. It is the Form that is *truly* beautiful, just as it is the primary dear that is *truly* dear.

5.7 *Non-sensory apprehension of the Forms*

We know from the *Phaedo* (65C–E, 75A–B) that the Forms cannot be grasped by sense perception but only by thought (*dianoia*) and reasoning (*logismos* 66A 1, 79A 3; cf. *logizetai* at 65C 5, *dianoeisthai* and *dianoia* 65E 3ff., *noēton* "intelligible" at 80B 1, 81B 7). So in *Republic* VI the first cut in the Knowledge Line divides the visible realm from the intelligible (509E). Accessible only to the intellect (*nous*), the Forms are located in intelligible space (*noētos topos*, 508C 1), where the Good stands to the intellect as the Sun stands to the faculty of sight.

In the *Symposium* Plato does not name either intellect or thought as the faculty for non-sensory cognition. Instead, Diotima speaks indirectly, even coyly, of "beholding [the Form of Beauty] with what is required" and "seeing it with that to which it is visible" (212A 1–3). These circumlocutions might seem opaque to an uninstructed reader. The meaning is immediately clear, of course, to anyone who knows the doctrine of the *Phaedo* and *Republic*.[30]

Why does Plato have Diotima refer so obliquely to non-sensory apprehension? Of course not everything can be compressed into this brief revelation. And perhaps Plato avoids naming *nous* here just as he avoids any reference to esoteric doctrines like recollection and the transcendental soul. After all, the term *nous* in ordinary Greek means simply "intelligence" or "good sense." The conception of *nous* as a faculty of reason or intellect, defined by contrast to sense perception, is a technical creation of the philosophers beginning with Parmenides. Diotima prefers not to speak in such technical terms. Above all, by avoiding the sensible–intelligible dichotomy here in the *Symposium*, Plato can make more uninhibited use of the metaphors for "seeing" and "beholding" in this, his first account of the beatific vision of the Forms.

5.8 Eponymy and other refinements

What is missing from Diotima's account? As we have just seen, the epistemic division between things sensible and intelligible is barely alluded to; and the knowledge–opinion distinction is passed over in silence in the final revelation (although it was mentioned earlier by Diotima, at 202A). One essential component of the classic doctrine of Forms that is entirely absent from Diotima's speech is the relation Plato calls *epōnumia*: that sensible things are "named after" the corresponding Form (*Phaedo* 102B 2, C 10, 103B 7–8; *Phaedrus* 250E 2; cf. *Rep.* X, 596A 7). Some such semantic relation may be regarded as implicit in the distinction between beautiful things and the Beautiful itself, when taken in conjunction with the claim that only the Form itself is *truly* beautiful. But to explicate this relation as an account of derivative naming or, in modern terms, predication, would introduce a degree of philosophical reflection that would probably seem out of place in Diotima's lesson on love.

Missing also from the *Symposium* is any explicit statement of the

---

30. A reader unfamiliar with Plato's work might nevertheless understand *Symp.* 212A 1–3 as a reference to *nous* if he or she was acquainted with Parmenides' use of *noein* or with Democritus' contrast between genuine and spurious cognition.

ontological deficiency of the many beautiful things. We have found a hint of this in the contrast between truth and image at the end of Diotima's lesson. Ontological inferiority is certainly *implied* by the Being–Becoming distinction, as reinforced by the distinction between Being and Appearance. But for an explicit statement we must turn to the *Phaedo*, to learn that sticks and stones *try* to be like the Equal itself but fall short (74D–75B).

Another typical feature of the theory that is absent from Diotima's account is the terminology for "forms" as such. The terms *eidos* and *idea* are not used to designate Form in the *Symposium*. This terminology makes its appearance only quite late in the *Phaedo* (102B 1, 103E 3, 104B 9ff.), before becoming standard in the *Republic* (V, 476A 5, 479A 1, etc.) Such hesitation on Plato's part to introduce the *eidos/idea* terminology for metaphysical Forms may seem strange, since these are precisely the terms that he applies to definienda in the *Euthyphro* and *Meno*. Hence to account for Plato's restraint on this point in the *Symposium* and *Phaedo* it is not enough to cite his general distaste for fixed terminology.

A more pertinent consideration here is that something new and important is being announced, which should not at the outset seem too familiar. Any reader acquainted with the terms *eidos* and *idea* for essences in the dialogues of definition must come gradually to see that these new metaphysical entities announced in the *Symposium*, and identified in the *Phaedo* as objects of prenatal, supersensible cognition, are after all what was being sought for all along in the request for definitions. We have seen that the link to the definitional project is established (inconspicuously in the *Symposium*, emphatically in the *Phaedo*) by the phrase for essence itself, *to ho estin*, "the what-it-really-is." This phrase, which is obviously Plato's own creation, points to what is central in his ontology, the concept of essential Being, or what the *Phaedrus* calls *to ontōs on*, "what is really real." Once this link between definition and metaphysics has been clearly established (at *Phaedo* 75D, 76D 8, 78D), Plato can return to the convenient use of the nondescript words *eidos* and *idea* for "form," "type," and "structure," words that were originally not distinctive of his theory at all, but that might equally well be used by a medical author or a writer in geometry.

It is a mistake, then, to suppose (as some critics have done) that the etymological connections of the terms *idea* and *eidos* with the verb *idein*, "to see," are in any way essential or decisive for Plato's conception of the Forms. The metaphor of vision for intellectual access to the Forms is useful but altogether dispensable. The expressions for "hunting," "grasping," "hitting upon" or simply "thinking" and "recognizing" (*gnōnai*) will do as well. The fundamental conception of the Forms is, from the beginning, linguistic rather than visual in its orientation. That is to say, this conception is dominated not by the metaphor of seeing or the notion of mental intuition, but rather by the notion of essential *Being* as specified by the *what-is-X?* question.

6. FORMS IN THE *PHAEDO*

The *Phaedo* presents the first general statement of Plato's philosophy, bringing together themes that are more briefly announced in the *Meno* and *Symposium*. In the complex structure of this dialogue, the doctrine of Forms appears at four different points. For an understanding of Plato's compositional technique, it will be useful to examine these four passages in their relationship to one another. This will mean retracing our steps to some extent. In effect, this section and the next take the form of a running commentary on Plato's exposition in the *Phaedo* and *Republic*.

The Forms first appear at *Phaedo* 65Dff. where Justice, Beauty, and the Good are mentioned together with other essences ("the *ousia* which each one really is"), as representing the truth and reality that is the goal of the philosopher's quest, the object of his loving desire. The notion of philosophical *erōs* here is an extension of the doctrine taught by Diotima. The philosopher's love is now a desire for knowledge of the Forms generally, rather than desire of the Beautiful alone. A second novelty is that such knowledge is to be gained only by separating the soul as far as possible from the body, so that knowledge can be fully achieved only by a disembodied soul. As we have remarked, in the language of the *Phaedo* the body corresponds epistemically to sense perception, the soul to thought and reasoning. So by the psyche in such contexts Plato means the rational soul, what he will elsewhere call *nous* or *to logistikon* ("the part that calculates").

The Forms reappear with the mention of the Equal itself at 74A, as part of Plato's restatement of the doctrine of Recollection. The objects recollected, which were left unspecified in the *Meno*, are here identified as the Forms. The perspectival "appearance" of equal sticks and stones is cited to demonstrate their deficiency with respect to the Equal itself. It is then argued that knowledge of the Form must be presupposed by our recognition of deficiency on the part of the objects of perception. The prenatal existence of the soul is thus inferred from our previous acquaintance with the Forms as objects of recollection, that is, as objects to which we must refer in interpreting the deliverances of sense perception (76D 9–E 2).

This argument for prenatal knowledge of Forms, as a precondition for sensory cognition, has been justly criticized by many commentators. (A similar conclusion is more convincingly presented at *Phaedrus* 249C: see below, §8.) But the rigor (or lack of it) of the argument for recollection is perhaps less important than the major synthesis it achieves. For it firmly embeds the transcendental psychology of the *Meno* in the Parmenidean metaphysics of the *Symposium*: "just as these Forms really exist, in this same way our soul must really exist even before we are born" (*Phaedo* 76E). And by identifying these Forms with the what-it-is (*to ho esti*) discussed in dialectical questions and answers (75D), the argument for recollection connects the new metaphysics and psychology with the essences pursued in non-metaphysical dialogues. The *Phaedo* thus brings together in a single exposition the philosophical concerns that partially emerge in the *Laches* and *Euthyphro* and are more fully disclosed in the *Meno* and *Symposium*.

In the third appearance of the Forms, in the argument from invariance that begins at 78B, the Forms are again identified with the essence (*ousia*) pursued in dialectic (78D); but the new point is Plato's insistence on their freedom from change and variation. Here we encounter the classic formula for invariance for the first time (78C 6). But in this context the ontological distinction between changeable and invariant entities is paired with the epistemic division between the visible and invisible, the objects of sense perception and the objects of rational thought (*dianoias logismos* 79A 3) respectively. The result is a division into two kinds of entities (*onta* 79A 6), the invariant-invisible and the changing-perceptible – a division that remains fundamental for Plato as late as the *Philebus* and *Timaeus*. The twin terms in which this division is formulated, by reference to both perception and change, reflect the union between Plato's epistemology and his metaphysics – precisely that union which will be consecrated in the paradoxical thesis that the Form of the Good is cause of both knowledge and reality, the source of both knowability and being (essence, *ousia*) for intelligible objects (*Rep.* VI, 508E–509B).

The last and most elaborate discussion of the Forms in the *Phaedo* begins at 100B, where they are introduced as the basis for the new rational method proposed by Socrates, as an alternative to Ionian natural philosophy. Plato is thus fully conscious of the historical function of the doctrine of Forms, as defining not only a new mode of causal explanation but a new conception of philosophy, one that differs from the Presocratic tradition both in its method and in its content. The method is Socratic discussion, the art of *logoi*, but given more rigorous structure now by the deductive techniques of hypothesis adapted from geometry. The content is again Socratic, but transformed. Socrates is said to have brought philosophy down from heaven to earth by focusing on the virtues and on what makes for a good life. But Plato redefines philosophy by identifying the Good, the Just, and the Noble (or Beautiful, *kalon*) as the basic constituents of reality. The principles of goodness, justice, and moral beauty are thus conceived as more fundamental and more intrinsically rational then the structure of the physical cosmos. And this cosmos must itself be derived from, and explained by, the principles of eternal Being and Good as defined by the doctrine of Forms. This derivation of the order of nature from reason working to make things good is desiderated by Socrates in the *Phaedo* and actually carried out in the *Timaeus*.

In the *Phaedo* the explanatory role of the Forms is developed on a more modest scale, as a basis for the final argument for immortality. The argument itself begins with a rather technical discussion (in which Socrates mockingly apologizes for "speaking like a textbook," 102D 3) concerning the way in which sensible individuals participate in Forms. In analyzing relations of relative size between himself, Phaedo and Simmias, Socrates introduces what looks like an unfortunate distinction between transcendent and immanent Forms – between Tallness itself and the tallness in us (102B–103C). Taken literally, this "separation" between the Forms and their instantiation in us leads to disastrous results for the theory, as Plato himself will show in the *Parmenides*. The reference to "the tallness in us" at *Phaedo* 102D 7 was probably intended only as a linguistic variant for *our being tall*. But the formula was a dangerous one. If we take it as Parmenides does, as positing a reduplication of the Form as an attribute or property in us, this separation of "the opposite in us" from the Opposite itself leads to the Greatest Objection of *Parmenides* 133B ff., which makes the Forms unknowable. Just as some of the initial difficulties for the theory of Forms raised at *Parmenides* 130E–131E depend upon taking the metaphor of participation quite literally and as it were physically, so the final objection of 133B–134E arises from a deliberate misreading of the notion of separation, a reading designed to force apart a given Form from its instantiation in us, in such a way as to reify both items.[31]

Plato was clearly aware of both dangers, as his critique in the *Parmenides* shows. Thus there is no trace of immanent forms (like "tallness in us") in the *Republic* or in any later work (except for the critical discussion in the *Parmenides*), just as there is no use made of the notion of participation of sensible things in Forms after a single reference in the *Republic* (v, 476D). In the *Timaeus* there are no immanent forms but only images of the Forms; and these images are construed neither as entities nor as properties of individuals but as fleeting qualifications of the Receptacle. The *Timaeus* has thus replaced the notion of participation by a careful elaboration of Plato's earlier conception of sensible things as "appearances" of Forms. (See above, §5.2.)

Regarded as a technical account of the relation between Forms and sense appearance, the *Phaedo* must be counted a failure. As a substitute for natural philosophy, the *deuteros plous* of the *Phaedo* does not achieve its goal. (For that we must await the *Timaeus*.) But that is not the only, or even the primary enterprise undertaken in this dialogue. What Plato does successfully achieve in the *Phaedo* is something perhaps more important: the creation of a rational religion for the educated classes of antiquity. In Hellenistic and Roman times, philosophy was cultivated above all as a guide to life, as a moral and spiritual religion. For all except the Epicureans, Socrates became the patron saint of the philosophic life. And the *Phaedo* portrays him in his noblest moment, sustained by the most moving and most otherworldly statement of Plato's philosophy.

This achievement of the *Phaedo* is symbolized in Plutarch's narrative of the death of Cato the Younger, who takes his own life at

---

31. In his exposition Socrates had used the term *choris* ("apart") only once, for the distinction between Forms and sensible particulars (129D 7). Parmenides seizes upon the term and immediately uses it three times, to separate similarity itself from the similarity "which we have" (130B 4ff.). See other passages cited above in n.25.

Utica rather than beg Caesar to spare it. At the climax of his exemplary action of discharging all domestic and political responsibilities, Cato spends his last night in the study of "Plato's dialogue on the soul," which he is said to have read through twice before falling on his sword.[32] The *Phaedo* had thus become a spiritual gospel for the educated aristocracy, the noblest intellectual consolation for one about to die.

7. FORMS IN THE *REPUBLIC*

The most substantial account of the Forms in all of Plato's work (with the possible exception of the second part of the *Parmenides*) begins in the *Republic* towards the end of Book VI and extends through the whole of Book VII. But just as the presentation of the Form of Beauty in the *Symposium* was not the statement of a general theory but a brilliant climax to Diotima's account of philosophical *erōs*; and just as the four expositions of the Forms in the *Phaedo* were all subordinated to the topic of the nature and destiny of the soul; so the long discussion in Books VI–VII of the *Republic* is not a treatise on the Forms but the theoretical framework for a program of higher education. The great passages on the Sun, the Line, and the Cave do not pretend to give a systematic account of human knowledge and the nature of reality. What Plato offers us is a set of powerfully suggestive images designed to portray the need for an experience of intellectual conversion and enlightenment, and so to justify a course of training that will permit the philosopher-kings to achieve an understanding of what is good for themselves and for the city. We are told just enough about the Forms for us to see why Plato thinks such training is necessary, and what its goals must be.

The other two discussions of Forms in the *Republic* are similarly subordinated to specific contexts in the construction of the good city. In the earlier passage at the end of Book v the distinction between Forms and their sensible participants, as the objects of Knowledge and Opinion respectively, is elaborated just far enough to draw the line between genuine philosophers and false claimants to this title. And the final reference to Forms, at the beginning of Book x, is clearly motivated by Plato's desire to undermine any

32. Plutarch, *Life of Cato the Younger* 68, 70.

claim to cognitive authority for the arts of imitation, and above all for poetry.

Despite these contextual limitations, the discussion of Forms in the *Republic* is much too rich for any attempt at completeness of coverage here. My aim is simply to mark the stages in a progressive exposition, and to note the elements of novelty and continuity at each stage.

The first introduction of Forms in Book v at 475E–476A builds directly on what was provided by the *Symposium* and *Phaedo*. Plato here takes from the *Symposium* the first Form to be mentioned, the Beautiful, but he construes this according to the pattern presented in the final section of the *Phaedo*, by conceiving the Forms in opposing pairs.[33] After the mention of Beautiful–Ugly, Socrates continues: "and the same account applies to Just and Unjust and Good and Bad and all the Forms (*eidē*)" (476A 4). The use of *eidē* here also picks up the terminology from the end of the *Phaedo* (102Bff.). Adapted from the *Symposium* is the epistemic framework in which opinion (*doxa*) figures as a middle term between Knowledge and Ignorance. What is entirely new is the mapping of these three terms (knowledge, opinion, ignorance) onto the corresponding ontological framework of Being and Not-Being, with a middle term as object for *doxa*, construed in Parmenidean language as "what is and is not" (479B).

When the intermediate position of *doxa* between knowledge and ignorance was briefly anticipated in Diotima's characterization of Eros at *Symposium* 202A, the contrast there (as also in the *Meno*) was between knowledge and *true* opinion. In *Republic* v this qualification has been dropped, and *doxa* is conceived as a general faculty of perspectival judgment, whether true or false. So conceived, *doxa* can take the whole realm of sensible appearance as its object, as knowledge in the strong sense takes the Forms as object. The Forms are now represented as *to pantelōs on*, "what is completely." The conceptual and linguistic echoes of Parmenides are even more conspicuous here in *Republic* v than in the Being–Becoming contrast in Diotima's description of the Form.[34] It is noteworthy,

33. See §9 on the role of opposites in the theory.
34. Besides the Parmenidean triad of Being, Not-Being, and What-is-and-is-not, there is the argument of 476E 7–477A 1: knowledge must be of something that is (*on*), because what-is-not (*mē on*) cannot be known (echoing Parmenides B.2, 7). See Kahn (1988b) for Plato's use of Parmenides here.

however, that in this context the object of *doxa* is not immediately identified as Becoming, since that would obscure the is-and-is-not structure of perspectival appearance. As we have seen, the characterization of this realm in terms of coming-to-be and passing-away enters only later, at VI, 485B 2, and then more systematically at 508D 7, where coming-to-be and perishing are explicitly recognized as object for *doxa*. Plato's revision of the Parmenidean scheme is thus completed by a full equation between two pairs of alternative descriptions for the same range of items: in epistemic terms, the domain of *doxa* (or appearance) and the objects of sense perception; in ontological terms, the realm of Becoming and what-is-and-is-not.[35]

At the end of Book V and beginning of Book VI we encounter the master image of the *Republic*, the figure of the philosopher with his gaze fixed upon the Forms. The figure itself recalls the beatific vision of the *Symposium*, but the Forms are initially described here by the formula for invariance from the *Phaedo* "being forever constant and in the same state" (479E 7, 484B 4). Once again Plato's formulation in the *Republic* brings together themes from the *Symposium* and *Phaedo*. On the other hand, because of the essentially this-worldly focus of the *Republic* on the life of the city, the transcendent psychology of the *Meno* and *Phaedo* will be held in abeyance until the end of Book X, after the proof of immortality. The psyche of Books IV and VIII–IX is the embodied, not the transcendent soul.

Book VI opens with the conception of the Forms as a model

35. In a moment of epistemic modesty, the Socrates of the *Republic* refers to his views on the Good as mere opinion (VI, 506B–E *doxai, to dokoun*). That has led some commentators to deny that *doxa* is necessarily limited to objects in the sensory realm. Why could we not have either true or false opinions about the Forms?

This issue can scarcely be settled in a footnote. But I believe that the passage just cited is a dramatic aside, without consequences for the doctrinal account of *doxa*. In every careful statement of the basic dichotomy, *doxa* and sense perception belong together as taking *to gignomenon* as their object (e.g. *Tim.* 28A 2), whereas the reality of the Forms is *adoxaston* (*Phaedo* 84A 8).

Such is Plato's doctrine. Is it reasonable? Yes, if *doxa* is necessarily limited to images (of Forms) and cannot unambiguously fix reference to the Form as such. For any image will inevitably represent more than one Form. Hence one could never distinguish between a false opinion about Form F and a (possibly true) opinion about Form G. The sophistical problem about the possibility of false statement and false belief becomes a *deep* problem when the Forms are the subject of discussion.

(*paradeigma*) according to which the philosophers, like painters, will shape the affairs of the city (VI, 484C–E). Later in Book VI, when Plato returns to the figure of the philosopher-king as painter, it is the notion of imitation and assimilation that connects the artist-ruler with his model (500C–501C). It is precisely this role of the Forms as pattern for the good life and the good city that provides the justifying principle for the rule of philosophy. And it is this same conception that makes it necessary for the training of the guardians to culminate in the "greatest study," the vision of the Form of the Good. We may note that, from a modern point of view, it is this monolithic conception of the Good, and the un-limited power of the guardians to shape the city according to their vision of it, that forms the most alarming feature of Plato's politi-cal thinking. Plato himself, who was no liberal pluralist, seems to have recognized the danger of such a scheme, as we can see from his very different construction of the "second best" city in the *Laws*.[36]

When the Forms are officially introduced for the second time, in the analogy between the Sun and the Good at the end of Book VI (507B), the Forms define the noetic domain over which the Good reigns, as the sun reigns over the visible world. This analogy is elab-orated by the geometric proportions of the Divided Line, in which the noetic-visible division is equated first with the dichotomy be-tween Knowledge and Opinion from Book V (509D–510A) and later, in the final restatement, with the Being–Becoming division first mentioned in Diotima's revelation (VII, 534A). As in Book V, the basic divisions of epistemology and ontology are thus mapped onto one another.

The Divided Line serves to introduce the conception of dia-lectic described above in Chapter 10 §2. As a deductive science mathematics must take for granted, as *hupotheseis*, certain primitive concepts and premises. Dialectic somehow rises above these as-sumptions to reach a non-hypothetical or unconditional first prin-ciple (*archē*), presumably to be identified with the Good. It then proceeds, "by, through, and to Forms, and concludes in Forms" (511C 1). Book VII gives a thorough account of the preliminary training program but not of dialectic itself, since this can only be

36. For discussion of these issues and the changes in Plato's political vision, see Kahn (1993b) and (1995).

grasped by someone who has been properly prepared (533A). Reading a literary work like the *Republic* is no substitute for the years of rigorous training.

What the reader can see, however, is that dialectic is presented as the consummation of the enterprise first sketched in the dialogues of definition. The dialectician is the one who is able "to give and receive an account (*logos*)" (531E, 533C 2; cf. 534B–D). What he has to give an account of is precisely the essence, "what each thing itself is," and ultimately "what good itself is" (532A 7–B 1; 533B 2; cf. 523D 4, 524C 11, E 6). The *logos* he investigates is thus a *logos tēs ousias*, an account of the essence (534B 3). To this extent the pursuit of definition remains as a central element in dialectic. Thus, retrospectively, Plato himself endorses a "unitarian" reading of the dialogues of definition.

In Book x Plato generalizes the doctrine of Forms to apply to any plurality identified by a single term, and thus to include artificial as well as natural kinds: "We are accustomed to posit a Form, one in each case, for each group of many things to which we apply the same name" (596A 6).[37] This is the most inclusive statement of the theory in the Corpus. In what follows, the terminology ("what bed is," *ho esti klinē* 597Aff.) shows that Plato still has the technical notion of Form as essence in view. But he has conveniently extended it to an entirely new domain, where the doctrine is presented in a way that is not prima facie consistent with what has gone before. Thus it is surprising to find that god is the maker of the Form of Bed (597B–D). (One wonders whether such a Form can still be eternal and exempt from coming-to-be.) Since beds are man-made, the Form of Bed must be god-made! Perhaps by this assertion Plato means simply to indicate that beds are artificial, not natural kinds.

8. FORMS IN THE *CRATYLUS, PHAEDRUS,* AND BEYOND

Stylistically the *Cratylus* belongs to Group I, and thus it is (as far as we can know anything about chronology) prior to the *Republic*. I

---

37. Myles Burnyeat reminds me that there is a weaker reading proposed by J. A. Smith: "we posit a single Form for each plurality, and we apply the name of the Form to members of the plurality." See Smith (1917). On either reading the formula needs to be qualified in some way, if it is not to lead to the Third Man difficulty.

have left it aside, however, because the two passages on the Forms, at the beginning and end of this dialogue, do not fit smoothly into the natural sequence of exposition that we have traced from the *Symposium* through the *Phaedo* and *Republic*. The contents of the *Cratylus* on the theory of naming, the problems of flux, Protagorean relativism and the paradox of false statement, all point ahead to discussion of these topics in the *Theaetetus* and *Sophist*. Hence scholars who judge by content have been inclined to date the *Cratylus* with a later group of dialogues. But since in the matter of dating Plato's change of style is our only reliable clue, I believe we must simply accept the fact that the *Cratylus* belongs chronologically with the *Phaedo* and *Symposium* in Group I. It is clear that Plato's philosophical concerns could operate on several tracks at the same time. What the *Cratylus* shows is that, even before the *Republic*, he already had problems in view that he would deal with more fully only in later works.

The first reference to the Forms in the *Cratylus* takes us by surprise, since the two Forms mentioned there are not familiar from any other Platonic text: the Form of Shuttle at 389B and the Form of Name at 389D. There can be no doubt that we are dealing with Forms in the strict sense, since here again the standard terminology is used: *auto ho estin kerkis* "what-itself-Shuttle-is" and *auto ekeino ho estin onoma* "that-itself-which-Name-is." The reference to shuttle here is the only example in the dialogues, outside of *Republic* x, where a Form for artefacts is mentioned.[38] And here the name is also treated as an artefact, the product of the namegiver. In sketching the ontology for a general theory of language or naming, Plato seems to indicate that a Form would be required for every well-defined structure or type of thing, and hence for artificial as well as for natural kinds.

In this early section of the *Cratylus* words are regarded as instruments by which we perform certain actions, namely, by which "we inform or instruct one another, and distinguish things the way they are" (388B). The point being made here, against Hermogenes' view of words as entirely arbitrary, is that underlying the conventional sounds of a language there must be some non-arbitrary nature or

38. But there is a comparable generalization in *Epistle* VII, 342D, where the fifth element (or Form) is mentioned for all body "artificial (*skeuaston*) as well as produced by nature."

structure that makes it possible for words to perform this function of informing and describing, just as the carpenter who makes a shuttle must conform to the structure that permits the shuttle to do its work by passing through the warp threads on the loom. In this case there will be a Form of Name in general, the semantic link between language and the world that I have called the sign relation.[39] And there must also be a Form corresponding to each particular name, which is the sign relation that connects words in any given language with a particular nature in the world. (Thus there will be a sign relation or name-Form connecting the Greek word *agathon* with the Form of the Good; and this same name-Form will also connect the English word *good* and the French word *bien* with the same object.)

The second reference to Forms in the *Cratylus*, at the very end of the dialogue, returns to a formulation that is more familiar from the *Phaedo* and *Republic*. "Do we say there is something that is Beautiful itself and Good and each one of the beings of this sort?" (439c 8; cf. *Phaedo* 65D, *Rep.* v, 476A; vi, 507B). The following contrast between the Beautiful itself and a beautiful face reads like an echo of *Symposium* 211A: "Let us therefore consider just this, not if there is a beautiful face or something of this sort, and all these seem to be in flux, but the Beautiful itself; isn't it always just as it is?" But here again we have something new: a systematic argument for the necessity of a principle of stability and definiteness in the world, in opposition to a "Heraclitean" doctrine of universal flux. Discourse and knowledge both require some fixity in their object. If things are capable of being described in language and grasped in cognition, then something definite must be the case. Things must in fact *be* in one way rather than in another; they cannot be continuously changing in every respect. In this context the argument against unlimited flux seems to imply an argument for the existence of completely invariant Forms. The *Cratylus* suggests, but

39. See Kahn (1973) 172: "By a sign relation I mean an ordered pair {N,O} such that N is a phonetic configuration in a particular language ... and such that speakers of this language regularly make use of N in order to identify O and to distinguish it from other objects or kinds." However, as Richard Ketchum has pointed out to me, the notion of an ordered pair is too restrictive here. Uniqueness of the phonetic name could hold at most within a single language; and even there the phenomenon of synonymy requires the sign relation to be a many–one function.

does not assert, that the necessary elements of stability in the phenomenal world must be derived from Forms that do not change at all.[40]

The argument against universal flux is more fully developed at *Theaetetus* 182c–183b (although in the *Theaetetus* version the Forms are not mentioned). The *Cratylus* states the argument very briefly, but it opens up a systematic analysis of change and stability that will be pursued not only in the *Theaetetus* but also in the *Sophist* and *Timaeus*. In this respect the ontological considerations of the *Cratylus* go beyond anything in the *Phaedo* and *Republic*, where issues of change and invariance are treated only tangentially, as part of the contrast between Being and Becoming.

The *Cratylus* thus contains more technical philosophical analysis than any other dialogue of Group I. The discussion of Forms as such in the *Cratylus* is, however, very incomplete. Nothing is said about the Being–Becoming opposition (although it is implicit in the argument against flux), and the Intelligible–Sensible dichotomy is not even alluded to. Hence the *Cratylus* does not fit into the ingressive exposition of metaphysical Forms I have been analyzing here. It clearly lies on an alternative path leading to the *Theaetetus* and *Sophist*.[41]

The last statement of the classic theory of Forms occurs in Socrates' great speech in praise of love in the *Phaedrus*, in the mythical account of the disembodied souls as winged charioteers, travelling outside the heavens in a cavalcade led by the gods. Plato here completes the account of recollection he began in the *Meno*, by an artistic depiction of the prenatal vision of Forms that makes recollection possible. This is, in effect, the condition that Socrates describes in the *Phaedo* as the final goal of every philosophic quest: for the soul itself (without the body) to see the truth itself.

This is a vision of bliss, beyond what any poet has ever achieved (247c 3), and Plato brings all of his literary powers to bear on this portrayal, to render it as vividly as possible. Here the soul "beholds Justice itself, beholds Temperance, beholds Knowledge, not the knowledge in which becoming is involved, nor that which is

40. For some speculation along this line, see Kahn (1973) 170.
41. We recall, however, that the concern with naming in the *Cratylus* does pick up a theme developed in the *Protagoras* and *Meno*: the many–one and one–many relations between names and things. See above, pp. 219ff. Cf. also the quotation from *Rep.* x, 596A (above, p. 363 with n.37).

located somewhere in something else among the things that we now call beings (*onta*), but the Knowledge that is truly knowledge in what is truly Being (ἐν τῷ ὅ ἐστιν ὄν ὄντως)" (247D 5–E 2). Only a soul that has shared this prenatal vision can be embodied in human form, "for a human being must understand what is said according to a Form, passing from many sense perceptions to a unity gathered together in rational thought (*logismos*). And this is recollection of those things which our soul once saw when it travelled together with a god and looked beyond what we now call reality and was able to rise up into the truly Real (τὸ ὄν ὄντως)" (249B–C).

Here for the last time[42] recollection is invoked in an explanation deriving human rationality from the soul's contact with the Forms. And here Plato explicitly presents the a priori element in human cognition as a necessary precondition for language comprehension and conceptual thought. I believe this passage is best understood as an allegorical anticipation of the Kantian view of a priori concepts as giving unity and structure to sensory experience. (We might also read it in terms of an even more modern nativist view of language acquisition.) If the *Cratylus* opens up a deeper insight into the ontological function of the Forms, the *Phaedrus* brings us back to the geometry lesson in the *Meno* and the innate conditions for rational judgment and understanding. But epistemology in the *Phaedrus* myth is only preliminary and subordinate to the principal function of recollection in this dialogue, which is to provide a new and richer account of how erotic experience can trigger and motivate the philosophic quest. Recollection here adds something lacking in the *Symposium* and only hinted at in the *Phaedo*: a link between philosophical *erōs* and the transcendent destiny of the soul.

The literary presentation of the doctrine of Forms, as basis and goal for the philosophic life, comes to a climax and conclusion in the myth of the *Phaedrus*. What I have tried to show in this chapter is that at least half a dozen dialogues, from the *Laches* and *Euthyphro* to the *Republic* and *Phaedrus*, can be read as the progressive exposition of a single, complex philosophical view of essential Forms,

---

42. Recollection is not explicitly mentioned in any work later than the *Phaedrus*, but it is alluded to in *Statesman* 277D 3. (See Diès' note in the Budé edition, p. 34, n.2.) Recollection is also implied at *Timaeus* 41E–42D, if the prenatal revelation to the souls is to be of any use to them when embodied.

a view different aspects of which are displayed in different contexts. On the whole, the exposition of this view remains at a rather general, non-technical level (with a few exceptions, such as the more detailed account of participation in *Phaedo* 102B–103C, and the discussion of flux and stability at the end of the *Cratylus*). What Plato offers in these dialogues is not so much a systematic theory as a suggestive sketch of the metaphysical and epistemic framework for his protreptic account of the life in philosophy. What he begins in the *Parmenides* and *Theaetetus* is something different: a critical review of problems posed for the technical development of the theory, and a painstaking analysis of some of the epistemological issues that the theory was supposed to resolve. When Parmenides and the Eleatic Stranger take over the leadership from Socrates, the Platonic dialogue enters a new phase, and the topic of this book comes to an end. There is no explicit reference to Forms in the *Theaetetus*. And when Forms return in the *Sophist* and *Timaeus*, there is a new protagonist and a new story to be told.

We may close, then, this discussion of the Forms in the Socratic dialogues by quoting the passage in which Plato has Parmenides, after a rigorous critique of the theory, express his own (that is, Plato's) abiding commitment to the fundamental assumption of the theory, despite such criticism. If in view of all these difficulties, says Parmenides to the youthful Socrates, "you do not allow that there are Forms of things, and if there is no Form delimited for each one, you will have no object to turn your thought to; . . . and you will utterly destroy the power of dialectic," that is, the capacity for philosophic discourse (*Parm.* 135B–C). Without the Forms, says Parmenides, no rational thought and no rational discourse. And the *Timaeus* will add, what the *Cratylus* implies: without the Forms no rational structure for the world.

So we end, after all, with the fundamental importance of the Forms for a theoretical understanding of nature and knowledge, as in the traditional accounts of Plato's thought. What I have tried to demonstrate, however, is that this is not where the theory began, but rather with Beauty and *erōs*, the virtues and the Good. Plato's epistemology and metaphysics were required by his basic enterprise, begun in the *Gorgias* but not successfully carried out there, of providing philosophic understanding and justification for the radical claims of the Socratic moral life.

9. AFTERWORD ON THE ROLE OF OPPOSITES
IN THE DOCTRINE OF FORMS

The ontological deficiency of sensible participants is often specified by their possessing contrary properties: they are both beautiful and ugly, equal and unequal, just and unjust, pious and impious (*Phaedo* 74Bff., *Republic* v, 479Aff., etc.). Also, in explaining why the guardians must study mathematics, Socrates distinguishes perceptions that provoke rational reflection from those that do not, and suggests that the epistemic advantage of the former is due to the fact that they result in contrary perceptions at the same time. Thus the sight of a finger does not provoke us to ask "What is a finger?" But the sight of something large coincides with that of something small, and similarly for the touch of something thick and thin, hard and soft. Such simultaneous perceptions of contrary qualities lead to a cognitive *aporia*; and the soul is thus inclined to resort to calculation and rational thought (*logismos* and *noēsis*) in asking whether these are two objects or one, and finally to ask "what is the large and the small?" (vii, 523–4).

The importance of contrariety here and in the expositions referred to above has led some interpreters to conclude that the doctrine of Forms was originally limited to concepts that entail the co-presence of opposites in particulars, and that natural kinds such as man and bee (or finger) were therefore not included in the primitive version of the theory. It would then be an even later stage of development that is represented by the Forms for artefacts: for Bed and Table in *Republic* x, and for Shuttle and Name in the *Cratylus*.

Aside from chronological doubts about any hypothesis of development that puts the *Cratylus* later than the central books of the *Republic*, there is no philosophical reason to tie the doctrine of Forms to pairs of opposite concepts that co-appear in sensible particulars. These pairs of opposites do offer the most sensational examples of things that are both F and not F, and hence they make for a rhetorically more compelling exposition. (The focus on pairs of opposites also connects up with an explanatory tradition in natural philosophy that goes back to Heraclitus and Anaxagoras, and probably to the Milesians as well.) But the criteria enumerated in our analysis of Diotima's revelation, as supplemented from the

Phaedo and *Republic*, do not in any way depend upon the co-occurrence of opposites. The contrasts between Being and Becoming, invariance and change, unity and plurality, accessibility to intellect and to sense perception, uniform reality and perspectival appearance – all of these criteria apply equally well to the Forms for Humanity and Fire as to those for Beauty and Equality. Human beings are not only subject to change and mortality; they also have many properties that are not essentially human (weight, size, mass, location). And of course any instance of any kind, whether natural or artificial, will appear differently from different perspectives and at different times.

I conclude that if we set aside the somewhat convoluted argument for the study of mathematics in *Republic* VII, the prominence of contrary pairs in the exposition of the doctrine of Forms is due to rhetorical and historical advantages (such as the explanatory role of the opposites in Presocratic philosophy), not to any deep philosophical motivation.

CHAPTER 12

Phaedrus *and the limits of writing*

1. TWO INTERPRETATIONS OF THE *PHAEDRUS*

The *Phaedrus* is, in a sense, the last Socratic dialogue. Not that Socrates disappears from Plato's work; the continuity of literary form is preserved by Socrates' presence in every dialogue except the *Laws*. He plays an important and unprecedented role in the *Parmenides*; he is the principal speaker in the *Theaetetus* and also, for one last time, in the *Philebus*. The *Theaetetus* even imitates the formal pattern of an aporetic dialogue. But in comparison with earlier dialogues the portrayal of Socrates in the *Theaetetus* is rather wooden and didactic, and even more so in the *Philebus*. The *Phaedrus* is the latest work in which Plato's talent as a writer is displayed in its full intensity. It is also the work in which Plato reflects most explicitly on the role of writing in philosophy. So it is fitting that we conclude this study of Plato as author of Socratic dialogues with a consideration of the *Phaedrus*.

This dialogue occupies a unique place among Plato's literary masterpieces. It does not have the dramatic power of the *Protagoras*, *Symposium*, and *Phaedo*, or the magnificent argumentative structure of the *Republic*. But in the *Phaedrus* Plato shows himself the master of a new kind of art. First a pastoral dialogue with the charming picture of Socrates wading through a cool stream on a hot day, stretching himself on the grass in a shady spot near a shrine to the nymphs, with the music of cicadas all around in the noonday heat. This romantic description of nature is unparalleled in Plato, and rare in Greek literature. There follows a series of three speeches on love, culminating in the famous allegorical myth in which the soul is depicted as a winged charioteer with two winged horses, driving with the gods in a cavalcade beyond the heavens in order to feast itself on a beatific vision of the Forms. After these speeches on *erōs* we have a critical discussion of rhetoric and the arts of persuasion. Here Plato argues that philosophical dialectic, the systematic study of unity and plurality, provides the foundation for all rational inquiry and all successful discourse. The dialogue concludes with remarks on the function and limits of writing in philosophy. This final section is the only passage in the dialogues in which Plato overtly comments on his own work as a writer.[1]

The interpretation of the *Phaedrus* poses a number of problems, and first of all the question of unity. How, for example, is the myth of the soul with its metaphysical theory of love related to the more technical discussion of rhetoric and dialectic in what follows? It is in the *Phaedrus* that we find, probably for the first time, the notion of organic unity for a work of literary art: "every *logos* should be composed like a living creature ... so as to lack neither head nor feet, but with middle, beginning, and end written to fit with one another and with the whole work" (264c). But the dialogue itself seems to lack the unity which it recommends. It apparently falls apart into two different pieces. The speeches on love in the first half, framed by the pastoral atmosphere and by flirtatious interaction between Socrates and Phaedrus, are followed in the second half of the dialogue by a quite different kind of discourse, where the topic of love disappears from view and the personality of the interlocutors is largely submerged as Socrates assumes the role of teacher in a didactic treatment of rhetoric. In the first part we have a splendid literary vision of love and the soul, in the second part a much drier discussion of speech-making and writing. And whereas the myth of the first part is built around the doctrine of Forms as known from the *Phaedo* and *Republic*, the philosophical center of the second part is an account of dialectic that ignores the metaphysical Forms but announces a logical technique of definition by Collection and Division – by determining unities and pluralities – that will be exemplified in Plato's later writings, the *Sophist, Statesman,* and *Philebus*.

Thus the *Phaedrus* naturally appears as a kind of Janus-dialogue, like a figure with two faces looking backwards and forwards. The first half connects up with Plato's earlier work: with the tripartite psychology of the *Republic*, with the discussion of love in the *Symposium*, and with the theory of Forms. The second half looks ahead

1. There is a parallel passage in the *Seventh Epistle*, to be discussed below in §5.

to the practice of rigorous dialectic in the Academy and to Plato's literary reflection of this mode of training in the so-called dialectical dialogues. The two parts are externally connected by the use, in the second part, of the speeches of the first part as examples (*paradeigmata*) of discourse composed with and without philosophic art (*technē*). But the dialogue as a whole can be seen as marking a transitional moment in Plato's lifework as an author: his farewell in the first part to the highly wrought literary products of his early and middle periods, and in the second part his project for a new mode of writing, designed to be an image (*eidōlon*, 276A 9) of the oral practice of dialectic as carried on in his school. The division between the two parts of the *Phaedrus* will thus reflect the shift in Plato's own literary work, from the dramatic dialogue focused on the personality of Socrates to the more didactic compositions of later years, in which the figure of Socrates as master dialectician can be replaced by Parmenides and an Eleatic stranger, by Timaeus, and by an anonymous Athenian in the *Laws*.

One chief advantage of this Janus view of the *Phaedrus* is that it provides an explanation for what might otherwise be regarded as a puzzling feature of the dialogue, namely that it contains so many reminiscences of Plato's earlier work, above all in the first half.[2] Since these reminiscences are even more numerous than are recognized by the commentators, and since they provide important evidence for the self-referential character of Plato's remarks about writing, it will be worthwhile to catalogue them here.

There are several backward references in the very first words of the *Phaedrus*. The mention in the second sentence of "Lysias son of Cephalus" recalls the opening scene of the *Republic*, which takes place in the house of Cephalus with Lysias present (*Rep.* 1, 328B 4). The first speaker in the *Republic* was Lysias' brother Polemarchus; he is mentioned in the *Phaedrus* as having devoted himself to philosophy (257B 4), which I take to be a discreet allusion to the conversation in *Republic* 1. The introduction of Phaedrus himself, in the opening sentence, reminds us of the *Symposium*, where Phaedrus proposes the topic of love and makes the first speech. He enters

---

2. This dyadic view of the *Phaedrus* does not imply a mechanical division between the two parts. For example, the forward-looking definition of the soul as self-mover is found in part one (245E), whereas the backward-looking reference to the critique of rhetoric in the *Gorgias* is developed in part two (260E, 270B).

this dialogue on his way to take a walk on the advice of the physician Acumenus (227A 5), whose son Eryximachus is mentioned as Phaedrus' companion (*hetairos*) later on in our dialogue (268A 9). It is of course precisely in this role as Phaedrus' companion that Eryximachus appears in the *Symposium*. At *Phaedrus* 242B 1–3 we are reminded both of the *Symposium* and of the *Phaedo* when Socrates says to Phaedrus: "of the speeches made in your lifetime no one has caused more to be made than you, whether speaking yourself or somehow forcing others to speak – I make an exception only for Simmias of Thebes." It is questions by Simmias that provoke major expository sections of the *Phaedo*. And of course the topic of *erōs* itself recalls the *Symposium*.

These and other literary echoes serve to connect the *Phaedrus* externally with earlier works, and above all with the three great dialogues that present the theory of Forms (*Symposium, Phaedo, Republic*). There are also more substantial philosophical connections, of which the following are worth noting. (1) The implied definition of *erōs* as desire for the beautiful at 237D follows the line of *Symposium* 201Bff. (2) The tripartite psychology of the *Republic* is presupposed in the allegorical account of the psyche at 246Aff. (3) The vision of the Forms at 247C–E clearly alludes to the doctrine of *Symposium–Phaedo–Republic*. (4) The myth of Er in *Republic* X is presupposed by the otherwise enigmatic reference to the soul's "allotment and selection of a second life" at 249B 2. (5) The notion of recollection at 249Cff. develops the thought of *Phaedo* 73–6, the only other passage in Plato where the Forms are recollected. (6) The reference to a beautiful body as "named after" Beauty itself (by *epōnumia*) at 250E 3 presupposes the doctrine of *Phaedo* 102B 2, C 10ff., where the term *epōnumia* is introduced. (7) The unexpected reference to bodily pleasures following on previous pain at 258E probably echoes a passage in the *Phaedo* (60B–C) and certainly implies a theoretical development along the lines of *Republic* IX (583Cff.). (8) Finally, the mention of "telling stories (*muthologein*) about justice" at 276E and writing a political treatise (*sungramma politikon*) at 277D represent, in my opinion, an unambiguous reference to Plato's own major work in political theory, the *Republic*.

Now there are passages in other dialogues where Plato seems to be alluding to his own thoughts and words in earlier works. But I doubt whether there is any other dialogue that shows a comparable density of self-referential reminiscences. The Janus view of the *Phaedrus* takes full account of this thick cluster of backward references.

However, recent work on the *Phaedrus* by Szlezák and Rowe has shown that there is a different interpretation of the dialogue, well grounded in the text, that does more justice to its implicit claim to unity.[3] If the entire dialogue is seen as concerned with the philosophical use of language or *logos* in general and writing in particular, compositions with *technē* and without *technē* (277B 1), then the beginning and end will indeed fit together like parts of a living whole. The discussion of writing in the final section of the dialogue is prepared, from the beginning, by repeated references to books and writers (228A 2, 230D 8, 235B 8, D 6, E 5). In fact, the issue of writing is raised from the very first moment, by the emphasis on Lysias' book which Phaedrus is hiding under his cloak (228D). The first speech, read off from this book, is thus represented as the written work of someone without knowledge, the most unscientific and inartistic (*atechnos*) of literary productions. The two speeches of Socrates have some of the advantages of oral discourse: they are represented as spontaneous and unrehearsed, and upon later study they reveal the marks of a dialectical analysis, with a careful definition of love in Socrates' first speech and a more systematic display of Collection and Division in the second one. Above all, the great second speech reflects the psychological theory of the *Republic*, the metaphysical theory of Forms, and the epistemology of recollection. It thus suggests how, if challenged, the author could defend his written work by drawing upon a more fully developed background theory.

Nevertheless, even the great speech on love and the soul is after all a set speech, "delivered like the speeches of rhapsodes, for the sake of persuasion without questioning and explanation" (277E 8). It is only the dialectical discussion of part two which shows how this speech could be utilized philosophically, in a conversational context where the questions and criticisms of the audience might be answered by an author who was able to explain and defend what he had written or spoken. As it stands, Socrates' great speech is an example not of dialectic but of philosophical rhetoric, designed to show how "the art which, as normally practiced, was a tool in the hands of the designing and ambitious, is capable of

3. See Szlezák (1985) Chapter 2; Rowe (1986a).

being turned by the philosopher to the better purpose of clothing in an attractive dress the results of his more abstruse speculations; and also of stimulating the minds of his disciples."[4]

In reflecting upon writing the dialogue reflects upon itself. In describing writing as a form of play (*paidia*) Plato calls attention to the playful elements in this as in other dialogues. And at the end of what appears to be a serious philosophical discussion of speaking and writing, Socrates says: "we have now played enough with this subject" (*pepaisthō metriōs hēmin ta peri logōn*, 278B 7). Here the written dialogue recognizes its own limitations. Plato carefully avoids the paradox of providing a written demonstration of the superiority of oral dialectic. The dialogue merely outlines, but does not attempt to exemplify, the fuller dialectical treatment that would be required for any adequate philosophical account of teaching and persuasion.

So much for a second interpretation of the *Phaedrus*. On our first view it is a transitional piece, one half looking backward to Plato's earlier work and to the theme of *erōs* developed in the Socratic literature, the other half looking forward to the dialectical methods of later dialogues. But the second interpretation treats the *Phaedrus* as a unified whole, devoted to the theme of the philosophical use of language. Different as they are, these two views are fully compatible with one another. The second interpretation looks only at the *Phaedrus*; the first interpretation locates the *Phaedrus* in relation to the rest of Plato's literary work. The two views converge on the role of writing in philosophy.

2. PLATO AS A COMMENTATOR ON HIS OWN WORK

If we take seriously the backward- and forward-looking aspects of the *Phaedrus*, we may expect Plato's reflections on writing to provide not only a comment on his own work but also some explanation for the very striking change in his mode of writing: his giving up the Socratic dialogue in the broadest sense, including works like the *Symposium* and *Phaedo*, in favor of a new, more technical kind of philosophical writing. The change is marked externally by the fact that not only does the personal portrayal of Socrates be-

---

4. W. H. Thompson (1868), xviii, quoted by Rowe (1986b) 109.

come less vivid and lifelike, but Socrates himself can be replaced as chief speaker, for example, by a visitor from Elea. These formal changes are accompanied by a more profound literary transformation, from highly readable works that belong among the masterpieces of European literature to difficult, technical discussion of philosophical problems in a crabbed, intricate style, where the conversational form often seems an artificial mask for what is essentially a didactic exposition. In the *Timaeus* this mask is finally dropped, and the dialogue assumes the form of an uninterrupted treatise. Let us look more closely at the reasons alleged by Plato for regarding any written work as inferior to the spoken word, to see if they can help us understand this radical transformation of his own literary activity.

Like a set speech that is not followed by questions from the audience, a written work can persuade but it cannot teach, that is, it cannot impart knowledge (276c 9). It is like a painting that seems to be alive, but remains silent if one asks it a question. A set speech or written work is equally unable to respond to questions; it simply repeats the same message each time it is interrogated (275D). Let us call this the failure of clarification. The second defect of a book is that it cannot adapt itself to the level of the audience: "once written, it tumbles about everywhere, and behaves the same among those who understand and among those who have no notion of the subject, and it does not know how to speak and to whom, and to whom it should remain silent" (275E 1–3). Call this the failure of adaptability. Together these two failures are what Plato has in mind when he denounces the naiveté of an author or reader who thinks there can be anything clear (*saphes*) and secure or reliable (*bebaion*) in a written work in philosophy (275c 6; cf. 277D 8–9). The clarity of a written text is only skin deep; it cannot dispel the misconceptions or confusions that arise in the mind of the reader.

In referring to the lack of stability or reliability, however, Plato is pointing to something else. In order to produce knowledge and understanding in the mind of his reader or hearer, the speaker or author must do more than avoid being misunderstood. He must be able to explain and justify his claims by a fuller argument, that is, by deriving them from more fundamental principles. In the language of the *Meno*, knowledge requires the bond of a rational, explanatory account (*aitias logismos*, 98A 3). The *Republic* goes further:

to achieve knowledge and understanding (*noēsis*) we must reach a universal principle that lies beyond or behind all assumptions (*archē anhupothetos*, *Rep.* VI, 510B 7). It must be something of this sort Plato has in mind in the *Phaedrus* when he claims that the philosopher who is author of a political treatise, "if he has knowledge of the truth, will be able to defend his writings when he is challenged to a test (*elenchos*), and will by his own arguments be able to show that what he has written is inferior" to the oral practice of dialectic, because he possesses "something more valuable (*timiōtera*) than his writings" (278C–D), namely, his dialectical mastery of the relevant subject matter.[5]

The language of Plato's self-description here as author of a political treatise calls to mind the requirement he places on the dialectician in the *Republic*: "He who is not able to define in argument (*logos*) the Form of the Good and distinguish it from all other things, as it were in combat pursuing his way through all tests (*elenchoi*), eager to examine the question according to the nature of the case and not according to opinion, and who cannot come through all these tests with his reasoning (*logos*) undefeated, you will say of such a one that he knows neither the Good itself nor any good thing, but if he grasps some image, he grasps it with opinion and not with knowledge" (*Rep.* VII, 534B–C).

Although the description of dialectical method is quite different in the *Republic* and the *Phaedrus*, the position of the dialectician is essentially the same. To put the thesis of the *Phaedrus* in the language of the *Republic*, the conviction that writing produces is inevitably opinion (*doxa*), not knowledge. To help the reader towards knowledge the written word must point beyond itself, to the living practice of philosophy that Plato calls dialectic. And the limits of writing, so explicitly indicated in the *Phaedrus*, are clearly implied in the *Republic* as well. For example, one of the things that the *Phaedrus* requires but does not provide is a psychological theory, an account of whether the psyche is "one and uniform in nature or multiform like the body" (271A 6). The *Republic* supplies us with such an account, but it does so only with a proviso: our present procedures, says Socrates, will never give us an accurate treat-

---

5. Here I am in general agreement with the view of Szlezák (1985), except that I do not believe that *timiōtera* at 278D 8 refers to any particular body of knowledge or any specific formulation of first principles.

ment; "it is a different, longer and harder way that leads to that goal."[6]

This is the first of several warnings in the *Republic* that for an adequate treatment of difficult matters one must refer to the practice of dialectic itself, which the *Republic* does not attempt to describe. For the psyche Plato offers a rudimentary theory; for the Good he offers only an image. "Let us leave alone for the present the question of what is the Good itself. To give my present view of this seems to me a greater work than our current effort can reach" (vi, 506E). And so when he is asked later for a detailed description of dialectic, Socrates replies: "Dear Glaucon, you would no longer be able to follow, though for my part there would be no lack of willingness. But you would no longer be looking at an image of what we are talking about but at the truth itself ... And what we insist upon is that only the power of dialectic could show this [and only] to one who is trained in the studies we have described; there is no other way" (vii, 533A).

Dialectic is a more difficult road than the philosophical exposition of the *Republic*; it is the "longer way round" twice referred to in the *Republic* (vi, 504B 2, c 9) and twice echoed in the *Phaedrus* (272D 3, 274A 2). Instead of describing dialectic the *Republic* specifies only its prerequisites (in the prolonged study of mathematics), its technique (question and answer), and its goal (the knowledge of essence or *what a thing truly is*, and ultimately a knowledge of *what the Good is*). The *Phaedrus* goes a step further in sketching the methods of Collection and Division. But both works make clear that the thing itself lies outside the dialogue and, the *Phaedrus* adds, beyond the reach of any written work.

Because of its concern with discourse and teaching, the *Phaedrus* tells us more. It specifies that for teaching to result in knowledge, that is, for the living word to be planted like a fertile seed in the soul of the learner, the following conditions must be satisfied: (1) knowledge of the subject matter on the part of the teacher, whether speaker or writer, (2) an appropriate audience, (3) a discourse adapted to the character and intellect of the audience, and

6. *Rep.* iv, 435D 3, repeated at vi, 504B–D. In Book x Plato hints at a more adequate psychology, that could determine whether the soul is really "multiform or uniform" (612A 4), with a clear indication that the tripartite theory does not account for the true nature of the psyche (611Bff.). The same problem is alluded to at *Phaedrus* 230A.

(4) the opportunity for clarification and justification by means of question and answer.

From Plato's own point of view, in the case of his writing only the first condition is actually satisfied: Plato as author will naturally assume that he has the requisite intellectual command of the subject matter. But the situation is quite different for the other conditions. Like any author of a written work, Plato cannot select his audience and hence cannot adapt his presentation to a specific audience, just as he obviously cannot respond to questions from the audience. However, these three conditions can be represented, or "imitated," by Plato's use of the dialogue form, in which Socrates does in fact present material differently to different interlocutors. What this form indicates, as a treatise or essay does not, is that human access to the truth is inevitably partial and perspectival, dependent upon the standpoint of the inquirer. In the dialogue form this perspectival condition is reflected in the fact that philosophical discourse takes place in an interaction between two or more persons, the minimum case of which is an interaction between teacher and learner. That is presumably why Plato maintains the dialogue form even in his later works, where the interlocutor is often a docile learner.

3. THE SHIFT IN THE LITERARY CHARACTER OF THE DIALOGUES

I want now to apply this theoretical analysis to the dialogues themselves, and to the contrast between the Socratic works (broadly understood) and the later dialogues. I suggest that this radical shift in dialogue type, foreshadowed in the dichotomous structure of the *Phaedrus*, signifies no fundamental change in Plato's conception of philosophy nor in his views concerning knowledge and reality. What is new is a different notion of philosophical writing corresponding to a different choice of the audience for whom the dialogues are intended. And this rhetorical shift on the author's part is reflected within the dialogues by his selection and characterization of the interlocutors. Phaedrus is perhaps the last non-philosopher to appear as a dialogue speaker until we reach Plato's latest and most "practical" work, the *Laws*. On the other hand in the *Parmenides, Theaetetus, Sophist, Statesman, Timaeus,* and *Philebus* –

in the six dialogues which, I suppose, directly follow the *Phaedrus* – Plato can deploy rigorous argument and elaborate technical method, because he has interlocutors whose interests are genuinely philosophical. Among earlier works only the *Phaedo* and the central books of the *Republic* are at all comparable. In the latter case Plato's brothers, in the former the two Thebans Simmias and Cebes participate, in effect, as promising young graduate students in philosophy. And it is no accident that these are the two contexts in which the theory of Forms is most fully discussed. The intellectual tone here, as in the later dialogues, is almost that of a philosophy seminar. How different is the urbane and at the end rowdy party atmosphere of the *Symposium,* the elaborate public contest of the *Protagoras,* the passionate moral conflicts of the *Gorgias* and *Republic* 1, the quibbling of the *Euthydemus,* the stubbornness of Meno or the fanaticism of Euthyphro.

If we assume that Plato's practice, throughout his literary career, corresponds *grosso modo* to the rhetorical theory of the *Phaedrus,* it follows that the philosophical content of each dialogue is adapted to the personality and understanding of the interlocutors. With this in mind it is easy to see that much of Plato's work, from the *Laches, Charmides,* and *Protagoras* to the *Meno* and *Symposium,* can be conceived as a sustained protreptic to philosophy. As the choice of interlocutors indicates, Plato's intended audience for these dialogues includes not only professional philosophers and beginners in philosophy but also the general public, and in particular the young men in search of themselves, in search of knowledge, or in search of a career, men who in the fifth century would have sat at the feet of the sophists and who in Plato's own day might be tempted by the lessons of Isocrates or Antisthenes. To attract these young men and to assure Socratic philosophy a place of honor and respect within Greek culture as a whole, Plato employed his talents lavishly to create a vivid, imposing portrait of Socrates, in works of such high literary quality that they would be guaranteed a broad and on the whole sympathetic audience. (Another, less strictly philosophical motive for Plato's early-middle compositions must have been his loving memory of Socrates and a desire to bring him back to life in the pages of these dialogues. This is, I take it, what Plato means by "treasuring up reminders for himself against the forgetfulness of age, and for anyone else who follows

the same track" [276D], that is, for other friends of Socrates or
members of the Academy. It is clearly Plato as author who is
speaking here, not Socrates.)

The *Phaedrus* is perhaps the last work that Plato designed for this
wider public. Here, as at the end of the *Tempest*, the magician
breaks his wand and embarks on a new course. The *Parmenides* and
Theaetetus, which belong in the same stylistic group and may have
followed soon afterwards, are works of philosophy written for philosophers. Plato's dramatic gifts are once again displayed, more
economically and perhaps for the last time, in the introduction to
these two otherwise formidably technical works. The *Sophist* and
Statesman are subsequently composed to illustrate the collections
and divisions described in the *Phaedrus*: here we have the written
image of the new dialectic. But both of these austere dialogues
occasionally practice definition by dichotomy in a strangely frivolous or even comic vein, in order to remind us of the aspect of
playfulness that the *Phaedrus* insists is inseparable from the written
work of a serious philosopher.

Thus the *Phaedrus'* strictures on writing apply to all of Plato's
work: retrospectively to the "Socratic" dialogues and prospectively
to the later, more didactic compositions. No doubt the sixty-year-
old author of the *Phaedrus* has had more occasion to reflect upon
the role of writing than when he composed the *Crito* and the *Ion* in
his earlier years. But his early practice is compatible with his later
theory. In view of the fact that Socrates, his model philosopher,
wrote nothing, Plato must have been attentive from the beginning
to the problematic status of writing within a Socratic conception
of philosophy. The existence of the Socratic dialogue gave Plato a
natural opportunity for his literary gifts; he was in the course of
time able to transform this modest genre into a high art form and
the perfect vehicle for his own conception of philosophy. But the
more philosophical content he poured into the dialogue form, the
more acute became his sense of limitations. Hence the warnings in
Republic IV–VII, and the fuller explanation of these limitations in
the *Phaedrus*.

If this view is correct, the author and his conception of writing
remain essentially the same for the Socratic and for the later dialogues; it is only the target audience that changes. But Plato's
conception of writing is scarcely separable from his conception of
philosophy. So our conclusion has interesting implications for the

apparent development or revision of the theory of Forms in the later dialogues and the relation of all this to the "unwritten doctrines." Plato's later philosophy is a formidable topic that could be properly treated only in another long book. I offer here a sketch of what I take to be the lines of continuity in Plato's work as a whole.

4. PHILOSOPHY AND DOCTRINE

For Plato philosophy is essentially a form of life and not a set of doctrines. Socrates could serve as model for the philosophic life because (in Plato's eyes) he was wholly committed to a life of strenuous search and inquiry, summed up in the phrase "the unexamined life is not worth living" (*Apology* 38A). Philosophical inquiry means a search for knowledge and truth in regard to the most fundamental issues: the nature of reality, the nature of human beings, the principles of right and wrong, and the structure of the good life. Because Socrates investigated many if not all of these questions, depicting his conversations can serve as a depiction of the philosophic life.

So much is likely to be common ground. Controversy begins when we ask: what role do doctrines or teachings play in the life of philosophy? What is it that the philosopher *knows*? Does the search for knowledge involve finding firm answers to questions, definitive solutions to problems? Or does it involve unending search? These questions were first raised in Hellenistic debates between skeptics and dogmatists; both sides tried to enlist Socrates and Plato among their supporters. Concerning Socrates I emphasized in Chapter 3 our lack of reliable documentation for any teachings that go beyond the familiar paradoxes. For Plato there is a larger story to tell. What follows is a summary of what I take Plato's position to be.

A coherent life of inquiry implies a commitment to finding the truth; one may or may not succeed, but inquiry means *trying* to find the truth. This effort presupposes the conviction that there is something there to be found, something independent of the search itself. If grasping the truth is at least part of what we mean by knowledge, then rational knowledge is possible only if there is something with a rational structure "out there," waiting to be grasped and known. In the language of the *Theaetetus*, knowledge entails truth and truth entails Being (*ousia, to on*), that is, that things are really so-and-so, that they exist in some determinate way rather than in other ways.[7] And this holds for the knowledge of right and wrong and the knowledge of what is good: there is something definite that is the case, something there to be known.

So ontological realism in a rather strong sense, including realism about the good and the beautiful, is inseparable from the philosophic life as Plato conceives it. But Platonism implies something much more specific about the kind of things there are for us to know. From early on, Plato's conception of philosophy is guided by a strong metaphysical vision. The objects of knowledge in a strict sense are not the objects of ordinary experience. Plato never gives up the otherworldly vision of reality that he presented in the *Symposium* as the teaching of Diotima, developed in the *Phaedo* in Socrates' characterization of philosophy as a preparation for death, and confirmed in the *Republic* by the allegory of the Cave, where ordinary human experience is represented by the prisoners who sit in darkness. Whatever developments and revisions may appear in later dialogues, the basic scheme of metaphysical and epistemic dualism is everywhere presupposed.

Since this claim is no longer non-controversial, I must say more. By Platonic dualism I mean the radical distinction between Being and Becoming, between eternal realities that remain unchanged and variable appearances that come and go. The former are accessible to knowledge and rational understanding (*nous*) strictly conceived; the latter are the objects of ordinary human experience, that is, of sense perception and opinion. This is not a dualism that Plato ever gives up. The *Philebus*, like the *Timaeus*, expressly contrasts the range of entities that come to be and perish with those entities "that are forever one and the same, admitting neither coming-to-be nor passing away" (*Phil.* 15A–B; cf. *Tim.* 27D 6–28A 4). The same ontological dualism underlies the account of dialectic in the *Statesman*. In this relatively late work dialectic is still recognized as the only mode of access to "the greatest and most precious" and most beautiful of entities, which are incorporeal

---

7. See *Theaetetus* 185C–186D. For the interpretation of οὐσία/εῖναι here as "being so," including existence, predication, and truth claim or assertion, see Kahn (1981).

and not available to the senses.[8] Even in a dialogue like the *Sophist*, where the critical distance from Plato's own theory is unusually great, we find clear allusions to this basic duality.[9] And although the metaphysics of invariant Being is scrupulously excluded from the *Theaetetus*, Plato's otherworldly vision is nowhere more strikingly expressed than in Socrates' outburst in that dialogue about escaping from the evils of this mortal life by "assimilation to the divine."

I conclude that Plato never wavers in his metaphysical vision. The reality which is the object of the philosopher's quest is always located in the unseen world of eternal, invariant Being, to be grasped only by rational discussion and intellectual understanding. It is true that, for particular purposes in individual dialogues, Plato will deliberately withhold mention of his larger metaphysical commitments. Thus the *Theaetetus* attempts (unsuccessfully) to define knowledge without reference to invariant Forms. And by introducing a Stranger from Elea as chief interlocutor in the *Sophist* Plato manages to establish a perspective as it were from outside his own school, so that the Platonic theory of Forms can be subjected to critical scrutiny, as one account of Being among others.[10] In a similar shift of perspective the terms *eidos* and *idea*, which serve in the middle dialogues to designate metaphysical Forms, are used in the later dialectic (from the *Phaedrus* on) as if they represented logical concepts or classes of things, without any strong metaphysical claim.

This extraordinary flexibility, both in language and in theoretical perspective, is a unique feature of Plato's work. I suggest that such systematic variation in the written expression of his thought

8. *Statesman* 285E 4–286A 7. Similarly in *Philebus* 58A 2, dialectic as the truest form of knowledge is concerned with true, invariant reality (περὶ τὸ ὂν καὶ τὸ ὄντως καὶ τὸ κατὰ ταὐτὸν ἀεὶ πεφυκὸς πάντως). See also *Philebus* 59A 7–C4, D4, 61E 1–3.

9. Thus "the darkness of not-being," in which the sophist takes refuge, is contrasted with the dazzling brightness of the region where the philosophical dialectician makes contact with "the form (*idea*) of eternal Being" (*Soph.* 253E–254A).

10. The "Eleatic" critique of the Forms in the *Sophist* continues, of course, the critical attitude introduced by Parmenides himself. But whereas the objections of the *Parmenides* can be seen as directed against a particular formulation of the theory (and one defended only by a very young Socrates), the view assigned to the Friends of Forms at *Sophist* 246B and 248A asserts the basic dualism which I take to be the distinctive feature of Plato's own position.

reflects Plato's view of the perspectival condition of human discourse and cognition, while at the same time representing his conception of dialectic as a discursive method for moving beyond any
and all conditions, in the attempt to gain access to a level of knowledge that is unconditioned. If so, it is surely a mistake to interpret
these frequent shifts in dialectical perspective as if they reflected
fundamental changes in Plato's philosophical position. On the contrary, it would seem that for Plato a shifting point of view is the
inevitable condition for any human grasp and, above all, for any
literary expression of an insight into unchanging reality.

On this interpretation, the variation in Plato's account of the
Forms reflects not merely his distrust of the written word, but his
deeper sense of the human condition as one in which the rational
soul's access to reality is limited by its incarnation and its con-
tinual involvement in sense perception, so that what we say and
think about intelligible reality is inevitably permeated by appearance and opinion (*doxa*). That is why there is not, and there cannot
be, any fully adequate, definitive statement of Plato's conception
of Forms. There can only be a variety of perspectively conditioned, context-dependent formulations.

This is not to deny the doctrinal significance of some of Plato's
changes in formulations. After the criticism of the *Parmenides*, for
example, Plato will abandon the concept of participation as an
account of the relation between sensible appearance and Forms.
Instead, in the *Sophist*, he makes use of participation solely for a
relation between Forms. The *Sophist* also introduces other substantive innovations, such as a concern for locating life, soul, and
reason among realities, and an insistence on recognizing change
(*kinēsis*) itself as a mode of being or reality (249B 2, D 4).

This new emphasis on the ontological status of life and soul is
reflected in the *Timaeus* by Plato's description of the model for
creation as an Intelligible Living Thing (*zōion noēton*). And so the
first item to be created is a cosmic Soul, a generated but invisible
entity, which moves itself in eternally invariant circular motion. In
the *Timaeus* the conception of nature as the work of divine artistry,
together with the recognition of Space or extension as the Receptacle for Becoming, represents a radical reshaping of the view
of how eternal Forms are related to a changing, sensible world.

Nevertheless, these innovations are all worked out within the
wider framework of the Being–Becoming dichotomy. If the onto-

logical status of the rational psyche (both cosmic and personal) is problematic, that is because it is at once a non-sensible object of reason and also, by definition, a self-mover. We see that in this case the distinction between Being and Becoming is apparently neither exclusive nor exhaustive. For Plato the soul constitutes an intermediate realm between eternity and mortality – a paradoxical view that is symbolically expressed in the myth of reincarnation, and in the strange mixing process by which the World Soul is created in the *Timaeus*. But this mediating role for the psyche is defined precisely by its position *in between* invariant Being and sensible Becoming.

In the development of Plato's political theory from the *Republic* to the *Laws*, we can trace a similar pattern of continuity and change within a stable theoretical framework. Although in his latest work Plato abandons the rule of philosopher-kings for the rule of law, and readmits the traditional family with its private property, he clearly regards this solution as a second best. At the level of ideal theory, his vision of the best form of government remains unchanged.[11]

As I see it, the same is true for Plato's metaphysical stance. If by the theory of Forms we mean a commitment to the general metaphysical framework described here as Platonic dualism, together with a conception of knowledge as access to a kind of reality that is essentially different from the ordinary objects of human perception, then there is no reason to suppose that Plato ever gave up such a theory or even considered giving it up. If, on the other hand, we mean by the theory of Forms the doctrine of participation as formulated in the *Phaedo* or in the introductory section of the *Parmenides*, then it is clear that Plato was not happy with this formulation and that in the *Timaeus* he has replaced it with something quite different.

Today the term "metaphysical realism" is sometimes used for a view that assumes that there is or could be some uniquely true description of reality, some definitive formula (whether in language or in thought) for the way the world is. In this rather special sense of the term, Plato is probably not to be counted as a metaphysical realist. Every formulation of Plato's theory is provisional; no statement will be the final account. We recall that the doctrine

---

11. For a fuller statement of this point, see Kahn (1995).

of Forms is presented in the *Phaedo* as an assumption or hypothesis, and that the discussion ends with Socrates' call to investigate further "the primary *hypotheseis*" (107B 5). The *Republic* offers us the prospect of a first principle beyond hypothesis (511B), but it does not venture to formulate such a principle. No doubt in oral discussion with a more specialized audience, Plato as the master of philosophical *logos* could make use of more technical language as the appropriate rhetorical device to be addressed to such an audience. The *agrapha dogmata* that Aristotle reports concerning the One and the indeterminate Dyad must represent some discussion of this kind.

If the unwritten doctrines are understood in this way, as an advanced but still provisional formulation, a kind of code or cipher for the ongoing attempt to comprehend the unity and plurality of things, then by definition they go beyond anything in the written corpus, which is frozen in place and can make no further progress towards understanding. But if these *dogmata* are taken as dogma, as definitive formulae of knowledge, direct depictions of intelligible reality, then they suffer from the same defects as written statements naively understood. The mistake of the esoteric interpretation of Plato is to suppose that the "unwritten doctrines" might be written down without losing their advantage over what we find in the dialogues. In the statement of first principles as in other statements, writing deprives philosophic thought of its natural life and motion, of its opportunity for continued clarification, correction, and justification. Once Aristotle writes down the unwritten doctrines, what he writes down is just one more inadequate sketch, one more unsatisfactory image of the goal and target of the philosophic life.

5. THE *SEVENTH EPISTLE* AND THE LIMITS OF LANGUAGE

At first sight the *Seventh Epistle* seems to express a mistrust of language more radical than anything we find in the *Phaedrus*. Whereas the *Phaedrus* deplores the limitations of the written word in philosophy and insists upon the superiority of oral teaching, the *Seventh Letter* launches a more general attack on the weakness of language as such (343A 1) and denounces speaking and writing in the same breath (341D 5, 343D 4–7). The *Letter* seems to imply that the most important philosophical insights are essentially incommunicable:

they are "not at all statable like other kinds of knowledge."[12] This
suggestion of ineffability has appeared to many observers to reveal
a streak of mysticism in the author of the *Letter* that is wholly incompatible with the commitment to reasoned discourse, to *logos*,
that is so characteristic of the dialogues.

I maintain that this appearance is incorrect, and that the description of dialectical training in the *Letter* is essentially equivalent
to the teaching of the *Phaedrus, Republic,* and *Parmenides.* What follows immediately upon the description of this kind of knowledge
as "not stable" is the further explanation that understanding
comes instead "after long intercourse with the subject and a shared
life" between teacher and pupil (341c 5–7). And the sequel makes
clear that the shared life is a life of *logos*: only after prolonged
training with words, definitions (*logoi*), examples and perceptions,
"making use of questions and answers in friendly tests and refutations (*elenchoi*) without ill will" can the subject be illumined by
reason and understanding (*phronēsis* and *nous*) as far as is humanly
possible (344B). We recognize here a new description of that long
process of philosophic training that leads to the vision of the Form
of the Good in the *Republic*, the kind of training that Parmenides
says will be required before anyone can give a proper account of
the Forms (*Parm.* 135c–d).

But if Plato's conception of dialectic is essentially the same in
the *Letter* as in the dialogues, why is he so much more sceptical here
about the vehicle of language as such, so much more insistent upon
the inherent vagueness and instability of words (343A–C)?[13] Note
that the two reproaches are the same here as in the *Phaedrus* – lack
of stability (*to bebaion*) and lack of clarity (*to saphes*) – directed now
at words in general, but above all at words "in unchangeable
form, as happens when things are written down" (343A 3). The *appearance* of stability is doubly deceptive; hence the written word is
the greater culprit. But the spoken word is in principle subject to
the same kind of limitations.

Could the aging philosopher have become more disillusioned
about his success in oral teaching? Perhaps so; but there is really

---

12. 341c 5: ῥητὸν γὰρ οὐδαμῶς ἐστιν ὡς ἄλλα μαθήματα.
13. The weakness of language (τὸ τῶν λόγων ἀσθενές) is unable to express the
    essence or whatness of things without expressing their quality (τὸ ποῖόν τι)
    as well (342E 3–343A 1).

no need to resort here to biographical conjecture. First of all, precisely because of his acute sensitivity to the seductions of language, Plato never likes to repeat himself exactly, and we must always be ready to find him expressing old thoughts in a new form. And in this case there is an obvious reason in the context of the *Letter* for him to emphasize the fallibility of *oral* as well as written communication. He is referring to Dionysius and others who have claimed to understand Plato's philosophy from hearing him expound it in person. To undermine all such claims Plato is obliged to insist upon the limitations of oral explanation as such, in a way that was not required by his discussion in the *Phaedrus*, which was designed specifically to subordinate the role of reading and writing in philosophy to the role of systematic training with an expert teacher. And it is precisely this kind of training which in the *Letter* is said to produce, under favorable conditions, the "leaping flame which kindles in the soul of the learner a fire that is able from then on to nourish itself" (341D 1).

I conclude, then, that the *Seventh Letter* does not contradict but only supplements what is said about the limits of language in the *Phaedrus*. But by generalizing these limitations to the spoken word, the *Letter* does raise the issue of ineffability and the specter of mysticism. To what extent does Plato actually mean that philosophic truth is ineffable?

By mysticism here I understand two things. One is the claim that the most important truths and insights cannot be communicated in language; the second is the claim that the highest human cognitive experience and deepest contact with reality is essentially non-rational or trans-rational, beyond the reach of intellectual understanding. The first claim may plausibly be derived from the second, but it is also possible to construe the two claims as independent of one another. (Thus one might deny the capacity of language properly to express an insight that is nevertheless fully rational, as, on one interpretation, Wittgenstein does for his own theory of meaning in the *Tractatus*. And, on the other hand, one might claim that trans-rational, mystical experience can be expressed in poetry, music, or dancing, but not in sober discourse.) The supreme example of philosophical mysticism in which these two claims are essentially linked is the system of Plotinus, whose notion of being "oned" with the One transcends all rational understanding and, *a fortiori*, all rational discourse. For Plotinus, discursive thought and language have the radical defect of introducing plurality of all kinds, including the fundamental distinction between thinking subject and object of thought. But for Plotinus it is precisely this distinction that has to be overcome in the experience of oneness.

I submit that in Plato's thought there is nothing mystical in this strong sense. The flame that leaps from one soul to another is not a trance experience nor the result of silent meditation, but the light of understanding that dawns after much rational discussion and explanation. Nowhere does Plato attempt to blur or transcend the distinction between knowing subject and the object known: psyche and *nous* are everywhere sharply distinguished from the Forms or, in the terminology of the *Seventh Epistle*, from the "fifth thing, which is knowable and truly real (*on*)" (342B 1). And the path to understanding such reality is wholly rational. It leads by way of mathematics and *dialegesthai*, the conversational analysis of unities and pluralities, essences and kinds.

The fact that Plato persists in calling the highest form of knowledge by a name that properly refers to linguistic communication, *dialegesthai*, is, I submit, conclusive evidence that he does not regard such knowledge as essentially ineffable. But Plato is painfully aware of how easy it is for a thinker to be misunderstood, whether in writing or in speaking. To some extent Plato's frustration with language has its roots in the experience which every writer and lecturer has had, of seeing how completely an audience can misconstrue one's most carefully chosen words. There is also the writer's sense of the gap between thought and expression, the sense that he or she has not succeeded in communicating just what they had in mind. The more profoundly original the thinker, the graver this problem will be. Bergson has given us a vivid account of the frustrations felt by a philosopher-author in the expression of his own ideas. Speaking of the philosophies of Berkeley and Spinoza but clearly with his own work in view, Bergson suggests that, when one penetrates to the inner unity of a complex philosophical system, the thought of the philosopher seems then to be concentrated in a single point.

In this point there is something simple, infinitely simple, so extraordinarily simple that the philosopher has never succeeded in saying it. And that is why he went on talking all his life. He could not formulate what he had in mind without feeling obliged to correct his formulation, then to correct his correction ... Thus all the complexity of his doctrine, which could go on *ad infinitum,* is only the incommensurability between his simple intuition and the means at his disposal for expressing it.[14]

Plato would presumably not share Bergson's notion of philosophical intuition. But he would, I think, share this sense of incommensurability between the simple clarity and certainty of his philosophical vision and the imprecision and ambiguity of even its finest literary presentation.

But for Plato there is something more. Words and sentences, whether written or spoken, belong to the sensible realm, the realm of Becoming. And there is only an arbitrary connection between words and what they denote.[15] Even the *meanings* of words, insofar as these are contained in human thought, belong to what Plato in the *Letter* calls the fourth factor: "knowledge and reason (*nous*) and true belief ... which are present not in sounds nor in bodily shapes but in souls" (342c). Although they are neither bodily nor visible, such thoughts are nevertheless caught up in a kind of Heraclitean flux, by virtue of being present in a mortal human soul.

So language is subject to this double liability. There is, first of all, no firm correlation between words and things, or between words and thoughts. And secondly, the best human thoughts are still perspectival and still ontologically defective by comparison with the unchanging timeless reality of the Forms. Hence the nature of reality, the nature of "true Being," is imperfectly reflected in our thought, and still more imperfectly expressed in our words.[16]

This is, I think, metaphysics and not mysticism. Call it what you will, it is the doctrine of the *Seventh Epistle.* And this doctrine, which represents Plato's final reflection on his own work as writer and as teacher, is in my view fully compatible both with the teaching and with the literary practice of the dialogues.

---

14. Bergson (1960) 119: "En ce point est quelque chose de simple, d'infiniment simple, de si extraordinairement simple que le philosophe n'a jamais réussi à le dire. Et c'est pourquoi il a parlé toute sa vie. Il ne pouvait formuler ce qu'il avait dans l'esprit sans se sentir obligé de corriger sa formule, puis de corriger sa correction ... Toute la complexité de sa doctrine, qui irait à l'infini, n'est donc que l'incommensurabilité entre son intuition simple et les moyens dont il disposait pour l'exprimer."

15. *Epistle* VII 343B.

16. See Friedländer (1958) 118–25 for a treatment of Plato's attitude to his own written work that is essentially in sympathy with the view presented here.

Appendix. On Xenophon's use of Platonic texts

In Chapter 3 §3 we examine a text concerning dialectic in *Memorabilia* IV.5–6 where the influence of Plato is, I believe, unmistakable. But this is not an isolated case. I consider here a number of parallel texts to demonstrate how pervasive is Xenophon's dependence on Platonic material.

The importance of this Platonic influence on Xenophon must not be exaggerated. His use of Platonic texts is essentially superficial, almost cosmetic in nature. Xenophon seems to have had no real sympathy with Plato's portrayal of Socrates. Thus his *Symposium*, though no doubt inspired by Plato's dialogue and largely devoted to the same theme, is as different from that work in tone and substance as anything one can well imagine. As von Fritz pointed out, it would be a mistake to think of Xenophon as trying to *compete* with Plato; he simply rejects and hence ignores the spiritualized view of Socrates that Plato presents.[1] In Antisthenes and Aeschines, on the other hand, Xenophon found more congenial representations of Socrates that he could to some extent absorb into his own portrayal.

A full study of the parallels between Xenophon and Plato would call for a separate monograph. What follows makes no claim to completeness. I simply note some eight or ten passages from the *Memorabilia* where the direct literary dependence of Xenophon upon Plato seems to me at least probable, and two from the *Symposium* where it seems certain.

1. (*Mem.* 1.6.14)

As for myself, just as someone else takes pleasure in a good horse or dog or bird, in the same way and even more so do I take pleasure in good friends.

1. von Fritz (1935) 19–45, esp. 43ff.

This is an unmistakable, in part verbatim echo of *Lysis* 211D–E, where horse, dog, and bird are all mentioned in a similar comparison. But the context is quite different, and Xenophon's discussion of friendship makes no real use of Plato's dialogue.

2. (II.6.6)

We do not judge a sculptor by his words (*logoi*), but when we see that he has already produced good statues, we have confidence in him and in his producing good work in the future.

This is closely related to the thought of *Laches* 185Eff. that the possession of a *technē* is to be revealed in the quality of the work produced. Verbatim agreement is limited to a single word (*pisteusai*), and one might perhaps think of this as a Socratic commonplace.[2] (Compare a similar passage at *Mem.* IV.2.12, in 5 below.)

3. (III.9.1–6) This is perhaps the most important passage in the *Mem.* for detailed use of a Platonic dialogue, namely the *Protagoras*. III.9 begins with the question whether courage is teachable or natural. (In the *Protagoras* the question of teachability is raised for virtue generally, but the final discussion focuses on courage.) After assigning a reasonable answer to Socrates ("human beings differ by nature, but training and practice can be decisive"),[3] Xenophon proceeds:

He made no distinction between wisdom (*sophia*) and temperance (*sōphrosunē*), but he judged that to know what is good and noble and do it, and to know what is shameful and avoid it, is both wise and temperate. (III.9.4)[4]

This is a free, slightly confused variation on *Prot.* 332A–333B, where Socrates argues for the identity of *sophia* and *sōphrosunē* by showing that they have the same opposite, namely folly (*aphrosunē*). There seems to be an echo of this argument from the opposite in Xenophon's sequel at III.9.6: "He said that madness (*mania*) was the opposite of wisdom, but he did not identify madness with lack of

2. Gigon (1956) 130f. notes the *Laches* parallel and asks "should we suppose a common source?" But that reflects his idiosyncratic refusal to recognize Xenophon's use of material from Plato.

3. Cf. *Protagoras* 351B 1–2.

4. The text is problematic, but this is roughly the sense. Delatte (1933: 113) translates: "He judged both wise and temperate the man who knows good and noble things to practice and shameful things to avoid."

knowledge (*anepistēmosunē*)." Xenophon's primary concern, however, is a somewhat unsuccessful attempt to render the central thesis of the *Protagoras*:

> He said that justice and all the rest of virtue was wisdom. For just deeds and all actions of virtue are noble and good. And men who know these things will choose nothing else instead, and men who do not have this knowledge are unable to act [virtuously], but even if they try, they fail [or make mistakes, *hamartanein*]. (III.9.5)

It seems that the theory of motivation here is intended to be the theory of rational choice (everyone prefers what is better, and of two evils no one chooses the greater) that Socrates develops at *Protagoras* 358c 7–d 4. This is Xenophon's major attempt to produce his own version of the Socratic connection between virtue and knowledge, but he does not carry the thought very far.[5]

4. (III.9.8) Immediately following the passages just quoted, which almost certainly draw on the *Protagoras*, Xenophon apparently makes use of a much later Platonic dialogue, the *Philebus*.

> In inquiring what envy (or malice, *phthonos*) is, Socrates discovered it to be a kind of pain, but neither pain at the misfortunes of one's friends nor at the good fortune of one's enemies; he said that only those feel envy (or malice) who are grieved at their friends' successes. (III.9.8)

This bit of psychological insight sounds like a correction of Plato's rather artificial discussion of *phthonos* in the *Philebus*, where it is defined as a mixture of pleasure and pain felt in the misfortunes of one's neighbors (48b 11) or one's friends (49c 3–6, 50a 2–3). Plato's discussion is much too complex and too directly motivated by the concerns of his own analysis of pleasure to be dependent upon Xenophon, but the converse is possible. Xenophon may have felt that Plato's account was not faithful to the natural sense of hostility in *phthonos*, and hence he jumped at the chance to find Plato in error. Note that Aristotle too defines *phthonos* as a kind of pain

---

5. Compare Delatte's comment (1933: 122): these problems are treated with a lack of unity and harmony which obscures the thought. "Xenophon's memories [!] are confused, or else he is unable to make sense of the philosophical material he has found in his papers and express it clearly." Writing before Gigon, it does not occur to Delatte that the material Xenophon is "incapable de dominer" might be found in the papers of another Socratic author. See also the discussion of this passage in Vlastos (1991) 99f.

(not pleasure) at the success of others.[6] It would not be surprising to find that Xenophon was acquainted with the *Philebus*. Among Platonic dialogues later than the *Theaetetus*, the *Philebus* is the only one in which Socrates plays the central role and in which the topic is one that would interest Xenophon.

5. (IV.2.12–18) In a long discussion with a certain Euthydemus, Xenophon's Socrates treats justice in terms that recall several passages in *Republic* I. First the proper work or function (*ergon*) of justice is compared to that of an art like carpentry (IV.2.12; cf. justice as a *technē* at *Rep.* I, 332D 2, with its *ergon* at 335D 11). In proceeding then to specify the product of justice, Socrates points out that many actions normally regarded as unjust, such as lying or stealing, may turn out to be just under special circumstances (IV.2.14ff.; cf. *Rep.* I, 331C). The suggestion is made here (as by Polemarchus in *Rep.* I, 332A 9ff.) that actions which are unjust when done to friends become just when done to enemies (IV.2.15–16). But in both texts this solution is rejected as unsatisfactory. (See 10 below for another echo of *Rep.* I.)

6. (IV.2.19–20) In the immediate continuation of his conversation with Euthydemus, Xenophon's Socrates develops the parallel between the knowledge of justice and the art of literacy (*grammatikē*) in a way that recalls the paradox of the *Hippias Minor*, namely that intentional wrongdoing is more virtuous than the same thing done unintentionally. Here the person who voluntarily (*hekōn*) writes or reads incorrectly is said to be "more skilled in literacy" than one who errs involuntarily (*akōn*), because the one who errs voluntarily "can, when he wants, also do this correctly." Similarly, says Socrates, the person who *voluntarily* lies and cheats is someone who knows what is just, and hence is himself more just than someone ignorant, who speaks falsely or calculates badly out of ignorance (IV.2.20–1). The parallels here to *Hippias Minor* 366C–367C (writing and calculating) and 375D–376B (voluntarily, involuntarily) are too close to be accidental.[7] But nothing is made of the paradox here except to baffle poor Euthydemus.

7. (IV.2.32–5) In the final phases of bringing Euthydemus to the self-recognition of his own ignorance, Socrates points out that

6. *Rhet.* II.9, 1387b21, cited by Hackforth (1945) 92n.
7. As was recognized long ago by Maier (1913) 54–6.

even health and wisdom (*sophia*) may be no more good than bad, since their results can sometimes be harmful as well as beneficial. All apparent goods, such as beauty, strength, wealth, reputation, and political power, may on some occasions be a source of disaster. Xenophon is here giving a garbled version of two Platonic arguments designed to show that only wisdom is a good that is always beneficial (*Meno* 87D–89A, *Euthydemus* 281A–E).[8]

8. (IV.4.5)

When Hippias arrived in Athens after some time he found Socrates saying to his interlocutors that it was extraordinary that if you want to have someone taught to be a shoemaker or a carpenter or a smith or a horseman, you are not at a loss where to send him, but that if you want yourself to learn justice or to have your son or your servant taught, you do not know where to go to find this.

This parallels several passages in Plato, most notably *Meno* 89Dff., on the impossibility of finding teachers of virtue.

9. (IV.4.6, immediately following the passage just quoted)

When Hippias heard this he said in mockery "Well, Socrates, so you are still saying the same old things I heard from you long ago?" "Yes," said Socrates, "and what is worse, Hippias, I not only always say the same things, but I say them about the same subjects."

This is a verbatim echo of *Gorgias* 490E 9–10, with Hippias in place of Callicles.[9]

10. (IV.4.9)

[Hippias claims that he has an irrefutable account of justice.] "But you will not hear it, Socrates, until you declare your own view of what justice is. For you are satisfied to make fun of others by questioning and cross-examining them all, but you yourself are not willing to give an account to anyone or to declare your opinion on any matter."

This is almost precisely the charge made against Socrates by Thrasymachus in *Rep.* I, 336C, 337A and E. (Compare also *Theaetetus* 150C 4–6.)[10]

8. Here again the parallel with *Euthydemus* 278Eff. was noted by Maier (1913) 57.
9. With Maier (1913: 53f.) Breitenbach (1967: 1831) notes Xenophon's borrowing from the *Gorgias* here, but he also sees a more unconvincing reference to the *Hippias Major*. See below, n.11.
10. Vlastos (1991: 105) notes the incompatibility between this complaint and Socrates' usual behavior in Xenophon.

Not all of these parallels are equally decisive. Some comments found in both Plato and Xenophon may be relatively commonplace, going back to earlier Socratic literature or even to the historical Socrates. Thus 10 is vaguely paralleled in the post-Platonic *Cleitophon*; and 2 and 8 might conceivably be independent reflections of a common tradition. In the case of 1, 3, 4, 5, 6, 7, and 9, however, the verbal and conceptual links seem to me too tight for any plausible explanation except the direct dependence of Xenophon upon Plato's text. A fuller study of the *Memorabilia* would no doubt reveal more candidates for this list.[11] But the general picture is not likely to be altered by further study. We have relatively few echoes of Plato in Books I and II (reflecting only the *Lysis* and *Laches*, if my analysis is correct), considerably more in Books III–IV, closely concentrated in three sections (III.9, IV.2, and IV.4–6) but making use of a relatively large number of Platonic dialogues including *Gorgias, Protagoras, Republic* I and probably at least one late work, the *Philebus*. Turning in a moment to Xenophon's *Symposium* we will find echoes there not only of Plato's *Symposium* but probably also of the *Theaetetus*. And this is more or less what we would expect if Xenophon began writing his *Memorabilia* in the 380s in the relative isolation of Scillus, but completed Books III–IV and the *Symposium* after his return to Athens in the 360s, when Plato was clearly the dominant intellectual figure and all of his dialogues would have been easily available.

11. The words "Hippias having come to Athens after some time" (*Mem.* IV.4.5) are described by Breitenbach as a "citation" from the first sentence of the *Hippias Major*. But in fact only one phrase (*dia chronou*) is literally the same in both texts, and Breitenbach does not notice that this point ("after some time") is required by what Hippias says in what follows: "you are still saying what I heard from you *so long ago* (*palai*)." So the parallel here is a case of genuine coincidence.

More intriguing are the resemblances between the *Hippias Major* (290Aff., 295C–D) and *Mem.* III.8.2–7 on utility and relativism in conceptions of what is good and beautiful. If I believed this dialogue were by Plato, these parallels might well figure as candidates for my list. Since I am convinced on other grounds that the *Hippias Major* was not written by Plato (see Kahn, 1985: 261–87), I am happy to see that two careful scholars, in independent studies of these parallels, have both come to the conclusion that Xenophon is *not* dependent here on the *Hippias Major*. Delatte (1933: 103–7) concludes that either the *Hippias Major* is borrowing from Xenophon or both are reflections of "relativist" passages in earlier Socratic literature. The second alternative seems more likely. It is confirmed by Caizzi (1964: 87f.), who argues that Xenophon's Socrates is here making use of concepts drawn from Antisthenes.

As has been noted by Gigon and others, the two earlier books of the *Memorabilia* show more signs of the influence of Antisthenes. And this discrepancy correlates neatly with the results Eucken has reached on the basis of his study of Isocrates, namely, that from Isocrates' point of view Antisthenes figures as the principal Socratic in the earlier period, down to the middle or late 380s, and Plato only gradually takes his place as Isocrates' chief rival. After about 380, however, when the Academy was becoming an international center and the *Gorgias*, *Protagoras*, and *Symposium* had appeared, Plato's position as heir to the Socratic tradition in philosophy was unchallenged. So Xenophon was then to some extent obliged to wrap himself in Plato's mantle in order to be taken seriously as an author on Socrates. Most of the themes drawn from Plato in the *Memorabilia* are not so much points of polemic as borrowed intellectual plumage to trick out Xenophon's philosophically colorless portrayal of Socrates. This is true also for the most philosophically significant of Xenophon's borrowings from Plato, his discussion of dialectic in *Mem.* IV.5–6 (above, pp. 76–9).

The points of connection between Xenophon's *Symposium* and Plato's dialogue of the same name are more obvious, more polemical, and more complex than in the *Memorabilia*. I limit my discussion to the two passages in Xenophon's dialogue where there is a direct reference to Plato's text.

In his long speech that concludes the discussion of love, Socrates begins by questioning a distinction between two Aphrodites:

11. (*Symp.* VIII.9–10)

Now whether there is one Aphrodite or two, the celestial (*ourania*) and the popular (*pandēmos*), I do not know. For Zeus seems to be the same, although he has many epithets. But I do know that the altars, temples, and sacrifices are different for the Celestial and the Popular Aphrodite; the cult is looser in the latter case, more chaste in the former. And one might imagine that the Eros sent by the popular goddess is bodily love, while the celestial goddess sends forth loves of the soul and of friendship and of noble deeds.

The distinction between two Aphrodites is argued for by Pausanias in Plato's *Symposium* (180Dff.), precisely as a basis for contrasting a celestial and a vulgar form of Eros. But Pausanias' conception of the higher love is strictly homosexual (181C) and does not exclude physical gratification. Xenophon's reference is doubly polemical, since he not only questions Pausanias' distinction between two Aphrodites (a point of only rhetorical interest) but he wants to identify vulgar love with physical pederasty. This is the essential message of Socrates' final speech and his personal exhortation to Callias: to keep his love for Autolycus pure, that is, not physically gratified (cf. VIII.12). So whereas in Plato's *Symposium* Socrates accepts the love of beautiful bodies as the first step on the ladder of philosophical *erōs* (210A), Xenophon's Socrates emphasizes his rejection of physical homosexuality.

A little later in the same speech Socrates refers to "Pausanias the lover of the poet Agathon" for his immoral suggestion, "in his defense of those who wallow in lasciviousness,"[12] that the bravest army would be composed of lovers and their loved ones (VIII.32). The old soldier Xenophon is shocked; he is clearly criticizing the tolerant attitude towards homosexuality that pervades the talk of love in Plato's *Symposium*. (Relying on his memory, however, Xenophon has here combined the military suggestion, that is actually made not by Pausanias but by Phaedrus in Plato's dialogue, with remarks on the sexual mores of Elis and Boeotia that do come from Pausanias' speech.)[13] And it is characteristic of Xenophon that his attention should be focused on these first two speeches in Plato's dialogue, which bear directly on contemporary practices and moral attitudes but are the least rich in philosophical and poetic content.

There is another passage in Xenophon's *Symposium* that seems to be indebted to his reading of Plato, combined in this case with ideas from Aeschines. This is the scene in which Socrates describes himself and Antisthenes as pander and procurer. It has been plausibly suggested by more than one scholar that in describing Socrates in these lurid terms Xenophon is influenced by the passage in Plato's *Theaetetus* where Socrates refers to himself as a midwife. For, says Socrates in the *Theaetetus*, midwives are also the best matchmakers (*promnēstriai*), although they do not announce this fact for fear of being taken for procurers (*proagōgoi*, 150A 2). The hypothesis that Xenophon is here dependent upon Plato is strik-

---

12. Loeb transl. by O. J. Todd.
13. Plato, *Symp.* 178E–179A, 182B. Xenophon's version apparently incorporates material based on his own knowledge of the military practices of Elis and Boeotia. See von Fritz (1935) 43n. for a correct account of the connections here. (Accepted by Ehlers, 1966: 118.)

ingly confirmed by the fact that sending students to Prodicus is given in both dialogues as an example of matchmaking in the relevant sense (*Theaet.* 151B, Xen. *Symp.* IV.62.)[14] If this connection is accepted, we can be sure of the late date of Xenophon's *Symposium* (inferred above on other grounds), since we know that the *Theaetetus* was not completed before the death of its namesake in 369 BC. And nothing could better illustrate how completely Xenophon alters the tone and significance of what he takes from Plato, even when the concrete content remains identical (as it does here in the example of matchmaking for Prodicus). The personal intimacy and intellectual intensity of Socrates' conversation with Theaetetus is replaced by a series of off-color jokes well suited to a drinking party in an officers' club.[15]

14. I am here following Caizzi (1964) 97–9. The same connection is established by Ehlers (1966: 114) on the suggestion of H. Patzer.
15. For further suggestions of Xenophon's dependence on Plato, see Maier (1913) 53–62. More recently, Vander Waerdt (1993) has argued that Xenophon's *Apology* is a direct reply to Plato's work of that name, and that in general the influence between these two Socratic authors "runs only in one direction," from Plato to Xenophon (p. 9).

Bibliography

Adam, J. (1902). *The Republic of Plato*, 2 vols., Cambridge
Adkins, A. W. H. (1960). *Merit and Responsibility*, Oxford
Allen, R. E. (1971). "Plato's Earlier Theory of Forms," in Vlastos (1971a)
   319–34
Annas, J. (1993). *The Morality of Happiness*, New York/Oxford
Arnim, H. von (1914). *Platos Jugenddialoge und die Enstehungszeit des Phaidros*,
   Leipzig/Berlin
Benson, H. H. (1990a). "The Priority of Definition and the Socratic
   Elenchus," in *Oxford Studies in Ancient Philosophy* VII, 19–65
   (1990b). "Meno, the Slave-boy, and the *Elenchus*," *Phronesis* 35, 128–58
Bergson, H. (1960). *La Pensée et le Mouvant*, Paris
Beversluis, J. (1987). "Does Socrates Commit the Socratic Fallacy?",
   American Philosophical Quarterly 24, 211–23
Blank, D. (1986). "Socrates' Instruction to Cebes: Plato, 'Phaedo' 101D–
   E," *Hermes* 114, 146–63
Blass, F. (1874). *Die Attische Beredsamkeit* II (1st edn.), Leipzig
Bloch, G. (1973). *Platons Charmides*, dissertation, Tübingen
Bluck, R. S. (1961). *Plato's Meno*, Cambridge
Bobonich, C. (1994). "Akrasia and Agency in Plato's *Laws* and *Republic*,"
   Archiv für Geschichte der Philosophie 76, 3–36
Bonitz, H. (1871). "Zur Erklärung des Dialogs Laches'," *Hermes* 5, 413–
   42, reprinted in *Platonische Studien*, Berlin, 1886, 210–26
Bostock, D. (1986). *Plato's "Phaedo"*, Oxford
Brandwood, L. (1990). *The Chronology of Plato's Dialogues*, Cambridge
Breitenbach, H. R. (1967). "Xenophon," *RE* 2. Reihe, IX A 2, 1567–928
Brunt, P. A. (1993). "Plato's Academy and Politics," in *Studies in Greek
   History and Thought*, Oxford
Burnet, J. (1964). *Greek Philosophy: Thales to Plato*, London
   (1977). *Plato's Euthyphro, Apology of Socrates, and Crito*, New York
Burnyeat, M. (1976). "Protagoras and Self-Refutation in Later Greek
   Philosophy," *Philosophical Review* 85, 44–69
Bury, R. G. (1909). *The Symposium of Plato*, edited with critical notes and
   commentary, Cambridge

Caizzi, Fernando Decleva (1964). "Antistene," *Studi Urbinati* 38, 48–99 (1966). *Antisthenis fragmenta*, Milan

Campbell, Lewis (1867). *The Sophistes and Politicus of Plato*, with a revised text and English notes, Oxford

(1896). "On the place of the *Parmenides* in the chronological order of the Platonic Dialogues," *Classical Review* 10, 129–36

Cherniss, Harold (1935). *Aristotle's Criticism of Presocratic Philosophy*, Baltimore

(1936). "The Philosophical Economy of the Theory of Ideas," *American Journal of Philology* 57, 445–56, reprinted in Vlastos (1971b) 16–27

Clay, Diskin (1988). "Gaps in the 'Universe' of the Platonic Dialogues," *Proceedings of the Boston Area Colloquium in Ancient Philosophy* III, ed. J. J. Cleary

Cohen, S. M. (1971). "Socrates on the Definition of Piety: *Euthyphro* 10A–11B," in Vlastos (1971a) 160–76

Crombie, I. M. (1963). *An Examination of Plato's Doctrines*, 2 vols., London

Davidson, D. (1980). "How is Weakness of the Will Possible?" in *Essays on Actions and Events*, 21–42, Oxford

Davies, J. K. (1971). *Athenian Propertied Families, 600–300 BC*, Oxford

Delatte, A. (1933). *Le troisième livre des souvenirs socratiques de Xénophon*, Paris

Deman, T. (1942). *Le témoignage d'Aristote sur Socrate*, Paris

Devereux, D. T. (1977). "Courage and Wisdom in Plato's *Laches*," *Journal of the History of Philosophy* 15, 129–41

Dittmar, H. (1912). *Aischines von Sphettos, Studien zur Literaturgeschichte der Sokratiker = Philologische Untersuchungen* 21, Berlin

Dodds, E. R. (1959). *Plato. Gorgias*, Oxford

Döring, Klaus (1972). *Die Megariker, Kommentierte Sammlung der Testimonien*, Amsterdam

(1984). "Der Sokrates des Aischines von Sphettos und die Frage nach dem historischen Sokrates," *Hermes* 112, 16–30

(1989). "Gab es eine Dialektische Schule?," *Phronesis* 34, 293–310

(1992). "Die Philosophie des Sokrates," *Gymnasium* 99, 1–16

Dover, K. J. (1974). *Greek Popular Morality in the Time of Plato and Aristotle*, Oxford

(1978). *Greek Homosexuality*, Cambridge, Mass.

(1980). *Plato: Symposium*, Cambridge

Düring, I. (1941). *Herodicus the Cratetean*, Stockholm

Ehlers, Barbara (1966). *Eine vorplatonische Deutung des sokratischen Eros: Der Dialog Aspasia des Sokratikers Aischines* (Zetemata 41), Munich

Eliot, T. S. (1932). "Shakespeare," in *Selected Essays 1917–1932*, New York

Erler, M. (1987). *Der Sinn der Aporien in den Dialogen Platons*, Berlin/New York

Eucken, C. (1983). *Isokrates: seine Positionen in der Auseinandersetzung mit den zeitgenössischen Philosophen*, Berlin

Ferrari, G. R. F. (1992). "Platonic Love," in Kraut (1992) 248–76

Fine, G. (1984). "Separation," in *Oxford Studies in Ancient Philosophy* II, 31–87

(1993). *On Ideas: Aristotle's Criticism of Plato's Theory of Forms*, Oxford

Flashar, H. (1958). *Der Dialog "Ion" als Zeugnis platonischer Philosophie*, Berlin

Frankena, William (1973). *Ethics* (2nd edn.), Englewood Cliffs, N.J.

Friedländer, Paul (1958). *Plato*, translation by H. Meyerhoff, vol. 1: *An Introduction*, London

(1964) *Plato*, vol. II: *The Dialogues, First Period*, London

Fritz, Kurt von (1931). "Die Megariker," *RE* Supplement Band V, 707–24

(1935). "Antisthenes und Sokrates in Xenophons Symposion," *Rhein. Museum* 84, 19–45

(1938). "Phaidon," *RE* XIX.2 1538–42

(1965). "Das erste Kapitel des zweiten Buches von Xenophons Memorabilien und die Philosophie des Aristipp von Kyrene," *Hermes* 93, 257–79

Fujisawa, N. (1974). "ἔχειν, Μέτεχειν and Idioms of 'Paradeigmatism' in Plato's Theory of Forms," *Phronesis* 19, 30–58

Gaiser, Konrad (1969). Review of Ehlers (1966), *Archiv für Geschichte der Philosophie* 51, 200–9

Gallop, D. (1975). *Plato, "Phaedo"*, translated with notes, Oxford

Geach, P. T. (1966). "Plato's *Euthyphro*," *The Monist* 50, 367–82, reprinted in *Logic Matters*, Berkeley and Los Angeles, 1972, 31–44

Giannantoni, Gabriele (1991). *Socratis et Socraticorum Reliquiae*, 4 vols., Naples

Gigon, Olof (1947). *Sokrates*, Bern

(1953). *Kommentar zum ersten Buch von Xenophons Memorabilien*, Basel

(1956). *Kommentar zum zweiten Buch von Xenophons Memorabilien*, Basel

Gomme, A. W. (1945). *A Historical Commentary on Thucydides*, vol. I, Oxford

(1956). *A Historical Commentary on Thucydides*, vol. II, Oxford

Gosling, J. C. B. and Taylor, C. C. W. (1982). *The Greeks on Pleasure*, Oxford

Grote, George (1875). *Plato and Other Companions of Socrates*, 3 vols. (3rd edn.), London

Guthrie, W. K. C. (1965). *History of Greek Philosophy*, vol. II, Cambridge

(1969). *History of Greek Philosophy*, vol. III, Cambridge

(1975). *History of Greek Philosophy*, vol. IV, Cambridge

Hackforth, R. (1945). *Plato's Examination of Pleasure*, Cambridge

Halperin, D. M. (1985). "Platonic *Erōs* and What Men Call Love," *Ancient Philosophy* 5, 161–204

Hawtrey, R. S. W. (1981). *Commentary on Plato's "Euthydemus"*, Philadelphia

Hermann, K. F. (1839). *Geschichte und System der Platonischen Philosophie*, Heidelberg

Herrnstein, R. J. (1990). "Rational Choice Theory, Necessary but Not Sufficient," *American Psychologist* 45, 356–67

Hirzel, R. (1895). *Der Dialog*, Leipzig

Inwood, B. (1992). *The Poem of Empedocles*, Toronto
Irwin, T. (1977). *Plato's Moral Theory*, Oxford
  (1995). *Plato's Ethics*, Oxford
Jaeger, W. (1944). *Paideia* vol. II, Berlin; English translation by G. Highet, 1944, Oxford
Kahn, Charles (1963). "Plato's Funeral Oration," *Classical Philology* 58, 220–34
  (1973). "Language and Ontolology in the *Cratylus*," in *Exegesis and Argument*, edd. E. N. Lee *et al.*, 152–76
  (1981). "Some Philosophical Uses of 'to be' in Plato," *Phronesis* 26, 105–34
  (1983). "Drama and Dialectic in Plato's *Gorgias*," in *Oxford Studies in Ancient Philosophy* I, 75–121
  (1985). "The Beautiful and the Genuine: A Discussion of Paul Woodruff's *Plato, Hippias Major*," in *Oxford Studies in Ancient Philosophy* II, 261–87
  (1988a). "On the Relative Date of the *Gorgias* and *Protagoras*," in *Oxford Studies in Ancient Philosophy* VI, 69–102
  (1988b). "Being in Parmenides and Plato," *La Parola del Passato* 43, 237–61
  (1990). "Plato as a Socratic," *Recherches sur la philosophie et le langage* 12, (Grenoble) 19–30; also published in *Studi Italiani di filologica classica* 3rd series 10 (1992), 580–95
  (1992). "Vlastos' Socrates," *Phronesis* 37, 233–58
  (1993a). "Proleptic Composition in the *Republic*, or Why Book I was Never a Separate Dialogue," *Classical Quarterly* N.S.43: 131–42
  (1993b). Foreword (pp. xvii–xxvii) to 1993 reprinting of G. R. Morrow, *Plato's Cretan City*, Princeton
  (1994). "Aeschines on Socratic Eros," in *The Socratic Movement*, ed. P. Vander Waerdt, 87–106
  (1995). "The Place of the *Statesman* in Plato's Later Work," in C. Rowe, ed., *Reading the Statesman*, Sankt Augustin, 49–60
Kahrstedt, U. (1927). "Lysikles," *RE* XIII, 2550–1
Karasmanis, Vassilis (1987). *The Hypothetical Method in Plato's Middle Dialogues*, unpublished dissertation, Oxford
Keyser, Paul (1991). "Review of G. R. Ledger," *Bryn Mawr Classical Review* 2, 422–7
  (1992). "Stylometric Method and the Chronology of Plato's Dialogues," *Bryn Mawr Classical Review* 3, 58–73
Klosko, G. (1988). "The 'Rule' of Reason in Plato's Psychology," *History of Philosophy Quarterly* 5, 341–56
  (1986). *The Development of Plato's Political Theory*, New York/London
Kraut, R. (1992). ed. *The Cambridge Companion to Plato*, Cambridge
Kube, J. (1969). *TEXNH und APETH, sophistisches und platonisches Tugendwissen*, dissertation, Frankfurt/Main, Berlin

Lebeck, Anne (1971). *The Oresteia*, Washington, D.C.

Ledger, G. R. (1989). *Recounting Plato*, Oxford

Lee, E. N., Mourelatos, A. P. D. and Rorty, R. M., edd., (1973). *Exegesis and Argument: Studies in Greek Philosophy Presented to Gregory Vlastos*, Assen

Lesky, A. (1957/58). *Geschichte der griechischen Literatur*, Bern

Long, A. A. and Sedley, D. N. (1987). *The Hellenistic Philosophers*, 2 vols., Cambridge

Lutoslawski, W. (1897). *The Origin and Growth of Plato's Logic*, London

Maier, H. (1913). *Sokrates, sein Werk und seine geschichtliche Stellung*, Tübingen

Mann, W. (1996). "The Life of Aristippus," in *Archiv für Geschichte der Philosophie* (forthcoming)

Mannebach, Erich (1961). *Aristippi et Cyrenaicorum Fragmenta*, Leiden/Köln

Marrou, H.-I. (1950). *"Histore de l'Éducation dans l'Antiquité"* (2nd edn.), Paris

McDowell, John (1980). "The Role of *Eudaimonia* in Aristotle's Ethics," in A. O. Rorty, ed. *Essays on Aristotle's Ethics*, Berkeley

McKim, R. (1985). "Socratic Self-Knowledge and 'Knowledge of Knowledge' in Plato's *Charmides*," *Transactions of the American Philological Association* 115, 59–77

Meinwald, Constance C. (1991). *Plato's "Parmenides"*, Oxford

(1992). "Farewell to the Third Man," in Kraut (1992) 365–96

Méridier, L. (1931). *Platon: Ion*, Budé, vol. v.1, Paris

Momigliano, A. (1971). *The Development of Greek Biography*, Cambridge, Mass.

Moravcsik, J. M. E. (1971). "Reason and Eros in the 'Ascent'-Passage of the *Symposium*," in J. P. Anton and G. L. Kustas, edd. *Essays in Ancient Greek Philosophy*, Albany, N.Y.

Müri, W. (1944). "Das Wort Dialektik bei Platon," *Museum Helveticum* 1, 152–68

North, H. (1966). *Sophrosune. Self-knowledge and Self-Restraint in Greek Literature*, Ithaca

O'Brien, M. J. (1958). "Modern Philosophy and Platonic Ethics," *Journal of the History of Ideas* 19, 451–72

(1963). "The Unity of the *Laches*," *Yale Classical Studies* 18, 131–47, reprinted in *Essays in Ancient Greek Philosophy*, edd. J. P. Anton and G. L. Kustas, 1971, Albany, N.Y. 303–16

(1967). *The Socratic Paradoxes and the Greek Mind*, Chapel Hill

Ostwald, M. (1986). *From Popular Sovereignty to the Sovereignty of Law*, Berkeley

Ostwald–Vlastos (1956). *Plato's Protagoras*, edd. M. Ostwald and G. Vlastos, New York

Patzer, A. (1970). *Antisthenes der Sokratiker*, dissertation, Heidelberg

(1975). "Resignation vor dem historischem Sokrates," in A. Patzer, ed. *Apophoreta für Uvo Hölscher*, Bonn

(1987). ed. *Der historische Sokrates*, Darmstadt

Patzer, H. (1965). "Die philosophische Bedeutung der Sokratesgestalt in den platonischen Dialogen," in *Parousia, Festgabe für J. Hirschberger*, Frankfurt

Penner, T. (1973). "The Unity of Virtue," *Philosophical Review* 82, 35–68

(1992). "Socrates and the Early Dialogues," in Kraut (1992) 121–69

Pohlenz, M. (1913). *Aus Platos Werdezeit*, Berlin

Price, A. W. (1989). *Love and Friendship in Plato and Aristotle*, Oxford

Robin, L. (1910). "Les 'Mémorables' de Xénophon et notre connaissance de la philosophie de Socrate," *Année philosophique* 21, 1–47; (= *La pensée hellènique des origines à Épicure*, 81–137)

Robinson, D. B. (1986). "Plato's *Lysis*: The Structural Problem," *Illinois Classical Studies* 11, 63–83

Robinson, Richard (1941). *Plato's Earlier Dialectic* (1st edn.), Ithaca

(1953). *Plato's Earlier Dialectic* (2nd edn.), Oxford

Robinson, T. M. (1979). *Contrasting Arguments. An Edition of the "Dissoi Logoi"*, New York

Ross, W. D. (1924). *Aristotle's Metaphysics*, 2 vols., Oxford

(1951). *Plato's Theory of Ideas*, Oxford

(1955). *Aristotelis Fragmenta Selecta*, Oxford

Rossetti, Livio (1973). "'Socratica' in Fedone di Elide," *Studi Urbinati* 47, 364–81

(1980). "Ricerche sui Dialoghi Socratici di Fedone e di Euclide," *Hermes* 108, 183–200

Rowe, C. J. (1986a). *Plato: Phaedrus*, with translation and commentary, Warminster

(1986b) "The Argument and Structure of Plato's *Phaedrus*," *Proceedings of the Cambridge Philological Society* N.S. 32, 106–25

Santas, G. X. (1964). "The Socratic Paradox," *Philosophical Review* 73, 147–64

(1971a) "Socrates at Work on Virtue and Knowledge in Plato's *Laches*" in Vlastos (1971a) 177–208

(1971b). "Plato's *Protagoras* and Explanation of Weakness," in Vlastos (1971a) 264–98

(1979). *Socrates, Philosophy in Plato's Early Dialogues*, London

(1988). *Plato and Freud, Two Theories of Love*, Oxford

Saunders, T. J. (1986). "'The Rand Corporation of Antiquity?' Plato's Academy and Greek Politics," in J. H. Betts *et al.*, edd. *Studies in Honour of T. B. L. Webster*, Bristol

Schofield, Malcolm (1984). "Ariston of Chios and the Unity of Virtue," *Ancient Philosophy* 4, 83–95

(1991). "Editor's Notes," *Phronesis* 36, 107–15

Scott, D. (1987). "Platonic Anamnesis Revisited," *Classical Quarterly* 37, 346–66

Sedley, David (1989). "Is the *Lysis* a Dialogue of Definition?," *Phronesis* 34, 107–8

(1995). "The Dramatis Personae of Plato's *Phaedo*," *Proceedings of the British Academy* 85, 3–26, reprinted in T. J. Smiley, ed. *Philosophical Dialogues: Plato, Hume, Wittgenstein*, Oxford

Sharples, R. W. (1985). *Plato: Meno*, Warminster and Chicago

Shorey, Paul (1933). *What Plato Said*, Chicago

Sidgwick, H. (1872). "The Sophists," *The Journal of Philology* 4, 288–307

Smith, J. A. (1917). "General Relative Clauses in Greek," *Classical Review* 31, 69–71

Snell, Bruno (1953). *The Discovery of the Mind*, tr. T. G. Rosenmeyer, Cambridge, Mass.

Sprague, R. S. (1962). *Plato's Use of Fallacy*, London
    (1972). *The Older Sophists*, Columbia, S.C.
    (1976). *Plato's Philosopher-Kings*, Columbia, S.C.

Stalley, R. F. (1983). *An Introduction to Plato's Laws*, Oxford

Strycker, E. de (1950). "Les témoignages historiques sur Socrate," *Mélanges H. Grégoire*, Brussels, 199–230. German translation in A. Patzer (1987) 323–54

Szlezák, T. A. (1985). *Platon und die Schriftlichkeit der Philosophie*, Berlin

Tatum, J. (1989). *Xenophon's Imperial Fiction: On the Education of Cyrus*, Princeton

Taylor, A. E. (1911). *Varia Socratica*, Oxford

Thesleff, Holger (1982). *Studies in Platonic Chronology*, Helsinki

Thompson, Dorothy Burr (1960). "The House of Simon the Shoemaker," *Archeology* 13, 234–40

Thompson, Homer (1954). Excavation report, *Hesperia* 23, 54f.

Thompson, W. H. (1868). *The Phaedrus of Plato*, with English notes and dissertations, London

Tigerstedt, E. N. (1970). "Furor Poeticus: Poetic Inspiration in Greek Literature Before Democritus and Plato," *Journal of the History of Ideas* 31, 163–78
    (1977). *Interpreting Plato*, Stockholm Studies in History of Literature 17, Uppsala

Tuckey, T. G. (1951). *Plato's "Charmides"*, Cambridge

Van der Ben, N. (1985). *The "Charmides" of Plato*, Amsterdam

Vander Waert, P. (1993). "Socratic Justice and Self Sufficiency: The Story of the Delphic Oracle in Xenophon's *Apology of Socrates*," *Oxford Studies in Ancient Philosophy*, 11, 1–48
    (1994). ed. *The Socratic Movement*, Ithaca

Vlastos, G. (1956). Introduction to *Plato's Protagoras*, edd. M. Ostwald and G. Vlastos, New York
    (1967). "Was Polus refuted?," *AJP* 88, 454–60
    (1971a). *The Philosophy of Socrates: A Collection of Essays*, New York
    (1971b). *Plato I: Metaphysics and Epistemology*, New York
    (1973). *Platonic Studies*, Princeton

(1987) " 'Separation' in Plato," in *Oxford Studies in Ancient Philosophy* v, 187–96

(1988). "Socrates," *Proceedings of the British Academy* 74, 89–111

(1990). "Is the 'Socratic Fallacy' Socratic?," *Ancient Philosophy* 10, 1–16

(1991). *Socrates, Ironist and Moral Philosopher*, Cambridge

(1994). *Socratic Studies*, ed. M. Burnyeat, Cambridge

(1995). *Studies in Greek philosophy*, ed. D. W. Graham, 2 vols., Princeton

Watson, G. (1980). "Skepticism about Weakness of Will," *Philosophical Review* 86, 316–39

Wilamowitz-Moellendorff, Ulrich von (1879). "Phaidon von Elis," *Hermes* 14, 187–9, 476f.

(1920). *Platon*, 2 vols., Berlin

Williams, Bernard (1985). *Ethics and the Limits of Philosophy*, Cambridge, Mass.

Winkler, John J. (1990). "Laying Down the Law: The Oversight of Men's Sexual Behavior in Classical Athens," in D. M. Halperin et al. edd. *Before Sexuality*, Princeton

Witte, B. (1970). *Die Wissenschaft vom Guten und Bösen, Interpretationen zu Platons "Charmides"*, Berlin

Woodbury, L. (1971). "Socrates and Archelaus," *Phoenix* 25, 299–309

Woodruff, Paul (1982). *Plato, Hippias Major*, Indianapolis

(1983). *Plato, Two Comic Dialogues*, Indianapolis

(1990). "Plato's early theory of knowledge," in S. Everson, ed. *Companions to Ancient Thought 1, Epistemology*, Cambridge, 65–75

Young, Charles M. (1994). "Plato and Computer Dating," in *Oxford Studies in Ancient Philosophy* xii, 227–50

Zeller, E. (1889). *Die Philosophie der Griechen*, vol. ii, Part One (4th edn.), Leipzig

Zeyl, D. J. (1980). "Socrates and Hedonism – *Protagoras* 351b–358d," *Phronesis* 25, 250–69

Indexes

SUBJECT INDEX

Academy, founding of, 52, 55–6
akrasia, see weakness of will
Alcibiades, dialogue of Aeschines, 18–23; date of, 28–9
Alcibiades, dialogue of Antisthenes, 19–20
anachronism: in Aeschines, 28, 34; in Xenophon, 32–3; relative lack of in Plato, 34–5
analogy, argument from, 4, 14, 93, 111–13, 115, 119–20, 142–5, 189; in Aeschines' *Aspasia,* 26; attributed to Socrates, 74; rejected by Eucleides, 14, 144; weakness of, 135, 143–5, 192, 194–5; Plato's departure from in *Charmides,* 202–3
aporetic dialogues, 57–8, 98–100, 156; as Plato's innovation, 41, 68, 128, 179; as reinterpretation of Socratic elenchus, 99–100, 179; *Laches* as introduction to, 58, 150–4; *Meno* as culmination of, 180; form imitated in *Theaetetus,* 98, 371
aporia, 94ff; pedagogical benefits of, 66–7, 99–100, 157, 178–80; used systematically in *Lysis,* 265, 283, 285, 290
appearance, perspectival, *see doxa*
aretē, see virtue
Aristotle as historian of philosophy, 79–87; his account of origins of Plato's philosophy, 81–3; his account of Presocratic philosophy, 79ff; his account of Socrates' philosophy, 83–7, 224, 226–7, 229
Aspasia, dialogue of Aeschines, 23ff; date of, 28–9
Aspasia, dialogue of Antisthenes, 8–9
autarcheia, see self-sufficiency

beauty: Form of, 260, 267ff, 274–5, 280, 340–5; and the Good, 267–71
being: Parmenidean origin of Plato's conception, 82, 342–3, 345; essential

Being specified by *what-is-X?* question, 355; *see also* essence; Forms
belief, *see doxa*

care of one's self, Socratic theme, 20–1, 73–4; and political activity, 52; and virtue 90–1; *see also* virtue
chronological order of the dialogues, 45–8, 101, 127–8, 148, 339
collection and division, *see* division, method of
courage: definition of in *Laches,* 164–70; as a form of knowledge in *Protagoras,* 211, 235–40, 254; examples common to *Laches* and *Protagoras,* 168–9
craft analogy, *see technē*
Cyrenaic School, *see* pleasure

definition: attributed to Socrates, 74, 84–5, 92–5; and methodological clarity, 93–5; two kinds of, 93–5, 155–7; epistemic priority of, 155ff, 180–2, 337; as test of expertise, 152–3, 156, 199; logic of, 170ff, co-extensivity for definiens and definiendum, 172ff, genus-species in, 172ff, the explanatory criterion, 174ff, search for unity in, 176–7, 348–9; cumulative lesson in *Laches, Euthyphro, Meno,* 178–9; sample definitions of color and figure in *Meno,* 177; distinctive of dialectic, 296; the definiendum points to the Forms, 178, 354; terminology for in Plato, 171–2, 354–5; *see also* dialogues of definition; Socratic fallacy; *what-is-X?* question
desire: contrast between sheer desire (*epithumia*) and rational desire (*boulesthai*), 141–2, 227n, 232, 245, 253, 262; Aristotelian analysis of, 262–3, 277–8; universal desire for good, 243ff,

recollection, doctrine of, 314, 317, 356, 374–
5, 387; as response to Meno's paradox,
150; as transition from true belief to
knowledge, 162; introduces fundamental features of Plato's metaphysics,
64, 163–4; as allegorical interpretation
of reincarnation, 67–8, 160; and
doctrine of Forms, 150, 366–7; and
philosophical *erōs*, 367; as anticipation
of Kantian *a priori* concepts, 367; as
anticipation of language acquisition
theories, 367
relations, reflexive and irreflexive, theory of
in *Charmides*, 184, 195–6
rhetoric: Aristotle's classification of, 129n;
in *Euthydemus*, 321ff; Gorgias' praise of,
134; in *Phaedrus*, 372ff, 381

self-sufficiency, as element of virtue, 7, 284
Seventh Epistle, authenticity of, 48n
shame, moral importance of, 134ff, 138,
140–2, 231
Simon, dialogue of Phaedo, 9ff
Socrates as historical figure, Ch. 4 *passim*;
traditional conceptions of his philosophy, 73–5; Aristotle's account of, 3,
79–88, 92–5; did he pursue definitions? 93ff; his influence on Plato, 39–
40, 49–51, 72; physiognomy of, 10–11,
233n; his philosophy reflected in
Apology, 89–90
Socrates in Plato's dialogues: as
embodiment of moral ideal, 72, 126,
145; as embodiment of philosophical
life, 39–40, 52, 97, 100 and *passim*;
avowal of ignorance, 89–90, 95–6, 191,
193, 197ff; as exponent of positive doctrine, 100 and *passim*; when does he
speak for Plato? 57–8, 65; contrast
between *Apology* and dialogues, 88ff;
self-critique in *Charmides*, 201ff; practi-
tioner of political *technē* in *Gorgias*, 130;
erotic nature of, 187–8, 233n, 270, 273–
4; *see also erōs*
Socratic fallacy, 157ff, 181–2; and Meno's
paradox, 161–2; committed only in
Hippias Major, 182
Socratic intellectualism, 73–4, 169, 272–3,
Ch. 7 *passim*; disavowal of in *Republic*?
243–4; and desire, 243–7; and Euripides, 227–30, 253; and hedonistic calculus in *Protagoras*, 238–9; and the
historical Socrates, 231, 232n; in *Protagoras* not endorsed by Plato, 232; pro-

treptic interpretation of, 228–32; and
Stoic psychology, 232
Socratic literature: Socratic dialogue as a
genre, 1ff; topics commonly treated, 4;
external form of, 19–20, 23, 33; Plato's
innovations in, 53, 57, 128; fictive
character of the genre, 2–3, 10, 22, 30,
32–5, in Aeschines, 27–8, 34–5, contrasted with Xenophon's historical
work, 33; literary contact between
authors, 3–4, 31–2, 121–4, between
Aeschines and Plato, 23, 28–9, between Xenophon and Plato, 32, 76–9,
393–401; and the historical Socrates,
71–95; *see also* literary form of Plato's
dialogues; Platonic dialogues
Sōkratikoi logoi, see Socratic literature
Socratic paradox, 72–3, 91–2, 127–9, 142–3,
224–6, 229–31, 233, 238, 281, 292;
underlies moral paradox in *Hippias
Minor*, 117, 131–2; and desire for good,
132, 138–9, 249–50, 263–4, 269, 277ff;
established in *Protagoras* by appeal to
hedonism and denial of weakness of
will, 238–57; moral and prudential
versions of, 247–52, 267–8; *see also*
desire; *erōs*; good
soul: health of, consisting in virtue, 215,
217–18, 247ff; parts of, in Plato, 243–4,
247n, 255–6, 260, 262–4, 273, 276–80,
374; *psychē* understood as rational soul,
355; transcendent character of essentially linked to Platonic metaphysics,
163, 268–71, 273–80, 331; *see also*
virtue; justice
sōphrosunē, see temperance
species–genus relation, *see* part–whole
Symposium, dialogue of Xenophon, 32
synopsis, method of, 299–300

technē, 21, 102ff, 129; defined by its subject
matter, 108ff, 129, 197; infallibility of,
132; and moral education, 148, 155,
213ff; and moral knowledge, 104, 129–
30, 139; politics as a *technē*, 130–1, 203,
206, 208; mastery of definitions as a
criterion of, 153, 155–6; un-Socratic
character of Plato's conception of, 40,
103ff, 130; dialectic as the highest form
of, 148, 150; why poetry is not a *technē*,
104–10; and principle of specialization,
105–6; in Xenophon, 394; *see also*
knowledge; political art; virtue,
teachability of

INDEX OF PASSAGES CITED

Aeschines
(fr.5 Dittmar) 20
(frs.7–8) 20, 90n
(fr.11) 21, 29
(fr.17) 24
(fr.19) 24n
(fr.22) 25
(fr.24) 25
(frs.26–7) 25

Anaxagoras
(fr.12) 334

Antisthenes
(*Alcibiades* fr.1 Dittmar) 8
(*Alcibiades* fr.3 Dittmar) 19n
(unknown dialogue = *SSR* v A 187) 122–3,
303n

INDEX OF ANCIENT NAMES

INDEX OF MODERN AUTHORS